CHAUCER STUDIES XLIV

CHAUCER'S DECAMERON
AND THE ORIGIN OF THE *CANTERBURY TALES*

CHAUCER STUDIES

ISSN 0261-9822

Founding Editor
Professor Derek S. Brewer

Editorial Board
Professor Helen Cooper
Dr Isabel Davis
Dr Robert Meyer-Lee
Dr William T. Rossiter

Since its foundation, the series Chaucer Studies has played a highly significant role in the development and promotion of research on Chaucer and his many cultural contexts. It is an ideal forum for the publication of work by both younger and established scholars, comprising innovative monographs and essay collections together with indispensable reference books. Chaucer scholarship just would not be the same without it.

Professor Alastair Minnis
Douglas Tracy Smith Professor of English, Yale University

The publisher welcomes new proposals for the series; monographs are particularly encouraged but volumes of essays will be included when appropriate. All submissions will receive rapid, informed attention. They should go in the first instance to Caroline Palmer, Editorial Director, at the following address:

Boydell & Brewer, PO Box 9, Woodbridge, Suffolk, IP12 3DF, UK

Previously published volumes in this series
are listed at the back of this book

CHAUCER'S DECAMERON AND THE ORIGIN OF THE *CANTERBURY TALES*

FREDERICK M. BIGGS

D. S. BREWER

First published 2017
D. S. Brewer, Cambridge

ISBN 978 1 84384 475 4

D. S. Brewer is an imprint of Boydell & Brewer Ltd
PO Box 9, Woodbridge, Suffolk IP12 3DF, UK
and of Boydell & Brewer Inc.
668 Mt Hope Avenue, Rochester, NY 14620–2731, USA
website: www.boydellandbrewer.com

The publisher has no responsibility for the continued existence or accuracy
of URLs for external or third-party internet websites referred to in this book,
and does not guarantee that any content on such websites is, or will remain,
accurate or appropriate

A CIP catalogue record for this book is available
from the British Library

This publication is printed on acid-free paper

Printed and bound in Great Britain by TJ International Ltd, Padstow, Cornwall

For Elizabeth's and Catriona's grandparents,
Charles R. and Margaret A. Biggs

Contents

List of Illustrations

The author and publishers are grateful to all the institutions and individuals
listed for permission to reproduce the materials in which they hold copyright. Every effort has been made to trace the copyright holders; apologies
are offered for any omission, and the publishers will be pleased to add any
necessary acknowledgement in subsequent editions.

Acknowledgments

Chapter 4 revises some material previously published in two articles: "The Miller's Tale and *Heile van Beersele*," *Review of English Studies* n.s. 56 (2005), pp. 497–523; and "The *Miller's Tale* and *Decameron* 3.4," *JEGP* 108 (2009), pp. 59–80.

In the pursuit of Chaucer's sources I have been fortunate in my teachers, colleagues, and students. Penn Szittya and his seminal article, "The Green Yeoman as Loathly Lady: The Friar's Parody of the Wife of Bath's Tale," introduced me to how Chaucer constructed arguments. Joe Grennen and Bob Kaske both appear in the following pages. Tom Hill taught me to pay attention to surprising details however small. Had I been smart enough to study with Alice Colby Hall and Giuseppe Mazzotta, this would be a better book. Jay Jasanoff introduced me to Old Irish and a year at the Dublin Institute for Advanced Studies under the direction of James Carney improved my skills. Although they would probably see it simply as the generosity that they extend to all scholars, the help of Piero Boitani, Helen Cooper, Bob Hanning, and Jane Roberts at different times and in different ways, has meant a great deal to me. A memorable conversation with Dan Wakelin marks the start of this book and several with Will Robins have contributed much to its arguments. Ray Anselment, Pete Beidler, Nick Bingham, Louise Bishop, Fred Cazel, Andrea Celli, Kenneth Clarke, Clare Costley King'oo, Kara Doyle, Francis Eaves, Josh Eyler, Tom Farrell, Suzanne Fein, Andy Galloway, Warren Ginsberg, Rohais Haughton, Brandon Hawk, Laura Howes, Dave Johnson, Rob Kinsey, Henrike Lähnemann, Bre Leake, Pami Longo, Jill Mann, Geoffrey Meigs, Andy Pfrenger, Gina Psaki, David Raybin, James Simpson, Tom Stillinger, Kisha Tracy, Elaine Treharne, Mike Twomey, David Wallace, Nicholas Watson, Charlie Wright, and Bob Yeager have all shaped my ideas, without in some cases agreeing with any of them. Dr William Rossiter, the reader for the press, who still "collegially" disagrees with "certain core principles of the argument," made many improvements and changed the title. Because of her unsurpassed command of Chaucer and publishing, Caroline Palmer has been the perfect editor.

Two students enter these pages at particular points: Betsy Passmore's dissertation on the Loathly Lady mapped out for me a tradition central to my claims about the Irish sources of the *Wife of Bath's Tale*, and Gretchen Hendrick's seminar paper on *Decameron* 3.9, the story of Gilette of Narbonne, as another source for this tale opened a new possible relationship that deserves a full scholarly hearing. Christine Romparto-Cooper and her husband, Giovanni

Romparto, offered timely help with some of Boccaccio's more idiomatic Italian. The medievalists in my most recent graduate seminar, Will Biel, Jake Couturiaux, Laura Godfrey, Micah Goodrich, and Katelyn Jaynes, were presented the tales in the order Chaucer wrote them; their own work again taught me of the limits of mine. Lindy Brady, who has just completed her first book, has read and talked me through the whole thing. For three more friends, Peter Calliauw, Jody Falco, and Jeffrey Steinman, and for Sheila McTighe, it will, I hope, bring back good memories. To all, thank you.

And genuine and various thanks to each named in the dedication. Let me mention only that many years ago on a crowded bus to her school in London with one of her teachers sitting not many seats away Catriona allowed me to tell her the *Miller's Tale*, including "a berd, a berd," a story that she has often retold. And recently, Elizabeth took time away from her dissertation to sort out the Common Plea that mentions a pepper mill. Their grandparents have been a constant help with my and their educations. My father, whose mother read him Chaucer, has died; my mother, who pretends to prefer Bede, has read and commented on many versions of this work.

List of Abbreviations

CCCM   Corpus Christianorum Continuatio Mediaevalis
DIL   *Dictionary of the Irish Language*, http://www.dil.ie/
DMA   *Dictionary of the Middle Ages*, 13 vols., ed. Joseph R. Strayer
           (New York: Scribner, 1982–89)
DMLBS   *Dictionary of Medieval Latin from Medieval Sources*, 17 vols.,
           ed. R. E. Latham et al. (London: Oxford University Press,
           1975–2013)
FFC   Folklore Fellows' Communications
McWilliam *The Decameron*, ed. and trans. G. H. McWilliam (2nd edn,
           London: Penguin, 1995)
MED   *Middle English Dictionary*, http://quod.lib.umich.edu/m/med/
S&A   *Sources and Analogues of* The Canterbury Tales, 2 vols., ed.
           Robert M. Correale with Mary Hamel (Cambridge: D. S.
           Brewer, 2002 and 2005)
Stockton *The Major Latin Works of John Gower:* The Voice of One
           Crying *and* The Tripartite Chronicle, trans. Eric W. Stockton
           (Seattle: University of Washington Press, 1962)
TLIO   *Tesoro della lingua italiana delle origini*, http://tlio.ovi.cnr.it/
           TLIO/
Wilson   *Mirour de l'omme (The Mirror of Mankind), by John Gower*,
           trans. William Burton Wilson, rev. trans. Nancy Wilson Van
           Baak (East Lansing: Colleagues Press, 1992)

Conventions for Citing Editions

Quotations and translations from the works of Boccaccio, Chaucer, and Gower are identified parenthetically by the standard editions discussed below. Many other texts cited in the following pages are referred to using a similar system, specifying the edition in question when first mentioned and then relying on parenthetical references.

The *Decameron* is quoted from the edition of Vittore Branca (Turin: Einaudi, 1980). Passages are identified by the day, novella, and section: for example, 8.1, 2 refers to the second section in the first *novella* of the Eighth Day. I have also consulted the edition of Amedeo Quondam, Maurizio Fiorilla, and Giancarlo Alfano, first published in 2013, 6th edn (Milan: BUR Classici, 2016). Translations are usually those of G. H. McWilliam, *The Decameron*, 2nd edn (London: Penguin, 1995) and are identified by the translator's name and page numbers: for example, McWilliam, p. 632. The main exceptions are the translations of 8.1 and 8.2, which are by John Scattergood in *S&A*, 2.570–80, that is volume 2, pages 570–80, the system used throughout this book to refer to volumes and pages in a multi-volume work. Unidentified translations are my own.

Chaucer's works are quoted from *The Riverside Chaucer*, 3rd edn, ed. Larry D. Benson (Boston: Houghton Mifflin, 1987). Passages in the *Canterbury Tales* are identified by fragment and line numbers: for example, VII, 1 refers to the opening line of the *Shipman's Tale*. Those in the *Book of the Duchess* are referenced by line numbers; those in the *Legend of Good Women* by text (either F or G) and line numbers; and those in *Troilus and Criseyde* by book and line numbers.

Quotations from Gower's *Confessio Amantis* are from the edition of Russell A. Peck, with Latin translations by Andrew Galloway, 3 vols., 2nd edn of vol. 1, TEAMS Middle English Texts Series (Kalamazoo: Medieval Institute Publications, 2003–06). These are identified by book and line numbers. When necessary, references are also made to the edition of G. C. Macaulay in the *Complete Works of John Gower. Vols. 2 and 3. The English Works* (Oxford: Clarendon Press, 1901), identifying Macaulay and using book and line numbers. The *Mirour de l'omme* is cited from the *Complete Works of John Gower. Vol. 1. The French Works*, ed. Macaulay (Oxford: Clarendon Press, 1899) by line numbers. The *Vox Clamantis* is taken from the *Complete Works of John Gower. Vol. 4. The Latin Works*, ed. Macaulay (Oxford: Clarendon Press, 1902); references are to line numbers. Translations of these last two works are by William Burton Wilson (revised by Nancy Wilson Van Baak),

Mirour de l'omme (The Mirror of Mankind), by John Gower (East Lansing: Colleagues Press, 1992) and Eric W. Stockton, *The Major Latin Works of John Gower:* The Voice of One Crying *and* The Tripartite Chronicle (Seattle: University of Washington Press, 1962); these are referenced by the translators' name and page numbers.

In addition to primary editions of complete works, I have also relied on extracts, particularly those gathered for the study of Chaucer's sources by the contributors to *S&A*. In the bibliography of primary sources, these are referred to only by the volume and page numbers of *S&A* on which they appear, but the contributors are identified in the text and the Bibliography of Secondary Sources.

The Bible is quoted from the *Biblia Sacra iuxta Vulgatam versionem*, 5th edn, ed. Roger Gryson and Robert Weber (Stuttgart: Deutsche Bibelgesellschaft, 2007); the translation is the Douay-Rheims.

Introduction

This book places the origin of the *Canterbury Tales* in the *Decameron*, arguing that Chaucer found in Boccaccio's work two new ways to write that allowed him to begin his own collection and that carried him through its first major revision, the creation of a second story for the Wife of Bath. My main evidence is, then, her tale, the one first assigned to her but now known as the *Shipman's Tale*, and a third also written, I argue, as he began the work, the *Miller's Tale*. These three show that Chaucer had learned to create from disparate materials new, short narratives that would embody the ideas he wished to explore.[1] When considered in relation to the ones with which they were originally paired, *Melibee*, which was first assigned to the Man of Law, and the *Knight's Tale*, they also demonstrate that he found in Licisca's outburst at the beginning of the Sixth Day of the *Decameron* how to build these tales into a frame that would not only announce the topics to be addressed but also engage in the debates carried out through the work. Finally, in making these claims I also argue that two of these narratives, the *Miller's Tale* and the *Wife of Bath's Tale*, were retold by others almost as soon as they had been written, the first serving as the basis for the anonymous Dutch *boerde*, *Heile van Beersele*, and the second for Gower's *Tale of Florent*. Indeed, the latter dates Chaucer's own initial work on the *Canterbury Tales* to before 1390 because it was in that year that Gower completed the first version of the *Confessio Amantis*.

These claims may strike some as unlikely because they rely on a distinctive kind of text. The tales of the Miller, Wife of Bath, and Shipman, the *Tale*

---

[1] Using the phrase "la realizzazione narrativa," Pier Massimo Forni has identified a similar use of sources by Boccaccio in the *Decameron*; see *Forme complesse nel* Decameron, Biblioteca di "Lettere italiane," Studi e Testi 42 (Florence: Olschki, 1992); *Adventures in Speech: Rhetoric and Narration in Boccaccio's* Decameron (Philadelphia: University of Pennsylvania Press, 1996); and "La realizzazione narrativa in Boccaccio," in *Gli zibaldoni di Boccaccio: memoria, scrittura, riscrittura*, ed. Michelangelo Picone and Claude Cazalé Bérard (Florence: F. Cesati, 1998), pp. 415–23. See also Francesco Ciabattoni and Forni, eds., *The Decameron Third Day in Perspective* (Toronto: University of Toronto Press, 2014); and in particular Martin Eisner's "The Tale of Ferondo's Purgatory (III.8)," pp. 150–69. William Robins notes that "the *Decameron* is predicated in part upon a disavowal of popular storytellers and *uomini di corte*, despite the fact (or rather because of the fact) that their repertoire has been ransacked by Boccaccio for compelling narrative material"; "The Case of the Court Entertainer: Popular Culture, Intertextual Dialogue, and the Early Circulation of Boccaccio's *Decameron*," *Speculum* 92 (2017), p. 5.

of Florent, and *Heile van Beersele* are similar to the many short, often comic narratives that circulated both orally and in collections throughout Western Europe from roughly the end of the eleventh century.[2] Because the works of Boccaccio focused on here, *Decameron* 3.4, 7.2, 8.1, 8.2, and 8.10, are part of this same tradition, establishing precise literary relationships among them would appear to be difficult, if not impossible.[3] While we are certain that Chaucer and Gower knew each other's works, scholars have long debated whether Chaucer used the *Decameron*. Expressing the current scholarly opinion, Helen Cooper returns the issue to the murky place between oral and literate sources when she argues that although Chaucer had heard or perhaps read parts of Boccaccio's work, he did not have direct access to it as he wrote.[4]

This book initially challenges the claim that we must remain agnostic about Chaucer's use of the *Decameron* by proposing a new source, 8.10, for the *Shipman's Tale*. The first two *novelle* of the Eighth Day, which have long been considered analogues for Chaucer's tale, have been identified by folklorists as examples of a tale type called the Lover's Gift Regained. Recognizing 8.10 as like them changes our understanding of their relationship as well. 8.2 is the simplest of the three. Set in Varlungo, a hamlet near Florence, it recounts how a parish priest, who has convinced the wife of one of his parishioners to sleep with him in exchange for his cloak, gets his garment back by informing her husband, at a moment when he knows the two are together, that he had left it as collateral for a mortar and pestle that he had borrowed. The exchanges in 8.1 are more elaborate. Here a German mercenary living in Milan punishes a woman whom he no longer considers

---

2   A useful introduction is *Medieval Comic Tales*, 2nd edn, ed. Derek Brewer (Cambridge: D. S. Brewer, 1996). On the Dutch *boerden*, see F. J. Lodder's dissertation, "Lachen om List en Lust. Studies over de middelnederlandse komische versvertellingen" (Leiden University, 1997).

3   Brewer claims that "there is no clear demarcation" between "oral and written forms" of these narratives; *Comic Tales*, p. xi. While he is certainly right in many cases, Boccaccio and Chaucer, I argue here, are exceptions.

4   *S&A*, 1.7–13; see note 24 for a review of the scholarship on Chaucer's possible use of the *Decameron*. As Cooper claims, "much of David Wallace's *Chaucerian Polity: Absolutist Lineages and Associational Forms in England and Italy* (Stanford: Stanford University Press, 1997) is devoted to the dialectic that can be constructed between them"; see also, Wallace, *Giovanni Boccaccio: Decameron* (Cambridge: Cambridge University Press, 1991), p. 111; and "Italy," in *A Companion to Chaucer*, 2nd edn, ed. Peter Brown (Oxford: Blackwell, 2008), pp. 221–22. Since Cooper's evaluation, see especially Robert R. Edwards, *Chaucer and Boccaccio: Antiquity and Modernity* (Basingstoke: Palgrave, 2002); Carol Falvo Heffernan, *Comedy in Chaucer and Boccaccio* (Cambridge: D. S. Brewer, 2009), which I reviewed in *JEGP* 110 (2011), pp. 409–11; and K. P. Clarke's *Chaucer and Italian Textuality* (Oxford: Oxford University Press, 2011). Warren Ginsberg in *Tellers, Tales, & Translation in Chaucer's Canterbury Tales* (Oxford: Oxford University Press, 2015) largely overlooks the issue, but comments near the end of the study, "I believe that Chaucer had at most only heard about the 'cento novelle contro la morte'" (p. 226).

worthy of his devotion by borrowing the money that she has asked for from her husband and then explaining later, when the three are together, that he has returned it to her. 8.10 is the most complicated of these *novelle*, subordinating its transactions to another common motif, the Deceiver Deceived. In it a Florentine merchant in Palermo must regain the proceeds of the sale of his company's goods, which he has loaned without collateral to the courtesan who has seduced him but then ended their affair. The similarities among the three narratives might be explained by noting that they are related by the theme of the day, "the tricks that people in general, men and women alike, are forever playing upon one another" (McWilliam, p. 548). They are linked, however, more closely in that each is a trick played by a man on a woman, making them closer to the more specific theme considered and then rejected by the queen of the day: "Dioneo volle ieri che oggi si ragionasse delle beffe che le donne fanno a' mariti; e, se non fosse che io non voglio mostrare d'essere di schiatta di can botolo che incontanente si vuol vendicare, io direi che domane si dovesse ragionare delle beffe che gli uomini fanno alle lor mogli" (7, *Conclusione*, 3; "yesterday, Dioneo insisted that we should talk, today, about the tricks played upon husbands by their wives; and but for the fact that I do not wish it to be thought that I belong to that breed of snapping curs who immediately turn around and retaliate, I should oblige you, on the morrow to talk about the tricks played on wives by their husbands," McWilliam, p. 548). The only other story told on the Eighth Day which concerns a conflict between a man and a woman is the brutal 8.7, in which a scholar gets revenge on a widow, who has made him spend a night in the snow as he tries in vain to sleep with her, by making her "spend a whole day, in mid July, at the top of a tower, where, being completely naked, she is exposed to the flies and gadflies and the rays of the sun" (McWilliam, p. 585). 8.1, 8.2, and 8.10 are associated, then, not only by their placement at the beginning and end of the day but also by their specific concern with the connection between sex and gifts or money.[5]

It is, however, the relationship of these three *novelle* to their likely source that provides the strongest evidence that Boccaccio wrote them as a group, constructing 8.1 and 8.10 from the narrative of 8.2. As discussed in more detail in Chapter 1, the events of 8.2 are indeed close to a folktale that circulated widely in India, the Near East, and Western Europe beginning in the twelfth century. However, a short Latin poem, the "Versus de mola piperis" ("A Poem about a Pepper Mill"), appears likely to have been the version from which Boccaccio worked:

---

[5] See the discussion of the relationships of the themes in the stories of this day in Giovanni Boccaccio, *Decameron*, ed. Amedeo Quondam, Maurizio Fiorilla, and Giancarlo Alfano, 6th edn (Milan: BUR Classici, 2016), pp. 1175–79.

Militis uxorem clamidis mercede subegit
Clericus, et piperis clam tulit ipse molam.
Mane redit, referensque molam presente marito.
Dixit, "mantellum redde; reporto molam."
"Redde," maritus ait. Respondet femina, "reddam;
Amplius ad nostram non molet ipse molam."[6]

(A clerk won a soldier's wife with, as payment, a cloak and that very one secretly took a pepper mill. The next morning he returns, giving the mill to the husband who is there. "Give me back the cloak; I am returning the mill," he said. "Give it back," says the husband. "I will," answers the wife, "but this one will grind no more at our mill.")

While there are a number of more immediate surprises here, the two objects, the *clamis* (cloak) and the pepper mill, contribute to an unexpected contrast: the coarse behavior is carried out by wealthy, upper-class people. Intrigued by this turn in a story usually told about the lower class, Boccaccio wrote separate *novelle* about people of different social standing, in which he also detailed the different economies themselves, the bartering of peasants in Varlungo, the loans of urban merchants in Milan, and the new economies of international banking and trade in Palermo.

We can be as certain as one ever is in proposing a new source relationship that Chaucer perceived this connection shared by these *novelle* because he combined elements of all three in the *Shipman's Tale*. Scholars have long considered 8.1 and 8.2 analogues to this tale, finding in the first a similar narrative and in the second parallels to its puns and lack of morality. Two analogues, however, can always be dismissed as too uncertain to be considered sources because they could suggest no more than a lost common ancestor. More striking, however, than similarities of plot and tone is Chaucer's use of the distinct economies depicted in all three *novelle*. Here let me note only that he invoked a peasant, feudal economy in Daun John's profession as a monk and the gifts that he distributes throughout the merchant's household. The urban setting of Saint-Denis is like that of Milan, and the relationship between the merchant and his wife personifies their bourgeois lives. Most remarkable, however, is Chaucer's attention to the merchant's activities as he travelled to the banking centers of Bruges and Paris to complete his deals; the impetus for this extension of the narrative is the backdrop of international commerce in 8.10. There is more to say, but even from these details it is certain that Chaucer found all three of these linked stories in the *Decameron* because he played a similarly literary trick of recombining them into a single tale.

---

6   This transcription is from Eton, Eton College, MS 125. See Chapter 2 and the Appendix for bibliography on this text.

It is, moreover, at least reasonable to assume that Chaucer knew these *novelle* well. The relationship of 8.10 to 8.1 and 8.2, which is crucial for understanding the sources of the *Shipman's Tale*, would have been no more apparent to those living in the fourteenth century than it is to modern readers. Unless someone—to suggest that it might have been Boccaccio himself indicates how unlikely this possibility is—explained it to him, Chaucer probably worked it out by reading these narratives closely.

This discovery about the sources of one tale has led to my more general claim about the origin of the *Canterbury Tales*. The development of a single idea into three such different *novelle* taught Chaucer a new way to write, not to retell stories, but rather to use odd details to create his own short narratives. Moreover, the relationships among them showed him how to develop complex arguments by juxtaposing conflicting tales on similar topics. Indeed, as already noted, the *novelle* of the Eighth Day are tied to those of the Seventh Day, and both sets are linked back to Licisca's extraordinary outburst recounted in the *cornice* of the Sixth Day. As I discuss in Chapter 3, from her dramatic account of her friend's wedding night Chaucer also learned how to construct frames for his narratives that would play a dramatic role in the debates that they developed. Specifically her status as a servant meant that, in addition to the conflict between men and women, this incident raises the issue of the inequality between the classes. We have, then, both the techniques and the topics that led Chaucer to begin writing the *Canterbury Tales*. The *Shipman's Tale*, originally assigned to the Wife of Bath, would oppose the already written *Melibee*, which would be told by the Man of Law, and the *Miller's Tale* would answer that of the Knight. Although the *Decameron* did not offer a source of the narrative of the new tale for the Wife of Bath, it was the narrative technique that Chaucer learned from Boccaccio that, as I discuss in Chapter 5, lies behind this remarkable tale.

Heile van Beersele and, to a greater extent, the *Tale of Florent* at first challenge but finally, I argue, confirm this proposal about the origin in the *Decameron* of the *Canterbury Tales*. As I discuss in Chapter 4, the garbled version of the *Miller's Tale* that appears in the Dutch *boerde* draws attention to the literary sophistication of Chaucer's original, constructed as it was from several different sources, including *Decameron* 3.4 and 7.2. Indeed, a review of its other analogues demonstrates that the *Miller's Tale* is ill-suited for popular dissemination and so is unlikely to have arisen as an oral folktale. Moreover, the early date of the manuscript in which *Heile van Beersele* is preserved offers some initial indication that Chaucer composed this tale early in his work on the project. The *Tale of Florent* engages these same issues, but does so more dramatically because more is known about Gower's methods of composition and the publication history of the *Confessio Amantis*. Although it emerges only briefly in the discussion of the sources of the *Canon's Yeoman's Tale* in Chapter 1 and then disappears until Chapter 5, the analysis of the Chaucer–Gower quarrel is a significant secondary focus of this book. Like the *Canterbury Tales* Gower's collection is deeply literary, employing both a complicated framing device and a wide variety of illustrative narratives. With perhaps only one other exception, the *Tale of Three Questions*, there is, however, no evidence that Gower constructed new narratives with the freedom that Chaucer learned from the *Decameron*. It is then much more likely that he created the *Wife of Bath's Tale*, which Gower then retold as the *Tale of Florent*. Indeed, I argue that Gower's rewriting of the tale caused the two authors to fall out. In any case if the direction of transmission is from the Wife's tale to the *Confessio Amantis*, Chaucer must have written both her original tale and the new one before 1390. Licisca's outburst began the *Canterbury Tales*.

There is much speculation in the pages that follow. The basic fact, however, of a source relationship between *Decameron* 8.1, 8.2, and 8.10 and the *Shipman's Tale* appears, to me at least, to be certain. Let me round off this introduction by mentioning two of the immediate historical contexts, uncertain as they still are, into which this discovery must fit.

Manuscripts of the Canterbury Tales *and Chaucer's Access* to the Decameron

A developing consensus about the nature of the manuscript of the *Canterbury Tales*, which was expressed by John H. Fisher in his presidential address to the Medieval Academy in 1988, has been challenged in radically different ways by Ralph Hanna and Linne R. Mooney. According to Fisher, "present opinion tends therefore to the hypothesis that the copy texts for both *Troylus* and *The Canterbury Tales* were bundles of vellum fascicles interlarded with marginal and interlinear emendations and inserted leaves from which different scribes elicited different texts after Chaucer's death."[7] Although his specific point of departure is not this "consensus" but rather N. F. Blake's more specific claim that, as the earliest manuscript,[8] Hengwrt is our sole authority for establishing what Chaucer actually wrote, Hanna explores the possibility that this manuscript might instead have been put together by "an early editor lacking access to the author's papers but attempting to assemble the poem piecemeal out of odd bits acquired from individual owners."[9] In sharp contrast Mooney builds from the identification of the scribe of both Hengwrt and Ellesmere as Adam Pinkhurst, whom she associates with the

---

7   John H. Fisher, "Animadversions on the Text of Chaucer," *Speculum* 63 (1988), p. 789.
8   Aberystwyth, National Library of Wales, Peniarth 392D. The manuscript can be found online at http://www.sd-editions.com/AnaAdditional/HengwrtEx/images/hgopen.html/.
9   Ralph Hanna, "The Hengwrt Manuscript and the Canon of *The Canterbury Tales*," in *Pursuing History: Middle English Manuscripts and Their Texts* (Stanford: Stanford University Press, 1996), p. 148.

Adam named in Chaucer's short poem "Adam Scriveyn," to argue that "the Hengwrt manuscript may have initially been supervised by the poet himself; the Ellesmere manuscript, even if copied after Chaucer's death, would nevertheless have been written by a scribe who had had a close working relationship with Chaucer through the years when he was writing the *Tales*."[10] These two positions are incompatible: if Adam had not only Chaucer's papers but the author himself to consult, it is difficult to explain, for example, why booklet 4 of the earlier manuscript would, as Hanna has argued, both reflect the "common procedure" of compilers of manuscripts who encounter disparate material they wish to include and remain "somewhat outside the categories of text" already copied.[11] In contrast, while my study provides some new evidence in support of Hanna's thesis for the independent circulation of individual tales,[12] it seems unlikely that an editor working as he proposes would miss only one tale (the Canon's Yeoman's) while also acquiring many of the links, which need not have circulated with their tales. Perhaps the new consensus is that these complicated issues cannot be settled, as Hanna puts it, "by a priori logical fiat."[13] My working assumptions, then, are that both Hengwrt and Ellesmere were written after Chaucer's death, that the mistakes in Hengwrt's order reflect the difficulty of untangling the materials he left unfinished, and that the many similarities among all of the manuscripts allow us to perceive much if not all of his plan.[14]

The main outline of Chaucer's contact with Italy has long been known to scholars, but the topic continues to yield new insights from examinations of questions both large and small. Derek Pearsall contextualizes the established facts in his biography: Chaucer probably learned Italian "as a boy from the Italian merchants with whom his father and his step-cousins, the Herons, had had business"; he travelled to Italy twice (1 December 1372 to 23 May 1373 and 28 May to 19 September 1378); and on 11 November 1373 he

---

10 Linne R. Mooney, "Chaucer's Scribe," *Speculum* 81 (2006), pp. 119–20. Jane Roberts offers substantial paleographic, linguistic, and art-historical evidence to challenge this conclusion; "On Giving Scribe B a Name and a Clutch of London Manuscripts from c. 1400," *Medium Ævum* 80 (2011), pp. 247–70. The Ellesmere manuscript, San Marino, Huntington Library, El 26 C 9, can be found online through the Huntington Digital Library, http://hdl. huntington.org/cdm/.

11 Hanna, "Hengwrt," p. 146.

12 Gower, I would argue, must have had access to the *Wife of Bath's Tale* almost as soon as it was written. Similarly, if the manuscript in which *Heile van Beersele* survives is, as the paleographers believe, early, the *Miller's Tale* seems also to have circulated, either in written or oral form, very quickly.

13 Hanna, "Hengwrt," p. 155. For a review of other approaches to the manuscript evidence as well as a discussion of fifteenth-century scribal practices, see Simon Horobin, "Compiling the *Canterbury Tales* in Fifteenth-Century Manuscripts," *Chaucer Review* 47 (2013), pp. 372–89.

14 See Larry D. Benson, "The Order of the *Canterbury Tales*," *Studies in the Age of Chaucer* 3 (1981), pp. 77–117. Beyond the scope of this project but influential to it is Donald R. Howard, *The Idea of the* Canterbury Tales (Berkeley: University of California Press, 1976).

represented the crown in Dartmouth, which he would later make the home of the Shipman, in arranging the return of a merchant-ship to its Genoese master.[15] Working on a much larger interpretive scale, David Wallace has considered Chaucer's intellectual engagement with Italy, aligning his understanding of Dante and Boccaccio with Florentine republicanism and Petrarch with Lombard tyranny.[16] Focusing more narrowly on manuscript production, K. P. Clarke has drawn particular attention to Boccaccio and Chaucer as glossators of their works.[17] However, two articles, one by Robert A. Pratt and the other by William E. Coleman, may serve to close this introduction.[18]

Starting from the premise that much of Chaucer's use of Italian literature dates to after his 1378 visit to Italy,[19] Pratt proposes the libraries of the Visconti brothers and co-dukes of Lombardy, Bernabò's in Milan and Galeazzo II's in Pavia, as the likely sources of his Italian books. This family, known for its lordly munificence, would have had reason to favor their English guests with gifts: whatever the actual purpose of the mission was, it apparently failed, making other ways for the Italians to ingratiate themselves with the representatives of the English crown appealing.[20] Moreover, Pratt speculates that the later practice of providing copies of rare materials in the family's libraries may already have been in effect.[21] Building on Pratt's arguments while focusing specifically on one manuscript of the *Teseida* in Galeazzo's library (Bernabò's collection was apparently destroyed when his nephews captured him and burned his castle in 1385), Coleman provides further reasons for Chaucer's undocumented visit to Pavia and identifies manuscript 881, now

---

[15] Derek Pearsall, *The Life of Geoffrey Chaucer: A Critical Biography* (Oxford: Blackwell, 1992), pp. 102–09.

[16] Wallace, *Chaucerian Polity*.

[17] *Chaucer and Italian Textuality*. While he acknowledges that "the majority of early manuscripts" contain the entire collection, Clarke discusses two that could support the claim that Chaucer knew a "fragmentary *Decameron*" (p. 97). One, Vatican City, Biblioteca Apostolica Vatican, Vat. lat. 9893 is particularly relevant because it is made up of three parts, covering the stories from Days I–III, IV–VII and VIII–X. The following pages discuss passages from all three parts.

[18] Their work is contextualized by Peter J. Lucas, "Borrowing and Reference Access to Libraries in the Late Middle Ages," in the *Cambridge History of Libraries in Britain and Ireland*, vol. 1, ed. Elisabeth Leedham-Green and Teresa Webber (Cambridge: Cambridge University Press, 2006), pp. 242–62. See also Rhiannon Daniels's chapter on the *Decameron* in *Boccaccio and the Book: Production and Reading in Italy 1340–1520* (London: Modern Humanities Research Association and Maney Publishing, 2009), pp. 76–136. These topics were addressed at a conference organized by Piero Boitani and Kenneth Clarke at Pembroke College, Cambridge in 2012, where I presented a first draft of Chapter 3.

[19] Robert A. Pratt, "Chaucer and the Visconti Libraries," *English Literary History* 6 (1939), pp. 191–99. The exception, according to Pratt, is Dante's *Commedia*, which he might have acquired on his first visit.

[20] Pratt, "Chaucer and the Visconti," pp. 198–99.

[21] Pratt, "Chaucer and the Visconti," p. 199.

lost but recorded in a 1426 catalogue, as a likely exemplar for his copy.[22] Chaucer would have wanted not only to pay respects to Bernabò's brother, but also to visit the grave of the recently deceased Lionel of Clarence, in the service of whose wife his career as a page had begun. A tour of Galeazzo's library, where amanuenses were available, seems almost inevitable. Although Pratt accepts Otto Schmidt's conclusion that many of this library's Italian manuscripts were acquired after 1378,[23] Coleman connects manuscript 881 to Chaucer since it lacks the parts of the work he seems not to have used: "the prose prologue, the introductory sonnets, Book XII, lxxxiv–lxxxvi, and the two concluding sonnets."[24] If Chaucer was offered or ordered a copy of the *Teseida*, might he not have asked for one of the *Decameron* as well? If so, manuscript 870 in the 1426 catalogue is a possible candidate for its exemplar:

Liber unus in vulgari grossi voluminis qui dicitur liber Decameron in papiro completus per d. Johannem Bocacium de Certaldo civem florentinum; qui incipit: *Ogni cosa* et finitur: *alcuna cosa giova laverlo leto Deo gratias amen.* cum clavis grossis platis ac assidibus copertis corio rubeo hirsute albicato.[25]

(A thick, one volume book on paper in Italian called the *Decameron* written by dottore Giovanni Boccaccio from the Florentine city Certaldo, which begins "Ogni cosa" and ends "alcuna cosa giova laverlo leto Deo Gratias. amen." With thick, flat clasps and fine bindings of rough, whitened red leather.)

Unlike manuscript 881, here Boccaccio is clearly identified as the author of the work.

This speculation may help us to visualize Chaucer's *Decameron*. A thick book in Italian written on paper.[26] Had Chaucer paid for it himself, he might well have economized by leaving it unbound or getting a limp binding.[27] At the time of his death, such a volume would have been an anomaly in England,

---

[22] William E. Coleman, "Chaucer, the *Teseida*, and the Visconti Library at Pavia: A Hypothesis," *Medium Ævum* 51 (1982), pp. 92–101.

[23] "Die Visconti und ihre Bibliothek zu Pavia," *Zeitschrift für Geschichte und Politik* 5 (1888), pp. 456–57.

[24] Coleman, "Chaucer, the *Teseida*," p. 98. Coleman also considers it significant that this manuscript lacked not only Boccaccio's commentary but also any attribution to him.

[25] Elisabeth Pellegrin, *La Bibliothèque des Visconti et des Sforza, ducs de Milan, au XVe siècle* (Paris: C.N.R.S., 1955), p. 267.

[26] Paris, Bibliothèque nationale de France, Italien 63, which provides the cover of this book, is a paper manuscript but, I assume, different from Chaucer's because of its illustrations. For further information on this manuscript, see http://archivesetmanuscrits.bnf.fr/ark:/12148/cc9591h.

[27] See Alexandra Gillespie, "Bookbinding," in *The Production of Books in England 1350–1500*, ed. Gillespie and Daniel Wakelin (Cambridge: Cambridge University Press, 2011), pp. 150–72.

where, unlike on the Continent, parchment continued to be the main writing surface, particularly for literary texts, through at least the mid-fifteenth century.[28] To speculate further: not realizing its value Chaucer's executors might well have passed it on to an Italian merchant or allowed it to fall into disrepair. What do we actually know about Chaucer's *Decameron*? If the claims of my study are correct, it was not only a well-read manuscript, but also an idea, a Decameron, which survives most clearly in the *Canterbury Tales*.

---

[28] See R. J. Lyall, "Materials: The Paper Revolution," in *Book Production and Publishing in Britain 1375–1475*, ed. Jeremy Griffiths and Derek Pearsall (Cambridge: Cambridge University Press, 1989), pp. 11–29; Orietta Da Rold, "Materials," in *Production of Books*, ed. Gillespie and Wakelin, pp. 12–33; and Paul Needham, "The Paper of English Incunabula," in the *Catalogue of Books Printed in the XVth Century Now in the British Library*, BMC, Part XI, England, ed. Lotta Hellinga ('t Goy-Houten: Hes & de Graaf, 2007), p. 312.

1

Boccaccio as the Source for Chaucer's Use of Sources

The literary relationship between the *Decameron* and the *Canterbury Tales* sketched out in the Introduction reveals a distinct attitude toward constructing brief narratives from diverse sources that separates these works from many others, including Chaucer's earlier writings. My claim is not that he had previously lacked imagination. The *Book of the Duchess*, usually considered his earliest major poem, is strikingly original both in its narratives and in the use of its dream vision to frame them. How, then, do its methods of composition differ from those of the three tales focused on here, and by extension, the *Canterbury Tales* as a whole? In a cogent discussion of the difficulties scholars face in establishing the chronology of Chaucer's works, which explains the "also" in the following quotation, Larry D. Benson, editor of the *Riverside Chaucer*, makes a simple and yet profound observation: "Chaucer's works also tend to reflect his reading and intellectual interests" (p. xxviii). After discussing a few of the examples, such as his translation of Boethius's *De consolatione philosophiae*, which "affected almost all that he wrote at that time," Benson introduces "the old, not altogether mistaken, division of Chaucer's career into the so-called French, Italian, and English periods" (p. xxix). While he qualifies this idea by noting that "these divisions are not mutually exclusive," he concludes the discussion, "yet his interests and ideas about poetry did change, and tracing such changes can be useful in determining the chronology of his works" (p. xxix).

In the tales that define the so-called English period Chaucer's reading becomes much more difficult to discover. As a writer he seemed always to have been conscious of his *mater*, the material from which he worked. Indeed, Arlyn Diamond begins her introduction to a collection of essays which grew out of sessions considering the sources of the *Canterbury Tales*, "Chaucer, with his trickster prescience, seems to have anticipated our fascination with his sources," calling attention to his naming of "the texts that matter to him" ("Virgile, Ovide, Omer, Lucan and Stace"; *Troilus and Criseyde*, V, 1792) and noting his "false clues" ("As writ myn auctour called Lollius"; *Troilus and Criseyde*, I, 394).[1] To return to the *Book of the Duchess*, the narrator's

---

[1] Arlyn Diamond, "Introduction" to the "Colloquium: The Afterlife of Origins," *Studies in the Age of Chaucer* 28 (2006), p. 217.

reading at the start of the poem (44–61) not only introduces the story of "Seys" and "Alcyone," which he then tells, but draws attention to two of the major sources of the work as whole, Ovid and Machaut. Colin Wilcockson writes confidently in his notes in the *Riverside Chaucer*,

> The Book of the Duchess was strongly influenced by French poetry, notably *Le Roman de la rose* and the works of Froissart and Machaut. A number of passages are closely translated, and the form of *The Book of the Duchess* owes much to Machaut's *Jugement dou Roy de Behaingne*, where the narrator overhears the stories of the bereaved or forsaken lovers. The notes indicate these source-passages, as well as debts to Ovid, Statius, and others. (p. 966)

Because it is widely accepted, as Wilcockson explains, that the *Book of the Duchess* was written to commemorate the death of Blanche, the wife of John of Gaunt, perhaps the English period can be explained by a new subject matter, the difficult-to-trace popular stories of "harlotrie," with a renewed focus on English settings such as the Oxford of the *Miller's Tale*.

To account for the new direction of the *Canterbury Tales* in this way is to miss the pervasive influence of the *Decameron*. Although the focus of this book is on what I argue are the first three tales that Chaucer wrote for his collection, many later ones are indebted to it as well. And yet a progression within these three is itself revealing. The *Shipman's Tale*, which I argue was written first, is most closely tied to narratives in the *Decameron*, specifically 8.1, 8.2, and 8.10. The *Miller's Tale*, written second, relies more loosely on 3.4 and 7.2, as well as other narratives. The *Wife of Bath's Tale*, the third, uses the *Decameron* only in its narrative technique. Boccaccio did indeed teach Chaucer to be original—to look for ideas that could become tales not primarily in other narratives but rather in the ideas that concerned him.

This chapter, then, provides some background for the ones that follow by considering how Chaucer used sources in the *Canterbury Tales*. After offering definitions of the key terms "source" and "analogue," I discuss the main reason—the lack of verbal echoes—that persuades the scholar on whose work I rely most in this study, Helen Cooper, to argue that although Chaucer had heard or perhaps read parts of Boccaccio's work, he did not consult it as he wrote. I then note some of the assumptions evident in the *Sources and Analogues of the Canterbury Tales*, edited by Robert M. Correale and Mary Hamel. Although most scholars contributing to this reference work expect to find Chaucer writing from an existing narrative, which he sometimes did, many conclude that their assigned tale did not have such a starting point. The discussion of the *Canon's Yeoman's Tale* in this section, although beyond the strict chronological limits of this book, is particularly significant because it introduces the quarrel between Chaucer and Gower and shows just how bitter it became. Finally, I turn to the folktale, which has appeared to scholars as a likely origin for several stories without clear antecedents and which returns us to the tales central to the claim of this book. Chaucer at times used popular traditions, but it was Boccaccio who showed him how.

Sources and Analogues

Initial definitions of two terms, "source" and "analogue," are required here. [2] Since my subject is the *Canterbury Tales*, I use "source" to refer to anything Chaucer used in composing his collection. As scholars have shown, he turned to many different kinds of material, each of which presents its own challenges. There can be no doubt, for example, that he knew the Bible, the book nonpareil of the Middle Ages, and that he used many other primarily literary traditions associated with it, although these may well have reached him in other, sometimes oral, forms, such as religious instruction, hymns, sermons, and casual conversations. In identifying these kinds of source, R. E. Kaske, who devoted much of his distinguished career to this subject, was less concerned with discovering a particular text than in sorting out what he called the "miscellaneous ragbag" of traditional Christian learning.[3] Others have demonstrated Chaucer's familiarity with other texts—for example, Boethius's *De consolatione philosophiae* and Innocent III's *De miseria condicionis humane*—and other traditions—such as astronomical lore and proverbs. Let me stress that I am using "texts" and "traditions" not as distinct entities, but rather as markers at opposite ends on a continuum. The Bible, for example, is more text than tradition, and yet, as Kaske notes, "throughout the Middle Ages the Latin Bible was continually being re-edited and revised, so that there were in effect many medieval "Vulgates," often differing appreciably according to time and place" (p. 5).[4] In contrast proverbs are more tradition than text, but the *Liber consolationis et consilii*, the ultimate if not direct source for *Melibee*, is, as Cooper puts it, "a *florilegium* of choice sayings organized into an argument."[5] All these texts and traditions are sources, if

---

[2] While useful in articulating some of the issues involved in establishing sources and differentiating them from analogues, Peter G. Beidler's terms, "hard source," "soft source," "hard analogue," "soft analogue," and "lost source," finally confuse the issue by considering analogues primarily as evidence for lost sources; see his "New Terminology for Sources and Analogues," in *Chaucer's Canterbury Comedies: Origins and Originality* (Seattle: Coffeetown Press, 2011), pp. 29–36; this essay was first presented and published as part of the "Colloquium: The Afterlife of Origins."

[3] R. E. Kaske, *Medieval Christian Literary Imagery: A Guide to Interpretation*, Toronto Medieval Bibliographies 11 (Toronto: University of Toronto Press, 1988), p. xvii.

[4] Kaske goes on to discuss the Vetus Latina and translations in other languages. At one end of this continuum I would imagine a particular manuscript that we could prove Chaucer used; at the other the basic structure of Middle English, a language that he would have heard from birth.

[5] Helen Cooper, *The Canterbury Tales*, Oxford Guides to Chaucer, 2nd edn (Oxford: Oxford University Press, 1996), pp. 313–15.

the correspondence any one of them offers is, to quote Kaske again, "precise or complex enough" and carries "an appropriate enough meaning for its context, that to consider it accidental would outrage probability" (p. xx). There are, then, many kinds of sources for the *Canterbury Tales* just as there is a differing degree of certainty in any proposed source relationship.

The *Canterbury Tales* is, however, primarily a collection of stories, and, if the thesis of this book is correct, it was through them that Chaucer, following the *Decameron*, set out to explore ideas. There is, therefore, a strong reason for seeking the sources of its narratives, the origins, whatever they may be, of each of its stories. It is in this sense that I will use the phrase "source of the narrative" for the source or sources, be they narrative or not, necessary to account for the unfolding of the events in each of Chaucer's tales. The search is not for the earliest version of a particular narrative or expression of the key idea that led to it, but rather for the one or ones from which Chaucer was most likely to have worked, because they allow us to see what he both accepted and changed. It is, moreover, in this more restricted context that I will use the term "analogue," a story that is neither the source of nor itself derived from one of Chaucer's tales, but similar to it in some significant way. Two stories may be analogues because they come from a common source, but they may also share certain illuminating features even though they appear in separate traditions. I will consider these definitions in more detail when turning to the two-volume study *Sources and Analogues of the Canterbury Tales* below.

Allusions and Verbal Echoes

Verbal echoes are generally considered the surest means of establishing a source relationship, more certain even than authorial assertions. Kaske offered the memorable, if admittedly "improbable," example, contrasting "a letter signed by Chaucer" insisting that at a particular point he had used the *Confessio Amantis* with "a passage in the writings ascribed to Zoroaster" that "offers an uncommonly precise and complex correspondence" to this part of one of his works (pp. xx–xxi). His conclusion: "we would have no choice but to reject the allusion to the *Confessio Amantis* and assume some sort of connection—direct, or more probably indirect—between our passage and the works of Zoroaster" (p. xxi). In this case, the situation is reversed. Even though Chaucer used a number of the Boccaccio's works including the *Filostrato*, the *Teseida*, and *De casibus virorum illustrium*, he never mentioned him by name and, indeed, when he had the Clerk identify the source for his tale, he invokes "Fraunceys Petrak, the lauriat poete" (IV, 31), not *Decameron* 10.10, Petrarch's acknowledged source. Were it not for the relationship of the *Shipman's Tale* to the *novelle* of the Eighth Day, this silence might well suggest Chaucer did not know whose works he had used in writing, for example, *Troilus*, the *Knight's Tale*, and the *Monk's Tale*, and, more specifically, that he had not read the *Decameron*. With the evidence, however, of the *Shipman's Tale*, it becomes clear that Chaucer specifically sought out Boccaccio's works and so was fully prepared to treat the *Decameron* with respect for its serious intent. The Clerk's decision to cite and use Petrarch is finally a comment on him and on the misogyny, as the Wife of Bath points out, of Latin learning. Following this line of thought, I would suggest that Chaucer did not mention his main source for the *Canterbury Tales* because to do so would oppose what he had learned from Boccaccio: to engage in the illusion that his tales, as part of a vast collection of amusing stories, simply reflect the views of his tellers.

A similar argument may lie behind the lack or, I would claim, avoidance of verbal echoes, the detail that most influences Cooper to argue that "Chaucer had read or heard the *Decameron* while in Italy—conceivably even from an Italian merchant in London—but did not have a copy of his own to set in front of him while he was writing."[6] She uses this possibility to explain why "the closest parallels show the kind of creative reinvention that would more plausibly come from thinking about Boccaccian ideas than from reworking his precise words" (*S&A*, 1.8–9). She discusses five kinds of similarity between the two collections; the following list recalls her main points: (1) they share similar frame narratives; (2) the *Decameron* offers a number of analogues for individual tales and prologues; (3) in each "the author remains as a first-person presence alongside the story tellers" and "they both use their presence to justify their work in strikingly similar terms"; (4) both "offer a wider range of tales than the typical single-genre medieval story-collection"; and (5) both "develop connections of theme and motif between tales" (*S&A*, 1.9–13). In the context of her fifth point, Cooper even mentions Licisca's outburst as "an approximate parallel" for Chaucer's "interplay between the characters of his frame and their counterparts within the tales" (*S&A*, 1.13). My views follow Cooper's very closely.[7] However, while she concludes that "the most obvious interpretation of this convergence is that it represents Chaucer's own elaboration of a model he recalled from the *Decameron*" (*S&A*, 1.13), I claim that he had read and studied this work much more closely, indeed learning from it to avoid verbal echoes because doing so allowed him to think in his own way.[8]

---

[6]   *S&A*, 1.8; and see the works cited in note 4 in the Introduction. The lack of verbal borrowings has led Warren Ginsberg to deny "textual contact" and instead argue for "cross-cultural translation"; "'Gli scogli neri e il niente che c'è': Dorigen's Black Rocks and Chaucer's Translation of Italy," in *Reading Medieval Culture: Essays in Honor of Robert W. Hanning*, ed. Robert M. Stein and Sandra Pierson Prior (Notre Dame: University of Notre Dame Press, 2005), p. 387.

[7]   I have turned often to Professor Cooper's *The Structure of the* Canterbury Tales (Athens: University of Georgia Press, 1983) and *Canterbury Tales* when I teach Chaucer. I am also grateful for her help and generosity through the years.

[8]   Daniel Wakelin concludes a review of the first volume of *S&A*, in which he expresses some skepticism about Chaucer's knowledge of the *Decameron*, with the point that since Chaucer

Let me make this discussion more concrete with two examples, the first from Boccaccio's handling of his likely source for 8.1, 8.2, and 8.10, and the second from Chaucer's use of the *Decameron* in the *Shipman's Tale*. As we will see in more detail in Chapter 2, the "Versus de mola piperis," quoted in the Introduction and Chapter 2, succeeds in part by mixing a few specific terms into a situation that implies more than it states. A priest lies with ("subegit") the wife of a soldier by giving her his cloak (*clamis*) and then secretly takes a pepper grinder (*mola piperis*). When he returns the grinder asking for his cloak back and the husband tells his wife to return it, she responds, "'that one will grind no more in our mill'" ("'amplius ad nostram non molet ipse molam'"). In 8.2 Boccaccio played on the sexual innuendo of "grinding," using it to introduce Belcolore, the wife of a farm-worker, as "atta a meglio saper macinar che alcuna altra" (8.2, 9; "able to know better how to grind than any other"; *cf.* McWilliam, p. 555, "who seemed better versed in the grinder's art than any other girl in the village").[9] Moreover, he returned to the metaphor in an exaggerated, if somewhat cryptic, form when the priest tries to convince Belcolore to sleep with him by claiming that the clergy do better work, "'perché noi maciniamo a raccolta'" (8.2, 23; "'we do our grinding when the millpond's full,'" McWilliam, p. 557).[10] When he reaches the story's climax, however, Boccaccio replaced the pepper grinder with a mortar, in part setting up the priest's final quip, "'dira'le...che s'ella non ci presterà il mortaio, io non presterò a lei il pestello; vada l'un per l'altro'" (8.2, 45; "'tell her that if she doesn't lend me her mortar, I shan't let her have my pestle. It's no use having one without the other,'" McWilliam, p. 560). More significant, however, for the argument of this book is that omitting the reference to pepper, a luxury during the Middle Ages,[11] is part of Boccaccio's setting of the story more specifically among the peasantry, where indeed many *fabliaux* take place. While there will be more to say on this topic in Chapter 2, the point here is that by not translating the Latin, he moved the narrative in a different direction, first to mock the morality of peasants but more profoundly to set up a larger reflection across the three *novelle* on the sexual morals of the lower, middle, and upper classes.

---

imagines his pilgrims to construct tales from memory "with nothing but their wit," "could not he himself have exercised similar freedom?" *Review of English Studies* 54 (2003), pp. 516–17.

9   I follow here Forni's analysis (*Adventures in Speech*, pp. 71–2), adding the relationship to Boccaccio's source.

10   The phrase hinges on the meaning of "a raccolta," "from a collection." McWilliam's translation follows Branca's note. Of course, shifts in scale are exactly what Boccaccio played with as he moved the story from the village to the world of international commerce.

11   Relying on a variety of evidence, including the *Canterbury Tales*, Paul Freedman argues strongly that spices such as pepper "were effective in claiming, conveying, and confirming social status"; see *Out of the East: Spices and the Medieval Imagination* (New Haven: Yale University Press, 2008), p. 5.

Similarly, Chaucer both used and modified a clause from 8.10 about the necessity of money for merchants. After putting in place an elaborate scheme to fleece a Florentine merchant, Salabaetto, of his company's money, Janco-fiore, a courtesan in Palermo, feigns unwillingness to accept the five hundred gold florins because she knows he is a merchant, "'e i mercatanti fanno co' denari tutti i fatti loro'" (8.10, 36; "'and merchants do all their business with money,'" McWilliam, p. 638). This comment is the source for the idea and indeed of the wording, except for the final striking metaphor, of a remark by the merchant in the *Shipman's Tale* as he asks the monk, daun John, to make sure that he returns the hundred francs he is borrowing:

> "But o thyng is, ye knowe it wel ynogh
> Of chapmen, that hir moneie is hir plogh." (VII, 287–88)

Merchants work with money.[12] Indeed, the idea stands out in the *Shipman's Tale* because it is not motivated by the plot. Jancofiore's protestation is only one of many means she uses to deceive Salabaetto, but it is particularly appropriate at this moment in the story because it should remind him not only that the money is not his but also that he should think like a merchant, as she will later do when he asks for a loan, securing his investment. In contrast the merchant in the *Shipman's Tale* trusts daun John and treats him as a friend. Immediately before this couplet, he assures the monk that he is welcome to all that he has:

> "O cosyn myn, daun John,
> Now sikerly this is a smal requeste.
> My gold is youres, whan that it yow leste,
> And nat oonly my gold, but my chaffare.
> Take what yow list; God shilde that ye spare." (VII, 282–86)[13]

---

[12] In their note on these lines in the *Riverside Chaucer*, J. A. Burrow and V. J. Scattergood suggest that it may be proverbial or reflect current economic conditions. They make the first point by quoting a couplet from "Money, Money!," a poem preserved in a fifteenth-century manuscript: "At al tymys the best ware is / Every redy money"; quoted from *Historical Poems of the XIVth and XVth Centuries*, ed., Rossell Hope Robbins (New York: Columbia University Press, 1959), p. 136. On the manuscript, London, British Library, Royal 17. B. 47, see the British Library online catalogue, which identifies "Money, Money!" (fol. 159 b) as in a fifteenth-century hand. Even if a commonplace in the fourteenth century, Boccaccio's use of it could be the source of Chaucer's. Burrow and Scattergood raise the possibility that Chaucer might have been aware that "supplies of money were low" by citing Sylvia L. Thrupp, *The Merchant Class in Medieval London 1300–1500* (Chicago: University of Chicago Press, 1948), p. 143.

[13] These lines may echo Jancofiore's speech as "ella gli cinse una bella e leggiadra cinturetta d'argento con una bella borsa" ("she fastened a dainty and beautiful little silver girdle round his waist with a fine purse to go with it") following their first night together: "'Salabaetto mio dolce, io mi ti raccomando: e così come la mia persona è al piacer tuo, così è ciò che ci è, e ciò che per me si può è allo comando tuio'" (8.10, 25; "'My darling Salabaetto, I

Moreover, as the story transpires, daun John will be all too willing to return the money. Perhaps the clearest evidence, however, that the merchant's remark is not motivated by the Shipman's narrative is the absence of any similar comment in the story most like his, *Decameron* 8.1. Here, after he has heard of Madonna Ambruogia's demand of two hundred gold florins before she will sleep with him, the German soldier, Gulfardo, approaches her husband for a loan:

> "Io son per fare un mio fatto per lo quale mi bisognan fiorini dugento d'oro, li quali io voglio che tu mi presti con quello utile che tu mi suogli prestar degli altri." Guasparuolo disse che volentieri e di presente gli annoverò i denari. (8.1, 10)

> ("I'm about to drive a bargain, for which I require two hundred gold florins. Would it be possible for you to lend them to me, at the same rate of interest as usual?" Guasparruolo willingly agreed to lend him the money, and counted it out for him right away; McWilliam, p. 553.)

The merchant's speech, as much else in the *Shipman's Tale*, reflects more deeply on economic matters than is required by the narrative.

Chaucer, however, changed not only the immediate context of the remark but also its wording. Again, I would argue that he did so in response to the *Decameron*, even though his striking metaphor, money is a merchant's plough, does not appear in this work. What would have surprised him was Boccaccio's modern sense, as evident in the passage just quoted from 8.1, that it is acceptable to make money from money because usury,[14] often asso-

---

implore you to remember that just as my person is yours to enjoy, so everything I have here is yours, and all that I can do is at your command,'" McWilliam, p. 636).

[14] For an overview, see the article by James A. Brundage, "Usury" in *DMA*, 12.335–39. Still useful for understanding Chaucer's immediate context is R. H. Helmholtz, "Usury and the Medieval English Courts," *Speculum* 61 (1986), pp. 364–80. John T. Noonan, *The Scholastic Analysis of Usury* (Cambridge, MA: Harvard University Press, 1957) has been augmented by Odd Langholm, *Economics in the Medieval Schools: Wealth, Exchange, Value, Money and Usury according to the Paris Theological Tradition, 1200–1350*, Studien und Texte zur Geistesgeschichte des Mittelalters 29 (Leiden: Brill, 1992); see pp. 586–89 for a summary and the passages listed in index under "Arguments against usury," p. 628. For an Italian perspective relevant for Boccaccio, see Lawrin Armstrong, *Usury and Public Debt in Early Renaissance Florence: Lorenzo Ridolfi on the* Monte Commune, Texts and Studies 144 (Toronto: Pontifical Institute of Mediaeval Studies, 2003). Gwen Seabourne considers usury in her discussion of loans in *Royal Regulation of Loans and Sales in Medieval England: Monkish Superstition and Civil Tyranny* (Woodbridge: Boydell Press, 2003); and Chris Briggs looks at the problem from the other end of the economic scale in *Credit and Village Society in Fourteenth-Century England* (Oxford: Oxford University Press, 2009); see especially the overviews on pp. 74–77 and 173–75. Mark Koyama's provocative thesis, that the ban on usury was sustained because it allowed certain elites to earn monopoly rents, leads to a wide review of the evidence; see "Evading the 'Taint of Usury': the Usury Prohibition

ciated with the Jews, was condemned during the Middle Ages, as it is in the opening lines of the tale that follows the Shipman's, the Prioress's:

> Ther was in Asye, in a greet citee,
> Amonges Cristene folk a Jewerye,
> Sustened by a lord of that contree
> For foule usure and lucre of vileynye,
> Hateful to Crist and to his compaignye. (VII, 488–92)[15]

One of the arguments used against this practice, as illustrated in a passage from Nicholas Oresme's *De moneta*, a work written perhaps as early as 1360 in response to the monetary policies of Philip VI and John II of France, is that since money, unlike grain, is sterile, it should not multiply:

> Quamuis omnis iniusticia sit quodammodo contra naturam, uerumptamen accipere lucrum ex mutacione monete est quodam speciali modo iniustum innaturale. Naturale enim est quibusdam naturalibus diuiciis se multiplicare, sicut cerealia grana
> que sata cum multo fenore reddit ager,
> ut ait Ouidius; sed monstruosum est et contra naturam quod res infecunda pariat, quod res sterilis a tota specie fructificet uel multiplicetur ex se, cuiusmodi est pecunia. Cum igitur ipsa pecunia affert lucrum, non exponendo eam in mercacione naturalium diuiciarum et in usum proprium ac sibi naturalem, sed eam transmutando in semetipsam, sicut mutando unam in aliam uel tradendo unam pro alia, tale lucrum uile est et preter naturam. Per hanc enim racionem probat Aristotiles primo Politice quod usura est preter naturam...

> (Although all injustice is in a way contrary to nature, yet to make a profit from altering the coinage is specifically an unnatural act of injustice. For it is natural for certain natural riches to multiply, like grains of corn, "which," as Ovid says, "when sown, the field with ample interest repays." But it is monstrous and unnatural that an unfruitful thing should bear, that a thing specifically sterile, such as money, should bear fruit and multiply of itself. Therefore when profit is made from money, not by laying it out in the purchase of natural wealth, its proper and natural use, but by changing it into itself, as changing one form of it for another, or giving one form

---

as a Barrier to Entry," *Explorations in Economic History* 47 (2010), pp. 420–42. Finally, for comparison, see Gower's *Mirour de l'omme*, 7213–344.

[15] For an essay that considers this passage in relation to the tale as a whole, see Kathy Lavezzo, "The Minster and the Privy: Rereading the *Prioress's Tale*," *PMLA* 126 (2011), pp. 363–82. Lavezzo's argument would be strengthened by showing that the examples of loaning money that she adduces were seen as usury. See also, more generally, a work she cites, Joseph Shatzmiller, *Shylock Reconsidered: Jews, Moneylending, and Medieval Society* (Berkeley: University of California Press, 1990), and the reviews of it by Gavin I. Langmuir in the *Journal of Economic History* 50 (1990), pp. 715–17 and William Chester Jordan in the *Jewish Quarterly Review* 82 (1991), pp. 221–23.

of it for another, such profit is vile and unnatural. It is by this reasoning that Aristotle proves, in the first book of the Politics, that usury is against nature...) [16]

In a tale that contrasts a monk's fictitious buying of "certein beestes" with a merchant's complicated yet abstract financial dealings, and both of these with an agreement struck between a wife and a monk to exchange sex for money, Chaucer's plough cuts at the edge of his society's accepted moral practice. By not translating, he, like Boccaccio, made the plot his own.

Sources and Analogues of the Canterbury Tales
and the Nun's Priest's Tale

Interest in Chaucer's sources has remained high because of both ongoing debates about the relative importance of the French and Italian literary traditions for his work and continued interest in translation theory.[17] A major opportunity, however, to reassess this topic with respect to his last and most complicated work was offered by the decision to revise one of the standard references in the field, the *Sources and Analogues of Chaucer's Canterbury Tales*, edited by W. F. Bryan and Germaine Dempster and published in 1941.[18] The new two-volume study, *Sources and Analogues of the Canterbury Tales*, edited by Robert M. Correale and Mary Hamel and published in 2002 and 2005, contains many individual contributions that advance our understanding of the materials Chaucer used and, indeed, of how he used them. The work as a whole, however, might have done more to reshape the field had the

---

16 *The De Moneta of Nicholas Oresme and English Mint documents*, ed. and trans. Charles Johnson (London: Nelson, 1956), pp. 25–26. Following the scholastics, Oresme associated this idea with Aristotle; see Langholm, who also notes pre-scholastic expression of this idea; *Economics*, pp. 57–58, 139–41, and 163–67.

17 I would like to thank Kara A. Doyle for allowing me to read chapters of her forthcoming book, and for discussing these topics with me. Attention has often moved beyond evaluating literary sources to considering questions of cultural difference and interaction; see, for example, the three opening chapters, "Italy" (Robert R. Edwards), "France" (Ardis Butterfield), and "England" (Kathy Lavezzo) in *Chaucer: Contemporary Approaches*, ed. Susanna Fein and David Raybin (University Park: Pennsylvania State University Press, 2010), pp. 3–64. On Chaucer's relationship to the French tradition, see also Ardis Butterfield, *The Familiar Enemy: Chaucer, Language, and Nation in the Hundred Years War* (Oxford: Oxford University Press, 2009). David Wallace provides a balanced assessment of Chaucer's literary debts in "Chaucer's Italian Inheritance" in the *Cambridge Companion to Chaucer*, ed. Piero Boitani and Jill Mann (Cambridge: Cambridge University Press, 2003) , pp. 36–57. In the same collection, see Roger Ellis, "Translation," pp. 443–58.

18 *Sources and Analogues of Chaucer's Canterbury Tales*, ed. W. F. Bryan and Germaine Dempster (1941; repr. New York: Humanities Press, 1958). This work replaced *Originals and Analogues of Some of Chaucer's Canterbury Tales*, ed. Frederick James Furnivall, Edmund Brock and W. A. Clouston (London: N. Trübner, 1872–88).

editors defined the key terms "source" and "analogue" more clearly or had they stepped back from the completed entries to place them in relationship to each other. The "Colloquium: The Afterlife of Origins," organized at the 2004 Congress of the New Chaucer Society by Arlyn Diamond and Nancy Bradbury and then published in *Studies in the Age of Chaucer* in 2006, considers some of these problems but also misses the main point: in the *Canterbury Tales* Chaucer was strikingly original in his selection of materials out of which to construct new narratives, an approach, I am arguing, he learned from the *Decameron*.[19]

While neither the earlier nor the more recent *Sources and Analogues* defines either term in their titles, contributors to both quite properly, if at times not entirely consistently, investigate the sources of the narratives, the materials from which Chaucer constructed his tales. Their method is not, then, a line by line accounting of each source but rather a broad review of the major texts and traditions that he used to shape each plot. Even to make this claim, however, draws attention not only to the wide variety of narratives Chaucer told—is the *Parson's Tale* something other than a treatise on penance?—but also to the different ways he blended material to construct his tales—where does the Canon's Yeoman's "prologue" end? So while, following Bryan and Dempster, Correale and Hamel claim they will leave to "literary critics... questions of how he adapted them [i.e. sources] for his own artistic purposes" (*S&A*, 1.viii), their contributors confront, although not always explicitly, two inter-related questions: what was Chaucer trying to achieve in each tale and what was the relative importance of the sources he used? Source study, in the case of a writer like Chaucer, is never mechanical.

Let me make this argument less abstract by considering the *Nun's Priest's Tale*. In 1941, James R. Hulbert included three texts in his chapter on the tale, *Le Roman de Renart*, *Reinhart Fuchs*, and two *exempla* from Valerius Maximus's *Factorum et dictorum memorabilium, libri novem*, the first two in an effort to establish the "version" of the cock and fox story from which Chaucer had worked.[20] His primary focus, then, was on the plot, and

---

[19] Stephen Knight notes Chaucer's originality in his review of volume 1 of *S&A*: "evidence from the other commentators in this book, when collated, is that Chaucer eschewed a primary model of working, even in one tale, and rarely did the same thing twice: a clear source, much modified, in The Clerk's Tale stands against a range of minor stimuli in The Squire's Tale. The subtext of this volume is the volatile nature of Chaucer's relation with his sources"; *Speculum* 79 (2004), p. 1058. Yet he makes this point in order to undercut Cooper's argument that "the *Decameron*...is Chaucer's primary model for his collection of stories"; (*S&A*, 1.13). Knight writes: "given the productive lability of Chaucer's method, a new sense of his dependence on a major source for the structure of the tales may in itself be epistemologically unlikely"; p. 1058.

[20] James R. Hulbert, "The Nun's Priest's Tale," in *Sources and Analogues*, ed. Bryan and Dempster, pp. 645–63. On animal narratives see Jill Mann, *From Aesop to Renard: Beast Literature in Medieval Britain* (Oxford: Oxford University Press, 2009).

although he concluded that "with the evidence at present available it is probably impossible" to decide which of the texts better represents the version Chaucer used, he clearly assumed that there was a single "immediate source," even if it might have been "oral or derived from an oral form" (p. 646). His third text, two excerpts from Valerius Maximus, offers what he identified as "analogues" for two of Chauntecleer's examples of true dreams (VII, 2984–3062 and 3064–104).[21] Although he did not say so explicitly, it appears he had included these passages mainly because they account for substantial parts of the tale and because they can be paralleled in an identifiable tradition. Finally, he commented that "no specific source can be cited" for the tale's "mock heroic and sermonistic development," but he speculated that "some passage in Chaucer's original, like the introduction to the story in *Renart*, may have suggested the mock heroic elaboration" (p. 646).

On the surface, Edward Wheatley's chapter in the 2002 volume looks similar to Hulbert's because he includes three versions of the cock and fox story, "Le Coq et le renard" (Fable 60 in Marie de France's collection), *Le Roman de Renart*, and *Le Roman de Renart le Contrefait*, to account for the main plot, and two passages from Robert Holcot's *Super sapientiam Salomonis* to cover Chauntecleer's two examples also discussed by Hulbert. Relying explicitly, however, on the publications of Robert A. Pratt,[22] Wheatley's analysis opens a radically different way to understand Chaucer's use of sources. Rather than assuming that he worked from a single version of the fable, Wheatley accepts and quotes Pratt's conclusion that he used all three of the ones he includes: "although his plot was based directly on Marie's, Chaucer developed and enriched it with a number of verbal expressions, motifs, and bits of action suggested by the *Roman de Renart* and *Renart le Contrefait*" (*S&A*, 1.451). In Pratt's words, which Wheatley again quotes, Chaucer discovered "the complete sequence of farmyard dream, discussion, enticement to sing with eyes closed, capture, chase, escape, and *moralité*" in the *Roman de Renart*; and in *Renart le Contrefait* "he found a dream worthy of Marie's style—simple, direct, and clear, for he recognized the qualities of the structure of her fable and allowed them to condition the neat, logical form of his basic narrative."[23] Without pursuing the implications of these multiple sources for the plot, Wheatley, still following Pratt, then mentions the "centrality of two *lectiones* from Robert Holcot's commentary on the Book of Wisdom...to Chauntecleer's two longest exempla about dreams," before turning to "Chauntecleer's briefer exempla of St. Kenelm (VII, 3110–

---

21 His commentary makes it clear that he considers these "analogues" not "sources" because Chaucer might have found them in a number of different places.

22 Robert A. Pratt, "Three Old French Sources of the Nonnes Preestes Tale," *Speculum* 47 (1972), pp. 422–44 and 646–68; and "Some Latin Sources of the Nonnes Preest on Dreames," *Speculum* 52 (1977), pp. 538–70.

23 "Three Old French," pp. 443–44.

21) and Andromache's prophecy to Hector (VII, 3141–50)" (*S&A*, 1.451). The sources of these passages, he notes, remain "unclear, largely because their brevity and consequent generality make them resemble a number of earlier texts," but in his discussion he mentions as "plausible" Pratt's view that "the Andromache exemplum came from lines 3123–40 of *Le Roman de Renart le Contrefait*" (*S&A*, 1.451–52). The remainder of Wheatley's remarks concerns other sources for other details: Pertelot's knowledge of laxatives and medical lore, references "to textual authorities ranging from Boethius to Bishop Bradwardyne," and "allusions that reinforce the mock-heroic nature of the conflict between the cock and fox" (*S&A*, 1.452). He concludes by referring to Derek Pearsall's edition of the tale, which outlines "major issues in the debates on its sources and analogues in greater detail than space will permit here," and some more recent publications which he characterizes as examining "only peripheral influences" (*S&A*, 1.452).[24] While Wheatley's emphasis is on the different versions of the cock and fox story, he views the tale as presenting a series of largely unrelated source problems, all of which deserve attention.

Restricting the question, however, to the precise sources of the narrative can reveal more about how this tale fits together. The starting point, I would argue, is to recognize that Chaucer wrote it with the "Literary Group," characterized by Cooper as "a debate on literature,"[25] already in mind.[26] The first two tales of Fragment VII, as Cooper shows, contrast the most basic feature of all stories, language. Through its puns, the *Shipman's Tale* undermines the idea that there is a simple correspondence between words and objects or actions while the *Prioress's Tale* asserts that all sound that matters, even a baby sucking on its mother's breast, means one thing, praise of the divine.[27] Chaucer's own tales of *Sir Thopas* and *Melibee* then focus on stories, using the criteria introduced by the Host in the *General Prologue* to judge the winner of the competition: the romance attempts to be pure *solaas* and the moral treatise, pure *sentence*. Finally, the *Monk's Tale* and the *Nun's Priest's Tale* investigate story collections, one containing multiple stories on one theme, the other a single story with multiple themes. Although beyond the scope of this study, I would argue that the idea for this grouping arose out of Chaucer's reflections on the failures of the *Shipman's Tale* to express his intended message for the Wife of Bath, and of *Melibee* to work effectively

---

[24] His reference is to *The Nun's Priest Tale*, ed. Derek Pearsall, Variorum Edition of the Works of Geoffrey Chaucer 2/9 (Norman: University of Oklahoma Press, 1984).

[25] Cooper, *Structure*, p. 161.

[26] Forni recognizes this starting point as significant for the *Decameron*: "the task of determining how one particular Boccaccian *novella* was born or put together, often cannot be separated from the investigation of how and why it was *put together with other novelle*" [original emphasis]; *Adventures in Speech*, p. 3.

[27] In Cooper's view, Chaucer's "concern is with the inadequacy of earthly language to express the spiritual"; *Structure*, p. 165.

for the Man of Law: he had, then, these two in hand as he started developing this theme of how, from their most basic level of language to their inclusion in collections, stories convey meaning and how these meanings change. That he was still thinking about Boccaccio is also indicated by the choice of the *De casibus* tradition for the *Monk's Tale*. With these tales and issues in mind, he sought a single tale that would do in a more generally recognizable way what he had already done in the *Shipman's Tale*: in itself to invoke others, although here it would be not just three *novelle* but many more. His tribute to the *Decameron* was to turn the simple vehicle of a beast fable into a profound reflection on literature.

With the fable of the cock and the fox, Chaucer selected a story that he must have read and heard many times and that he could assume his audience would immediately recognize. His use of sources, however, remained distinctly literary, indeed to a degree, as Cooper has made clear particularly in discussing the relationship of the *Nun's Priest's Tale* to the *Canterbury Tales* as a whole,[28] that he might have expected his audience would recognize. In choosing Marie de France's Fable 60 as the main source for the plot, he immediately lit on a genre recognizable by its simple narrative form, which he preserved even while expanding it in many directions. In doing so, he also introduced his main concern, the nature of story collections, because it is in these that since the time of Aesop animal fables have often travelled. At the same time, the tale's mock heroic style clearly alludes to this fable's elaboration in the beast-epics of Renart, his other main sources for the story of the cock and fox. With their greater length, these expanded versions would appear more suitable for individual circulation with, perhaps, greater claims of authorial weight.[29] In this choice of sources, then, Chaucer set one of the central topics of the tale and the fragment that it concludes, the ways stories change both as they are rewritten and retold and as individual versions appear in new contexts, an idea—or, might one say, *the* idea?—central to the *Canterbury Tales* as a whole.

In the Andromache *exemplum Le Roman de Renart le Contrefait* also provided Chaucer with a more obvious way to develop this theme, by turning the tale itself into a collection of stories that reflects on the others in the *Canterbury Tales*. Its context in the beast-epic, if not the source for this self-reflexivity, appears well suited to it. Here the rooster, frightened by his dream,

---

[28]   Cooper, *Structure*, pp. 165–95 and *Canterbury Tales*, pp. 350–2. In the latter, Cooper cites Alan T. Gaylord, "*Sentence* and *Solaas* in Fragment VII of the *Canterbury Tales*: Harry Bailly as Horseback Editor," *PMLA* 82 (1967), pp. 226–35.

[29]   The qualifications here acknowledge present and perhaps permanent limitations in our understanding of Chaucer's use of sources. Could he have used one fable but two epics because he wanted to challenge expectations about how these genres circulated? Could he have chosen for similar reasons Marie de France to represent an anonymous tradition in contrast to a "literate" one now associated with Pierre de Saint Cloud but which circulated in many redactions?

turns to a hen, Pinte, for "tresbon conseil" (31304; "very good counsel"), [30]
recalling the theme of *Melibee*. She responds both by denigrating women's
advice ("se bien en vient, c'est aventure," 31311; "if any good should come
from it, it is by chance") and by claiming that many women do indeed give
wise counsel, before summing up with a passage reminiscent of both the
Wife of Bath's *Prologue* and her *Tale*:

> "Mais certes ce est chose voire,
> S'elles disoient Euvangilles,
> Semble a pluseurs que ce sont guiles,
> Et pour ce coire ne les voeullent,
> Combien que maint bien dire soeulent
> Et monlt grans biens en advenissent,
> Si les pluseurs mieulx les creïssent." (31316–22)

("but certainly it's the truth that even if women quote the gospels, it seems
to many people that these sayings are ruses, and for this people don't want
to believe women, however many good things they are accustomed to
saying. And many great thing would happen to them, if some men believed
women better.")

Pinte then uses Andromache's advice to Hector not to go to battle on the
day when he was slain by Achilles as the first of two examples to support
her point (31323–40). Chaucer changed many details. Relying on a tradition
recorded in Dares Phrygius's *De excidio Troiae historica*,[31] he specified the
source of Andromache's fear as a dream, reassigned the *exemplum* to Chauntecleer, and placed it last in the series of examples. The story, however, still
figures prominently in a debate between men and women, which recalls his
own that extends back through the "Marriage Group" to Licisca and Tindaro,
and transforms the simple plot of the beast fable into a collection of stories.
In these ways it contributes to Cooper's understanding of the *Nun's Priest's
Tale* as "the *Canterbury Tales* in miniature."[32] Aided, then, by his choice of
sources for the cock and fox narrative, Chaucer made the *Canterbury Tales*
into a source of the narrative of this tale.

The texts and to some extent the analyses in the 1941 and 2002 *Sources
and Analogues* volumes establish that, contrary to the expectation of a single
version of the story that can be identified as the one used in the tale, Chaucer
deliberately invoked several—at least two (a beast-fable and a beast-epic)
but more likely three—for the cock and fox story, and, indeed, did so to
place this part of the work into the developing structure of the *Canterbury*

---

[30] The texts and translations here and in the following discussion are from *S&A*, 1.475–87 by
line number.

[31] See Susan H. Cavanaugh's note on line 3141 in the *Riverside Chaucer*, ed. Benson, p. 938.

[32] Cooper, *Structure*, p. 180.

Tales. Now the *Nun's Priest's Tale* is, I admit, remarkable in part because of the bewildering mirroring effect achieved by drawing on so many different works, including the collection in which it appears, and thus might seem unlikely to reveal much about Chaucer's use of sources elsewhere. The same assumption, however, that he must have worked from a primary source, and the likelihood that instead his starting point for at least some of the tales was less a particular story than a position—an idea—in a developing argument that needed illustration, can be found in four other chapters of *Sources and Analogues*, which discover too few—indeed no—sources of the narratives.

Tales with No Source: Sir Thopas, Squire, and Cook

In their chapter in *Sources and Analogues* on the *Canon's Yeoman's Tale*, Carolyn Collette and Vincent DiMarco immediately assert that it has "neither any known major sources nor analogues that suggest the earlier existence of a primary source," and for this reason they consider it "extraordinary among the *Canterbury Tales*" (*S&A*, 2.716). DiMarco, however, had begun his own essay on the *Squire's Tale*: "with the exception of the long Confession of Nature in the *Roman de la Rose*, half a dozen passages of which Chaucer adapts at various points in the *Squire's Tale*, no close literary source of the poem has come to light, and the fragmentary nature of the narrative, as well as the strong likelihood of Chaucer's dependence on oral reports and reminiscences of travelers and merchants, renders the possibility of finding a written source for the story unlikely indeed" (*S&A*, 1.169). Similarly, Joanne A. Charbonneau opens her analysis of *Sir Thopas*, which she calls "the most imitative and derivative of all the *Canterbury Tales*," by noting that it "has no known single source or analogue, but instead borrows extensively from romances and ballads with echoes from these popular works in virtually every line" (*S&A*, 2.649). Finally, John Scattergood concludes his chapter on the *Cook's Tale*: "though too little of it has survived for one to be confident about generalizing, it does appear that in the *Cook's Tale* Chaucer is not using the type of source material he usually used, but contemporary documents of a non-narrative sort"; his last suggestion is that the tale was "perhaps based on a contemporary incident" (*S&A*, 1.86). All these scholars, then, assumed that Chaucer worked, except perhaps in the case of the tale they were considering, from "a primary source," "a literary source," a "single source or analogue," or "a contemporary incident." The belief that Chaucer simply retold others' tales runs deep.

If the sources of these narratives, however, are not other narratives, what are they? The *Squire's Tale* and *Sir Thopas* might seem to present a different problem than do the tales of the Canon's Yeoman and the Cook (if this is long enough to be considered at all) because even if not based on existing narratives, they represent particular genres, the interlace romance and the tail-rhyme romance.[33] One might imagine Chaucer deciding, independently of writing the *Canterbury Tales*, to parody these genres much as he translated the *Consolation of Philosophy*. The unfinished state, however, of both indicates that they were probably written for the collection. Chaucer did of course leave works—the *House of Fame*, the *Legend of Good Women*, and even the *Canterbury Tales*—incomplete. These two, however, are unfinished in order to take part in arguments in their immediate contexts. As Cooper notes, "the sense of a double text is far stronger in *Sir Thopas* than in other tales of the Canterbury sequence that are affected by their dramatic context": for the reader it is "a *tour de force* of Chaucer's art, a virtuoso piece by an accomplished master," while at the same time for the fictional audience, as articulated by the Host, it is "drasty rymyng...nat worth a toord" (VII, 930).[34] This effect is heightened by breaking off the performance: the events remain simply events rather than a completed plot,[35] and so can be judged both as success and failure. In this way *Sir Thopas* corresponds to *Melibee*, a successful translation of a popular moral treatise, but one that failed to begin the debate on marriage because it is simply too static to initiate a story collection, a problem Chaucer highlighted when he tried to correct it by translating the story of Custance for the Man of Law. In other ways *Sir Thopas* is, however, *Melibee*'s opposite: a fragmentary, poetic tale of *solaas*. His already written successful/failed tale, *Melibee*, led Chaucer not to a particular tail-rhyme romance but rather to the genre as a whole, which he could both invoke brilliantly and allow to fall apart. As with the *Nun's Priest's Tale*, the main sources of *Sir Thopas*'s narrative are not themselves narratives.

The fragmentary nature of the *Squire's Tale* ties it more tightly to its immediate context, the "Marriage Group," by extending the technique, which Chaucer learned from the Licisca episode, of blending the frame into the unfolding arguments of successive tales. It is less an unfinished argument than an argument that is finished by breaking it off. As we will see in more detail in Chapter 3, Licisca's claim, which she is not allowed to complete, that women should control their sexuality is taken up both in the following tales and again in the frame when first the women and then the men travel to the *Valle delle Donne*. At this point in the "Marriage Group" Chaucer's topic was not who should have power in sexual relationships but more specifically the role of children in marriage. He introduced it, just as Boccaccio had included the servants in the Introduction to the First Day, in the *General Prologue*. His estates satire begins appropriately with the Knight, and yet is immediately complicated because the next pilgrim, the Squire, is not just a

---

[33] Cooper, *Canterbury Tales*, pp. 218–19 and 300–04.

[34] Cooper, *Canterbury Tales*, p. 305.

[35] For a discussion of how conclusions shape narratives, see Frank Kermode, *The Sense of an Ending: Studies in the Theory of Fiction: With a new Epilogue* (New York: Oxford University Press, 2000).

step lower on the social scale, but, more significantly, his son (I, 79). In the tales about marriage, the role of children had been present from the start, since *Melibee*, originally assigned to the Man of Law and expected to begin the debate, opens with not just Prudence's beating but also their daughter's receiving of "fyve mortal woundes" (VII, 971). Unlike the French and Latin versions of the treatise,[36] Chaucer named this daughter Sophie (Latinized, as Cooper notes, in some manuscripts to "Sapience"),[37] but then, following his sources, gave her no further role in the tale. When considered, however, not as a moral treatise but rather as a story, it becomes remarkable that Prudence and, indeed, the readers would not care about her brutal treatment. Both the *Shipman's Tale* and the new tale for the Wife of Bath contain no references to the main characters' children, a silence carried over conspicuously into the Wife's Prologue, establishing that the debate on marriage concerns primarily two people. The topic of children, however, re-emerges in the *Clerk's Tale*,[38] in which Walter is asked by his people to marry so his heir can rule them when he dies, and indeed is amplified when he tests his wife by pretending to kill their children. The *Merchant's Tale* echoes the first theme when January announces one of his reasons for marrying: "'Yet were me levere houndes had me eten / Than that myn heritage sholde falle / In straunge hand'" (IV, 1438–40). It then challenges this assumption and more generally the view that men can control their wives' sexuality by mocking both January's performance on his wedding night (IV, 1805–57) and his foolish pride in May's (feigned?) pregnancy even after he has seen what she and Damien do in the pear tree (IV, 2354–415). By leaving the chronology of events unclear the *Merchant's Tale* provides no way to know whose child May is carrying.

The Squire then advances this argument less through the narrative of his tale, which concerns Cambyuskan and his three children (V, 28–33), than through its formal qualities—both its engagements with the *Knight's Tale* and its fragmentary state. Chaucer's point, to anticipate my argument, is that interlace romance, like descendants, may sometimes carry on too long and so this line of debate must be cut off to return the focus to marriage as a relationship between two people. The tale immediately establishes the Squire as the Knight's son when he gets no further than the description of the first feast before he demonstrates his father's habit of listing things he will not discuss:

---

[36] See *S&A*, 1.332, note to 1.1.

[37] Cooper, *Canterbury Tales*, p. 313.

[38] It has also appeared in the *Summoner's Tale* in which the Friar responds to the wife's news that since his last visit her child has died with an account of the revelation he and others in his convent had received of this event (III, 1851–957). That he is lying is obvious since if true this miracle would have been the first thing he would have said to her.

> I wol not tellen of hir strange sewes,
> Ne of hir swannes, ne of hire heronsewes. (V, 67–68)[39]

Moreover, it develops the relationship between the two tellers by having the Squire turn to interlace romance, a genre that provides for seemingly infinite expansion, in order to construct a tale that will be like but longer than his father's. The real conflict, however, between the two, as DiMarco's brilliant chapter in *Sources and Analogues* allows us to perceive, appears in the tale's handling of sources, which contrasts the exotic and political East to the western European world of courtly romance.

Although Chaucer would have received most if not all of his information from western sources, the two parts of the tale that the Squire completes divide East from West. His immediate source for the first is likely to have been an Old French romance, the *Meliacin* of Girart d'Amiens, and yet he perceived in it—perhaps aided by his knowledge of the related romance, *Cleomadés* of Adenet le Rois and other versions of this tale—an originally oriental story, which would later be known from the *Thousand and One Nights* as the *Tale of the Enchanted Horse*.[40] As Cooper writes, "many medieval romances of course abound in Oriental settings and marvels, but such elements in the *Squire's Tale* go beyond incidents and motifs."[41] The opening line sets it in the capital of the Mongol Empire ("At Sarray, in the land of Tartarye"; V, 9) and the first words of the knight who arrives unexpectedly on the "steede of bras" (V, 81) reveal that he has been sent by "the kyng of Arabe and of Inde"; V, 110). However, to quote Cooper again, "most strikingly of all, the means by which the two main plots are connected, with one story starting off an apparently unrelated one in a series of accumulating narrative, is much more typical of Oriental than Western story-collections or interlaced romances."[42] In contrast the second part, Canacee's encounter with the falcon betrayed in love, could not be more local in origin because it is derived from Chaucer's own earlier writings. While DiMarco discusses some possible Eastern analogues to the falcon's story, he prints only three passages: one from the *Consolation of Philosophy*, the source for the example of a well-cared-for yet caged bird fleeing to the woods when able; a second from the *Roman de la Rose*, as a possible source for the description of the tree on which the falcon rests (V, 409); and the "Tale of the Captive Bird and Traveler" from Alexander Neckam's *De naturis rerum*, since an earlier critic, Albert C. Friend, had called attention to it "in speculating on how the falcon

---

[39] From his opening, the Knight too announces subjects he will not discuss (the battle between the Athenians and the Amazons, the besieging of Hippolyta, the wedding feast, and a storm (I, 875–92), a rhetorical strategy that culminates in the long account of what he will not say about Arcite's funeral rites (I, 2919–66).

[40] See *S&A*, 1.169–71.

[41] Cooper, *Canterbury Tales*, p. 220.

[42] Cooper, *Canterbury Tales*, pp. 220–21.

would come to find her mate again" (*S&A*, 1.176 and 180–82). Instead, its main sources are identified by Cooper: "the whole falcon episode could be described as being by the *Parliament* out of the *Anelida*."[43] Even if Chaucer did not expect his readers to know his earlier works, they would have recognized this part of the tale as in the tradition of French court poetry. As such it fits the portrait of the Squire in the *General Prologue* (I, 79–100).

The surprise, then, is the Eastern origin of the first part, which could be explained as an attempt on the Squire's part to compete with the distinctive setting of his father's tale in the mythical history of Athens. DiMarco's research, however, into contact between Öz Beg Khan, who ruled the Golden Horde (Chaucer's "Tartarye") from 1313–41, and el-Melik en Nasir, who ruled the Mamluk Sultanate (Chaucer's "Arabe and Inde") from 1291–92, 1298–1308 and 1309–40, offers a more compelling reason to view this setting as relevant. The historical relationship, which included exchanges of gifts and a marriage, undermined Western hopes for an alliance with the Mongols to advance their interests in the Crusades. As DiMarco writes,

> the best that could realistically be expected now of crusading ventures from the middle of the [fourteenth] century were the melancholy and temporary successes enumerated in the portrait of the Knight—the ultimately inconsequential campaigns in North Africa and Moorish Spain; the rape, then abandonment of Alexandria; raids in Asia Minor and beleaguered Cilicia (which was to be destroyed in reprisal by the Mamluks in the 1370s and 1380s); and finally, the redirection of crusading activity by the Teutonic Order to a theatre far indeed from the Holy Land, against (among other) the Orthodox Christians of the Baltic North.[44]

Drawing on recent political events, Chaucer used the Squire, apparently unknowingly because the tale contains no overtly critical comments, to tell a tale that points to his father's failure. In this stalemate across generations, there is no further place for the debate on the importance of children for understanding marriage to go.

Chaucer then broke off the *Squire's Tale* in a way that calls attention to his theme, the inability of children to resolve the question of how power should be apportioned in marriage. Feigning to be unaware that the Squire is still mid-story, the Franklin interrupts, praising his eloquence as a sign of his nobility and contrasting him to his own son, who refuses to live virtuously.

---

43   Cooper, *Canterbury Tales*, pp. 221–22. See also Charles A. Owen, Jr., "The Falcon's Complaint in the *Squire's Tale*," in *Rebels and Rivals: The Contestive Spirit in* The Canterbury Tales, Studies in Medieval Culture 29, ed. Susanna Greer Fein, David Raybin, and Peter C. Braeger (Kalamazoo: Medieval Institute Publications, 1991), pp. 173–88.

44   Vincent DiMarco, "The Historical Basis of Chaucer's Squire Tale," in *Chaucer's Cultural Geography*, ed. Kathryn L. Lynch (New York: Routledge, 2002), p. 67; repr. from *Edebiyât*, n.s. 1 (1989), pp. 1–22.

From his opening words, he focuses on the main topic of the Loathly Lady's speech at the end of the *Wife of Bath's Tale*, "gentillesse": "'In feith, Squier, thow hast thee wel yquit / And gentilly'" (V, 673–74). Yet he qualifies this judgment by noting that he is still young ("considerynge thy yowthe"; V, 675) and that he will become the equal in eloquence of any on the pilgrimage, most obviously his father, "'if that thou lyve'" (V, 679). In contrast, his own son, although often "snybbed" (V, 688), prefers to play dice and talk with a page "'Than to comune with any gentil wight / Where he myghte lerne gentillesse aright'" (V, 693–94). Although the Host then mocks the discussion ("'Straw for youre gentillesse!'"; V, 695), Chaucer used the exchange to establish that the question of power in marriage cannot be resolved by focusing on offspring because they will eventually act independently of their parents. This complicated argument, played out through the frame and tales, again shows that the sources of the narrative of the *Squire's Tale* are less particular stories than distinctive motifs and ideas that Chaucer drew from a variety of places—French romance, his own writings, and the political realities of the contemporary Middle East—to effect a dramatic shift in the course of a larger argument.

In this context our inability to identify existing narratives as sources for the tales of the Cook and the Canon's Yeoman appears less extraordinary: in both cases they fit into developing arguments and rely on themes drawn from contemporary life. Moreover, the fragmentary nature of the *Cook's Tale* links it directly to *Sir Thopas* and the *Squire's Tale*. As suggested above and as will be discussed in more detail in the Chapter 3, the issue of class, which first led Chaucer to write the *Miller's Tale* as a response to the Knight, developed into a profound reflection on hierarchies more generally. One of the surprises of the "First Fragment" turns out to be that even as the following tales challenge the Knight's self-interested faith in a divinely ordered universe, they themselves show an ordered falling away from an ideal.[45] This point can be made most simply by considering the settings: the classical pinnacle of learning, Athens of the *Knight's Tale*, is followed first by Oxford and then, tellingly, by Cambridge. London, Chaucer joked further, is as far from Athens as one can go. The descent also takes place in the genres, which move from epic, invoked in the epigraph to the *Knight's Tale*, through romance and *fabliau* to "a litel jape," the Cook's characterization of his tale, a progression which, incidentally, explains Chaucer's use of the cruder French *fabliau* tradition as the source of the *Reeve's Tale* rather than Boccaccio's reworking of the central motif of switched cradle in *Decameron* 9.6. Moreover, the sexual activity increases from the unrealized desires of courtly love, to marriage, adultery, and finally prostitution. Given these constraints, the random events in an

---

[45] See Cooper, *Canterbury Tales*, p. 121, and *Structure*, pp. 109–20.

apprentice's life all but write themselves, and the incomplete ending becomes a final way to question the Knight's certainty.

The Canon's Yeoman's Prologue *and* Tale *and Gower's* Confessio Amantis

The extraordinary feature that an investigation of the sources of the *Canon's Yeoman's Tale* reveals is not its independence from any particular narrative, but rather the degree to which its content and its place in the *Canterbury Tales* combine into an inquiry into what can be known of the secular and the divine. As with the relationship of *Sir Thopas* to *Melibee*, Chaucer developed this tale in relation to an existing work, in this case his translation of the legend of St. Cecilia, written, as is clear from a reference to it in the prologue to the *Legend of Good Women* (F 426, G 416), before he began the *Canterbury Tales*. Sherry L. Reames has shown that the *Second Nun's Tale* translates in succession (or at least largely in succession) two of the many abridgements of the late fifth- or early sixth-century *Passio S. Caeciliae*, one found in the immensely popular *Legenda aurea* and the other encountered "exclusively in breviaries and office lectionaries written for the Vatican, the Franciscans, or other communities that followed their lead in adopting the 'use of the Roman curia'" (*S&A*, 1.495). Even if, then, his change in sources at line 349 was caused by no more than a shift in the texts available to him,[46] it still indicates that Chaucer was aware that there were at least two versions of the legend, and indeed, the discussion at the end of the one in the *Legenda aurea* about a discrepancy in the records concerning when Cecilia was martyred indicates that there were, as he would almost certainly have known, many more. It may be, then, that he was drawn to constructing a new tale, the *Canon's Yeoman's*, to pair with his translation of the Cecilia legend not only because of the *Vita's* themes of secular and spiritual blindness and because of its striking closing image of the Saint surviving the attempt to execute her in a boiling bath,[47] but also because he perceived that even this sacred story was subject to change in transmission.[48] As Chapters 4 and 5 argue, the tales of both the Miller and the Wife of Bath were written as serious challenges to two of the

---

[46] Reames considers the possibility that Chaucer worked from a source which had already combined these two versions "remote"; *S&A*, 1.495. I would suggest that he used both to focus more sharply on Cecilia herself.

[47] The key article on this topic remains Joseph Grennen's "Saint Cecilia's 'Chemical Wedding': the Unity of the *Canterbury Tales* Fragment VIII," *JEGP* 65 (1966), pp. 466–88. Grennen, however, argues that the contrast reveals Chaucer's view of alchemy as "an unwittingly sacrilegious distortion of the central mystery of the Christian faith" (p. 467). See also Cooper, *Canterbury Tales*, pp. 363–65, with further bibliography.

[48] For example, as Reames notes, one of the distinctive features of the version in the *Legenda aurea*, compiled by the Dominican friar, Jacobus de Voragine, is the claim that before dying, Cecilia gave "her property to the poor, as the mendicants would have recommended, instead

fundamental principles of fourteenth-century society, the assumptions that the aristocracy should have power over the rest of the population and that men should control women. There is, then, reason to entertain the possibility that Chaucer wrote the *Canon's Yeoman's Tale* not to affirm the religious message articulated in the legend of St. Cecilia but rather to transform that message into a secular form.[49]

Although the transformation takes place, as I will argue in a moment, in the merging of the tale with the frame, the likely sources of the Yeoman's rant repay consideration even if conclusions must remain preliminary since new material on alchemy may yet emerge.[50] It appears, indeed, to have been the wealth of possible sources that led Collette and DiMarco to present the material as they have in their chapter in *Sources and Analogues*. They include nineteen extracts, identifying fourteen as analogues and placing five more in an appendix illustrating "differing opinions about the value and utility of alchemy in Chaucer's world" (*S&A*, 2.743).[51] Both sections, however, contain works that Chaucer certainly knew. The *Roman de la Rose*, parts of which he translated, is a good example of the tradition he wrote against: while deploring the trickery of some of its practitioners, Jean de Meun characterized alchemy as "art veritable" (16054; "a true art"), adding "Qui sagement en ouverrait / Granz merveilles i trouverrait" (16055–56; "whoever worked wisely in it would find great miracles").[52] The case of Gower, however, is more complicated not only because two of the three passages that Collette and DiMarco quote as analogues from book 4 of the *Confessio Amantis* are indeed similar to ones in the *Canon's Yeoman's Tale* but also because as contemporaries, either Gower or Chaucer could have been the other's source. While in Chapter 5 I argue that the *Tale of Florent* depends on the *Wife of Bath's Tale*, here it appears more likely that, as one might expect from knowing that the *Confessio Amantis* was published in 1390 and the *Canter-*

---

of dividing it among her own followers"; *S&A*, 1.494. In contrast, the Franciscan/Vatican version follows the original *passio* in this matter.

49   The reading offered here complements that of David Raybin, "'And pave it al of silver and of gold': The Humane Artistry of the *Canon's Yeoman's Tale*," in *Rebels and Rivals*, ed. Fein, Raybin, and Braeger, pp. 189–212.

50   For the introduction of alchemy into the Latin West in the thirteenth century, see Chapter 1 of William R. Newman, *The Summa Perfectionis of Pseudo-Geber: A Critical Edition, Translation and Study*, Collection de travaux de l'Académie internationale d'histoire des sciences 35 (Leiden: Brill, 1991), pp. 1–56. More generally, see Robert Halleux, *Les textes alchimiques*, Typologie des sources du Moyen Âge occidental 32 (Turnhout: Brepols, 1979).

51   They obscure the issue further by including extracts from John Lydgate and Thomas Norton, two authors who, they correctly assert, used Chaucer's tale.

52   The text is from the Guillaume de Lorris and Jean de Meun, *Le Roman de la Rose*, 3 vols., ed. Félix Lecoy, Les Classiques français du Moyen Âge, 92, 95, and 98 (Paris: Honoré Champion, 1965–70), 2.238. The translation is by Charles Dahlberg, *The Romance of the Rose* (1971; repr. Hanover: University Press of New England, 1986), p. 272. Compare *S&A*, 2.746–47.

bury Tales left unfinished in 1400, Chaucer responded directly to Gower's writing on alchemy while making several fundamental changes to it.

Let me work out from a key piece of evidence that is part of the first passage that Collette and DiMarco quote. After identifying his topic as alchemy, which concerns the multiplying of silver and gold (IV, 2459–60), Genius brings together two topics, the association of the metals with the planets and the distinction between the metals ("bodies") and volatile substances ("spirits"):

> The bodies whiche I speke of hiere
> Of the planetes ben begonne.
> The gold is titled to the sonne,
> The mone of selver hath his part,
> And iren that stant upon Mart,
> The led after Satorne groweth,
> And Jupiter the bras bestoweth,
> The coper set is to Venus,
> And to his part Mercurius
> Hath the quickselver, as it falleth,
> The which, after the bok it calleth,
> Is ferst of thilke fowre named
> Of spiritz, whiche ben proclamed;
> And the spirit which is secounde
> In sal armoniak is founde.
> The thridde spirit sulpher is;
> The ferthe suiende after this
> Arcennicum be name is hote. (IV, 2466–83)[53]

Similarly, near the beginning of his tale, the Canon's Yeoman explains:

> The firste spirit quyksilver called is,
> The seconde orpyment, the thridde, ywis,
> Sal armonyak, and the ferthe brymstoon.
> The bodyes sevene eek, lo, hem heere anoon:
> Sol gold is, and Luna silver we threpe,
> Mars iren, Mercurie quyksilver we clepe,
> Saturnus leed, and Juppiter is tyn,
> And Venus coper, by my fader kyn. (VIII, 822–29)

Differences between these two passages are immediately apparent. The Genius begins with the bodies, the Canon's Yeoman with the spirits, and, while the Genius joins the two groups with the seventh body and first spirit, mercury (quicksilver), the Yeoman begins the list of spirits with this substance but then places it in the middle of the list of bodies. Moreover, "bras," "sulphur," and "arcennicum" appear in the *Confessio* where "tyn," "brymston," and "orpy-

---

[53]   Collette and DiMarco begin their quotation nine lines earlier, with the beginning of Gower's discussion of alchemy.

ment" are used in the *Canterbury Tales*, although the first is the most significant because the others are merely different names for the same thing. Finally,
where Gower used a series of verbs to relate the substances to the planets
("is titled," "hath," "stant," "groweth," "bestoweth," and "is"), Chaucer relied
primarily on the copula, with even his two variants, "threpe" and "clepe,"
implying no more than identity. These differences, however, should not
obscure the fundamental similarity of the two passages perhaps best exemplified by their unlikely inclusion of mercury in both groups.

The discussion of minerals in Vincent of Beauvais's *Speculum naturale*, which Pauline Aiken has established as a major source for Chaucer's
alchemical lore,[54] allows us to perceive not only how close the two Middle
English passages are but also why it is more likely that Chaucer here used
Gower. As a compendium of earlier writings, Vincent's encyclopedia contains
many distinct traditions that could lead to differing conclusions. It is striking,
however, that he did not associate seven metals with the seven planets, an idea
often assumed to be ubiquitous in classical astrology,[55] even though he did,
for example, include Isidore's claim that there are "seven kinds of metals."[56]
For this idea, Gower or Chaucer probably turned to either Albertus Magnus
or Raymond Llull,[57] who, in associating metals with planets, continued a

---

[54] "Vincent of Beauvais and Chaucer's Knowledge of Alchemy," *Studies in Philology* 41
(1944), pp. 371–89. I will quote Vincent's work from the *Speculum quadruplex sive Speculum maius* (Graz: Akademischen Druck- u. Verlagsanstalt, 1964–65), which reprints the
Douai 1624 edition. It was written around 1256–59; see the appendix on "Medieval Encyclopedias" by Michael W. Twomey in Kaske, *Medieval Christian*, pp. 198–99. Aiken notes
that much of the material in the *Speculum naturale* also appears in the *Speculum doctrinale*,
but she finds some details that Chaucer used only in the former.

[55] In her note on these lines, Jill Mann states, "the idea that each of the planets was connected
with a metal goes back to Greek astrology; alchemists habitually used the planetary names
to denote metals"; *The Canterbury Tales*, ed. Jill Mann (London: Penguin, 2005), p. 1074.
She then cites Eric John Holmyard, *Alchemy* (Harmondsworth: Penguin, 1957). In discussing
the use by the Greeks of Babylonian astrology, Holmyard writes: "the old idea that the
planets were connected with metals was also adopted, so that the Sun, the Moon, Mars,
Mercury, Venus, Jupiter, and Saturn were often metaphorically used to signify gold, silver,
iron, mercury or quicksilver ('argent vive'), copper, tin, and lead" (p. 21), but he provides
no references. I have not found the connection between planets and metals discussed in
Nicholas Campion, *The Dawn of Astrology: A Cultural History of Western Astrology, Vol. 1:
The Ancient and Classical Worlds* (London: Continuum, 2008) or in any other work.

[56] VII.iii, col. 426, quoting *Etymologies* XVI.xviii; see *Etymologiarum sive Originum librii
xx*, ed. W. M. Lindsay (Oxford: Clarendon, 1911) and Stephen A. Barney, W. J. Lewis, J. A.
Beach, and Oliver Berghof, *The* Etymologies *of Isidore of Seville* (Cambridge: Cambridge
University Press, 2006), p. 329. It should be noted that one of Isidore's metals, *electrum*,
is an alloy, and a second, aes, may be as well since the Latin term, like the Greek χαλκός,
is ambiguous; see *A Greek–English Lexicon*, rev. edn, Henry George Liddell, Robert Scott,
Henry Stuart Jones, and Roderick McKenzie (Oxford: Clarendon Press, 1961), *s.v.* and *A
Latin Dictionary*, Charlton T. Lewis and Charles Short (Oxford: Clarendon Press, 1969), *s.v.*

[57] For Llull, see the *Arbor Scientiae*, CCCM 180a, ed. Pere Villalba i Varneda (Turnhout:
Brepols, 2000), p. 496. A search "plumb* + saturn*" in the database Cetedoc (see

Neoplatonic tradition found in Proclus's commentary on the *Timaeus*.[58] It seems, however, not to have received a definitive form in the classical world in part because the early Greeks and Romans did not systematize a list of pure metals.[59] In any case, in considering "Plato's" explanation of the formal cause of metals,[60] Albertus wrote:

> And in the same way, he says, the other [metals] are formed. For this reason they call the seven kinds of metals by the names of the seven planets: naming lead, *Saturn*; tin, *Jupiter*; iron, *Mars*; and gold the Sun (*Sol*); copper,

www.brepolis.net) reveals similar passages in his *Tractatus novus de astronomia, Liber de regionibus sanitatis et infirmitatis, Liber de praedicatione*, and the *Liber de ascensu et descensu intellectus*. On Llull's Neoplatonism, see Josep Enric Rubio, "Thought: The Art," in *Raimundus Lullus: An Introduction to his Life, Works and Thought*, CCCM 214, ed. Alexander Fidora and Josep E. Rubio, trans. Robert D. Hughes, Anna A. Akasoy and Magnus Ryan (Turnhout: Brepols, 2008), p. 245. See also Anthony Bonner, "Llull as Alchemist and Cabalist," in *Doctor Illuminatus: A Ramon Llull Reader*, ed. Bonner (Princeton: Princeton University Press, 1993), pp. 59–61.

58   Proclus, *Commentary on Plato's* Timaeus, vol. 1, trans. Harold Tarrant (Cambridge: Cambridge University Press, 2007), p. 136. Proclus includes only four metals and planets. Citing Proclus, Olympiodorus lists seven metals and planets; see Cristina Viano, *La matière des choses; le livre IV des Météorologiques d'Aristote et son interprétation par Olympiodore* (Paris: Vrin, 2006), pp. 167–70 and 214–15. An association of the planets with seven metallic substances occurs earlier in the *Contra Celsum*, where Origen attributes it to his adversary's knowledge of "Persian mysteries" about Mithras; see *Origen: Contra Celsum*, trans. Henry Chadwick (Cambridge: Cambridge University Press, 1953), pp. 333–34; and especially Chadwick's note for further bibliography. For the Greek text, see *Origenes Werke*, vol. 2, ed. Paul Koetschau (Leipzig: Hinrichs, 1899), p. 92. See also the discussion in Robert Halleux, *Le problème des métaux dans la science antique* (Paris: Les belles lettres, 1974), pp. 151–60.

59   See Plato, *Timaeus*, trans. Donald J. Zeyl (Indianapolis: Hackett, 2000), 60b7–c6; Aristotle, *Meteorologica*, 2nd edn, ed. and trans. H. D. P. Lee (Cambridge, MA: Harvard University Press, 1962), p. 6; Earle R. Caley and John F. C. Richards, *Theophrastus on Stones: Introduction, Greek Text, English Translation, and Commentary* (Columbus: Ohio State University, 1956), p. 1; and book 33 of Pliny's *Natural History*, trans. H. Rackham (Cambridge, MA: Harvard University Press, 1938–63), 9.2–122. One should note that Theophrastus's work on metals has been lost. For a general overview, see R. J. Forbes, *Studies in Ancient Technology*, vol. 7 (Leiden: Brill, 1963); and for an overview of a still emerging field, see Paul Lettinck, *Aristotle's* Meteorology *and its Reception in the Arab World* (Leiden: Brill, 1999), pp. 28–89 and 301–12. A pivotal work for this discussion because it considers mercury as a spirit but associates the six metals with their planets was attributed to the ninth-century physician Abū Bakr Muḥammad b. Zakariyyā' al-Rāzī (but now considered pseudo-Razi) and translated in the twelfth century by Gerard of Cremona as *De aluminibus et salibus* or *De spiritibus et corporibus*; see Robert Steele, "Practical Chemistry in the Twelfth Century, Rasis *De aluminibus et salibus*. Translated by Gerard of Cremona," *Isis* 12 (1929), pp. 10–48. Vincent used this work in writing his encyclopedia.

60   See Dorothy Wyckoff's assertion that "in the *Timaeus* Alexandrian alchemists found the notion of 'prime matter' (*materia prima*) from which the four elements were created, and the suggestion that the elements can be transmuted into each other"; Albertus's "references to Plato as an alchemist," however, "are too vague to be identified with any certainty"; *Book of Minerals*, trans. Wyckoff (Oxford: Clarendon Press, 1967), p. 281.

Venus; quicksilver, *Mercury*; and silver the Moon (*Luna*); and declare that by different numbers in their composition they acquire the constitutions of the seven planets.[61]

It is this Neoplatonic tradition that underlies Gower's more expressive verbs, providing a first indication that it was indeed he who knew it. Chaucer, in contrast, returned to the copula used by Vincent of Beauvais to assert the relationship between gold and the sun when he introduced the metals near the beginning of book 7 of the *Speculum naturale*: "scilicet sol, id est, aurum, Luna, argentum, stannum, aes, ferrum, plumbum" (VII.iv, col. 427). Moreover, combining the tradition of seven metals with the distinction between "bodies" and "spirits" led to the awkward need to place mercury in both categories.[62] In the *Speculum doctrinale*, Vincent included it among the spirits:

> Spiritus quidem sunt quatuor, scilicet sal ammoniacum, et sulphur, argentum viuum et arsenicum. Corpora vero sex, scilet aurum, argentum, aes, etc. (XI.cv, col. 1054)[63]

> (There are indeed four spirits, sal ammoniac, sulpher, quicksilver and arsenic. Truly there are six bodies such as gold, silver, copper, etc.)

Indeed, because Vincent never listed mercury among the six metals, it seems more likely that Chaucer revised Gower's list to make this unlikely doubling less prominent. Finally, it is difficult to imagine that, had Gower been using Chaucer, he would have changed "tyn," a metal, to "bras," an alloy; Gower presumably translated "stannum" in this way without much thought. For these reasons, then, it seems likely that Chaucer had not only the *Speculum naturale*, but also the *Confessio Amantis* in mind as he wrote.

Establishing this direct relationship allows us to see the next passage Collette and DiMarco quote from the *Confessio Amantis* (IV, 2580–99) as a significant source of the narrative of the *Canon's Yeoman's Tale* because it provided the main idea that Chaucer wrote against, that alchemy is a "science...trewe" since in the past its practitioners succeeded (IV, 2597–99). To challenge the second claim he replaced Gower's third person critique of

---

61 Wyckoff, *Book of Minerals*, p. 168.

62 Mercury is identified as a metal "quamvis sit elementum ductilissimum" ("inasmuch as it is the essential constituent element of malleable bodies") at the beginning of Alfred of Sareshel's Latin translation of selections from Avicenna's *The Physics of the Healing*, which both circulated separately and was added to Latin versions of Aristotle's *Meteora*; E. J. Holmyard and D. C. Mandeville, eds., *Avicennae De congelatione et conglutinatione lapidum, being selections of the* Kitâ al-Shifâ'*; the Latin and Arabic texts* (Paris: Paul Geuthner, 1927), p. 50. The translation is from their rendering of the Arabic text, p. 34.

63 Quicksilver is not considered a metal in Pseudo-Geber's (Paulus de Tarento's?) *Summa perfectionis* and, indeed, unlike the metals, which are associated with planets, it "is called mercury in the custom of the ancients" ("mercurius appellatur antiquorum usu"); see Newman, *The* Summa Perfectionis, pp. 333–37 and 669–71.

contemporary alchemists with a first person account of the experiences of living in this fraudulent but all-consuming world,[64] a shift that makes the supporting theme the two works share appear no more than analogous. As Collette and DiMarco note, however, the two passages are similar because both "complain of the difficulties and expense in preparing the Elixir" (*S&A*, 2.726).[65] Gower wrote,

> Bot now it stant al otherwise;
> Thei speken faste of thilke ston,
> Bot hou to make it, nou wot non
> After the sothe experience.
> And natheles gret diligence
> Thei setten upon thilke dede,
> And spille more than thei spede;
> For allewey thei finde a lette,
> Which bringeth in poverte and dette
> To hem that riche were afore:
> The lost is had, the lucre is lore,
> To gete a pound thei spenden fyve... (IV, 2580–91)

In the corresponding passage, Chaucer too linked the search for philosophers' stone to poverty, and yet this passage is memorable for the obsessive frustration of its tone characteristic of the tale as a whole:

> A! Nay! Lat be; the philosophres stoon,
> Elixer clept, we sechen faste echoon;
> For hadde we hym, thanne were we siker ynow.
> But unto God of hevene I make avow,
> For al oure craft, whan we han al ydo,
> And al oure sleighte, he wol nat come us to.
> He hath ymaad us spenden muchel good,
> For sorwe of which almoost we wexen wood... (VIII, 862–68)

In a tale about multiplication,[66] it is first the personal frustration of failure that increases.

---

[64] On this topic, see Lee Patterson, "Perpetual Motion: Alchemy and the Technology of the Self," *Studies in the Age of Chaucer* 15 (1993), pp. 25–57. Patterson compares the Canon's Yeoman to the Wife of Bath and the Pardoner (p. 38); the former's *Prologue* provides another example of a "tale" with narrative sources, in this case the tradition of anti-feminist writing, similar to those under consideration here. Ralph Hanna and Traugott Lawler begin their chapter: "*The Wife of Bath's Prologue* is surely among the most original and vital of Chaucer's poems, and yet it is also the one most deeply involved in literary tradition"; *S&A*, 2.351.

[65] Their sentence concludes, "yet each remains hopeful of the outcome," which misrepresents Chaucer's tale.

[66] See Joseph E. Grennen, "The Canon's Yeoman and the Cosmic Furnace: Language and Meaning in the 'Canon's Yeoman's Tale,'" *Criticism* 4 (1962), pp. 225–40.

With these two sources from the *Confessio Amantis* in mind Chaucer's inclusion of other material becomes more intelligible. Moving beyond Gower, he linked alchemists' inevitable poverty to their turning to fraud. In the *Prologue*, the Yeoman, for example, implies this connection in one of his first responses to the Host:

> "We blondren evere and pouren in the fir,
> And for al that we faille of oure desir,
> For evere we lakken oure conclusioun.
> To muchel folk we doon illusioun,
> And borwe gold, be it a pound or two,
> Or ten, or twelve, or manye sommes mo,
> And make hem wenen, at the leeste weye,
> That of a pound we koude make tweye.
> Yet is it fals, but ay we han good hope
> It for to doon, and after it we grope." (VIII, 670–79)[67]

Continuing the autobiographical form of the *Prologue*, the following *Tale* offers further reflections on the Yeoman's experience of alchemy (VIII, 720–49), lists (drawn mainly from Vincent of Beauvais) of materials related to the practice (VIII, 750–897), and a general account of one of the Canon's failed experiments (VIII, 898–971) before turning to an extended description of a canon's (the Canon's?)[68] deception of a London priest (VIII, 972–1387). The last section was probably suggested by the brief accounts of alchemists' fraud such as those found in Llull's *Libre de Meravelles* and in Juan Manuel's *El Conde Lucanor*, both printed by Collette and DiMarco (*S&A*, 2.731–34). Chaucer, however, changed them substantially, allowing his account to complement his larger shift to a first person narration. While both Llull and Juan Manuel described men who claimed to be alchemists in order to become rich, Chaucer discussed not just the corrupt canon, whose motives we do not learn, but also the priest, who, by taking part in the false experiments, becomes convinced that alchemy is a "noble craft" (VIII, 1247). Indeed the final couplet of this part of the tale focuses on him:

> Thus maketh he his introduccioun,
> To brynge folk to hir destruccioun. (VIII, 1386–87)

Alchemy has transformed this priest and will continue to multiply through him.

It is, however, in his final use of sources that Chaucer wrote most strongly against Gower's claim that alchemy itself is valid since it was once practiced

---

[67] See also VIII, 739–45.

[68] See Joseph E. Grennen, who suggests the two canons reflect the difference between "ordinary quicksilver" and "true philosophic mercury"; "The Canon's Yeoman's Alchemical Mass," *Studies in Philology* 62 (1965), p. 547.

effectively. Indeed, Collette and DiMarco's passage about the failure of alchemy in Gower's day, part of which I quoted earlier, concludes with this point:

> Bot noght forthi, who that it knewe,
> The science of himself is trewe
> Upon the forme as it was founded.... (IV, 2597–99)

This claim then led Gower to name the great alchemists of the past—"Hermes" (IV, 2606), "Geber" (IV, 2608), "Ortolan Morien" (IV, 2609), and "Avicen" (IV, 2610)—and, after again noting the failures of contemporary alchemists to understand their writing (IV, 2613–26), to conclude his discussion:

> Bot thei that writen the scripture
> Of Grek, Arabe, and of Caldee,
> Thei were of such auctorité
> That thei ferst founden out the weie
> Of al that thou hast herd me seie;
> Wherof the cronique of her lore
> Shal stonde in prise foreveremore. (IV, 2626–32)

Gower, then, viewed alchemy as one of the great discoveries of the past.

Following Gower, Chaucer also turned at the end of his tale to the alchemical tradition, yet with devastating effect. The Yeoman's personal frustration with the practice of alchemy shifts its focus to its writings, which appear equally elusive and fraudulent. He turns first to a pointlessly complicated discussion about altering mercury (the "dragon") by means of sulphur ("his brother"), which allows him to identify Hermes as the "philosophres fader" (VIII, 1434), [69] before concluding:

> "Lat no man bisye hym this art for to seche,
> But if that he th'entencioun and speche
> Of philosophres understonde kan;
> And if he do, he is a lewed man.
> For this science and this konnyng," quod he,
> "Is of the secree of the secretes, pardee." (VIII, 1442–47)

Only a "lewed man" would pretend to gain any real knowledge from this self-proclaimed occult science. The Yeoman then uses "Senior" (Senior Zadith)[70] to construct a dialogue in which Plato provides evasive answers to a disciple, who at one point comments, "This is *ignotum per ignocius*" (VIII, 1457),

---

[69]   The Yeoman refers to the "Rosarie" (*Rosarium philosophorum*) of "Arnold of the Newe Toun" (Arnaldus de Villa Nova), which identifies Hermes as the "philosophres fader." The main source for the passage is Arnaldus's *De lapide philosophorum*; see Collette and DiMarco, *S&A*, 2.738–40.

[70]   See Collette and DiMarco, *S&A*, 2.741–42.

before admitting that he will not reveal the truth about the philosophers' stone:

> "Nay, nay," quod Plato, "certein, that I nyl.
> The philosophres sworn were everychoon
> That they sholden discovere it unto noon,
> Ne in no book it write in no manere.
> For unto Crist it is so lief and deere
> That he wol nat that it discovered bee,
> But where it liketh to his deitee
> Men for t'enspire, and eek for to deffende
> Whom that hym liketh; lo, this is the ende." (VIII, 1463–71)

With these two examples, Chaucer used the Yeoman to contradict Gower, characterizing all alchemical writing as failing to contain the knowledge it professes to have. By doing so he identified Gower as in his own craft of writing a fraud.

In the *Canon's Yeoman's Prologue* and *Tale* Chaucer constructed a new narrative from the discussion of alchemy in the *Confessio Amantis*. Moreover, the narrative itself provides evidence of a falling out between the two authors, which, as I argue in Chapter 5, was caused by Gower's rewriting of the *Wife of Bath's Tale* in the *Tale of Florent*. Finally, the Yeoman's prologue and tale are also directly relevant to my larger argument because, like the role of the Squire and his tale in the "Marriage Group," they too use the technique Chaucer learned from Licisca's interruption at the beginning of the Sixth Day, the intertwining of the frame and the individual stories. Here prologue and tale themselves become the literary equivalent of an alchemical experiment: when the Canon and his Yeoman approach the pilgrims, a reaction takes place in which one sticks but the other flies off.[71] The addition brings the number of pilgrims to thirty, and so, as a multiple of ten, more similar to the ten members of the *Decameron*'s *brigata*. Chaucer, then, had anticipated their arrival from the opening of his work just as Boccaccio had prepared for the interruption of Licisca and Tindaro by naming them in the First Day's *Introduzione* (98–101; McWilliam p. 21). Moreover, in asking the Yeoman if his master could "telle a myrie tale or tweye, / With which he glade may this compaignye" (VIII, 597–98), the Host also recalls the terms of the initial story-telling competition, with the reduction of four tales to perhaps one or two indicating his, or Chaucer's, awareness that thirty tales would fill the journey and/or accomplish the aims of the collection. The *Canon's*

---

[71] See Joseph E. Grennen, who argues that "the alchemists in this poem are presented in a double focus; they are human beings with a more than ample amount of stupidity, and at the same time the physical apparatus—materials and instruments—of a cosmic alchemy carrying out its inscrutable and inevitable alterations on them"; "Chaucer's Characterization of the Canon and his Yeoman"; *Journal of the History of Ideas* 25 (1964), p. 279.

Yeoman's Prologue and *Tale*, then, invite us to reflect on the destination of the pilgrimage. In pointed contrast with the *Second Nun's Tale*, the Yeoman's message is secular: distrust claims of higher knowledge based on evidence not directly experienced. This insight has real value in this world, allowing one to change one's ways and to mitigate the evil spread by others. In the *Canon's Yeoman's Prologue* and *Tale* Chaucer affirmed Boccaccio's secular stance.

Folktales, Fabliaux, *and* Exempla

As the Introduction has indicated, the relationships of Boccaccio, Chaucer, and Gower to popular traditions lie at the center of this study and so are discussed in the following chapters as well. I introduce the topic here, however, because folktales, considered broadly to include both *fabliaux* and *exempla*,[72] are often mentioned by the authors of chapters in both the 1941 and the 2002/05 versions of *Sources and Analogues* to account for the plots of otherwise unsourced Canterbury tales. This section, then, provides a chance to compare the tales of the Shipman, Miller, and Wife of Bath as well as one more, the *Pardoner's Tale*. Indeed, doing so not only points out a significant change in Chaucerian scholarship that reflects more fundamental developments within the discipline of folklore, but also allows us to sharpen our understanding of these authors' uses of this kind of material. In 1941 scholars generally viewed folklore as the study of a vast, interconnected series of oral stories from which an author such as Chaucer might have drawn one of his narratives. Although this assumption appears most clearly in John Webster Spargo's analysis of the *Shipman's Tale*, it can be found in the other chapters as well. In 2002/05 two of the chapters, those on the tales of the Shipman and Miller, instead emphasize written sources, and, indeed, shortly after the publication of the second volume of *Sources and Analogues* Russell A. Peck has argued that the *Tale of Florent* is the source of the *Wife of Bath's Tale*.[73] My point here is that Chaucerians, like scholars of folklore, now perceive

---

[72] See, as starting points, the entries by Carl Lindahl, Nicola Chatten, and John McNamara on these terms in *Medieval Folklore: A Guide to Myths, Legends, Tales, Beliefs, and Customs*, ed. Lindahl, McNamara, and John Lindow (Oxford: Oxford University Press, 2002), pp. 142–48, 126–28 and 122–24. There is, of course, much in these entries with which I would not agree; specifically, "the supremely educated Chaucer and Gower, two of the most respected artists and thinkers of their time, have this in common with the tellers of oral folktales: both believe that *familiar stories are always the best*, that the art of storytelling lies not in surprise, surface variation, or superfluous innovation but in retelling a well-known story so well that an audience thoroughly familiar with its contents will still respond with excitement, experiencing it as if for the first time" [original emphasis]; p. 143.

[73] Russell A. Peck, "Folklore and Powerful Women in Gower's 'Tale of Florent,'" in *The "Loathly Lady" Tales: Boundaries, Traditions, Motifs*, Studies in Medieval Culture 48,

more complicated relationships between oral and written traditions. Even in Peck's work, however, the older view often remains unchallenged. In contrast scholars who focus exclusively on links among written texts fail to perceive genuine popular traditions within these works. Boccaccio and Chaucer, but not Gower, used these largely oral traditions, which indeed they recognized as such, to create new, literary short narratives.

In his chapter on the *Shipman's Tale* in the 1941 *Sources and Analogues*, Spargo turns to folklore to explain "the absence of an authentic source."[74] Returning to a possibility that has been suggested at least since the time of Thomas Tyrwhitt's edition of the *Canterbury Tales* (1775–78),[75] he continues, "if we had one, it would probably be an Old French *fabliau* very similar to the *Shipman's Tale*" (p. 439). By relying, however, on his earlier monograph, *Chaucer's Shipman's Tale: the Lover's Gift Regained*,[76] the rest of his brief discussion makes it clear that his interest is not in a particular *fabliau*, a written source, but rather in the oral tradition that would, in his view, underlie it and all other versions of the tale. Indeed, he identifies himself as a firm advocate of the Finnish historical-geographical school of folklore exemplified in the Aarne-Thompson *Types of the Folktale* (1961) and Stith Thompson's own *Motif-Index of Folk-Literature* (1955–58) when he writes in the monograph, "a written version of a tale is an accident" (p. 9).[77] This approach, which was widely influential in folklore departments at least from the time of Antti Aarne's *Verzeichnis der Märchentypen* (1910), sets out from largely nineteenth-century and later collections of material, such as the Grimm brothers' *Kinder- und Husmärchen* (1812), to construct, in Thompson's phrase, "a complete life history of a particular tale."[78] At its center is the perception that traditional narratives, types, remain constant as they are passed orally among communities and down through time. To account for

---

ed. S. Elizabeth Passmore and Susan Carter (Kalamazoo: Medieval Institute Publications, 2007), pp. 100–45.

[74] John Webster Spargo, "The Shipman's Tale," in *Sources and Analogues*, ed. Bryan and Dempster, p. 439.

[75] In his "Introductory Discourse to the Canterbury Tales," Tyrwhitt commented of the *Shipman's Tale*, "this tale is generally supposed to be taken from the *Decameron*. D[ay] viii. N[ovella] 1. but I should rather believe that Chaucer was obliged to some old French *Fableour*, from whom Boccace had also borrowed the ground-work of his Novel."

[76] FFC 91 (Helsinki: Suomalainen Tiedeakatemia, Academia Scientiarum Fennica, 1930).

[77] Antti Aarne and Stith Thompson, *The Types of the Folktale: A Classification and Bibliography*, 2nd edn, FFC 184 (Helsinki: Suomalainen Tiedeakatemia, Academia Scientiarum Fennica, 1961); and Thompson, *Motif-Index of Folk-Literature: A Classification of Narrative Elements in Folktales, Ballads, Myths, Fables, Medieval Romances, Exempla, Fabliaux, Jest-Books, and Local Legends*, 6 vols. (Copenhagen: Rosenkilde and Bagger, 1955–58). See also Hans-Jörg Uther, *The Types of International Folktales: A Classification and Bibliography based on the System of Antti Aarne and Stith Thompson*, FFC 284–86 (Helsinki: Suomalainen Tiedeakatemia, Academia Scientiarum Fennica, 2004).

[78] See Stith Thompson, *The Folktale* (New York: Holt, Rinehart and Winston, 1946), p. 430.

minor changes within a type, such as the Dragon Slayer (type 300),[79] folklorists also identify motifs, "the smallest element in a tale having a power to
persist in tradition."[80] As Alan Dundes has pointed out, the terminology here
is problematic because individual motifs are often themselves tale types.[81] For
those considering Chaucer's sources, this overlapping between largely static
tales and constantly varying motifs has created the false impression that identifying motifs is itself proof of an actual narrative's existence in oral tradition and that scholars can themselves combine these motifs to reconstruct
lost tales. Moreover, in contrast to Spargo's extreme position noted earlier,[82]
Thompson himself recognizes the complicated interchange between oral and
literate versions of a tale; he writes: "that many of our European and Asiatic
folktales go back to a literary source is as clear as any fact of scholarship
can be made."[83] For these two reasons, Spargo's list summarizing all of the
versions he considers related to the type of the Lover's Gift Regained (A. The
Broken or Removed Article; B. Horse and Wagon as Gift; C. Borrowing from
the Husband and Returning to the Wife; D. Accidental Discovery of Identity;
E. Piece of Cloth as Gift; F. Jewelry as Gift; G. Anser venalis; Goose (or
Animal) as Gift) can no longer simply be assumed to have been available to
Chaucer as he wrote his tale.[84]

The article that relates the general point of the previous paragraph to the
Shipman's Tale, Peter Nicholson's "The Medieval Tale of the Lover's Gift
Regained,"[85] is discussed briefly in John Scattergood's chapter in the new
Sources and Analogues, but the insights most important to the arguments of
this book are overlooked because of Scattergood's emphasis is on possible
literary sources, specifically *Decameron* 8.1 and 8.2. In correcting Spargo's
account of history of the Lover's Gift Regained, Nicholson suggests the possibility that 8.10 is related, perhaps as 8.1 is, to the type. His discussion of 8.1
is worth quoting at length first because it offers a concise summary of this
novella's relationship to the folktale:

[79] See Thompson's discussion in *Folktale*, pp. 24–32.

[80] Thompson, *Folktale*, p. 415.

[81] Alan Dundes, "From Etic to Emic Units in the Structural Study of Folktales," in *The
Meaning of Folklore: The Analytical Essays of Alan Dundes*, ed. Simon J. Bronner (Logan:
Utah State University Press, 2007), p. 92; repr. from the *Journal of American Folklore* 75
(1962), pp. 95–105. The Postscript, "The Motif-Index and the Tale Type Index: A Critique,"
in the edited collection develops the argument with new bibliography.

[82] In the monograph, Spargo discusses examples of literary texts influencing later ones, but the
one example of the "numerous imitations of Decameron VII, 2 which can possibly lay claim
to a popular rather than a literary origin," receives special attention and is finally dismissed
as being "as much a 'literary' version as any of the others listed below"; p. 24.

[83] Thompson, *Folktale*, p. 176.

[84] Spargo, "Shipman's Tale," p. 440. Spargo proposed this list at the end of his monograph,
and it was indeed accepted in the 1961 revision of *Types of the Folktale*, type 1420.

[85] *Fabula: Journal of Folklore Studies* 21 (1980), pp. 200–22.

The first striking thing about it is that it is clearly derived from the *Lover's Gift Regained* story which Boccaccio told in its more traditional form in *Decameron* 8.2. All of the motivating elements of the more widely distributed tale are present here as well. The central event is the exchange of love for a payment. There are only three main characters (plus only the soldier's friend in Boccaccio's version). The scheme is at the expense of the woman alone, and the seducer attains the same reward without suffering any cost. The conclusion is the familiar scene in which the woman must choose in the presence of her husband between concealing the bargain and insisting on her right to the gift, and for exactly the same reasons as in the better known tale she chooses to give up her prize. The ultimate popular background for both authors is to be found then in the same traditional story that we identify with the help of the Eastern and German analogues. (pp. 216–17)

In this context Nicholson turns to 8.10:

The juxtaposition of two tales [8.1 and 8.2] so close in subject is not at all unusual in Boccaccio's collection. The eighth day ends with another story very similar to 8, 1 that, unnoticed to Spargo, tells equally of a "lover's gift regained," and that provides a particularly important example of Boccaccio's procedure. The tale appears to have been designed to round off the themes introduced by the first two stories of the day. (p. 218)

After summarizing 8.10 and noting A. C. Lee's identification of the source for its final trick in "a device that has a long previous history in narrative fiction" (a point that I discuss in more detail in Chapter 2), Nicholson concludes the paragraph by raising the possibility that 8.1 and 8.10 are both Boccaccio's literary adaptations of the Lover's Gift Regained:

The design of the *Decameron* encouraged exactly the sort of innovation that made it possible to juxtapose two previously unrelated stories like 8, 1 and 8, 10, or two literary variations whose ultimate roots in popular literature are provided by precisely the same tale. And as 8, 10 illustrates, the specific nature of the innovations in *Decameron* 8, 1 can be traced to exactly the themes that characterize Boccaccio's work as a whole. (p. 218)

While it seems clear that Nicholson favors the second alternative, with its implication that Boccaccio created 8.1 and 8.10,[86] he does not pursue this

---

[86] Of the first two *novelle* of the day he writes: "the best explanation of the similarity between 8, 1 and 8, 2 is not that the two stories circulated together, but that their source was the same, and that Boccaccio himself was responsible for the creation and deliberate juxtaposition of the two different versions of the lover's bargain"; p. 219. A more precise relationship between 8.1 and 8.2 (and between these two and 8.10) is also unnoticed in the edition of Quondam, Fiorilla, and Alfano, pp. 1179–204; see in particular the comment on 8.1: "La novella, che non ha una fonte precisa ma rielabora un tema ben diffuso nella tradizione folklorica, presenta ancora una volta il tipico triangolo amoroso," p. 1180.

insight. Instead, 8.10 falls out of his argument and, when he then turns to the relationship of 8.1 to the *Shipman's Tale*, he concludes "without settling the precise nature of Chaucer's source" (p. 222).

We can go further. Chaucer recognized precisely what Nicholson suggests: Boccaccio had told the same story three times, in its traditional form in 8.2, but again in literary adaptations in the urban setting of Milan (8.1) and in the world of international commerce (8.10). Chaucer proved that he had perceived this narrative strategy by combining all three *novelle* back into one tale. In contrast to Nicholson, who claims that "Chaucer showed no familiarity with the more traditional tale of the *Lover's Gift Regained*" (p. 219), I would note here that his lover, as in 8.2, is a member of the clergy. Indeed, as a monk, daun John is an apt representative of the older, feudal economy of the village, a point emphasized by his attending to the holdings of his monastery in his claim that he needs money to buy beasts and by his association with gifts. Moreover, the setting of 8.2 in the hamlet of Varlungo is recalled in the detail that Chaucer's monk and merchant are friends because they "were bothe two yborn in o village" (VII, 35). At the other extreme in 8.10, Boccaccio's Florentine merchant working for Pisan employers and aided by a family friend living in Naples, who serves as "trasorier di madama la 'mperatice di Constantinopoli" (8.10, 42; "treasurer to Her Highness the Empress of Constantinople," McWilliam, p. 639), finds expression in Chaucer's merchant's complex dealings through the recently established banks of Bruges and Paris. As an old market town, Saint-Denis itself, where the merchant and his wife live, is equidistant between the village and the new centers of finance. It is, then, undeniable that the idea that binds these three *novelle* together, developments in economic systems, is the main source of the narrative of the *Shipman's Tale*.

As I argue, however, in more detail in Chapter 2, Chaucer was drawn to *Decameron* 8.1, 8.2, and 8.10 in part because he perceived their relationship to what we would call popular tradition and what he would have recognized as different from, for example, the work by Boccaccio, the *Teseida*, that he had used in writing the *Knight's Tale*.[87] The issue might appear to be complicated by the "Versus de mola piperis," which both Boccaccio and Chaucer probably knew since it has already been found in fifteen manuscripts from the thirteenth to the fifteenth century and seems likely to appear in more.[88] Are we not, then, considering a question of literary history exclusive of oral tradition? Again, Nicholson's analysis is revealing. By considering similar narratives surviving from the twelfth to the sixteenth century in India, the Near

---

[87] Chaucer's keen awareness of generic distinctions is played out in the contrast between the epigram from Statius, announcing a martial theme, and the final phrase of his first sentence: "And eek hir yonge suster Emelye" (I, 871). Epic has descended into romance. See Cooper, *Canterbury Tales*, pp. 63–64.

[88] These manuscripts are discussed in Chapter 2 and the Appendix.

East and northern Europe (Germany and the Netherlands), he demonstrates that the type represented by the "Versus" and 8.2 (as distinct from 8.1; see p. 220) circulated independently from any particular literary form (pp. 205–07). It did so, as he makes clear in his summary, because the story is well suited to oral performance:

> The consistency of the tradition is due, therefore, not to specific details that recur from text to text, but to a framework of a tale that could be constantly renewed, including a motivating device, the exchange of love for a gift; and a set of assumptions about character that occur in invariable combination in all the known versions to shape the dénouement.... The plot moves so quickly, and the tale circulated so far, because the expectations of behavior for each of the three characters could be supplied immediately from the previous narrative experience of every reader or listener wherever the story was told. (pp. 206–07)

While it is then possible, although unlikely, that these two fourteenth-century authors knew only written versions of the Lover's Gift Regained such as the "Versus de mola piperis" both almost certainly would have recognized the relationship of these versions to other similar stories in the popular tradition. That they did so can be seen in Panfilo's characterization of 8.2 as an "amorazzo contadino" (8.2, 5; "a tale of country love," McWilliam, p. 555) and in Chaucer's initial plan of contrasting the *Shipman's Tale* (told by the Wife of Bath) to the bookish *Melibee* (originally assigned to the Man of Law). The literary tradition, too, remains part of the argument since the stable form of the "Versus" would have aided Boccaccio in writing his *novelle*; had he known it, this Latin poem would have helped Chaucer to perceive his Italian precursor's brilliant literary exercise.

Recognizing Chaucer's literary use of popular tradition as mediated by Boccaccio in the *Shipman's Tale* allows us to reconsider the general problems related to sources of the tales of the Miller, Wife of Bath, and Pardoner. Writing in 1941, Stith Thompson began his chapter in the first *Sources and Analogues*: "though no direct literary source has ever been discovered for the *Miller's Tale*, and though such future discovery seems unlikely, the presence of the tale in oral tradition of the poet's day is well established."[89] It is immediately striking, however, that only one of the ten analogues he cites, *Heile van Beersele*, is (according to his dating) from the fourteenth century.[90] While there will be more to say about this work in a moment and in Chapter 4, let me note here that it does not conform to Folktale Type 1361, as established by Thompson:

---

[89] Stith Thompson, "The Miller's Tale," in *Sources and Analogues*, ed. Bryan and Dempster, p. 106.

[90] The date of this *boerde* is, of course, essential to my argument and is discussed in Chapter 4.

A priest persuades the man to sleep in a hanging tub to escape the coming flood [K1522]. Meantime he dallies with the man's wife. Another lover comes to the window. The priest presents his rump to be kissed [K1522; *recte* K1225]. The other lover the second time burns the priest with a hot iron [K1577]. The priest yells: 'Water!' The husband thinks the flood has come, cuts the tub ropes, and falls.[91]

In *Heile*, the prostitute just happens to keep a tub hanging in her ceiling, and here the priest does not mention a second flood until after he has done the "wiekewake" three times.[92] Indeed, the only examples of the type that might be independent of the *Miller's Tale* are from Germany. Three, by Hans Sachs, Valentin Schumann, and Kaspar Cropacius, are from the sixteenth century. An anonymous version in the late seventeenth-century collection, *Lyrum Larum*, and another bowdlerized one recorded in the nineteenth century in Northern Germany (Schleswig-Holstein) indicate oral circulation, but well after Chaucer's time.[93]

In part because of the nature of these analogues, Peter G. Beidler proposes that *Heile van Beersele* itself was Chaucer's source, or, to use his words, "the closest we have to Chaucer's source" (*S&A*, 2.249).[94] In Chapter 4 I argue that there are internal reasons, most importantly the two mentioned in the previous paragraph, to view *Heile* as descending directly from the *Miller's Tale*. Here I would like to consider the more general point: it is simply more likely, given the pattern we are establishing of Chaucer's free handling of sources elsewhere in the *Canterbury Tales*, that it was he, rather than an anonymous Dutch writer or indeed oral tradition itself, who created this tale. A broad overview of his likely sources may underline this point. The main source of his narrative of the lover's elaborate plot to sleep with a wife in her own home is *Decameron* 3.4, long recognized as an analogue to this tale. For the tubs, Chaucer turned to *Decameron* 7.2, a retelling of a story in Apuleius's *Metamorphoses or Golden Ass*;[95] his addition was to wind them into the rafters so one can crash brilliantly to the ground in the tale's final moments. His "misdirected kiss" probably did come from a *fabliau* such as

---

[91] *Types of the Folktale*, p. 405.

[92] Peter G. Beidler re-edits the text for his entry in *S&A*, 2.267–75; "wiekewake" appears in line 75. In his discussion, Thompson characterizes the "*flood* episode" here as "garbled"; "Miller's Tale," in *Sources and Analogues*, ed. Bryan and Dempster, p. 112.

[93] All are discussed in Chapter 4.

[94] The distinction is, for my argument, unimportant. There is always the possibility in source study of uncovering a more immediate source, in this case, say, a Dutch manuscript of *Heile* with Chaucer's notes in the margins explaining how he adapted it. Instead it appears to me that Beidler qualifies his claim because he still accepts an outdated understanding of folklore.

[95] The tale from Apuleius is printed and translated by Larry D. Benson and Theodore M. Andersson in *The Literary Context of Chaucer's Fabliaux: Texts and Translations* (Indianapolis: Bobbs-Merrill, 1971), pp. 6–9.

De Berangier au lonc cul because here it is a woman who plays this trick on a man as an expression of her power over him.[96] Finally, the branding derives from the tradition of linking punishments in Hell to the parts of the body that committed the sin, fitting into a pattern of religious imagery that runs through the tale concerning judgment and misjudgment. There is reason to believe that Chaucer assembled all of these pieces; it defies belief that they would appear together first in a garbled form in a Dutch *boerde*.

The issues at stake in considering the sources of the *Wife of Bath's Tale* are similar to those related to the sources of the *Miller's Tale*, and yet here the main popular traditions, the Loathly Lady and the question, have been less clearly defined, and the proposed direct source, Gower's *Tale of Florent*, is both closer to Chaucer and more obviously literary. After discussing Chaucer's original plan to assign the *Shipman's Tale* to the Wife of Bath, Bartlett J. Whiting continues his chapter in the 1941 *Sources and Analogues*: "in the Wife's new tale two motifs are joined, that of the Loathly Lady transformed through love, and that of the man whose life depends on the correct answering of a question."[97] For the first, he refers to D 732 ("Man disenchants loathsome woman by embracing her"); for the second H 530 ff. (the introductory entry for Riddles, which are covered in 530–899) and H 1388.1 ("*Question: What is it women most desire*. Answer: Sovereignty").[98] In the 2005 *Sources and Analogues*, John Withrington and P. J. C. Field begin their chapter: "*The Wife of Bath's Tale* makes use of two folklore motifs: in one a 'Loathly Lady' is transformed into a beautiful woman, while the other involves answering the question 'What is it that women most desire?'" (*S&A*, 2.405). Their note is to D 732 and H 1388.1. These chapters, then, pick out two of the same motifs, although both the reference to "H 530 ff." and minor differences in wording are revealing. However, even though these motifs might seem more closely related to each other than the elements joined in Type 1361 discussed in connection with the *Miller's Tale*, they have not been identified as a type, presumably because they appear together only in two places other than in Chaucer and Gower: a late fourteenth- or early fifteenth-century poem, *The Weddyng of Sir Gawen and Dame Ragnell*, and a ballad, *The Marriage of Sir Gawain*, preserved in the "Percy Folio" from around 1650.[99] These works, which appear to derive from the *Wife of Bath's Tale* and *Florent*, do not provide enough evidence of oral circulation of the combined motifs even after Chaucer's time to justify an entry in the *Types of the Folktale*.

It is, however, not only the lack of a tale type but also the imprecision

---

96 Benson and Andersson include *Berangier* "as an example of the 'misdirected kiss,'" but comment that Chaucer "probably did not" know it; *Literary Context*, p. 11.

97 Bartlett J. Whiting, "The Wife of Bath's Tale," in *Sources and Analogues*, ed. Bryan and Dempster, p. 223.

98 Thompson, *Motif-Index*, 2.84, 3.423–49, and 3.501.

99 Both may be found in *S&A*, 2.420–48.

of the motifs as they have been defined that has opened the way for much scholarly speculation, culminating in Peck's claims that the story existed in folk tradition and that Gower was the source of the later versions. Prior to Peck much scholarship had focused on the question of the transmission of the Loathly Lady from what Withrington and Field refer to as "early Irish analogues" to fourteenth-century England, a journey that allowed for hypothetical transformations within the motif and its combination with others.[100] Peck both embodies this tradition and changes it radically: "there is, in effect, no contradiction between Lang's 'Nobody can write a new fairy tale' and the proposition that Gower compiles the English narrative that Chaucer and the 'Ragnell'-poet follow in their Loathly Lady narratives."[101] While the first possibility harkens back to an understanding of folklore that is no longer widely accepted (Andrew Lang's *Lilac Fairy Book* was published in 1910), the second raises a significant question for this study because it is tied closely to an understanding of Chaucer's use of sources. The *Wife of Bath's Tale* could, of course, rely directly on *Florent* without contradicting my claim about the importance of the *Decameron* to other tales and to the *Canterbury Tales* as a whole; indeed the completion of the first version of the *Confessio Amantis* in 1390 and the conventional dating of the *Wife of Bath's Tale* to the mid-1390s favor this view.[102] However, as with *Heile van Beersele* and the *Miller's Tale*, there is reason to look further, because Chaucer often created strikingly original narratives from disparate materials. In spite of Peck's claims of Gower's relationship to folk tradition, the sources of the narratives in the *Confessio Amantis* are overwhelmingly literary,[103] as Peck himself acknowledges when he writes, "no English writer of the fourteenth century was more intelligently in touch with Ovid and classical narratives than Gower."[104] Peck, as one might expect given his thesis in this article, begins that thought with an "although" and the end of his sentence is, technically, accurate: "Although no English writer...than Gower, his 'Tale of Florent' seems more attuned to Celtic folk motifs than to classical literary sources, though Ovidian motifs do lurk in the

---

[100] Withrington and Field (*S&A*, 2.405, notes 2 and 3) give priority to three studies: G. H. Maynadier, *The* Wife of Bath's Tale*: Its Sources and Analogues* (London: Nutt, 1901); Sigmund Eisner, *A Tale of Wonder: A Source Study of* The Wife of Bath's Tale (Wexford: John English, 1957); and John K. Bollard, "Sovereignty and the Loathly Lady Tale in English, Welsh and Irish," *Leeds Studies in English* 17 (1986), pp. 41–59. Field returns to the question in "What Women Really Want: the Genesis of Chaucer's *Wife of Bath's Tale*," *Arthurian Literature* 27 (2010), pp. 59–85. I was an associate advisor for S. Elizabeth Passmore's dissertation, "The Loathly Lady Transformed: A Literary and Cultural Analysis of the Medieval Irish and English Hag-Beauty Tales" (University of Connecticut, 2004).

[101] Peck, "Folklore," p. 105.

[102] Andrew Lang, *The Lilac Fairy Book* (London: Longmans, Green, 1910). On the date of the *Wife of Bath's Tale*, see the explanatory notes by Christine Ryan Hilary in the *Riverside Chaucer*, ed. Benson, p. 872. Cooper does not offer a date in the *Canterbury Tales*, p. 156.

[103] See Chapter 5.

[104] Peck, "Folklore," p. 101.

background" (pp. 101–02). However, Celtic elements in *Wife of Bath's Tale*—the reference to "Britons," the Arthurian setting, and especially the allusion to the "elf-queene, with heir joly compaignye" (III, 860) that anticipates the appearance of the hag following a dance "Of ladyes foure and twenty, and yet mo" (III, 992)—appear nowhere in *Florent*. Since the precise motif on which the *Wife of Bath's Tale* depends—the transformation of a Loathly Lady connected not with the enchantment of an evil stepmother as in *Florent* but rather with the theme of sovereignty—occurs in Irish sources, Chaucer must have found it there.[105] It appears more likely, then, that Gower made the *Wife of Bath's Tale* more conventional as he retold it than that he worked directly from the Irish tradition to construct a new tale.

In Chapter 5 I develop the argument that the *Wife of Bath's Tale* was written before the *Tale of Florent* by considering Chaucer's other main narrative source, the anti-feminist tradition identified by Margaret Schlauch that appears in the hag's choice of her being either ugly and faithful or beautiful and unfaithful. It is this question that underlies the one, with its answer, that has received more attention: What is it that women most desire? Although given a separate entry in the *Motif-Index* (H1388.1), this question occurs only in the four English texts (the *Wife of Bath's Tale*, *Florent*, the *Weddyng*, and the *Marriage*),[106] and, indeed, outside of the context of Chaucer's tale makes less sense, as the grandmother's response to Florent's correct answer indicates:

> "Ha! Treson! Wo thee be,
> That hast thus told the privité,
> Which alle wommen most desire!
> I wolde that thou were afire." (I, 1659–62)

Starting instead from the anti-feminist tradition that a beautiful woman is never faithful, Chaucer considered the effect of a woman asking, "What is

---

[105] I consider the question of transmission in Chapter 5. Let me anticipate that discussion here by noting only that the assumption of an involved oral journey for an ancient source to more modern forms appears much less certain now than it did to practitioners of the historical-geographical school of folklore. The Irish motif of the Loathly Lady circulated in fourteenth-century Ireland, a country with which England had much direct contact.

[106] Not included in this list are two texts that David F. Johnson, P. J. C. Field, and Lindy Brady have identified as relevant to the discussion: an interpolation, *Hoe Walewein wilde weten vrowen gepens* ("How Walwein Wanted to Know the Thoughts of Women"), into the Dutch translation of *La Vengeance Raguidel*, and the Latin *Arthur and Gorlagon*; see Johnson, "Questing in the Middle Dutch *Lancelot Compilation*," in *The Grail, the Quest and the World of Arthur*, Arthurian Studies 72, ed. Norris J. Lacy (Cambridge: D. S. Brewer, 2008), p. 95; Field, "What Women Really Want," pp. 75–80; and Brady, "Antifeminist Tradition in *Arthur and Gorlagon* and the Quest to Understand Women," *Notes & Queries* n.s. 59 (2012), pp. 163–66, and "Feminine Desire and Conditional Misogyny in *Arthur and Gorlagon*," *Arthuriana* 24.3 (2014), pp. 24–25. I will return to this problem in Chapter 5.

it, then, that you men want?" In this tale of reversals, where the rapist knight pleads to be spared the violation of his body through a deal he has agreed to, power is the obvious answer to the misogyny embodied in rape. Chaucer's interest in the Celtic motif of the Loathly Lady is not that of an antiquarian preserving old tales, but of an author seeking vivid ways to explore the imbalance of gender relationships in his own day. Gower again missed or changed the point by altering the Loathly Lady's offer.

My final example of the value of rethinking Chaucer's relationship to folklore is, I admit, the most speculative, but returns us to the question of his use of the *Decameron*. The opening of Mary Hamel's chapter in the 2002 *Sources and Analogues* echoes the assumptions of the Finnish school of folklore: "the *Pardoner's Tale* of the three 'riotours' who find Death is a version of a folktale with a remarkably wide range, from Chaucer's England to the Near and Far East and sub-Saharan Africa; it very likely originated as a tale of the Buddha as Bodhisattva from the fourth or third century B.C." (*S&A*, 1.279).[107] When she turns, however, in her second paragraph to the versions "closest" to Chaucer, their dates immediately stand out: one is from ca. 1400, three from the early fifteenth century (one dated to 1406), one from the mid-fifteenth century, and the last from 1576. Hamel writes of the latest: "though the last two were printed a considerable time after Chaucer's death, they are included because they undoubtedly reflect a much earlier oral circulation of the tale, and moreover have more in common with the *Pardoner's Tale* than any other medieval analogues" (*S&A* 1.279–80). As one would expect, collections of *exempla*, which were used in sermons, are plentiful from the twelfth century onward, and many of the most important have been edited and catalogued.[108] While it is always possible that the Pardoner's narrative has yet to be discovered in an earlier manuscript, the evidence we now have suggests that Chaucer wrote a tale which was then adapted for later collections. I have argued that his source was *Decameron* 10.3, in which Nathan offers to exchange his old age for Mithridanes's youth after the latter has turned down a chance to kill him,[109] but to do so here would take us far beyond the scope of this study. Even this possibility, however, may serve as a reminder that more remains to be said about Chaucer's debt to the *Decameron*.

[107] Her note refers to *Originals and Analogues* (ed. Furnivall, Brock, and Clouston) "for texts of Eastern versions."

[108] See Kaske, *Medieval Christian*, pp. 88–89; and the *Thesuarus Exemplorum Medii Aevi* (ThEMA), hosted by *Le Groupe d'Anthropologie Historique de l'Occident Médiéval*, http://lodel.ehess.fr/gahom/thema/.

[109] "*Fanti e Famigliari nel* Decameron *and Some Followers in the* Canterbury Tales," Boccaccio: Rome 2013 (conference), "Sapienza" Università di Roma, June 2013.

2

The Shipman's Trade in Three *Novelle* from the *Decameron*

Focusing only on the first and second *novelle* of the Eighth Day of the *Decameron*, scholars have failed to appreciate the related last story of this section, 8.10, which Chaucer also used in writing the *Shipman's Tale* and which thus proves that he knew Boccaccio's collection. The first step in supporting this claim is to note that Chaucer's insight is itself remarkable: he saw something, Boccaccio's literary play with a single source, that modern critics have largely overlooked.[1] Moreover, it seems likely that he was able to perceive the relationships among these *novelle* because he knew Boccaccio's immediate source for them, the "Versus de mola piperis" ("A Poem about a Pepper Mill"), and recognized its relationship to the popular tradition that folklorists call the Lover's Gift Regained. Chaucer then watched Boccaccio exploit one of the enigmatic features of the poem, its placing of upper-class characters into a situation better suited to peasants, the subject of many of these traditional tales.[2] Boccaccio divided these elements, creating a more complicated, if shorter, story for bourgeois characters in 8.1 before resetting in 8.2 the basic narrative of the "Versus" among the inhabitants of a village. It is all but certain that he did so since he returned to the story in 8.10, extending his range beyond the village and the city into the world of international commerce.

Scholars have overlooked these source relationships because 8.10 is substantially more complicated than either 8.2 or 8.1, involving another common story type (although one not recorded in the *Types of the Folktale*), the Deceiver Deceived, as well as a specific motif, which appears in Petrus Alphonsi's *Disciplina clericalis* and the *Gesta Romanorum*, someone who refuses to repay money left with him until it appears someone else may

---

[1] The exception, to my knowledge, is Nicholson, whose article, "Medieval Tale," is considered in Chapter 1 and informs my discussion here.

[2] Stressing the diversity of the material, Norris J. Lacy provides a useful introduction to a significant part of the broader tradition of short, comic tales in *Reading Fabliaux* (Birmingham: Suma Publications, 1999). I agree with his conviction that that "medieval audiences had certain generic assumptions" (p. 53) against which individual texts can work in different ways. On the question of class, see his chapter "Courtliness and the Fabliaux," pp. 46–59.

entrust him with more.[3] Chaucer, then, would have seen not only Boccaccio's literary brilliance in retelling one story in three settings but also his transforming this short narrative by combining it with other motifs, a technique he would use to good effect in constructing other tales.

In the *Shipman's Tale* Chaucer stayed within the parameters of the three *novelle*, but made the story his own by turning it to a different purpose. Boccaccio's narratives, particularly 8.10, present many different themes, but when taken together and considered in the context of the *cornice*, one stands out: in the words of Neifile, the teller of 8.1, "affermo colei esser degna del fuoco la quale a ciò per prezzo si conduce" (8.1, 3; "I declare that any woman who strays from the path of virtue for monetary gain deserves to be burnt alive," McWilliam, p. 552).[4] Recognizing but not following this theme, Chaucer instead developed his tale as it was originally written for the Wife of Bath to investigate the economic basis of marriage.

Like Boccaccio, who began the Eighth Day with his Milan version of the Lover's Gift Regained, Chaucer too focused on the urban middle class, and yet he used details from both the agrarian and the international settings of 8.2 and 8.10 to show not that money and sex should be kept separate, but that there is a financial basis to the sexual relationship that concerned him: marriage. From the peasant tale he took, perhaps most significantly, the remarkable scene, which occupies a third of 8.2 and a quarter of the *Shipman's Tale*, in which the lover and the wife, each recognizing the other's desire, move their conversation to a shared end. In this barter economy, business and sex speak the same language and reach mutual agreements. 8.1, as is well recognized,[5] provided him with not only his basic plot but also the conventional moral assumption—that relationships between men and women should not involve economic considerations—that he wrote against. Influenced, however, by Boccaccio's elaboration of the Lover's Gift Regained in 8.10 with its backdrop of international commerce and its forceful female protagonist, who controls both her money and her sexuality, Chaucer extended his story so that it ends not with a verbal exchange between the wife and her lover but rather with the husband and wife in bed making a new deal, which again points to

---

3   This source is discussed by A. C. Lee, *The* Decameron*: Its Sources and Analogues* (1909; repr. New York: Haskell House, 1966), pp. 266–70.

4   McWilliam's translation, while free, catches the sense of the passage. I would call attention to "per prezzo" ("for a price") since the noun will appear twice more in the *novella*. Branca, moreover, notes other places in the *Decameron* where Boccaccio expresses similar ideas (p. 891, note 1).

5   Using his terminology for source study (see Chapter 1, note 2), Peter G. Beidler considers 8.1 a "hard analogue" that is the tale's "most likely source"; "Just Say Yes, Chaucer Knew the *Decameron*: Or Bringing the *Shipman's Tale* Out of Limbo," in *Chaucer's Canterbury Comedies*, p. 161; repr. from *The* Decameron *and the* Canterbury Tales*: New Essays on an Old Question*, ed. Leonard Michael Koff and Brenda Deen Schildgen (Teaneck: Fairleigh Dickinson University Press, 2000), pp. 25–46.

a basic connection between sex and money. Instead of accepting bourgeois morality as the norm against which to judge all society, Chaucer took details from the lives of both peasants and international merchants to point out the inequality in conventional views of marriage. A perfect tale, or so he thought, for his Wife of Bath. That it did not turn out this way is the subject of the next chapter; here I will discuss the traditional form of the Lover's Gift Regained and its expression in the "Versus de mola piperis," then consider Boccaccio's three *novelle* and what each contributed to the *Shipman's Tale*, and finally discuss how Chaucer's tale differs from these sources.

Before proceeding let me briefly reframe this argument in a way that makes it more speculative and yet introduces a possibility that will appear elsewhere in this study: among the tricks that Chaucer learned from Boccaccio was to provide particular settings for short narratives in order to enhance their meanings.[6] While some *fabliaux* are associated with identifiable locations, many, like "Versus de mola piperis," can be placed only generally by their characters and situations.[7] Boccaccio changed the Lover's Gift Regained simply by writing it into Varlungo, Milan, and Palermo, and he then exploited the possibilities offered by each. That Chaucer understood this idea is indicated, as we will see, by not only the appropriateness of his choice of Saint-Denis for the *Shipman's Tale* but also his elaborate engagement with Oxford in the *Miller's Tale*. He learned from Boccaccio not where things happened but why the where mattered.

Folktales and a Pepper Mill

While excluding many of the stories that earlier scholars, particularly John Webster Spargo,[8] had discussed in connection with the folktale type known

---

6   On this topic, see Robert W. Hanning, "Before Chaucer's *Shipman's Tale*: The Language of Place and the Place of Language in *Decameron* 8.1 and 8.2," in *Place, Space, and Landscape in Medieval Narrative*, ed. Laura L. Howes, Tennessee Studies in Literature 43 (Knoxville: University of Tennessee Press, 2007), pp. 181–96.

7   Interest in the settings of the *fabliaux* has been bound up with arguments over the bourgeois or aristocratic nature of the genre; see Marie-Thérèse Lorcin, *Façons de sentir et de penser: les fabliaux français* (Paris: H. Champion, 1979), pp. 7–29; and Raymond Eichmann and John DuVal, eds., *The French Fabliau B.N. MS. 837*, 2 vols., Garland Library of Medieval Literature A/16, 17 (New York: Garland, 1984–85), 1:xix–xx. Guérin's *De Berangier au lonc cul*, which will be discussed later, begins with a criticism of the Lombards; Benson and Andersson, *Literary Context*, pp. 10–11. See also the beginning of *Des .III. bocus menesterels*, where Durant claims to have forgotten the setting of his story; Eichmann and DuVal, eds., *French Fabliau*, 2.137.

8   Spargo, *Chaucer's Shipman's Tale*. Spargo discusses the texts and traditions I will consider in the following paragraphs, providing useful translations and commentary. I will, however, refer not to his work, but rather to more recent editions and translations.

as the Lover's Gift Regained (1420),[9] Peter Nicholson accepts a group, which includes both the "Versus de mola piperis" and *Decameron* 8.2, as "a single tradition" that circulated orally from twelfth-century India to twentieth-century Western Europe.[10] Much still remains unclear about these texts and the traditions to which they belong; his conclusions, however, remain on the whole plausible. All share, he notes, "a basic plot," although they may differ slightly in their conclusions:

> The seducer meets a woman and arranges an exchange for her love. He regrets the loss of his gift and devises a way to exploit the presence of her husband or another figure in order to have his gift returned.... It is the ending more than anything else that provides the recognizable identity to the tale: the woman is confronted with the lover's clever prevarication, and in order to conceal her role in the actual bargain she is forced to give up her prize. The variations in the ending also provide the only basis for classifying the surviving texts. When the seducer presents his claim for the gift he maintains either that it was taken from him unjustly or that it was part of a different sort of bargain than actually took place. (p. 207)

Both variations in the endings appear in the popular twelfth-century Sanskrit *Śukasaptati*.[11] In tale 38 after giving the wife of a merchant a ring before sleeping with her, a Brahmin takes one of the bed posts to her husband saying, "'the bed broke...and your wife took away my ring.'"[12] The husband returns the ring. In tale 35 a merchant having given a ring to the wife of another merchant then goes to her husband in the market to demand the sesame that he claims to have paid for with the gift; the husband again demands the ring's return (p. 122).[13] A third story in this collection, tale 34, is less close since it involves villagers in the role of the husband. Here a Brahmin uses his sari to seduce a girl who guards a field; to get it back he takes some grain before he follows her to the village, where he cries, "'for five ears of grain this

9   Aarne and Thompson, *Types of the Folktale*.
10   Nicholson, "Medieval Tale," p. 207.
11   The two versions, known as the *textus simplicior* and the *textus ornatior*, are both edited and translated by R. Schmidt. The critical edition of the first was published in the *Abhandlungen für die Kunde des Morgenlandes* 10.1 (Leipzig, 1893); and the translation in *Die Śukasaptati [textus simplicior]. Aus dem Sanskrit übersetzt* (Kiel: C. F. Haeseler, 1894). The critical edition of the second was published in the *Abhandlungen der Bayerischen Akademie der Wissenschaften* 21.2 (1898–99), pp. 317–416; and the translation in *Die Śukasaptati [textus ornatior] aus dem Sanskrit überetzt* (Stuttgart: W. Kohlhammer, 1899). For further details on other editions and translations of the work by Schmidt, see Ludwik Sternbach, *The Kāvya-Portions in the Kathā-Literature*, 3 vols. (New Delhi: Meharchand Lachhmandas, 1971–76), 3.209–11. Sternbach also discusses the origin of the work and the fourteenth-century Persian translation, from which it was further disseminated.
12   *Shuka Saptati: Seventy Tales of the Parrot*, trans. A. N. D. Haksar (New Delhi: HarperCollins, 2000), p. 129. This is a translation of the *textus simplicior*.
13   The corresponding tale in the *textus ornatior* is 45.

girl has taken my garment'" (p. 120). [14] Since she was "too embarrassed to say anything," the villagers make her return the sari (p. 120). A contemporary Arabic version in Ibn al-Jawzī's *Akhbār al-adhkiyā'*, which appears in later collections as well, corresponds to the first variation: the lover claims a broken water glass was the reason for his "gift."[15] Finally a ballad, "Een boerman hadde eenen dommen sin," which appears in *Het Antwerps Liedboek* (1544) and which Nicholson considers independent of the *Decameron* (p. 206),[16] also represent the first variation. Here a peasant claims that the wife has confiscated his wagonload of wood because of one crooked stick; as Nicholson notes, in "some versions there is a bawdy double meaning in his indignant complaint: 'I tell you the crooked burns just like the straight / As soon as they come by the fire'" (p. 206). Even if one were to challenge the premise that these narratives are directly related through oral transmission, arguing instead that written versions explain some correspondences and the chance creation of similar stories at different times others, they indicate that basic plot is well suited to popular performance.

The form of the "Versus de mola piperis" also supports the claim that the narrative circulated not only in manuscripts but also orally since it both is easier to understand if one recognizes the story and seems likely to have been retold as well as recopied and reread. The poem relies heavily on direct statements, and yet leaves much unstated:

> Militis uxorem clamidis mercede subegit
> Clericus, et piperis clam tulit ipse molam.
> Mane redit, referensque molam presente marito.
> Dixit, "mantellum redde; reporto molam."
> "Redde," maritus ait. Respondet femina, "reddam;
> Amplius ad nostram non molet ipse molam."[17]

---

14 See tale 44 in the *textus ornatior*.
15 See the edition of Muhammad Mursī Khūlī (Cairo: Matābi' al-Ahrām al-Tijārīyah, 1970). This collection is one of the major sources used by Ulrich Marzolph, *Arabia ridens. Die humoristische Kurzprosa der frühen abad-Literatur im internationalen Traditionsgeflecht*, 2 vols. (Frankfurt am Main: Klostermann, 1992), vol. 2, no. 1166, who also lists an earlier version from 1166. See also Hasan M. el-Shamy, *Types of the Folktale in the Arab World: A Demographically Oriented Tale-Type Index* (Bloomington: Indiana University Press, 2004), p. 798 (1420A), which records a new version from Egypt; and *'Abbasid Belles-Lettres*, Cambridge History of Arabic Literature, ed. Julia Ashtiany, T. M. Johnstone, J. D. Latham, R. B. Serjeant, and Rex Smith (Cambridge: Cambridge University Press, 1990), which acknowledges how much work remains to be done in this field; p. xii. On Ibn al-Jawzī, see the first chapter of Merlin Scartz, *A Medieval Critique of Anthropomorphism: Ibn al-Jawzī's Kitāb Akhbār aṣ-Ṣifāt* (Leiden: Brill, 2002), pp. 3–32.
16 *Het Antwerps Liedboek*, 2 vols., ed. Dieuwke E. van der Poel, Dirk Geirnaert, Hermina Joldersma, Johan Oosterman, and Louis Peter Grijp (Tielt: Lannoo, 2004), 1.84–85 (no. 35). They comment that this song is also known from the *Rostocker liedboek* (1478) and other German and Low German sources (2.110); see also their discussion of sources (2.23–24).
17 This transcription is from Eton, Eton College, MS 125.

(A clerk won a soldier's wife with, as payment, a cloak and that very one secretly took a pepper mill. The next morning he returns, giving the mill to the husband who is there. "Give me back the cloak; I am returning the mill," he said. "Give it back," says the husband. "I will," answers the wife, "but this one will grind no more at our mill.")

In spite of the abrupt first clause and the final punning one, the middle of the poem all but requires the reader to know the story in order to follow it. Without prior knowledge, we are put in a position similar to that of the husband, who appears both sharp in understanding the connection the clerk implies between the cloak and the pepper mill and then foolish in not working out the rest of deal. We may understand the larger context, but still be puzzled, momentarily, by the clerk's actions and demand. Moreover, we must supply the emotions of all the characters, which seem an intrinsic part of the story but which are not mentioned. Finally, several terms invite us to speculate about the social standing of the participants. As noted in the Introduction, pepper was a luxury item throughout the Middle Ages, and so owning a pepper mill is likely to be an indication of wealth.[18] From the second half of the twelfth century, moreover, *miles* may be translated most naturally as 'knight', a member of a distinct order of society "with its own rites and rules."[19] On the other hand, a *clericus* could, of course, belong to different professions, including a clergyman, an educated person in some particular employment, or just a student.[20] This one has a *clamis*, originally the rich cloak worn by a Greek military official, and which kept some of its distinction in Latin, where it was used of imperial, royal, and papal garments

---

[18] Pepper is the focus of Paul Freedman's "Spices and Late-Medieval European Ideas of Scarcity and Value," *Speculum* 80 (2005), pp. 1209–27. He cites *Le Viandier*, written around 1300, and more tellingly two poems by Eustache Deschamps which specifically mention pepper in the context of the hardships, such as lice, of life in Bohemia to show that "pepper lost some of its prestige toward the end of the Middle Ages"; p. 1215. He cites *The Viandier of Taillevent: An Edition of All Extant Manuscripts*, ed. Terence Scully (Ottawa: University of Ottawa Press, 1988) and the *Œuvres complètes*, 11 vols., ed. Marquis de Queux de Saint-Hilaire and Gaston Reynaud, Sociéte des anciens textes français (Paris: Firmin Didot & cie, 1878–1903), 7.88–90. He concludes, "notwithstanding such remarks, pepper enjoyed the status of a necessary luxury throughout the Middle Ages and beyond, an expensive condiment, but one within reach of a substantial proportion of the population"; p. 1215. The reference in the entry on *mola* in the *DMLBS* to "unam moldam piperialem" should be to Kew, The National Archives, CP 40/ 519 m. 499r. The date of the roll is 1390, and the entry records a debt case from Kent involving William and Agnes Frost and Thomas Deborn. The pepper mill is included in a long list of goods which includes, for example, two garments or coverings, a rug, a spinning wheel, a ladder, and a silver amulet. It can be found at http://aalt.law.uh.edu/AALT6/R2/CP40no519/519_1168.htm. I would like to thank Elizabeth Biggs for tracking down this reference and explaining it to me.

[19] See Giles Constable, *Three Studies in Medieval Religious and Social Thought* (Cambridge: Cambridge University Press, 1995), p. 332. See also the *DMLBS, s.v.*

[20] See the entry in the *DMLBS, s.v.*

as well as those of the clergy.[21] Even if pretension—a possibility, as we will see in a moment, that Boccaccio might have exploited when the priest in 8.2 explains the value of his own cloak—it suggests a clerk of high standing. The surprise, then, of the final pun is not that a woman would risk it in the presence of her husband but that the wife of a knight would say such a thing. This witty poem seems certain to provoke discussion and retelling through either repetition or paraphrase.

As Nicholson notes, the manuscript evidence attests to the poem's "widespread circulation" from the thirteenth through the fifteenth centuries.[22] Four more manuscripts may be added to his eleven, one of which is known only from a nineteenth-century edition, and others may well appear, since a short Latin verse seems likely to be overlooked in cataloguing.[23] Here I will mention briefly only the four manuscripts that are currently in English collections, which call attention to Chaucer's possible access to the work, since 8.2 itself establishes Boccaccio's knowledge of it. Three were written in the thirteenth century: Cambridge, Trinity College, O. 2. 45, at Cerne Abbey after 1248;[24] London, British Library, Harley 2851, also in England in the second half of the century;[25] and Eton, Eton College, 125, in either France or England some time during the century. This third manuscript was, according to N. R. Ker, "in England by s. xv at latest and at Eton by 1500."[26] In all three the "Versus de mola piperis," a rubric used in the Trinity College manuscript, appears among other similar short poems in Latin. The manuscripts themselves, however, are quite different. Trinity O. 2. 45, part of which became disassociated from the rest and is now preserved as London, British Library, Egerton 843, is composed mainly of mathematical, computistical, and other scientific works, with a noticeable emphasis on puzzles and enigmata. Harley 2851 contains a wide variety of often unusual religious and secular texts both in prose and verse, the largest group of which are described by H. L.

---

[21] See Lewis and Short, *Latin Dictionary*, *s.v.*; *Mittellateinisches Wörterbuch bis zum ausgehenden 13. Jahrhundert*, ed. Paul Lehmann, et al. (Munich: Beck, 1967–), *s.v.*; and the *DMLBS*, *s.v.*

[22] Nicholson, "Medieval Tale," p. 203.

[23] See the Appendix for a list of the manuscripts.

[24] M. R. James, *The Western Manuscripts in the Library of Trinity College, Cambridge*, 4 vols. (Cambridge: Cambridge University Press, 1900–04), 3.150–60. The catalogue is available at http://sites.trin.cam.ac.uk/james/.

[25] Online catalogue bl.uk/catalogues/illuminatedmanuscripts. The contents have been most fully described by H. L. D. Ward, *Catalogue of Romances in the Department of Manuscripts in the British Museum*, 3 vols. (London: Printed by order of the Trustees, 1883–1910), 2.401, 669 and 748; and 3.503–09.

[26] N. R. Ker, *Medieval Manuscripts in British Libraries*, 5 vols. (Oxford, 1969–2002), 2.742–45. See also M. R. James, *A Descriptive Catalogue of the Manuscripts in the Library of Eton College* (Cambridge: Cambridge University Press, 1895), pp. 56–57, where the contents are described more fully. The copy of James's catalogue at Eton contains many corrections by the author, but none on this poem.

D. Ward in his *Catalogue of Romances in the British Museum*, which itself provides a good indication of their genres. Eton 125 has as its main text Peter Comestor's *Historia scholastica*, but in the margins a contemporary hand (s. xii–xiii) has recorded around 140 poems of various lengths; our poem appears in later group of verse (s. xiii) written mainly on the last folio of the manuscript and on following flyleaves. A fourth manuscript that survives in England, Cambridge, Gonville and Caius College 249 (277), was written in 1464, and so is too late for Chaucer to have known. However, because here the poem stands independent of other verse on a flyleaf at the front of the volume among notes pertaining to events of the fifteenth and sixteenth centuries, it may well have been jotted down by someone who had memorized it. The "Versus de mola piperis" attracted the attention of a variety of readers.

Decameron *8.2*

In 8.2 Boccaccio retold the basic, comic plot of the "Versus de mola piperis," setting it in the peasant village of Varlungo. In his version the woman, Belcolore, is married to not a knight but a farmer, Bentivegna del Mazzo, and her admirer is a particular kind of *clericus*, the local parish priest. The story unfolds as expected, but with some differences. The priest does not take a pepper mill as he leaves, but rather the next day sends a boy to borrow a mortar, a more appropriate object in a rural setting, and waits to return it, again through an intermediary, until he knows that husband and wife will be eating together. Belcolore's aggrieved response, "dirai cosí al sere da mia parte: 'La Belcolor dice che fa prego a Dio che voi non pesterete mai piú salsa in suo mortaio'" (8.2, 44; "say this to your master from me: 'Belcolore says that she prays to God that you will not again grind more sauce in her mortar,'" *S&A*, 2.580),[27] opens the way for a rejoinder by the priest: "'dira'le, quando tu la vedrai, che s'ella non ci presterà il mortaio, io non presterò a lei il pestello; vada l'un per l'altro'" (8.2, 45; "'tell her, when you see her, that if she will not lend me the mortar I shall not lend her the pestle; one goes with the other'"; compare *S&A*, 2.580). Boccaccio, moreover, continued the story, telling us first that Bentivegna does not understand his wife's comment, attributing it to his reprimand, and that Belcolore refuses to speak to the priest "insino a vendemmia" ("until the grape harvest"):

> Poscia, avendola minacciata il prete di farnela andare in bocca del luci-fero maggiore, per bella paura entro, col mosto e con le castagne calde si

---

[27] This translation is by John Scattergood; compare McWilliam, p. 596. In this chapter I rely on Scattergood's translations of the first two *novelle*. He does not include the introductory materials, so in these cases references are to McWilliam. McWilliam at times departs from the literal sense to catch the flavor of the text.

rappatumò con lui, e piú volte insieme fecer poi gozzoviglia. E in iscambio delle cinque lire le fece il prete rincartare il cembal suo e appiccovvi un sonagliuzzo, e ella fu contenta. (8.2, 46–7)

(After that, because the priest had threatened to have her sent to be chewed by the great Lucifer, and because of the great fear she had of it, and what with the fermented grape juice he sent her and the roast chestnuts, she made her peace with him and they caroused and revelled more times together subsequently. And instead of the five lire the priest had a new skin put on her tambourine and added a little bell to it, and she was satisfied; *S&A*, 2.580).

Even with these changes and additions, the plot 8.2 remains close to its source, the "Versus de mola piperis." Moreover, unlike 8.1, it provides a source for the punning at the end of the *Shipman's Tale*, a first indication that Chaucer used this *novella*.

There is a readily apparent reason behind these changes and many of the other elaborations in the tale, which Chaucer would have recognized. They express the teller's and the *brigata's* disdain for the lack of morals among the lower class. This attitude appears even as Panfilo introduces his story as "uno amorazzo contadino, piú da ridere per la conclusione che lungo di parole" (8.2, 5; "a tale of country love, more amusing for its ending than conspicuous for its length," McWilliam, p. 555). He then reinforces it as he sets the story in his opening lines: "dico adunque che a Varlungo, villa assai vicina di qui, come ciascuna di voi o sa o puote avere udito..." (8.2, 6; "I tell you then, once in Varlungo, a village very close to here [i.e. Florence], as each of you ladies knows or may have heard...," *S&A*, 2.574). The village is so insignificant that, although it was close enough to Florence now to be incorporated into the city, there is no reason to assume that members of the upper class *brigata* would even have heard of it.

This disdain carries over into the descriptions of the main characters, who unlike in 8.1 are all mocked. Indeed, Panfilo specifically identifies the priest, as a representative of his profession, as the butt of his tale:

Belle donne, a me occorre di dire una novelletta contro a coloro li quali continuamente n'offendono senza poter da noi del pari esse offesi, cioè contro a' preti, li quali sopra le nostre mogli hanno bandita la croce, e par loro non altramenti aver guadagnato il perdono di colpa e di pena, quando una se ne posson metter sotto, che se d'Allessandria avessero il soldano menato legato a Vignone. (8.2, 3)

(Fair ladies, it behooves me to relate a little story against a class of persons who keep on offending us without our being able to retaliate. I am referring to the priests, who have proclaimed a crusade against our wives, and who seem to think, when they succeed in laying one of them on her back, that they have earned full remission of all their sins, as surely as if they had brought the Sultan back from Alexandria to Avignon in chains; McWilliam, pp. 554–55).

It is then the priest whom he first describes:

> ...fu un valente prete e gagliardo della persona ne' servigi delle donne, il quale, come che legger non sapesse troppo, pur con molte buone e sante parolozze la domenica a piè dell'olmo ricreava i suoi popolani; e meglio le lor donne, quando essi in alcuna parte andavano, che altro prete che prima vi fosse stato, visitava, portando loro della festa e dell'acqua benedetta e alcun moccolo di candela talvolta infino a casa, dando loro la sua benedizione. (8.2, 6–7)

> (...there was a priest, capable and vigorous in the service of women, who, though he did not know how to read well, yet with many good and holy aphorisms entertained his parishioners on Sundays, at the foot of the elm-tree. And, when the men had gone elsewhere, he was better than any priest who had been there before at visiting their wives, bringing for them, into their houses, feast-day stuff, and holy water, and sometimes some small candle-ends, and giving them his blessing; *S&A*, 2.574).

Perhaps the only surprise here is the elm: would not a priest address his congregation inside the church? Following Branca's note and so offering analogues in 8.6 and 4.1, John Scattergood comments: "in country villages, elm trees were often situated close to the church, and groups often gathered in their shade."[28] In light, however, of Panfilo's general disdain for his rural setting, this wording may simply suggest that the local church is as insignificant as its priest's sermons and so is subsumed by the tree. In any case the priest himself steps out of the *fabliau* and broader anti-clerical tradition as a typical lecherous clergyman.[29] Here, as one would expect from the basic structure of the Lover's Gift Regained, he may get the last word in the exchange over the mortar and, finally, Belcolore's continuing favors on his own terms; the wife's final comment in the "Versus" if defiant is still one of defeat. Yet the priest in 8.2 remains an object of ridicule. Boccaccio even involves him in the *novella*'s central pun when he explains to Belcolore that priests are better lovers "'perché noi maciniamo a raccolta'" (8.2, 23; "'it's because we do our grinding when the millpond's full,'" McWilliam, p. 557).[30] The "grinder's art," an apt phrase from McWilliam's translation although one without an exact source in the Italian, is shared by both main characters.

---

28 *S&A*, 2.574, note 21. The note in the edition of Quondam, Fiorilla, and Alfano follows this reading, p. 1213, note 6.

29 See Per Nykrog, *Les Fabliaux: Nouvelle édition* (Geneva: Droz, 1973), pp. 62 and 133; Howard Bloch, *The Scandal of the Fabliaux* (Chicago: University of Chicago Press, 1986), p. 63; and Lorcin, *Façons de sentir*, pp. 181–86.

30 In this case, McWilliam's translation is better; see Branca, ed., *Decameron*, p. 900, note 1.

In spite, moreover, of Panfilo's initial claim that he speaks for all husbands wronged by priests, his depiction of Bentivegna del Mazzo, while briefer than that of the priest, is no more sympathetic. Rather than simply having him find out that Bentivegna is away from home, Panfilo describes an encounter between the two men as he sets the narrative in motion:

> Ora avvenne un dí che, andando il prete di fitto meriggio per la contrada or qua or là zazeato, scontrò Bentivegna del Mazzo con uno asino pien di cose innanzi, e fattogli motto il domandò dove egli andava.
> A cui Bentivegna ripose: "Gnaffé, sere, in buona verità io vo infino a città per alcuna mia vicenda: e porto queste cose a ser Bonaccorri da Ginestreto, ché m'aiuti di non so che m'ha fatto richiedere per una comparigione del parentorio per lo pericolator suo il giudice del dificio." (8.2, 13–14)

> (Now, one day about noon when the priest was wandering here and there about the country,[31] it happened that he encountered Bentivegna del Mazzo, with a donkey laden with things in front of him, and greeted him and asked him where he was going.
> To which Bentivegna replied: "Truly, sir, in good faith, I am going as far as the city for something I need to do. And I am carrying these things to master Bonaccorri da Ginestreto to get him to help me, because the judge of penal causes has cited me before the court by means of his attorney to answer a peremptory summons," *S&A*, 2.574–75).

Scattergood notes: "The unsophisticated Bentivegna garbles the difficult words in this passage: *vicenda* for 'accenda', *parentorio* for 'perentorio', *pericolatore* for 'procuratore', *dificio* for 'maleficio'."[32] While he is correct in continuing, "The implication is that he is very much out of his depth with the law," I would add that Bentivegna's other attempts to sound sophisticated, such as "in buona verità," "infino a città," and "per alcuna mia vicenda," indicate that he does not belong in the city at all. Moreover, the reason for this particular scene becomes clear when at the *novella*'s end, he responds to the return of the mortar:

> ma Bentivegna con un mal viso disse: "Dunque toi tu ricordanza al sere? Fo boto a Cristo che mi vien voglia di darti un gran sergozzone: va rendigliel tosto, che canciola te nasca! e guarda che di cosa che voglia mai, io dico s'e' volesse l'asino nostro, non ch'altro, non gli sia detto di no." (8.2, 43)

> (but Bentivegna looking very cross, said, "So then, you are taking a pledge from the priest? I have a mind to give you a good hard smack in the face.

---

[31] McWilliam translates "while the priest was strolling aimlessly about the village" (p. 556); Scattergood offers "when the priest was wandering here and there about the district" (*S&A*, 2.574).

[32] *S&A*, 2.576, note 27.

Give it back to him immediately, a plague on you. And look to it that whatever he wants, I tell you, even if it is that donkey of ours, and more, he is not to be refused," *S&A*, 2.580).

Branca glosses "toi tu ricordanza" as "prendi tu pegno,"[33] but it seems Bentivegna has again garbled legal usage since *ricordanza* means "memory" or "recollection." Moreover, by specifying the donkey, which Branca notes is emphatic since it is their most important possession, Boccaccio anticipated 9.10, the story of Father Gianni's attempt to turn a peasant's wife into a mare.[34] Understanding this country matter no better than he does the affairs of the city, Bentivegna is a fit subject for ridicule.

Even the most complicated character, Belcolore, who served as a model for Alison in the *Miller's Tale*, remains part of the mocked peasant world. As seen in a passage quoted above, the *novella* ends with her content with having a new skin and bell for her tambourine. As with the priest and Bentivegna, Panfilo sets up this conclusion in his opening description:

...nel vero era pure una piacevole e fresca foresozza, brunazza e ben tarchiata e atta a meglio saper macinar che alcuna altra; e oltre a ciò era quella che meglio sapeva sonare il cembalo e cantare *L'acqua corre la borrana* e menar la ridda e il ballonchio, quando bisogno faceva, che vicina che ella avesse, con bel moccichino e gente in mano. (8.2, 9)

(The truth is that she really was a pretty and fresh country lass, brownskinned, and very sturdy, and was better at grinding than anybody else. And beyond that, she knew how to play the tambourine and sing "The water runs in the mill-race," and lead the round dance and the skipping dance, when the occasion presented itself, better than any of her neighbours, with a fine and dainty handkerchief in her hand; *S&A*, 2.574).

A comparison with the *Miller's Tale* proves illuminating here since it helps us to understand not only Chaucer's debt to the *Decameron* but also the earlier work itself. While less elaborate than the opening remarks about Alison (I, 3233–70), the passage in the *Decameron* introduces several themes that the Miller will also use. Like Belcolore, "una piacevole e fresca foresozza,"[35] Alison is a "wenche" (I, 3252), "moore blisful on to see / Than is the newe pere-jonette tree" (I, 3247–48); "prymerole" (I, 3268) may indeed play on the sound of "piacevole." While Alison is "long as a mast" (I, 3264), but Belcolore is "tarchiata," both women sing and dance and both use clothing to attract attention. Finally, Panfilo goes further than the Miller in noting

---

33 Branca, p. 903, note 7.
34 Lee notes the source of this *novella* in the *fabliau*, "De la demoiselle qui vouloit voler en l'air"; *Decameron*, p. 291.
35 Branca glosses the last word as "contadinotta," "peasant girl"; p. 896 note 8. See also *TLIO, s.v.*

that Belcolore "atta a meglio saper macinar che alcuna altra"; yet Alison too would be a catch "For any lord to leggen in his bedde, / Or yet for any good yeman to wedde" (I, 3269–70). In spite, however, of the explicit disdain evident in these passages, the two women are both appealing and, as we learn in the course of their tales, more aware of their situations than the tellers realize. In any case in all these features Belcolore embodies the world of the village, and so, like the priest and Bentivegna, is ridiculed by Panfilo.

There are, however, two related features of 8.2 that work powerfully against Panfilo's explicit mockery of the village: the pervasive use of Tuscan dialect and a cumulative sense that Varlungo's barter economy, based on mutual understanding, works. As McWilliam writes, "the wordplay and outlandish Florentinisms of the story of Belcolore are no mere ornaments: they are a function of the narrative itself."[36] Considering, moreover, not just the names "Bentivegna del Mazzo" and "Belcolore," he calls attention to,

> a whole gallery of other characters, whose sole *raison d'être* is to heighten the humour by the very sound of their curious Florentine names: Ser Bonaccorri da Ginestreto, Lapuccio, Naldino, Biliuzza, Lotto *rigattiere*, Buglietto, Binguccio dal Poggio and Nuto Buglietti. None of these has any real function in the narrative: they are simply personalities who flash momentarily into being and then subside, like sparks from a catherine-wheel.[37]

Recognizing this pervasive play on the sounds of words, Chaucer introduced new puns into the *Shipman's Tale*, perhaps the most significant of which revolves around *paye(n)*. This verb appears prominently at the tale's start in the discussion of a husband's need to "pay" for his wife's expenses; here it coincides largely with our modern usage. By the tale's end, however, as the wife asserts that she "wol not paye...but abedde" (VII, 424), Chaucer invoked the association of *pay* with "to please" and "to pleasure" (Latin *pacare*, which gave the direct source of the Middle English word in the Old French *paier*, and also Italian *piacere*).[38] The shift in meanings takes place, as we will see in a moment, when the wife uses the word in both senses as she explains to daun John that/how she will repay the "lene" (loan/gift) of the hundred francs. Chaucer's respect for Boccaccio's use of language may help

---

[36]   G. H. McWilliam, "On Translating the *Decameron*," in *Essays in Honour of John Humphreys Whitfield*, ed. H. C. Davis, D. G. Rees, J. M. Hatwell and G. W. Slowey (London: St George's Press, 1975), p. 80. See futher the introduction to the *novella* in the edition of Quondam, Fiorilla, and Alfano, p. 1182.

[37]   McWilliam, "On Translating," p. 80.

[38]   The merchant's "*Quy la?*" (VII, 214) in the *Shipman's Tale* may also derive from Boccaccio's use of local idiom, as may the northern dialect in the *Reeve's Tale*. I will also argue elsewhere that the description of John as a "gnof" in the *Miller's Tale* derives directly from the Tuscan interjection "gnaffé" used both in 8.2 and 3.4.

us notice that, perhaps without realizing it, Panfilo betrays a shared identity with his peasant characters.

This issue of Boccaccio's, as opposed to his teller's, attitude toward the lower class is of such importance to my study that I will pursue it here, as I will similar issues in connection with 8.1 and 8.10, by briefly considering some other *novelle* set in Florence. As Chaucer would certainly have noticed, Belcolore's story is followed immediately by the first of those concerning Calandrino, which feature the anarchic pair of artists, Bruno and Buffal-macco, Boccaccio's dark doubles. The themes that run through these *novelle* are too varied even to survey here; yet let me note that Bruno and Buffal-macco terrorize not only their foolish friend (8.3 and 8.6), but also the rich, pretentious and deeply stupid physician from Bologna, Maestro Simone (8.9). Moreover, this series ends with a story (9.5) remarkable for its cutting across class lines. Bruno and Buffalmacco, hired to paint the new villa of a wealthy Florentine, employ Calandrino and another friend to help them. When Calan-drino falls in love with the prostitute whom the owner's son has brought to the otherwise empty villa, all five (the three painters, the prostitute and the son) devise a plan to humiliate him, setting him up to be discovered by his wife in the arms of the prostitute. The *novella* concludes with Calandrino receiving a brutal beating and returning to Florence to live under his wife's control. Taken together, these *novelle* suggest that art opens a wide spectrum of stories that, in the words of the teller of 9.5, "festa e piacer possa porgere" (9.5, 4; "promote...joy and pleasure," McWilliam, p. 668). Yet even here the resolution both mocks social inferiors and supports conventional morality. Through his own art, Boccaccio lived only vicariously among the lower class.

If the shared dialect evident in 8.2 does not itself, then, dissolve class barriers, the *novella* still creates the image of people within a community who also express their understanding of each other through not only their language but also the goods and services they exchange. Money, in contrast, does not belong here. Boccaccio introduced the topic of gifts in the initial description, quoted earlier, of the priest, who uses "feast-day stuff, and holy water, and sometimes some small candle-ends" to ingratiate himself with his female parishioners. With Belcolore he goes further as described in a lyrical passage memorable for its merging of gifts with a rural setting: "e quando le mandava un mazzuol d'agli freschi, ch'egli aveva i più belli della contrada in un suo orto che egli lavorava a sue mani, e quando un canestruccio di baccelli e talora un mazzuolo di cipolle malige o di scalogni" (8.2, 11; "sometimes he brought her a small bunch of fresh garlic, of which he had the best in the neighborhood in his kitchen garden, which he tended with his own hands, and sometimes a little basket of broad beans, and at times a bunch of spring onions or shallots," *S&A*, 2.574). In this context, another detail already quoted, Bentivegna's donkey "pien di cose" for the lawyer who will represent him seems both incongruous and normal: how else would a peasant pay for these services?

The question of the relationship of barter and monetary economies is indeed central to the *novella*. When Belcolore turns down the priest's offers ("un paio di scarpette o...un frenello o...una bella fetta di stame," 8.2, 25; "a pair of shoes or a silk headband, or a length of fine carded wool," *S&A*, 2.576),[39] she asks instead for "un servigio" (a service) before she will do what he wants:

> "Egli mi conviene andar sabato a Firenze a render lana che io ho filata e a far racconciare il filatoio mio: e se voi mi prestate cinque lire, che so che l'avete, io ricoglierò dall'usuraio la gonnella mia del perso e lo scaggiale dai dí delle feste che io recai a marito, ché vedete che non ci posso andare a santo né in niun buon luogo, perché io non l'ho...." (8.2, 28)

> ("It is necessary for me to go to Florence on Saturday to take in the wool I have spun and to get my spinning-wheel repaired, and if you would lend me five lire, which I know that you have, I shall redeem from the pawnbroker my dark purple gown and the fancy belt I wear on feast days which I had in my dowry, for you see I cannot go to church or to any fine place because I do not have them" *S&A*, 2.576).

This passage contains a number of related problems. Belcolore claims to be asking not for money but for a loan ("e se voi mi prestate"), something that she will return to the priest. There is, however, no indication that she means to do so, and indeed the priest does not consider it: he expects to lose whatever he gives her. The unnaturalness of this situation would have been compounded, I would argue, in Chaucer's mind by *usuraio*, a word not used in British sources to refer to a pawnbroker,[40] although it is quite possible that this service would have been associated with lending money. Moreover, it is not clear where Belcolore wishes to go in her fine clothes: as Branca explains, the phrase "a santo" is unclear, probably implying "to church,"[41] and yet combined with "in niun buon luogo" it appears simply vague.

The most obscure feature, however, of this passage, at least from our perspective, is the money itself. In fourteenth-century Florence, *lire* would not have referred to coins or indeed a pound of silver, although the word remained in use in accounting since, when it was introduced, the value of a gold florin was set to it.[42] Unless using local dialect, Belcolore, then, asks not for a specific number of coins, but for an abstract monetary unit. Indeed, this amount in the currency of the village, which would have been silver and debased, would have entailed at least sixty *soldi*, or up to 1,200 *denari*. Panfilo indicates the enormity of assembling these coins when the priest, after

---

[39] See Branca's notes on the last two items; *Decameron*, p. 900, notes 4 and 5.
[40] The *DMLBS* has entries on *usurator* and *usuratrix*, but does not list this meaning.
[41] Branca, *Decameron*, p. 901, note 2.
[42] See "Appendix II: Money of Account," in Peter Spufford, *Money and Its Use in Medieval Europe* (Cambridge: Cambridge University Press, 1988), pp. 411–14.

the fact, reflects "che quanti moccoli ricoglieva in tutto l'anno d'offerta non valeva la metà di cinque lire" (8.2, 39; "that however many candles' ends he might receive in a year by way of offerings would not make up half the value of the five lire," *S&A*, 2.578). Moreover, Boccaccio had anticipated this point moments before: when asked by Belcolore about the value of his cloak, the priest replies: "'Io voglio che tu sappi ch'egli è di duagio infino in treagio, e hacci di quegli nel popolo nostro che il tengon di quattragio'" (8.2, 35; "'I want you to know that this is Flanders cloth from Douai, from as far away as Trouai, and there are those among our people who would claim they have got from Quadrouai'"; compare *S&A*, 2.578 and McWilliam, p. 558).

The starting point for unravelling this passage is Branca's identification of "duagio" as "il panno fine di Douai in Fiandra." He continues, "Treagio e quattragio sono nomi di immaginarie stoffe ancor più preziose, forgiati dal serie su una falsa facile etimologia per meglio infinocchiare la Belcolore."[43] Scattergood makes this explanation more explicit:

> The priest seeks to impress here by citing a faraway place and by arithmetical progression. *Douai* is indeed in Flanders and was a cloth-making town. But he also uses a pun on *due* (two) and Douai, and invents two other towns based on *tre* (three) and *quattro* (four).[44]

The punning here also plays on the names of coins, which were associated sometimes with the cities where they were minted and their denominations. Underlying "duagio" is also, then, the *doubles tournois*, two-denier pieces associated with mints in Tours.[45] Moreover, the Florentine economy used "black four *denaro* pieces" called *quattrini*,[46] which underlie the priest's "quattragio." Through this punning used first to call attention to the naivety of the peasants, Boccaccio introduced the complex idea of the multiplication and debasement of currencies.

Even without, however, a clear understanding of the urban much less the international economy in which Belcolore and others in the village participate by spinning wool, the local economy works. The story itself shows us why. Although as a version of the Lover's Gift Regained the narrative is based on deception, Boccaccio added many details that emphasize the shared understandings of the characters, especially the priest and Belcolore, who, like Alison, is an equal participant in the events. As the story opens, Panfilo provides a glimpse into their awareness of each other's games, even if we may find it difficult to understand exactly what they are doing: "e, quando si

43 Branca, *Decameron*, p. 902, note 3. This reading is accepted in the edition of Quondam, Fiorilla, and Alfano, pp. 1183 and 1219. See also *TLIO*, *s.vv.*

44 *S&A*, 2.578, note 30.

45 See Peter Spufford's opening discussion of currencies in his *Handbook of Medieval Exchange* (London: Royal Historical Society, 1986), pp. xix–xx.

46 Spufford, *Handbook*, pp. xix–xx and *Money*, pp. 329–30.

vedeva tempo, guatatala un poco in cagnesco, per amorevolezza la rimorch-
iava, e ella cotal salvatichetta, faccendo vista di non avvedersene, andava pure
oltre in contegno" (8.2, 12; "and when he saw the opportunity, he would gaze
at her in a surly manner, to rebuke her in an affectionate way, and she would
respond in a huff, making a pretence of not noticing. She kept her distance
in a really reserved manner…," *S&A*, 2.574). This game comes into the open
when the priest visits her house.[47] Belcolore at first feigns surprise at his
proposition: "'o fanno i preti cosí fatte cose?'" (8.2, 22; "'but do priests do
these sorts of things?'" *S&A*, 2.576). However, when he can merely promise
her five lire, she reveals much greater knowledge of his past:

> "Sí," disse la Belcolore "tutti siete cosí gran promettitori, e poscia non
> attenete altrui nulla: credete voi fare a me come voi faceste alla Biliuzza,
> che se n'andò col ceteratoio? Alla fé di Dio non farete, ché ella n'è dive-
> nuta femina di mondo pur per ciò: se voi non gli avete, e voi andate per
> essi." (8.2, 30)

> ("Indeed," said Belcolore, "you all make such great promises, but after-
> wards you keep none of them. Do you think you can do with me what you
> did with Biliuzza, whom you dazzled with your words? By my faith in God,
> you are not going to do that; and she went to the bad for what you caused.
> If you do not have it with you, go and fetch it," *S&A*, 2.578).

Again, dialect obscures parts of this statement, and yet the phrase "femina di
mondo" seems to imply prostitution.[48] Belcolore wants money or its equivalent, but she is also aware of the priest's reputation and, more importantly,
her own.

In light of many of the details added to 8.2, the concluding passage of the
novella, quoted above, may appear less a final mocking of the inhabitants of
Varlungo than a partially understood account of the next stage of the priest's
and Belcolore's dealings. Like his teller, Boccaccio, I believe, intended it
the first way, using the plot of the "Versus de mola piperis" as a whole to
laugh at the peasants' lack of morals, and yet in doing so he revealed much
of how their world works. It does so, at least as depicted here, independently
of money, which the villagers seem not to understand. Instead, they use their

---

[47] If Belcolore's opening question "che andate voi zaconato per questo caldo?" (8.2, 17; "what
are you doing gadding about in this heat?" *S&A*, 2.576) does echo by way of a local
synonym the earlier description of the priest, "per la contrada or qua or là zazeato" (8.2,
13; translated above), then the two share more than a dialect. In any case, Richard Guerin
has argued that Belcolore's comment underlies daun John's advice to the merchant in the
Shipman's Tale to beware of the heat (VII, 260–62); see "*The Shipman's Tale*: The Italian
Analogues," *English Studies* 52 (1971), pp. 412–19. See also Hanning, "Before Chaucer's
Shipman's Tale," pp. 191–92.

[48] See the edition of Quondam, Fiorilla, and Alfano, p. 1218, note 30.

distinctive language to arrive at agreements for the exchange of goods and services.

Chaucer placed the contrasts between three economies, rural, urban, and international, which Boccaccio alluded to in 8.2 and would explore further in the opening and final *novelle* of the Eighth Day, at the center of the *Shipman's Tale*. Our focus here is on the first, the world of the village, which, as 8.1 shows, is not necessary for the plot, and so all the more remarkable for the role it plays in this tale. It appears, indeed, in the opening description of daun John, which explains the friendship between the monk and the merchant:

> This yonge monk, that was so fair of face,
> Aqueynted was so with the goode man,
> Sith that hir firste kneweliche bigan,
> That in his hous as famulier was he
> As it is possible any freend to be.
> And for as muchel as this goode man,
> And eek this monk of which that I bigan,
> Were bothe two yborn in o village,
> The monk hym claymeth as for cosynage,
> And he agayn; he seith nat ones nay,
> But was as glad therof as fowel of day,
> For to his herte it was a greet plesaunce.
> Thus been they knyt with eterne alliaunce,
> And ech of hem gan oother for t'assure
> Of bretherhede whil that hir lyf may dure. (VII, 28–42)

This passage, which anticipates the later deal that will be struck in the tale between the monk and the wife, places their common origin from the same village ("o village") at the center of their relationship. Because of it, they claim to be related and begin to support each other in all they do, "knyt with eterne alliaunce." The final term, "bretherhede," returns to the kin structures common to all communities, while the simile—their association makes them "glad...as fowel of day"—contributes to the rural tone of the passage.

The professions of the two men differ sharply; here the focus will remain on the monk, an apt representative of the feudal economy because monasteries in the late fourteenth century were deeply involved in the manorial system of agriculture.[49] In his choice of *clericus*, Chaucer exploited some of the anti-clerical themes he also used in the portrait of the Monk in the *General Prologue*, who is not just "a manly man" (I, 167) fond of "a fat swan" (I, 206), but also an "outridere" (I, 166) more at home outside than within his monastery. The tale, however, stresses not this monk's love of hunting but his connection to his house's estates:

---

[49] I return to this point at the end of this chapter.

> This noble monk, of which I yow devyse,
> Hath of his abbot, as hym list, licence,
> By cause he was a man of heigh prudence
> And eek an officer, out for to ryde,
> To seen hir graunges and hire bernes wyde... (VII, 62–66)

It is this business that provides him with an excuse to borrow money from the merchant:

> "O thyng, er that ye goon, if it may be,
> I wolde prey yow: for to lene me
> An hundred frankes, for a wyke or tweye,
> For certein beestes that I moste beye,
> To stoore with a place that is oures.
> God helpe me so, I wolde it were youres!" (VII, 269–74)

Even the wording here is odd. By indicating that he would like "to stoore" the animals with the merchant until he can return the money, daun John appears to equate the two, even perhaps implying that any benefit from owning the "beestes" until the loan is repaid should be the merchant's. Moreover, the merchant's response develops this theme since he offers John not just his gold but also his goods:

> "O cosyn myn, daun John,
> Now sikerly this is a smal requeste.
> My gold is youres, whan that it yow leste,
> And nat oonly my gold, but my chaffare.
> Take what yow list; God shilde that ye spare." (VII, 282–86)

While I will argue in a moment that there is further reason to view the hundred francs not as a unit of exchange but rather a physical commodity, there are other parts of the tale suggestive of a peasant economy that require attention first.

Throughout the *Shipman's Tale*, Chaucer associated daun John, as Boccaccio had the priest in 8.2, with gifts. Indeed, the introductory passage quoted above continues:

> Free was daun John, and manly of dispence,
> As in that hous, and ful of diligence
> To doon plesaunce, and also greet costage.
> He noght forgat to yeve the leeste page
> In al that hous; but after hir degree,
> He yaf the lord, and sitthe al his meynee,
> Whan that he cam, som manere honest thyng,
> For which they were as glad of his comyng
> As fowel is fayn whan that the sonne up riseth.
> Na moore of this as now, for it suffiseth. (VII, 43–52)

The Shipman also specifies the items—"a jubbe of malvesye, / And eek another ful of fyn vernage, / And volatyl, as ay was his usage" (VII, 70–72)—that he brings before the merchant leaves for Bruges. Daun John has free access to his monastery's cellars, which allows his gifts to be much more valuable than the "moccoli" of Varlungo; yet they allude to the same economic system. With these passages in mind, it is readily understandable why John is welcomed back for the rendezvous: "In al the hous ther nas so litel a knave, / Ne no wight elles, that he nas ful fayn / That my lord daun John was come agayn" (VII, 310–12).

Moreover, the reference to the "cinque lire" in 8.2 may make us more aware of the significance of another seemingly minor detail in the *Shipman's Tale*, the merchant's remark to his wife that she has enough silver to run the house in his absence. The most prominent currency in the tale, the hundred francs already mentioned, is of course gold and of the merchant's worth there can be little doubt since he spends much of one morning reckoning with his "bookes and bagges many oon" in his "countour-hous" (VII, 75–88). So it is surprising that his wife follows a remark about his sexual deficiencies (in a phrase that mixes economics and country life) with a complaint about his tight-fistedness:

> "As helpe me God, he is noght worth at al
> In no degree the value of a flye.
> But yet me greveth moost his nygardye." (VII, 170–72)

The merchant himself confirms this charge in his instructions to his wife on how she should run the house in his absence:

> "For which, my deere wyf, I thee biseke,
> As be to every wight buxom and meke,
> And for to kepe oure good be curious,
> And honestly governe wel oure hous.
> Thou has ynough, in every maner wise,
> That to a thrifty houshold may suffise.
> Thee lakketh noon array ne no vitaille,
> Of silver in thy purs shaltow nat faille." (VII, 241–48)

While obviously better off than Belcolore, the wife does not have access to the sums, here indicated by the form of currency, silver rather than gold, which she desires.

At this point it should be clear that Chaucer indeed kept something of Varlungo in the *Shipman's Tale*: the relationship between the merchant and the monk is based on their common origin in the same village; daun John engages in the feudal economy of his monastery, carrying its practices in the form of wine and fowl into the merchant's house; and even the merchant expects his wife to run their domestic economy on not gold, the currency of commerce,[50] but silver. It is in this context, I would argue, that we need to place Chaucer's most important borrowing from 8.2,[51] the wife's explanation of her need for "an hundred frankes" (VII, 181), even though this passage takes us beyond the village. As in 8.2, it occurs within the lengthy exchange between daun John and the merchant's wife; indeed, immediately after she accuses her husband of being cheap (quoted above), she claims women desire their husbands to be "hardy," "wise," "riche," "free," "buxom," and "fressh abedde," VII, 173–77), before continuing:

> "But by that ilke Lord that for us bledde,
> For his honour, myself for to arraye,
> A Sonday next I moste nedes paye
> An hundred frankes, or ellis I am lorn.
> Yet were me levere that I were unborn
> Than me were doon a sclaundre or vileynye;
> And if myn housbonde eek it myghte espye,
> I nere but lost; and therfore I yow preye,
> Lene me this somme, or ellis moot I deye.
> Daun John, I seye, lene me thise hundred frankes.
> Pardee, I wol nat faille yow my thankes,
> If that yow list to doon that I yow praye.
> For at a certeyn day I wol you paye,
> And doon to yow what plesance and service
> That I may doon, right as yow list devise.
> And but I do, God take on me vengeance
> As foul as evere hadde Genylon of France." (VII, 178–94)

The bargains here and in 8.2 are, as Scattergood comments, "strikingly similar."[52] Like Belcolore, the merchant's wife claims to need money for clothing, in this case apparently to pay for items she has already acquired or perhaps for ones she has promised to buy. Moreover, as with Belcolore, the ambiguity of her explanation may make us wonder if she is telling the truth. In any case, as Scattergood notes, her request that the priest "loan" her the money corresponds exactly to Belcolore's "prestate." There is, I would like to note here, a major difference: if given "cinque lire," Belcolore claims "e io sempre mai poscia farò che voi vorrete"—she will *always* do what the priest wants—and, as the story unfolds, even when the priest deceives her, she eventually returns to him because he provides appropriate gifts. The wife in the *Shipman's Tale* may imply more, but actually offers "to pay" daun John only once, "at a certeyn day," just as she "moste nedes paye" the hundred francs "A Sonday next." Indeed here the tale ends without any sense that their affair

---

[50] I return to this point at the end of the chapter.
[51] As Scattergood notes, this detail "cannot be paralleled elsewhere," making 8.2, in his opinion, a "possible" source for the tale.
[52] *S&A*, 2.567.

will continue. We will, then, need to return to this scene after discussing 8.1 and 8.10. Its origin, however, like the tale itself is in the hamlet of Varlungo.

Decameron *8.1*

In contrast to 8.2, in which Panfilo's stated purpose of telling a story against priests dissolves more generally into a ridiculing of the lower class, Neifile's urban adaptation of the Lover's Gift Regained supports, with a few possible exceptions, her main point: a woman who gives herself for money deserves to be burned alive. The plot, in which a man borrows money from a husband so he can return it to the wife when he sleeps with her, could of course be told to illustrate the deviousness of men. Here blame falls almost entirely on the woman, with even the punning conclusion of the "Versus de mola piperis" no longer present. The qualification in the previous sentence is intended to register a pervasive undercurrent in this *novella*, a criticizing of the woman *because* she represents a bourgeois, mercantile attitude toward love, and so a critique of that economic system itself. Chaucer's response to this theme will require further discussion; yet even from the outset it is clear that while he relied more heavily on the plot of this *novella* than that of either 8.2 or 8.10, he studiously avoided Neifile's explicit message.

In a passage at the beginning of 8.1 omitted from Scattergood's text and translation in *Sources and Analogues*, Neifile explains that her story, unlike those of the previous day, concerns a trick played by a man on a woman: "e per ciò, amorose donne, con ciò sia cosa che molto si sia detto delle beffe fatte dalle donne agli uomini, una fattane da uno uomo a una donna mi piace di raccontarne" (8.1, 2; "and since we have talked a great deal, fond ladies, of the tricks played by women upon men, I should like to tell you of one which was played by a man upon a woman," McWilliam, p. 587). However, like the stories of the Seventh Day, which threaten to harm the reputation of women, hers does too: "non già perché io intenda in quella di biasimare ciò che l'uom fece o di dire che alla donna non fosse bene investito, anzi per commendar l'uomo e biasimar la donna" (8.1, 2; "my intention being not to censure the man for what he did or to claim that the woman was misused, but on the contrary to commend the man and to censure the woman," McWilliam, p. 552). Indeed, she claims, the story should be considered not a "beffa" (trick) but rather a "merito," something of value:[53]

> per ciò che, con ciò sia cosa debba essere onestissima e la sua castità come la sua vita guardare né per alcuna cagione a contaminarla conducersi (e questo non possendosi, così appieno tuttavia come si converrebbe, per la fragilità nostra) affermo colei esser degna del fuoco la quale a ciò per

---

[53] McWilliam's "reprisal" catches the point of the story but not the immediate meaning.

prezzo si conduce; dove chi per amor, conoscendo le sue forze grandissime, perviene, da giudice non troppo rigido merita perdono.... (8.1, 3–4)

(For a woman should act at all times with the greatest decorum, and guard her chastity with her life, on no account permitting herself to defile it; and although it is not always possible for us to observe this precept to the full on account of our frailty, nevertheless I declare that any woman who strays from the path of virtue for monetary gain deserves to be burnt alive, whereas the woman who yields to the forces of Love, knowing how powerful they are, deserves a lenient judge who will order her acquittal; McWilliam, p. 552.)

Neifile, then, condemns only women who give themselves to men not for love but for money. As with Panfilo, there can be no doubt about the narrator's attitude toward her material, although here her stated intention does indeed match her telling of the story.

The opening description of the lover, Gulfardo, contains perhaps the most significant details that could move the blame away from the woman, placing it instead on the society in which she lives. Neifile begins with him:

Fu adunque già in Melano un tedesco al soldo, il cui nome fu Gulfardo, pro' della persona e assai leale a coloro ne' cui servigi si mettea, il che rade volte suole de' tedeschi avvenire. E per ciò che egli era nelle prestanze de' denari che fatte gli erano lealissimo renditore, assai mercatanti avrebbe trovati che per piccolo utile ogni quantità di denari gli avrebber prestata. (8.1, 5)

(Now there was once in Milan a German mercenary soldier, whose name was Gulfardo, a brave man and very loyal to those with whom he took service, an uncommon characteristic amongst Germans. And because he was most reliable in paying back any money he borrowed, many merchants could be found who, at a low rate of interest, would lend him any amount of money; *S&A*, 2.570).

Unlike the "Versus de mola piperis" in which the husband is a *miles*, here it is the lover who follows this profession, although not as a knight (*cavaliere*) but rather as a mercenary ("al soldo"). Even worse, he is a German. As Branca notes, this description recalls Petrarch's reference to "bavarico inganno" in *Italia mia* (Canzone 128), a poem that criticizes Italian rulers for employing German mercenaries.[54] However bad the woman may be, Gulfardo seems destined to be worse. Moreover, this way of referring to mercenaries by their pay may draw attention to the currency, *denari*, at the root of the word for money, which stands in sharp contrast to the "fiorini dugento d'oro" (8.1, 7;

[54] Branca, p. 891, note 8. See Francesco Petrarca, *Canzoniere*, 2 vols., ed. Ugo Dotti (Rome: Donzelli, 1996), 1.384–93.

"two hundred gold florins," *S&A*, 570) at the center of the story. The name of these gold coins in turn calls attention to their origin in Florence, whose "republican *libertas*," as David Wallace has discussed,[55] stands in sharp contrast to the "dynastic despotism" of Milan, the setting of 8.1. In spite, however, of all of these possible warnings, Neifile's admiration of Gulfardo appears genuine: he is "a brave man and very loyal" and he falls in love and courts his lady as a conventional courtly lover should:

> Pose costui, in Melan dimorando, l'amor suo in una donna assai bella chiamata madonna Ambruogia, moglie d'un ricco mercatante che aveva nome Guasparruol Cagastraccio, il quale era assai suo conoscente e amico: e amandola assai discretamente, senza avvedersene il marito né altri, le mandò un giorno a parlare, pregandola che le dovesse piacere d'essergli del suo amor cortese e che egli era dalla sua parte presto a dover far ciò che ella gli comandasse. (8.1, 6)

> (While he was living in Milan, this man fixed his affection on a beautiful woman called Madonna Ambruogia, wife of a very wealthy merchant whose name was Guasparruolo Cagastraccio, who was his good acquaintance and friend. He loved her most discreetly, without the husband or anyone else noticing, and one day he sent word to her asking her courteously if she might be pleased to grant him her love, and that for his part he was ready to be at her service in whatever she might command; *S&A*, 2.570).

Boccaccio has used Gulfardo's profession and background less to undercut this character than to keep the *novella*'s setting firmly in Milan's middle class.

In contrast, Neifile's characterization of Madonna Ambruogia, whose name associates her with Milan's patron saint, Ambrose, is damning from the start. While she may be the beautiful object of Gulfardo's initial desire, her response to his request reveals her character:

> La donna, dopo molte novelle, venne a questa conclusione, che ella era presta di far ciò che Gulfardo volesse dove due cose ne dovesser seguire: l'una, che questo non dovesse mai per lui esser manifestato a alcuna persona; l'altra, che, con ciò fosse cosa che ella avesse per alcuna sua cosa bisogno di fiorini dugento d'oro, voleva che egli, che ricco uomo era, gliele donasse, e appresso sempre sarebbe al suo servigio. (8.1, 7)

> (The lady, after much inconsequential talk, came to the conclusion that she was ready to be at his service in whatever Gulfardo wished on the following two conditions: the first was that he must never reveal the affair to anybody; the second was that, since for some business of her own she had need of two hundred gold florins, she wished that he would, because he was a rich man, give them to her, and immediately forever she would be at his service; *S&A*, 2.570).

---

[55] *Chaucerian Polity*, p. 1.

Most revealing here is the phrase "dopo molte novelle," which Branca glosses "ciance, discorsi vani" (p. 891, note 12), because it shows her to be not only indecisive but also incapable of behaving as she expects Gulfardo to do, to remain silent about the affair.[56] Moreover, unlike Belcolore who at least claims she needs money to reclaim her best clothing from a pawnbroker, Madonna Ambruogia simply wants it to satisfy her own unspecified desires. She lives, in other words, in a world of bourgeois consumerism. It is in this context that her promise to be "appresso sempre" at his service sounds hollow: she is not offering eternal love but instead asking him to pay for a single service.

The story unfolds, praising Gulfardo, condemning Madonna Ambruogia and, most interestingly, associating the action, because of her initial reply, with a business deal. Gulfardo's response to her decision reveals a dramatic change in his attitude:

Gulfardo, udendo la 'ngordigia di costei, isdegnato per la viltà di lei la quale egli credeva che fosse una valente donna, quasi in odio transmutò il fervente amore e pensò di doverla beffare: e mandolle dicendo che molto volontieri e quello e ogni altra cosa, che egli potesse, che le piacesse... (8.1, 8)

(Listening to her avarice, Gulfardo became offended at the baseness of someone he believed to be an honourable lady, and his passionate love turned almost to hate. He decided he should trick her, and sent back word that he would very willingly do that and whatever other things, within his power, that she wanted which would please her; *S&A*, 2.570).

The beautiful woman has turned out not to be "una valente donna," and so, no longer in love, he may trick her. McWilliam's translation of *beffare* as "beat her at her own game" may at first seem too free, and yet it catches the sense of the passage: just as Madonna Ambruogia promises not a service but a lasting relationship, Gulfardo too lies as he offers "ogni altra cosa" (with the careful qualification, "che egli potesse") "che le piacesse."

It is this mercantile context that explains the next developments in the story. Gulfardo's message back to her continues with a surprising detail. In following her orders, he will tell only one person:

e per ciò mandassegli pure a dire quando ella volesse che egli andasse a lei, ché egli gliele porterebbe, né che mai di questa cosa alcun sentirebbe, se non un suo compagno di cui egli si fidava molto e che sempre in sua compagnia andava in ciò che faceva. (8.1, 8)

---

[56] Branca, p. 891, note 12. Scattergood's note suggesting she is trying to "negotiate a position," seems less likely since it is not clear that she expects her talk to reach him; *S&A*, 2.570, note 1. In contrast, Chaucer might well have noticed that the central discussion between Belcolore and the priest is reduced in 8.1 to a phrase.

(For this purpose she was to go ahead and send him word when she wished him to go to her, and he would bring the money with him, and nobody, moreover, would hear anything of it except a colleague of his, whom he trusted much, and who was always party to whatever he did; *S&A*, 2.570).

This violation of her initial condition that no one should know of the affair could simply show how foolish Madonna Ambruogia is; she is, in Neifile's words, a "cattiva femina" (8.1, 9; a "worthless woman," *S&A*, 2.570). It might also show, however, that it is sensible to have a companion when moving such a large sum. In any case when Madonna Ambruogia tells him to come to her and to bring the two hundred gold florins ("a lei dovesse venire e recare li dugento fiorin d'oro"),

> Gulfardo, preso, il compagno suo, se n'andò a casa della donna; e trovatala che l'aspettava, la prima cosa che fece, le mise in mano questi dugento fiorin d'oro, veggente il suo compagno, e sí le disse: "Madonna, tenete questi denari e daretegli a vostro marito quando sarà tornato." (8.1, 12)

(Gulfardo, taking his colleague with him, went to the lady's house. Finding her waiting for him, the first thing he did was to put into her hands those two hundred gold florins, in the sight of his companion, and said these very words to her: "Lady, take this money and give it to your husband when he returns," *S&A*, 2.572).

The third party here not only ensures Madonna Ambruogia's downfall at the end of the *novella*, but also makes it clear that this affair is being carried out as a business deal.

Madonna Ambruogia's response confirms that she views it as one. Before taking Gulfardo to her bedroom, she counts the money:

> e versatigli sopra una tavola e trovatigli esser dugento, seco forte contenta gli ripose. E tornò a Gulfardo e, lui nella sua camera menato, non sola-mente quella notte ma molte altre, avanti che il marito tornasse da Genova, della sua persona gli sodisfece. (8.1, 13–14).

(Having spread it out on a table, and having found that there were two hundred florins, she put it away very pleased with herself. And she turned to Gulfardo and, having led him to her bedroom, she gratified him with her body, not only on that night but on many others before her husband returned from Genoa; *S&A*, 2.572).

The penultimate phrase, "della sua persona," reinforces the sense that the transaction here is merely physical.[57] Perhaps more revealing, however, is

---

[57] Hanning points out that the "merchant's wife mimics the actions of a careful moneylender seated at his table in the public space of the market"; "Before Chaucer's *Shipman's Tale*," pp. 184–85.

Madonna Ambruogia's first response to Gulfardo's speech: "la donna gli prese e non s'avide perché Gulfardo dicesse cosí, ma si credette che egli il facesse acciò che il compagno suo non s'accorgesse che egli a lei per via di prezzo gli desse..." (8.1, 13; "the lady took it and did not perceive why Gulfardo had spoken as he did, but believed he did that so that his companion would not be aware that he was giving it to her as a payment," *S&A*, 2.572). Scattergood comments: "*prezzo* properly means 'price,' such as one might pay for an item purchased."[58] As she justifies Gulfardo's speech in her own mind, she identifies the real nature of the transaction.

The commercial themes are drawn together at the *novella's* conclusion, which offers a source for the idea behind Chaucer's pun on *tally*. Once Gulfardo knows that Guasparruolo has returned from Genoa and is with his wife, he,

> se n'andò a lui e in presenza di lei disse: "Guasparuolo, i denari, cioè li dugento fiorin d'oro che l'altier mi prestasti, non m'ebber luogo, per ciò che io non potei fornir la bisogna per la quale gli presi: e per ciò io gli recai qui di presente alla donna tua e sí gliele diedi, e per ciò dannerai la mia ragione." (8.1, 15)

> (went to him and said to him in her presence: "Guasparruolo, the money, those two hundred gold florins that you lent me the other day, they were of no use to me because I could not complete the business for which I took them, and so I brought them back here immediately to your wife and gave them to her, and so cancel my debt," *S&A*, 2.572).

The key phrase here is the last, "dannerai la mia ragione," which according to Branca's note is a technical expression for cancelling a debt, the opposite of registering one on a tally (p. 893, note 7).[59] The entire passage, however, is remarkable for its detail. A merchant would understand that deals sometimes fall through, and that the interest on the loan of two hundred florins would be substantial. In this situation Gulfardo would have had reason to act quickly. Madonna Ambruogia cannot, of course, deny she has received the money, so can only comment, "'mai sí che io gli ebbi, né m'era ancor ricordata di dirloti'" (8.1, 16; "'yes, I did receive it, but until now I did not remember to tell you of it,'" *S&A*, 2.572). Completing his deal with Gulfardo and repeating the word *ragione*, Guasparruolo declares, "'Gulfardo, io son contento: andatevi pur con Dio, ché io acconcerò la vostra ragione'" (8.1, 17; "'Gulfardo, I am satisfied. Go with God for I shall properly adjust your account,'" *S&A*, 2.572). Neifile then sums up the story:

---

[58] *S&A*, 2.572, note 17.
[59] See also, Florence Edler, *Glossary of Mediaeval Terms of Business: Italian Series 1200–1600* (Cambridge, MA: Medieval Academy of America, 1934), *s.v.*

Gulfardo partitosi, e la donna rimasa scornata diede al marito il disonesto prezzo della sua cattività: e cosí il sagace amante senza costo godé della sua avara donna. (8.1, 18)

(Gulfardo went away, leaving the scorned lady to hand over to her husband the dishonourable payment for her worthless conduct, and thus the shrewd lover, without payment, took his pleasure of his avaricious mistress; *S&A*, 2.572).

The two transactions have merged here, and yet it is only the woman who is blamed.

While Neifile's views are clear in the contrast between "il sagace amante" and "sua avara donna" and in the assigning of "il disonesto prezzo" to Madonna Ambruogia's "cattività," it is still possible that Boccaccio introduced the commercial language into the *novella* in order to challenge this conclusion, placing the blame instead on the mercantile world (and, more specifically, Milan) in which both characters live. Neifile's message, however, resonates with other *novelle*, suggesting that it does reflect the author's views as well. Here I would call attention to 3.7, the story of Tedaldo, again set in Florence, which illustrates the other half of Neifile's equation: a woman who gives herself for love is to be blamed only if she ends the relationship. The plot is straightforward. Tedaldo, "a noble youth," wins the love of Monna Ermellina, "a lady of impeccable breeding" married to Aldobrandino Palermini, but then, for no reason he can understand and in spite of all his efforts, is refused. He leaves Florence, finding work with a wealthy merchant in whose service he too becomes one. Seven years pass, until one day, hearing a song he had written about his love for his mistress, he decides to return to Florence disguised as a pilgrim. Here he discovers Aldobrandino in prison and about to be executed for his own murder. The story plays out as one might expect: Tedaldo, having discovered the true murderers and learned from Ermellina that she regrets having followed the advice of a friar to break off their affair, arranges everything so Aldobrandino is freed and he can continue his affair with Ermellina.

3.7, one of the *Decameron*'s longer *novelle*, cannot of course be taken as representing Boccaccio's views. In conjunction with 8.1, however, it suggests that, as Neifile states, a woman who gives herself for love deserves a lenient judge. At the core of this *novella* is Tedaldo's long speech, while still in disguise, to Ermellina, explaining that, unlike robbery or murder, "l'usare la dimestichezza d'uno uomo una donna è peccato naturale" (3.7, 45; "for a woman to have intimate relations with a man is a natural sin," McWilliam, p. 285).[60] The larger problem in interpreting the *Decameron* is whether Boccaccio finally supported this transgression of conventional morality or

---

60   This translation follows Branca, p. 402, note 1.

instead wrote in support of marriage or perhaps better still, a renunciation of even this relationship. In either case it appears unlikely that he intended the emphasis on commercial transactions in 8.1 to challenge Neifile's judgment.

The central action of the *Shipman's Tale* follows 8.1 more closely than it does 8.2 or 8.10. Daun John borrows money from the merchant and returns it to his wife when he sleeps with her. Here, then, the differences between the two narratives may be more revealing than their similarities. As in 8.2 but not 8.1, the two lovers are equal partners in the affair and neither is condemned. While both may lie—daun John, for example, about his reasons for having frequented the merchant's house and the wife about her husband's sexual prowess—they seem aware of the reasons behind other's claims, using the ambiguity of language to reach a conclusion both desire. That a valuable gift changes hands is not an issue: both seem to accept that there is an economic basis to relationships. Indeed, it is precisely this elision of business and sex, which Neifile condemns in a mercantile setting, that caught Chaucer's attention. Let me, however, conclude this section with another difference between 8.1 and his tale. While the last words of 8.1 focus on Gulfardo, its final action, projected into the future, will be Madonna Ambruogia's returning of the money to her husband. The *Shipman's Tale* ends with that conversation.

Decameron *8.10*

The last *novella* of the Eighth Day, told as is customary by Dioneo and so not necessarily tied to the day's theme, is less similar to the "Versus de mola piperis" than either 8.2 or 8.1 is. Here there is neither a soldier nor a priest, not even a wife. The affair, moreover, begins before the loan is requested, and the loan itself is then subsumed into a second deal, which returns to the lover not just his initial gift but a substantially larger sum. Finally, the end of the tale calls attention less to the recovery of the gift than to the fitness of the final turn of events in which the deceiver is deceived. For these reasons, it is understandable that critics have overlooked 8.10 when considering the sources of the *Shipman's Tale*. If, however, 8.1 adapts the rural narrative of 8.2 to an urban setting, 8.10 transforms it for a world of international commerce. In 8.2 Belcolore's wool may be destined for the international market, and in 8.1 Guasparruolo leaves Milan for business in Genoa, and yet 8.10 unfolds against the backdrop of transnational trade. It features a young Florentine merchant, known as Salabaetto, with a load of woolen goods owned by his Pisan employers and left over from a fair in Salerno, who arrives in Palermo looking for amusement. He is eventually helped out of the difficulty he gets into by a compatriot and close family friend, Pietro dello Canigiano, who, serving as treasurer to the Empress of Constantinople, lives in Naples. The depiction of this world of international commerce is the source for the deals of the Shipman's merchant, who travels first to Bruges and then to Paris to transact his business. Indeed, although played out on a more restricted geographical scale and put to a different purpose, this economic setting profoundly affects Chaucer's story.

The motif of the Deceiver Deceived, which Dioneo announces before beginning his narrative and which draws attention away from the motif of the Lover's Gift Regained, is one that Chaucer would have known and that he may have used, following Boccaccio's lead, in the *Reeve's Tale*. Rather than exercising his privilege to talk on a topic of his choice, Dioneo claims that his story will not only fit in with the others of the day but surpass them:

> Graziose donne, manifesta cosa è tanto piú l'arti piacere quanto piú sottile artefice è per quelle artificiosamente beffato. E per ciò, quantunque bellissime cose tutte raccontate abbiate, io intendo di raccontarne una tanto piú che alcuna altra dettane da dovervi aggradire, quanto colei che beffata fu era maggior maestra di beffare altrui che alcuno altro beffato fosse di quegli o di quelle che avete contate. (8.10, 3)

> (Gracious ladies, it goes without saying that the more cunning a person is, the greater our satisfaction in seeing that person cunningly deceived. And hence, whilst the stories you have told have all been excellent, the one I propose to relate should afford you greater pleasure than any of the others, inasmuch as it concerns the duping of a lady who knew far more about the art of deception than any of the men or women who were beguiled in the tales we have heard so far; McWilliam, p. 632).

Although perhaps more difficult for us to recognize because examples have not been collected in the *Types of the Folktale*, this motif would have been readily apparent in the Middle Ages because it is illustrated in the fable of the fox and the stork. In response to the fox, who has served him a liquid dinner he cannot eat, the stork places his meal in a glass vessel so the fox can see and smell it but, without a long beak, cannot reach it. A popular version, formerly attributed to Walter of England but now identified as the elegiac *Romulus*,[61] summarizes the action "fallitur audens fallere,"[62] "daring to deceive, he is deceived." This motif, central for the *Reeve's Tale*, occurs as a concluding moral, "A gilour shal himself bigyled be" (I, 4321). In my opinion Boccaccio used it not to compete with the main theme of 8.10 but to emphasize it.

Dioneo opens his story with a detailed account of a commercial practice

---

[61] See Mann, *From Aesop to Reynard*, pp. 11–12 and note 59. As Mann explains, the work was also known as the "Anonymous Neveleti."

[62] Léopold Hervieux, *Les fabulistes latins*, 5 vols., vols. 1–2 in 2nd edn (Librairie de Firmin-Didot et Cie, 1893–99), 2.332. See also *L'Esopus attribuito a Gualtiero Anglico*, ed. and trans. Paola Busdraghi. Favolisti latini medievali e umanisitici 10 (Genoa: Università degli studi di Genova, Dipartimento di archeologia, filologia classica e loro tradizioni, 2005); and Laura Gibbs, *Aesop's Fables* (Oxford: Oxford University Press, 2002), p. 81.

that is both central to the story he tells and strongly suggestive of its international setting. The description itself appears to be simply objective:

> Soleva essere, e forse che ancora oggi è, una usanza in tutte le terre marine che hanno porto cosí fatta, che tutti i mercatanti che in quelle con mercatantie capitano, faccendole scaricare, tutte in un fondaco, il quale in molti luoghi è chiamato dogana, tenuta per lo comune o per lo signor della terra, le portano; e quivi, dando a coloro che sopra ciò sono per iscritto tutta la mercatantia e il pregio di quella, è dato per li detti al mercatante un magazzino nel quale esso la sua mercatantia ripone e serralo con la chiave; e li detti doganieri poi scrivono in su il libro della dogana a ragione del mercatante tutta la sua mercatantia, faccendosi poi del loro diritto pagare al mercatante o per tutta o per parte della mercatantia che egli della dogana traesse. E da questo libro della dogana assai volte s'informano i sensali e delle qualità e delle quantità delle mercatantie che vi son, e ancora chi sieno i mercatanti che l'hanno; con li quali poi essi, secondo che lor cade per mano, ragionan di cambi, di baratti e di vendite e d'altri spacci. (8.10, 4–6)

> (In the seaports of all maritime countries, it used to be the practice, and possibly still is, that any merchant arriving there with merchandise, having discharged his cargo, takes it to a warehouse, which in many places is called the *dogana*, and is maintained by the commune or by the ruler of the state. After presenting a written description of the cargo and its value to the officers in charge, he is given a storeroom where his merchandise is placed under key; the officers then record all the details in their register under the merchant's name, and whenever the merchant removes his goods from bond, either wholly or in part, they make him pay the appropriate dues. It is by consulting this register that brokers, more often than not, obtain their information about the amount and value of the goods stored at the *dogana* together with the names of the merchants to whom they belong. And when a suitable opportunity presents itself, they approach the merchants and arrange to barter, exchange, sell, or otherwise dispose of their merchandise; McWilliam, pp. 632–33).

It is into such a *dogana* that Salabaetto checks goods valued at around five hundred gold florins.

While it seems odd to question a contemporary account of a practice no longer followed, especially one written by someone who began his career, as Boccaccio did,[63] working as a banker in Naples and so well aware of local and international business conventions, there are some details here that open this description to question. Dioneo's uncertainty about whether it still functions in his own day could be affectation—a way of holding himself above commercial matters. His assertion, however, that it functioned "in tutte le

---

[63] See Vittore Branca, *Boccaccio: The Man and His Works*, trans. Richard Monges (New York: New York University Press, 1976), pp. 16–18.

terre marine," which Branca glosses as "città marinare" (p. 1009, note 2), might be intended to raise doubt. The *dogana* itself, an originally Arabic word used elsewhere to refer to "customs," a "customhouse," or more generally "customs administration,"[64] seems to play too large a role here as a warehouse, the custom's office, and a mercantile exchange, with its *doganieri* ("officers in charge") recording names, goods, and values in a *libro della dogana* ("their register").[65] This book is used not only to assess customs but also to inform *sensali* ("brokers"), a second term glossed by Branca as from Arabic,[66] of available goods so they can arrange deals, specified by the perplexing list "di cambi, di baratti e di vendite e d'altri spacci." Barter and sale are obvious options, but "cambio" was apparently used then, as now, to refer to exchanges of currency.[67] More ominous, however, is the final unspecified "d'altri spacci." Even if this description simply records a contemporary practice, Boccaccio introduced it into 8.10 in a way that not only fits the needs of his story but also suggested the pervasive influence of merchants both locally and internationally.

The following description links this system to a particular place, Palermo, the setting of the *novella*, and a particular group in this community beyond merchants, the courtesans. As he did in both 8.2 and 8.1, Boccaccio again associated business with sex. Even if the *dogana* is neutral, these women are not:

> La quale usanza, sí come in molti altri luoghi, era in Palermo in Cicilia, dove similemente erano, e ancor sono, assai femine del corpo bellissime ma nemiche dell'onestà, le quali, da chi non le conosce, sarebbono e son tenute grandi e onestissime donne. E essendo non a radere ma a scorticare uomini date del tutto, come un mercatante forestiere vi veggono, cosí da' libro della dogana s'informano di ciò che egli v'ha e di quanto può fare: e appresso con lor piacevoli e amorosi atti e con parole dolcissime questi cotali mercatanti s'ingegnano d'adescare e di trarre nel loro amore: et già molti ve n'hanno tratti, a' quali buona parte della loro mercatantia hanno delle mani tratta, e a assai tutta; e di quegli vi sono stati che la mercatantia e 'l navilio e le polpe e l'ossa lasciate v'hanno, sí ha soavemente la barbiera saputo menare il rasoio. (8.10, 7–8)

---

64 Edler, *Glossary*, *s.v.* The other term used here, *fondaco*, is also borrowed from Arabic. Edler lists six definitions, which I abbreviate: "store or private warehouse," "public warehouse (usually in connection with a custom-house, in S. Italy and N. Africa)," "privately owned common warehouse (in Pisa)," "a public warehouse tax," "warehouse with dwelling-quarters, assigned to foreign merchants," and "a board which regulated provisions, and the weights and measures used in selling them." See also *TLIO, s.v.*

65 Edler includes an entry on *doganiere*, "collector of customs," as well as various kinds of accounting books, including *libro debitori e creditori* and *libro (de') filatori*. She does not, however, list *libro della dogana*.

66 See further, Edler, *Glossary*, *s.v.*

67 Edler, *Glossary*, *s.v.*

(Among the many seaports where this system prevailed was Palermo, in Sicily, which was also notable, and still is, for the number of women, lovely of body but hostile to virtue, who to anyone unfamiliar with their ways are frequently mistaken for great ladies of impeccable honesty. Their sole aim in life consists, not so much in fleecing men, as skinning them wholesale, and whenever they catch sight of a merchant from foreign parts, they find out from the *dogana* register what goods he has deposited there and how much he is worth: after which, using all their charms and amorous wiles, and whispering honeyed words into the ears of their unsuspecting victim, they attempt to ensnare him into falling in love with them. In this way they have enticed a large number of merchants to part with a substantial proportion of their goods, and a great many others to hand over the entire lot, whilst some of them have been know to forfeit not only their merchandise, but their ships as well, and even their flesh and their bones, so daintily has the lady-barber known how to wield her razor; McWilliam, p. 633).

The *dogana* and the courtesans do not just exist "similemente" in Palermo: they are connected, the women learning from the *libro della dogana*, just as the *sensali* do, about the merchants' affairs. Also significant here are the bodies, the women using their deceptively beautiful ones to shave—the controlling idea here being that they are barbers—the "merchandise, ships, flesh, and bones" from the men. The *novella's* main character, Jancofiore,[68] is one of these.

Dioneo's narrative is remarkable for the details, which tie into the final deception, then lavished on the seduction and affair, as Jancofiore convinces Salabaetto of both her love and her wealth through a series of gifts and staged events. When she sends a maidservant to invite him to a meeting at a "bagno," it is with an "anello," a ring (8.10, 11). This meeting is elaborately described; let me note only the "paio di lenzuola sottilissime listate di seta e poi una coltre di bucherame cipriana bianchissima con due origlieri lavorati a maraviglie" (8.10, 14; "a pair of sheets, fine as gossamer and edged all around with silk, over which they placed a quilt of whitest Cyprian buckram, together with two exquisitely embroidered pillows," McWilliam, p. 634), which two female slaves place, as Salabaetto watches, on a mattress prior to their owner's arrival. That same night, when she invites him to dine at her house, he finds more beautiful objects and fabrics, which confirm his estimation of her:

Poi, nella camera entratisene, sentí quivi maraviglioso odore di legno aloè e d'uccelletti cipriani, vide il letto ricchissimo e molte belle robe su per le stanghe. Le quali cose, tutte insieme e ciascuna per sé, gli fecero stimare costei dovere essere una grande e ricca donna. (8.10, 24)

---

[68] Dioneo does not consistently use the honorific before her name, suggesting that when he does, he does so ironically. Salabaetto, not surprisingly, calls her "Madonna." I will omit it.

(Then entering the bedroom, he smelled the wondrous fragrance of eagle-wood and little bird-shaped cookies, and saw the rich bed and many beautiful robes on pegs. All these things together, and each in particular, led him to the firm conviction that she was a great and wealthy lady; compare McWilliam, p. 636).

The next morning, "ella gli cinse una bella e leggiadra cinturetta d'argento con una bella borsa" (8.10, 25; "she fastened a dainty and beautiful little silver girdle round his waist, with a fine purse to go with it," McWilliam, p. 636) and her speech asserts a commitment similar to marriage: "'Salabaetto mio dolce, io mi ti raccomando: e cosí come la mia persona è al piacer tuo, cosí è che ci è, e ciò che per me si può è allo comando tuio'" (8.10, 25; "'my darling Salabaetto, I implore you to remember that just as my person is yours to enjoy, so everything I have here is yours, and all that I can do is at your command,'" McWilliam, p. 636). This speech, as noted in Chapter 1, provides a model for the description in the *Shipman's Tale* of the merchant's and daun John's "eterne alliance" (VII, 40) and the merchant offering him "nat oonly my gold, but my chaffare" (VII, 285).

The relationship continues in this way with Salabaetto receiving gifts from Jancofiore worth "ben trenta fiorin d'oro, senza aver potuto fare che ella da lui prendesse tanto che valesse un grosso" (8.10, 27; "at least thirty gold florins, without ever managing to persuade her to take so much as a silver groat in return," McWilliam, p. 637) until he sells the goods in the *dogana*, "a contanti e guadagnonne bene" (8.10, 26; "for ready money at a substantial profit," McWilliam, p. 637). Jancofiore learns of the sale not from him but "da altrui" (8.10, 27; "from others"; compare McWilliam, p. 637), and so the next day stages an evening that begins with her offering him yet more gifts before she is called away; she returns distraught, claiming to have learned that she must send a thousand florins within a week to her brother in Messina or else he will be executed. Salabaetto immediately offers the five hundred florins he has received from the sale of the goods, which she accepts.[69] Even though her behavior toward him promptly changes, it is only several months after the date by which she had promised to return the money that Salabaetto realizes that he has been fooled, and that "né scritta né testimonio" (8.10, 40; "without written evidence or a witness"; compare McWilliam, p. 639) there is nothing he can do, so he leaves, not to return to Pisa to be held accountable by his employers, but rather to Naples, the current residence of "nostro compar Pietro dello Canigiano, trasorier di madama la 'mperatrice di Constantinopoli...grandissimo amico e di Salabaetto e de' suoi" (8.10, 42; "a compatriot of ours, Pietro dello Canigiano, who was treasurer to Her Highness the Empress of Constantinople...a very close friend of Salabaetto and

---

[69]   In her feigned unwillingness to accept this offer, she makes the comment about merchants doing all their business with their money, discussed in Chapter 1.

his family," McWilliam, p. 639). It is Canigiano who devises the plan that regains the lover's gift.

The conclusion of the *novella* capitalizes effectively on the topics—the mercantile practices of Palermo, assurances of lasting cooperation, the appearance of wealth, and, above all, deceit—already introduced. Following Canigiano's plan, Salabaetto returns to Palermo with a shipment of goods valued, as he checks them into the *dogana*, at two thousand gold florins, and announces that he is waiting for another shipment valued at three thousand more, a sum ten times the worth of his original cargo. Hearing of these new resources, Jancofiore decides to return the original money "per potere avere la maggior parte de' cinquemilia" (8.10, 45; "to be able to have the greater part of the five thousand"; compare McWilliam, p. 640). When they meet, Salabaetto cuts off her excuses:

> "Madonna, nel vero egli mi dispiacque bene un poco, sí come a colui che mi trarrei il cuor per darlovi, se io credessi piacervene; ma io voglio che voi udiate come io son crucciato con voi. Egli è tanto e tale l'amor che io vi porto, che io ho fatto vendere la maggior parte delle mie possessioni: e ho al presente recata qui tanta mercatantia che vale oltre a dumilia fiorini e aspettone di Ponente tanta che varrà oltre a tremilia; e intendo di fare in questa terra un fondaco e di starmi qui per esservi sempre presso, parendomi meglio stare del vostro amore che io creda che stea alcuno innamorato del suo." (8.10, 47–48)

> ("To tell the truth, my lady, I was a little displeased, like one who would myself pull out my very heart to give it to you, if I thought it would please you. But I would like you to hear how vexed I am with you. So great and particular is the love I bear for you, that I have sold the greater part of my possessions, and now I have brought here a consignment of goods worth over two thousand florins. Moreover, I am expecting a further consignment from the West worth more than three thousand, and I intend to start a business in Palermo and settle here for good, for I consider myself more fortunate in loving you than any other lover in the world"; compare McWilliam, pp. 640–41.)

This admission that he was displeased at how he has been treated makes his protestations of love, including the claim that he would pull out his heart to give her, which resonates with the corporeal imagery noted earlier, all the more powerful. Equally significant, however, is Salabaetto's plan to open "un fondaco," translated by McWilliam as "business" and yet the same word that Dioneo used in apposition to *dogana* at the start of the tale.[70] Having learned his lesson, he will run the same kind of establishment. The mirroring continues as Jancofiore then returns the same florins ("quegli medesimi che

---

70 Branca suggests instead a more general meaning of *azienda mercantile* ("mercantile company"); p. 1020, note 4.

esso portati l'avea," 8.10, 53; "the very florins he had given her," McWilliam, p. 641). Although played out against a banking system that can convert goods to money, transferring credit across countries, it is striking that the same coins return to Salabaetto.

With the lover's gift regained, the *novella* shifts to Deceiving the Deceiver, or as Dioneo puts it: "ma Salabaetto, volendo col suo inganno punire lo 'nganno di lei...." (8.10, 56; "but Salabaetto, wishing with his own treachery to punish her treachery..."; compare McWilliam, p. 642). His story, sprung on Jancofiore one evening some time after their affair had resumed, is that he must raise a thousand florins to pay off pirates who have captured his second shipment. In explaining that she knows someone ("alcuna persona") who could lend it to him, but who would require collateral ("sicuro di buon pegno") and charge high interest ("grossa usura"; "trenta per centinaio"), she makes a suggestion that is both extreme in itself and, I would suggest, the source of the wife's pun on "wed" at the end of the *Shipman's Tale*: "'e io per me sono acconcia d'impegnar per te tutte queste robe *e la persona* per tanto quanto egli ci vorrà sú prestare, per poterti servire'" (8.10.60, emphasis added; "'now I personally would be prepared for your sake to offer him all I possess, *myself included*, as security for whatever sum he will lend,'" McWilliam, p. 643). Jancofiore offers her body as collateral just as in Chaucer's tale the wife tells her husband: "'Ye shal my joly body have to wedde'" (VII, 423). In any case the response convinces Salabaetto that Jancofiore will indeed be lending her own money, even though she goes through the pretence of having him borrow it from a *sensale* (8.10, 63) and use the goods already in the *dogana*—although he will keep the key to them—as collateral:

e per ciò,[71] come il dí fu venuto, ella mandò per un sensale di cui ella si confidava molto e, ragionato con lui questo fatto, gli diè mille fiorin d'oro li quali il sensale prestò a Salabaetto e fece in suo nome scrivere alla dogana ciò che Salabaetto dentro v'avea; e fattesi loro scritte e contrascritte insieme e in concordia rimasi, attesero a' loro altri fatti. (8.10, 63)

(early the next morning, she sent for a broker who was privy to most of her secrets, and having explained the situation to him, she gave him a thousand gold florins, which the broker lent to Salabaetto, having first ensured that all the goods that Salabaetto had at the *dogana* were transferred to his own name. Various documents were signed and countersigned by the two men, and when all was settled between them, they went their separate ways to attend to their other affairs; McWilliam, p. 643).

Unlike the earlier deal, this one is secure.

---

[71] "And for this reason," i.e. because she considers the goods in the *dogana* acceptable collateral and agrees he should keep the key. McWilliam omits this phrase.

The story turns first to Salabaetto, indicating how he should have behaved at the start. He returns to Naples with the "millecinquecento fiorini d'oro":

e di quindi buona e intera ragione rimandò a Firenze a' suoi maestri che co' panni l'avevan mandato. E pagato Pietro e ogni altro a cui alcuna cosa doveva, piú dí col Canigiano si diè buon tempo dello inganno fatto alla ciciliana; poi di quindi, non volendo piú mercatante essere, se ne venne a Ferrara. (8.10, 64)

(from here he sent to Florence to his employers, who had sent him with the clothing, a proper and complete remittance; and having paid Pietro and everyone else with whom he had [outstanding] affairs, he had [gave himself] a good time with Canigiano over the trick he had played on the Sicilian woman; then from there, not wishing any longer to be a barterer, he made his way to Ferrara; compare McWilliam, pp. 643–44).

If not simply an oversight on Boccaccio's part, sending the "ragione," here apparently a letter of credit, to Florence rather than directly to his employers in Pisa, is yet another reference to the international banking system that serves as a background to the story. The final comments concerning his decisions to leave commerce and to travel to Ferrara are more ambiguous since, as Branca points out in his note on the passage, this city was another major center for Florentine businessmen at this time. Taken together, however, Salabaetto's actions here emphasize that one should conduct business first and then relax in the company of men by ridiculing women.

The *novella* ends not with their male retelling of the events but rather with Jancofiore as she discovers what has happened. While focusing on her defeat, this dramatically apt conclusion provides her with a remarkable agency. Just as it took Salabaetto several months to realize he had been duped, so too she waits "ben due mesi" before acting, yet when she does, it is decisively:

fece che il sensale fece schiavare i magazzini. E primieramente tastate le botti che si credeva che piene d'olio fossero, trovò quelle esser piene d'acqua marina, avendo in ciascuna forse un baril d'olio di sopra vicino al cocchiume; poi, sciogliendo le balle, tutte, fuor che due che panni erano, piene le trovò di capecchio; e in brieve tra ciò che v'era, non valeva oltre dugento fiorini. (8.10, 65–66)

(she got the broker to force a way into the warehouse. And having first of all tested the casks, which were supposed to be full of oil, she discovered that they were filled with sea-water, apart from about a firkin of oil that was floating at the top of each cask, near the bung-hole. Then untying the bales, she found that all except two (which consisted of woollens) were filled with tow. And in fact, to cut a long story short, the whole consignment was worth no more than two hundred florins; McWilliam, p. 644).

As with the fox and stork, the deceiver has been deceived in the same way that she first tricked her target, with the appearance of wealth, including fabrics. The concluding sentences then remind the audience precisely of the deals and introduce a proverb:

> Di che Iancofiore tenendosi scornata, lungamente pianse i cinquecento renduti e troppo piú i mille prestati, spesse volte dicendo: "Chi ha a far con tosco, non vuole esser losco." E cosí, rimasasi col danno e con le beffe, trovò che tanto seppe altri quanto altri. (8.10, 67)

> (Because of this, the humiliated Iancofiore lamented long over the five hundred returned [florins] and even more over the one thousand lent, often saying: "One who deals with a Tuscan should not be shady." And so, left with the loss and the mockery, she discovered that some people know more than others; compare McWilliam, p. 644.)

She is humiliated ("scornata") and left with the loss of money ("danno"), the consequences of the *beffa*, and the realization that she has been outwitted. Dioneo, however, might have gone much further, as a comparison to 8.1 suggests. Unlike Madonna Ambruogia, who as she returns the five hundred florins to her husband returns herself as well, Jancofiore, who has proven herself to be a woman of considerable resources because she loaned her own thousand florins, remains independent.

Moreover, in lamenting both the five hundred and the thousand florins, Jancofiore here reminds the reader that Boccaccio has indeed added to, if not multiplied, his initial narrative of the Lover's Gift Regained with the second deal. Its detail, including the role of Canigiano, who was a well-known contemporary of Boccaccio, lends it the appearance of representing, albeit in an exquisitely narrated form, a real event. As Lee, however, notes, this part of the conclusion adapts a story told by Petrus Alphonsi in his twelfth-century *Disciplina clericalis*, which was then included with some minor changes in the thirteenth-century *Gesta Romanorum*.[72] The earlier work tells of a Spaniard who discovers that the person with whom he has left a thousand talents before going on a journey then denies ever having seen him. The man despairs of getting his money back until an old woman offers to help him. She has him first find a friend "de terra tua, cuius factis et dictis fidem habere possis" ("from your country, whom you trust in both actions and words"), and then buy ten well-made chests, fill them with pebbles and arrange to

---

[72] See the *Disciplina clericalis*, ed. Alfons Hilka and Werner Söderhjelm (Heidelberg: Carl Winter's Universitätsbuchhandlung, 1911), pp. 22–23. The translation is by P. R. Quarrie, *The* Disciplina clericalis *of Petrus Alfonsi* (Berkeley: University of California Press, 1977), p. 129. See also the text and translation by Jacqueline Genot-Bismuth, *Disciplina clericalis/ La Discipline de Clergie*, Moïse le Séfarade, alias Pierre d'Alphonse (Paris: Editions de Paris, 2001). The story is chapter 118 in the *Gesta Romanorum*; see the edition of Hermann Oesterley (Berlin: Weidmannsche Buchhandlung, 1872), pp. 461–63; and the translation by Charles Swan (1876; repr. New York: Dover Publications, 1959), pp. 210–12.

have ten men carry them to his deceiver's house "unus post alium uenientes ordine longo" ("in a long file one after the other").[73] The man himself is to arrive after the first has reached the deceiver's house. On the day, the woman and the man's friend are the first to appear, explaining that the man wishes to leave his treasure with the deceiver for safe-keeping while they travel to Mecca. As they are speaking, the first chest arrives, and shortly after, the Spaniard himself. The deceiver immediately returns the Spaniard's money, fearing if he does not do so, the friend will not entrust his to him. There are of course many differences between this narrative and 8.10, but the basic idea of returning a first sum in order to get a larger one is at the center of both. Although Chaucer used this technique of putting together different stories in the *Shipman's Tale* only in combining Boccaccio's three *novelle*, it underlies his practice in other Canterbury tales, particularly those, as we shall see, of the Miller and the Wife of Bath.

One more challenge of this conclusion, however, is the difficulty of weighing the final proverb, "One who deals with a Tuscan should not be shady." As Branca points out in his note, it is found often in the works of authors from this region; here, of course, Dioneo places it in the mouth of a Sicilian, perhaps as something she has heard but now experienced. It stresses that it is not the Tuscans who are "shady": they merely know how to repay those who are. As such, this message appears to represent Boccaccio's final take on the story. Salabaetto has proven to be somewhat foolish even to the end as he both renounces commerce and departs for Ferrara, itself a commercial center, and yet, with the aid of another Florentine, he has extricated himself from his difficulty, causing more harm to the person who has harmed him. The verbal triumph of the proverb confirms this judgment, and, moreover, recalls the topic of the Sixth Day: "di chi, con alcun leggiadro motto tentato, si riscotesse, o con pronta risposta o avvedimento fuggí perdita o pericolo o scorno" (5, *Conclusione*, 3; "those who, on being provoked by some verbal pleasantry, have responded, or with a prompt retort or action have avoided loss, danger or scorn"; compare McWilliam, p. 441). It is revealing that seven of the *novelle* (6.1–6 and 6.9) are either set in Florence or concern Florentines. Even here, however, Boccaccio's views are difficult to fix since 6.10, the light-hearted story of Friar Cipolla, a friar who must think quickly when coal is substituted for the "relic," a feather of the Angel Gabriel, he intends to use in his sermon, is set in Certaldo, the village near Florence that the author claimed as his home town. This *novella* in which Boccaccio, identifying with Friar Cipolla, showed off his ability to create brilliant stories from nothing and laughed at himself, demonstrates the difficulty of attributing any position to him. The plot, however, of 8.10, this *novella*'s relationship to both 8.1 and 8.2, its role (as I discuss in the next chapter) in the argument raised

---

[73] *Disciplina*, ed. Hilka and Söderhjelm, p. 23; trans. Quarrie, p. 200.

by Licisca, and finally its engagement with the stories of the Sixth Day all suggest that "altri," Florentine men, really are smarter than "altri," Sicilian women.

While Chaucer's greatest debt to 8.10 is not to follow this judgment, instead appreciating Jancofiore's control of her money and sexuality, the extent and the nature of his borrowings can be seen most clearly in the way he wove the merchant's international deal into the plot. For the Lover's Gift Regained to work, all that must happen is for the husband to be away as the infidelity occurs and then present when the gift is returned, which is indeed what "Versus de mola piperis" presents. 8.2 and 8.1 are both slightly more complicated: one begins when the priest sees Bentivegna leaving for Florence, and in the other Guasparruolo's business trip to Genoa allows the already arranged deal to take place. Neither, however, suggests the careful attention to the commercial setting of 8.10, which Boccaccio wove tightly into his narrative. Chaucer did the same; with, however, an important difference. By linking the *dogana* to the courtesans and by making the main increases in the transactions imaginary and dependent on lies, most of this *novella*'s commerce is based on deceit. Salabaetto's original goods are real and bring an undisclosed profit when he sells them, and yet this detail is overwhelmed by Jancofiore's claim that she needs twice this amount to save her brother from death, and Salabaetto's own fabricated claims that he returns to Palermo with merchandise valued at ten times the worth of the original shipment. Both manipulate the *dogana* and its officials. The Florentine banking system works; the focus, however, is on Sicilian corruption. In contrast, the merchant's affairs in the *Shipman's Tale* may defy complete explanation, but they return a real profit, and so stand in sharp contrast to daun John's lie as he requests one hundred francs to buy "beestes." Indeed, Chaucer's interest throughout the tale is less in condemning lies than in recognizing that ambiguous language allows real transactions to take place. It is this insight that allowed him to present Boccaccio's concern with the relationship between business and sexuality as something not to condemn but rather to explore.

Commerce lies immediately behind what appears to be the main action at the opening of the *Shipman's Tale* just as it does in 8.10. Salabaetto must check his employers' goods into the *dogana* before he can see what amusements Palermo has to offer. Similarly the Shipman's merchant has been working on a deal, which he sets aside for a few days to engage in pleasure:

> But so bifel, this marchant on a day
> Shoop hym to make redy his array
> Toward the toun of Brugges for to fare,
> To byen there a porcioun of ware;
> For which he hath to Parys sent anon
> A messager, and preyed hath daun John
> That he sholde come to Seint-Denys to pleye

With hym and with his wyf a day or tweye,
Er he to Brugges wente, in alle wise. (VII, 53–61)

While the type of the Lover's Gift Regained would not lead us to expect that this deal will play a role in the story, Chaucer provided some indication that it does by including in its opening description the most specific account in the tale of what the merchant does: he goes to Bruges "to byen there a porcioun of ware." As we struggle with the details at the end of the tale to figure out what has happened, we may return to it to recognize that a real transaction lies behind the other events of the story.

Chaucer then developed these topics of the real work of merchants and the difficulty of understanding it by describing this merchant in his counting house. For the deal between the wife and her lover to take place, all that must happen is for the husband not to be present. In contrast, the Shipman provides a vivid description of the merchant reconciling his cash and his books:

The thridde day, this marchant up ariseth,
And on his nedes sadly hym avyseth,
And up into his countour-hous gooth he
To rekene with hymself, wel may be,
Of thilke yeer how that it with hym stood,
And how that he despended hadde his good,
And if that he encressed were or noon.
His bookes and his bagges many oon
He leith biforn hym on his countyng-bord.
Ful riche was his tresor and his hord,
For which ful faste his countour-dore he shette;
And eek he nolde that no man sholde hym lette
Of his acountes, for the meene tyme
And thus he sit til it was passed pryme. (VII, 75–88)

Before entering a new, complex deal, he wants accurate information about his financial status. With its many "bookes" and "bagges," this description also suggests that it is genuinely difficult for him to get this information. His money, it seems, has the odd ability to change, either increase or decrease, on its own. Lying behind this description and the tale as a whole is the complicated question of usury, making money from money, which in one line of medieval thought was considered unnatural since it, unlike agricultural products, is sterile.[74] The Shipman here provides an image that is reassuring because it depicts a merchant engaged in his craft and unsettling because the commercial world itself appears out of control.

Moreover, Chaucer returned to these ideas in two passages in which the merchant reflects on his profession. The first is spoken to his wife when she

---

[74] See the discussion in Chapter 1.

interrupts him in his accounting following her own conversation with daun John in the garden:

> "Wyf," quod this man, "litel kanstow devyne
> The curious bisynesse that we have.
> For of us chapmen, also God me save,
> And by that lord that clepid is Seint Yve,
> Scarsly amonges twelve tweye shul thryve
> Continuelly, lastynge unto oure age.
> We may wel make chiere and good visage,
> And dryve forth the world as it may be,
> And kepen oure estaat in pryvetee,
> Til we be deed, or elles that we pleye
> A pilgrymage, or goon out of the weye.
> And therfore have I greet necessitee
> Upon this queynte world t'avyse me,
> For everemoore we moote stonde in drede
> Of hap and fortune in oure chapmanhede." (VII, 224–38)

There are several significant points here. Business may be "curious" not just because it is "worrisome" as glossed in the *Riverside Chaucer* or "pains-taking," as suggested by the *Middle English Dictionary*, but because it is genuinely obscure, like an occult or magic art (see the *Franklin's Tale* V, 1120). Moreover, merchants "justified," as the note in the *Riverside Chaucer* indicates, "their profits by emphasizing the risks (**hap, fortune**)." Perhaps most significant, however, is the claim that merchants must keep their situation, "estaat," private, since this idea resonates strongly with 8.10: Salabae-tto's difficulties arise because Jancofiore learns of the sale of his goods and he is then able to trick her when he keeps control of the key to the warehouse. It also recalls the conversation that has just taken place in which daun John and then the wife swear that they will not reveal anything the other says:

> "For on my portehors I make an ooth
> That nevere in my lyf, for lief ne looth,
> Ne shal I of no conseil yow biwreye."
> "The same agayn to yow," quod she, "I seye.
> By God and by this portehors I swere,
> Though men me wolde al into pieces tere,
> Ne shal I nevere, for to goon to helle,
> Biwreye a word of thyng that ye me telle,
> Nat for no cosynage ne alliance,
> But verraily for love and affiance." (VII, 131–40)

Although the wife pointedly ends her speech by claiming that love is stronger than any other relationship, echoing two of the terms, "cosynage" and "alli-ance," used earlier to describe the relationship of daun John and her husband, the context suggests it is precisely the point where they overlap, in marriage, that makes business deals similar to sexual relationships.

The second passage, addressed to daun John after he has requested the loan of a hundred francs to buy "beestes," balances the first by indicating that, for all one may manipulate appearances, a merchant's success also rests on his real assets. The merchant in the tale is more than willing to loan the monk money, even claiming "'My gold is youres'" and "'nat oonly my gold, but my chaffare'" (VII, 284–85); but he continues,

> "But o thyng is, ye knowe it wel ynogh
> Of chapmen, that hir moneie is hir plogh.
> We may creaunce whil we have a name,
> But goldlees for to be, it is no game.
> Paye it agayn whan it lith in youre ese;
> After my myght ful fayn wolde I yow plese." (VII, 287–92)

In contrast to 8.1 and 8.10, there is no explicit mention of interest here: this is a deal between friends. As discussed in Chapter 1, however, in the metaphor of money as a "plogh" Chaucer cut close to the problem of usury, playing on the idea that money is a tool that prepares the ground for another commodity, grain, to increase. The merchant then links his activity ("we may creaunce") to both reputation ("name") and real wealth ("But goldlees...."). As in 8.10, the appearance of wealth can be profitable, but here it is tied not to false practices but to the core of real commerce.

Again following 8.10, the *Shipman's Tale* then binds its two transactions tightly together. After completing the first part of his deal in Bruges and stopping briefly at home in Saint-Denis, the merchant travels to Paris. While the Shipman specifically states that he visits his friend "to pleye; / Nat for to axe or borwe of hym moneye" (VII, 337–38), the merchant does explain his situation to daun John:

> How he hadde wel yboght and graciously,
> Thanked be God, al hool his marchandise,
> Save that he moste, in alle maner wise,
> Maken a chevyssaunce, as for his beste,
> And thanne he sholde been in joye and reste. (VII, 344–48)

Daun John's response to this information is to claim that he wishes he could loan the merchant money, especially because of the kindness the merchant had just shown him:

> "And if that I were riche, as have I blisse,
> Of twenty thousand sheeld sholde ye nat mysse,
> For ye so kyndely this oother day
> Lente me gold; and as I kan and may,
> I thanke yow, by God and by Seint Jame!" (VII, 351–55)

This topic leads him into an account of how he returned the money the merchant had lent him to his wife. While both characters would deny that they are discussing business, their friendship and their deals have become intimately linked, more intimately than the merchant realizes. Moreover, this exchange is then used by the husband on the morning following his return to Saint-Denis, when his wife refuses to continue having sex with him:

> "By God," quod he, "I am a litel wrooth
> With yow, my wyf, although it be me looth.
> And woot ye why? By God, as that I gesse
> That ye han maad a manere straungenesse
> Bitwixen me and my cosyn daun John.
> Ye sholde han warned me, er I had gon,
> That he yow hadde an hundred frankes payed
> By redy token; and heeld hym yvele apayed,
> For that I to hym spak of chevyssaunce;
> Me semed so, as by his contenaunce." (VII, 383–92)

Here the merchant admits that daun John might have interpreted their conversation as about business and recognizes that their discussion may have changed their relationship. He concludes the speech by asking that his wife in the future keep him better informed of debts that have been paid in his absence, again linking the transactions and preparing for the final punning on "taillynge" where sex and business merge.

Finally the details we are given about the merchant's own deal, which reflect the scope of the transactions in 8.10, influence our perception of the end of the tale. Although the hundred francs remain only to be played out between husband and wife, the merchant has made "A thousand frankes aboven al his costage" (VII, 372)—his money has multiplied spectacularly. Indeed, this result has consequences within the tale:

> His wyf ful redy mette hym atte gate,
> As she was wont of oold usage algate,
> And al that nyght in myrthe they bisette;
> For he was riche and cleerly out of dette. (VII, 373–76)

While in 8.10 the appearance of money had led to an ultimately unhappy affair, here financial loss and gain are both intertwined into the marriage relationship.

The Shipman's Tale

From Boccaccio's retelling of the Lover's Gift Regained in three distinct economic settings, Chaucer created a single tale, one indeed that allowed him to investigate unexpected continuities, the most important of which is the similarity between sexual and business deals. He wrote the tale to point out that marriage is both, with the consequence that women need control of both their bodies and their money. He would have been well aware that the economies—agrarian, urban, and international—that Boccaccio depicted were to some extent distinct parts of the world in which he lived: an older feudal system based on barter and debased silver survived longest in monastic establishments; relying increasingly on gold, mercantile monetary exchange thrived particularly in cities; and with their ability to transfer credit and debt even across international boundaries, the emerging banks opened new opportunities for commerce. His reason for building these settings into his tale differed from that of his sources. By mocking Belcolore's Varlungo for its lack of morals and by overlooking Salabaetto's youthful indiscretions abroad, Boccaccio allowed the settings of 8.2 and 8.10 to reinforce the conventional sexual morality of 8.1. It is women who sell their bodies for money who deserve punishment, while in the name of love, men should enjoy their favors without economic consequences. Chaucer pointed out the injustice of these assumptions by emphasizing the continuities across these economic divides. Just as it is, for example, a Florentine and a family friend, Canigiano, who extricates Salabaetto from his foolish mistakes, his monk and merchant create their bond because of their common origin. Chaucer, in other words, recognized that much of the mentality of Varlungo remained in the world of international affairs. In this way he suggested that marriage itself is not a simple business transaction, a one-time cash payment, but rather a long-term relationship that requires continual renegotiation.

While an economic history of Western Europe in the fourteenth century is beyond the scope of this study, a few general comments about the end of a feudal economy, the changes in currency, and the role of fairs may help situate this reading of the *Shipman's Tale*. The shibboleth "the rise of a money economy" cannot in itself provide a context for Chaucer's reflections on its transactions since, as M. M. Postan noted, "historians have frequently taken it for granted that a money economy, like the bourgeoisie, arose at a single point of English history, usually at a point best suited to their argument."[75] However, largely due to the Black Death (1348–50), which occurred when Chaucer was a boy, late fourteenth-century England witnessed the end of an agrarian system, so plentifully recorded in the manorial records,[76] that relied

---

[75] M. M. Postan, "The Rise of a Money Economy," *Economic History Review* 14 (1944), pp. 123–34; reprinted in *Essays on Medieval Agriculture and General Problems of the Medieval Economy* (Cambridge: Cambridge University Press, 1973), p. 29.

[76] The classic study by J. A. Raftis, *The Estates of Ramsey Abbey*, Studies and Texts 3 (Toronto: Pontifical Institute of Mediaeval Studies, 1957), has been superseded by Mark Bailey, *The Decline of Serfdom in Late Medieval England: From Bondage to Freedom* (Woodbridge: Boydell & Brewer, 2014). See also, Christopher Dyer, *Making a Living in the Middle Ages:*

heavily on the exchange of labor services and produce even while allowing for the substitution of money in the form of, for example, rent and wages, in these transactions. In the decades following the plague, renters and wage-earners became the norm, resulting in the end of serfdom.[77] This gradual change may well have been apparent to Chaucer not only from anecdotal evidence but also from more public sources such as the passing and enforcing of new laws governing labor,[78] petitions in Parliament such as those in 1376 and 1378 concerning servants leaving the land,[79] and, indeed, the demands of the peasants in 1381 at Mile End for an end to villeinage, the controlling of rents, and the ability to negotiate wage labor contracts.[80] Of course, payment in kind did not end with serfdom,[81] nor indeed was it limited to agrarian society: one need only recall the example of Edward III's gift in 1374 of a pitcher of wine a day for life to Chaucer, and Chaucer's commuting of this gift in 1378 for an annuity of twenty marks to illustrate that goods and

The People of Britain 850–1520, New Economic History of Britain (New Haven: Yale University Press, 2002), pp. 373–5. The records have been interpreted in different ways; see, for example, A. R. Bridbury, "The Farming out of Manors," *Economic History Review*, 2nd ser. 31 (1978), pp. 503–20; reprinted in *The English Economy From Bede to the Reformation* (Woodbridge: Boydell Press, 1992), pp. 133–53. Bridbury is responding to M. M. Postan, "The Chronology of Labour Services," *Transactions of the Royal Historical Society*, 4th ser. 20 (1937), pp. 169–93; reprinted in Postan, *Essays on Medieval Agriculture*, pp. 89–106. For recent overviews, see Dyer, *Making a Living*, pp. 106–86; and Richard Britnell, *Britain and Ireland 1050–1530*, Economic and Social History of Britain (Oxford: Oxford University Press, 2004), pp. 223–47 and 473–90.

[77] Dyer, *Making a Living*, p. 278 and *passim*. See also Britnell, who identifies the Peasants' Revolt of 1381 as roughly the time when "the established method of estate administration generally ceased to function"; *Britain and Ireland*, p. 430.

[78] These include the so-called Ordinance of Labourers (1349) and the Statute of Labourers (1351); in the *Statutes of the Realm* (S. I.: s. n., 1810), the first titled the "Statute of Labourers" and the second "Statute the Second," pp. 307–09 and 311–13. Both are available in translation online at Fordham's Internet History Sourcebooks Project, https://sourcebooks.fordham.edu/. Issues related to the status of laborers continued arise in the following decades; see "Increased severity against labourers at the Parliament of Cambridge," *English Historical Documents. Vol. IV. 1327–1485*, ed. A. R. Myers (New York: Oxford University Press, 1969), pp. 1002–04 and the petitions mentioned in the following note. See also Harry A. Miskimin, *The Economy of Early Renaissance Europe 1300–1460* (Englewood Cliffs: Prentice Hall, 1969), p. 45; and J. L. Bolton, *The Medieval English Economy 1150–1500* (London: J. M. Dent, 1980), pp. 209 and 213.

[79] W. M. Ormrod, ed., "Edward III: Parliament of April 1376, text and translation," sections 61 (X) and 117 (LVIII); G. Martin, ed., "Richard II: Parliament of October 1377, text and translation," section 88; and Martin, ed., "Richard II: Parliament of October 1378, text and translation," section 69; in *The Parliament Rolls of Medieval England, 1275–1504*, ed. Chris Given-Wilson, et al., internet version at http://www.sd-editions.com.ezproxy.york.ac.uk/AnaServer?PROME+0+start.anv+id=GENINTRO, accessed 1 January 2017. See also Bolton, *Medieval English Economy*, p. 214.

[80] The relevant section from the *Anonimalle Chronicle* is translated in *English Historical Documents. Vol. IV*, p. 135. See also Bolton, *Medieval English Economy*, p. 215.

[81] See Dyer, *Making a Living*, p. 279.

money remained at times interchangeable.[82] It seems reasonable, however, that Chaucer would have perceived the exchange of goods and services as more representative of an older, rural economy and the use of money as more characteristic of a newer, urban one.[83] In this context, his choice of professions for the lover, a monk, and the husband, a merchant, is significant, as they suggest at least a two-fold contrast within the tale.

Attention to the physical form of money, which was changing in England and in Europe as a whole during Chaucer's life, indicates that the contrast is rather indeed three-fold. Due to the exploitation of mines in Hungary, by the mid-fourteenth century gold had overtaken silver as the primary metal for minting in Europe,[84] and was particularly important for the expansion of international trade. In preparation for the Hundred Years War, Edward III turned to Florentine bankers, specifically the Bardi and the Peruzzi, to borrow perhaps as much as one and a half million gold florins,[85] and while much of this money was initially dispersed in northern France and the Low Countries, from 1344 he minted nobles of fine gold in England, which transformed the currency.[86] It may, indeed, be relevant for Chaucer's reassignment of the tale after taking it from the Wife of Bath that the obverse of this coin depicts the King standing in a ship.[87] In any case Edward debased silver coinage four times (1344, 1345, 1346, and 1351) and gold coinage twice (1346 and 1351); in 1352, however, he accepted the Statute of Purveyors, which barred further debasement, a policy that remained in effect throughout the rest of Chaucer's life.[88] Given Chaucer's many connections with financial dealings—one might mention, for example, the sixteen pounds contributed by Edward III to his ransom in 1360 and his twelve year service as the controller of customs on the wool export—it would not be surprising to find that he was acutely aware of the physical form of money.

As we have seen, the money central to the *Shipman's Tale* is the "hundred frankes," which the wife claims that she needs to settle a debt (VII, 178–86), and which daun John then borrows from her husband (VII, 269–73 and 293–94) and returns to him through her although she does not at first realize this (VII, 313–17, 356–59, and 388–90). In all these cases, it is identified as one hundred francs, and indeed when John explains that he has returned it,

[82] Martin M. Crow and Clair C. Olson, *Chaucer Life-Records* (Oxford: Clarendon Press, 1966), pp. 112 and 304–05. See also Pearsall, *Life of Geoffrey Chaucer*, p. 95.

[83] For a discussion of what we can know of Chaucer's political views, see Pearsall, *Life of Geoffrey Chaucer*, pp. 143–51.

[84] *The Cambridge Economic History of Europe. Volume II. Trade and Industry in the Middle Ages*, 2nd edn, ed. M. M. Postan and Edward Miller (Cambridge: Cambridge University Press, 1987), p. 831.

[85] *Cambridge Economic*, ed. Postan and Miller, p. 833.

[86] *Cambridge Economic*, ed. Postan and Miller, p. 835.

[87] *Cambridge Economic*, ed. Postan and Miller, p. 835.

[88] Britnell, *Britain and Ireland*, pp. 456–57.

he specifies that it is "the same gold" (VII, 357). There is, then, a slippage of language at the end of the tale when the wife confirms to her husband that "He [daun John] took me certeyn gold" (VII, 404) since *certain* in Middle English means not only "specified" and "fixed" but also "a definite but unspecified amount."[89] Just as in 8.10, in which Jancofiore too returns the exact gold, the francs here are as much gift as money. Again, as noted, in contrast to this gold transaction is the husband's telling remark to his wife prior to his departure that she has enough "silver" in her purse to cover his expenses while he is away (VII, 248), revealing that he is in fact cheap at least in his dealings with her.[90] Finally, both these situations contrast with the merchant's own strikingly more profitable dealings, which focus not on the exchange of physical money for actual goods but rather on the agreements that make the exchange possible.

The sheer size of the merchant's deal, the lack of specificity as to the commodity involved ("a porcioun of ware," VII, 56, with his comment that "chaffare is so deere," VII, 328, referring to goods or perhaps even more generally to trade),[91] and its distance from the main action of the story all make it seem abstract. More significant, however, are the financial transactions themselves: the merchant does not simply buy goods but obtains credit ("byeth and creaunceth," VII, 303; "make a chevyssaunce," VII, 329) by entering into a formal bond ("For he was bounden in a reconyssaunce," VII, 330) to repay "twenty thousand sheeld" (VII, 331), which Kenneth S. Cahn asserts is "approximately thirteen thousand gold franks."[92] He fulfils this obligation by taking some of his own francs and some that he has borrowed from friends to "certeyn Lumbardes" (VII, 367) in Paris. What lies behind these transactions is, as Cahn has explained following the ground-breaking studies of Raymond de Roover, the international banking system that allowed merchants to borrow money in one place and repay it in another, using the local currency, in this case shields or *écus* in Bruges and francs in Paris.[93] This system, which stands in the background of 8.10, is central to the *Shipman's*

---

[89]   *MED, s.v.*

[90]   See Albert H. Silverman, "Sex and Money in Chaucer's Shipman's Tale," *Philological Quarterly* 32 (1953), p. 331; Murray Copeland, "*The Shipman's Tale*: Chaucer and Boccaccio," *Medium Ævum* 35 (1966), p. 18; and Carol Falvo Heffernan, "Chaucer's 'Shipman's Tale' and Boccaccio's *Decameron* VIII, i: Retelling a Story," in *Courtly Literature: Culture and Context*, ed. Keith Busby and Erik Kooper (Amsterdam: John Benjamins, 1990), pp. 265–66.

[91]   *MED, s.v.*

[92]   Kenneth S. Cahn, "Chaucer's Merchants and the Foreign Exchange: An Introduction to Medieval Finance," *Studies in the Age of Chaucer* 2 (1980), p. 116.

[93]   Cahn also claims, but without supporting evidence, that *shield* here does not refer to a coin, but rather that 'in the Middle Ages to sell shields meant to borrow sterling' (82). See Raymond de Roover, *Money, Banking and Credit in Mediaeval Bruges: Italian Merchant-Bankers, Lombards, and Money-Changers. A Study in the Origins of Banking* (Cambridge, MA: Medieval Academy of America, 1948), p. 221.

Tale. Here, as the borrower, the merchant would almost certainly have had to spend money on the financial side of these transactions, although prohibitions against usury obscure to some extent how lenders were paid for their services. The statement that Chaucer's merchant was bound "to paye" twenty thousand shields without specifying how much he in fact received might suggest, as is sometimes assumed, that interest was assessed by requiring more to be returned than was lent; a second possibility is that he was charged for a fictitious exchange of gold into silver. It seems, however, most likely, as de Roover has explained, that interest was built into the transaction by valuing local currency more highly: in Bruges the merchant would have to agree to repay more francs in Paris than the shields would be worth when he arrived there.[94] His profit, which he estimates at "a thousand frankes aboven al his costage" (or, as Cahn notes, about seven per cent of the amount of the deal) will come from having bought something that he can resell at a higher price. Unlike the wife's silver or the definite hundred francs, this money appears fluid and liable to increase in ways that defy understanding. That Chaucer might have been aware of these new transactions is further suggested by his dealings with Matthew Cheyne (Cennini) and Walter de Bardes, and, as David Wallace speculates, his "secrees busoignes" in Florence in 1373 "may have been to negotiate with the Bardi or with other Italian banking houses."[95] Gifts, currency, and financial instruments overlap in the tale.

It is, however, the settings of the *Shipman's Tale* that resonate most strongly with the three-fold division of agrarian, urban, and international economies of late fourteenth-century Europe. The merchant and his wife live in Saint-Denis, famous for its fair already in existence when in 634 or 635 Dagobert awarded its tolls and revenues to the local church, and given new life in the eleventh and twelfth centuries.[96] Probably during the twelfth century and certainly by the thirteenth, six fairs held in four towns in Champagne— Troyes, Provins, Lagny, and Bar-sur-Aube—had overtaken the Saint-Denis. In their prime, as O. Verlinden writes, "the Champagne fairs were indeed the centre of the international commercial activity of the western world," providing not only a location to exchange goods but also the necessary financial support of loans and money-exchange.[97] Although Verlinden expresses doubt about its relevance for the formative period of the Champagne fairs,[98] a late fourteenth-century work, *Les Coustumes, stylle et usaige de la court et chancellerye des foires de Champaigne et de Brye*, describes how visiting

---

[94]   *The Bruges Money Market around 1400* (Brussels: Paleis des Académiën, 1968), pp. 32–34.

[95]   Wallace, *Chaucerian Polity*, pp. 12–13.

[96]   O. Verlinden, "Markets and Fairs," in the *Cambridge Economic History of Europe. Volume III. Economic Organizations and Policies in the Middle Ages*, ed. M. M. Postan, E. E. Rich and Edward Miller (Cambridge: Cambridge University Press, 1963), pp. 120 and 125.

[97]   Verlinden, "Markets and Fairs," p. 132

[98]   Verlinden, "Markets and Fairs," p. 130.

merchants would deposit their money with Italian money changers who would then handle the financial aspect of their deals.[99] By Chaucer's day, however, even these fairs had begun to decline for various reasons, including the disruptions of war and the opening of new sea routes.[100] In their place, cities, particularly Bruges but also Paris and Florence, became the centers of commerce and finance; de Roover, who places the shift earlier than Verlinden, concludes that it "involved such a drastic change in the methods of doing business that the transition from one system to the other could be called, without exaggeration, 'the commercial revolution of the end of the thirteenth century.'"[101] As he describes it, "merchants ceased to visit the fairs and began to conduct all their business from the counting-house, using partners, factors, or correspondents to represent them in foreign parts."[102] Verlinden concurs: "from Bruges—the principal nodal point for the long-distance trade of the whole of north-west Europe—any kind of merchandise could be brought without interruption to all the towns in the north-west area."[103] In Chaucer's day, then, Saint-Denis was an old fair town, looking both back on a simpler economic time and forward to the emerging international banks. Even as he acknowledged change, Chaucer's interest in this tale was in continuities in these economic systems.

Some of the ways in which the *Shipman's Tale* links these economic concerns to sexual relationships have already been discussed, but let me draw them together here by focusing briefly on how the tale is constructed—largely as a series of well-drawn exchanges. The first and longest involves daun John and the wife, who meet apparently by chance early in the morning as the merchant counts his money.[104] The conversation becomes more serious after the monk seemingly inadvertently blurts out an inappropriate remark about his hosts' private affairs (VII, 107–09), but finds himself not reproved but

[99] See Félix Bourquelot, ed., *Étude sur les foires de Champagne: sur la nature, l'étendue et les règles du commerce qui s'y faisait aux XIIe, XIIIe et XIVe siècles*, Mémoires présentés par divers savants à l'Académie des Inscriptions et Belles-Lettres de l'Institut Impérial de France, 2nd series, vol. 5 part 2 (Paris: L'Imprimerie impériale, 1865), pp. 352–54. See de Roover, *Money, Banking and Credit*, p. 263.

[100] Verlinden, "Markets and Fairs," pp. 133–34.

[101] Verlinden, "Markets and Fairs," pp. 134 and 136; and de Roover, *Money, Banking and Credit*, pp. 11–12.

[102] De Roover, *Money, Banking and Credit*, p. 11.

[103] Verlinden, "Markets and Fairs," p. 137. It is also worth noting that similar changes were taking place in England where the fairs of the early fourteenth century were gradually replaced in importance by trade in urban centers, particularly London; see Britnell, *Britain and Ireland*, p. 324.

[104] Peter G. Beidler's has suggested that this scene may derive from the French *fabliau*, *Aloul*; see "Chaucer's French Accent: Gardens and Sex-Talk in the *Shipman's Tale*," in *Comic Provocations: Exposing the Corpus of Old French Fabliaux*, ed. Holly A. Crocker (New York: Palgrave Macmillan, 2006), pp. 149–69. This text, however, does not offer parallels for the details discussed here.

encouraged to continue. After the two exchange vows of silence, their talk grows both more intimate and more precise, as the wife explains that she needs a hundred francs. Both clearly understand the agreement they then reach: "he caughte hire by the flankes, / And hire embraceth harde, and kiste hire ofte" (VII, 202–03); and "forth she gooth as jolif as a pye" (VII, 209). Two more conversations follow. When the wife tells her husband to come down to dinner, he reflects on his profession and then explains his immediate plans (VII, 212–50), and after dinner, daun John asks the merchant for the loan (VII, 255–96). These exchanges lead to the consummation of the affair:

> The Sonday next the marchant was agon,
> To Seint-Denys ycomen is daun John,
> With crowne and berd al fressh and newe yshave.
> In al the hous ther nas so litel a knave,
> Ne no wight elles, that he nas ful fayn
> That my lord daun John was come agayn.
> And shortly to the point right for to gon,
> The faire wyf acorded with daun John
> That for thise hundred frankes he sholde al nyght
> Have hire in his armes bolt upright;
> And this acord parfourned was in dede.
> In myrthe al nyght a bisy lyf they lede
> Til it was day, that daun John wente his way,
> And bad the meynee "Farewel, have good day!"
> For noon of hem, ne no wight in the toun,
> Hath of daun John right no suspecioun. (VII, 307–22)

As clear as the deal seemed in the garden, it is presented again as an "acord" that is then fulfilled: a hundred francs buy daun John a night of pleasure. Also worth noting, however, is that it is his previous gifts that allow him the opportunity to make this new deal happen.

There is, then, a final exchange between the merchant and daun John in Paris, which, as already mentioned, both is and is not about business, before the concluding scene with the husband and wife, which again, as already noted, intertwines business and sex both in its puns and explicitly in its content. In this context I would draw attention to the wife's explanation of why she claims to have thought that daun John had intended the money for her:

> "For, God it woot, I wende, withouten doute,
> That he hadde yeve it me bycause of yow
> To doon therwith myn honour and my prow,
> For cosynage, and eek for beele cheere
> That he hath had ful ofte tymes heere." (VII, 406–10)

Her claim is that she considered it not a payment but a gift, one that although given to her was for both of them in return for hospitality daun John had received from them. Following her punning on "taille," she returns to this topic:

> "For by my trouthe, I have on myn array,
> And nat on wast, bistowed every deel;
> And for I have bistowed it so weel
> For youre honour, for Goddes sake, I seye,
> As be nat wrooth, but lat us laughe and pleye." (VII, 418–22)

These lines return us to the opening of the tale:

> A marchant whilom dwelled at Seint-Denys,
> That riche was, for which men helde hym wys.
> A wyf he hadde of excellent beautee;
> And compaignable and revelous was she,
> Which is a thyng that causeth more dispence
> Than worth is al the chiere and reverence
> That men hem doon at festes and at daunces.
> Swiche salutaciouns and contenaunces
> Passen as dooth a shadwe upon the wal;
> But wo is hym that payen moot for al!
> The sely housbonde, algate he moot paye,
> He moot us clothe, and he moot us arraye,
> Al for his owene worshipe richely,
> In which array we daunce jolily.
> And if that he noght may, par aventure,
> Or ellis list no swich dispence endure,
> But thynketh it is wasted and ylost,
> Thanne moot another payen for oure cost,
> Or lene us gold, and that is perilous. (VII, 1–19)

This passage stresses the danger of what may happen if a husband does not financially support his wife, as well as the futility of these expenses. The tale itself supports the first since it appears to be the wife's desire for money that leads to the affair. The second, however, is harder to judge. In contrast to the deal between daun John and the wife, which only appears to involve real money, the merchant's affairs, which will directly affect the way he and his wife live, have resulted in a substantial gain. Chaucer did not tell us how much the merchant figures out at the end of the tale, and yet his final words to his wife suggest compromise: "be namoore so large" (VII, 431). Similarly, daun John's future relationships with both wife and husband are opaque, and yet it is difficult to conclude that anyone has been hurt. One might even claim that if conventional morality is ignored, gifts and more generally the appearance of wealth have allowed all three to engage in pleasurable sex and the merchant and his wife to re-establish their wedding vows, while at the same time the merchant makes a substantial profit.

Why Chaucer considered this ambiguous tale appropriate for the Wife of Bath is discussed further in the next chapter. Here let me suggest that still under the sway of Boccaccio's three brilliant *novelle* he might well have thought he had made a strong statement. Business deals and sexual relationships are more similar than different, and marriage itself is where, in all their ambiguity, they meet.

3

Licisca's Outburst:
The Origin of the *Canterbury Tales*

By establishing that Chaucer relied heavily on three *novelle* from the Eighth Day of the *Decameron* in writing the *Shipman's Tale*, the previous chapter allows us to consider when and why he did so. The thesis of this chapter and, indeed, of this book is that his use of 8.1, 8.2, and 8.10 points to both the conceptual and temporal origin of the *Canterbury Tales*. From them Chaucer learned a new way to write, not to retell the stories of others, but rather to create new narratives from disparate places that would allow him to develop complex arguments. His tales, moreover, would stand in dialogue with each other just as Boccaccio's *novelle* develop a more complex discussion of the relationship between morality and class by telling the same story in differing economic settings. If this claim is correct, then it also seems likely that Chaucer would have paid attention to the *cornice*, Boccaccio's framing of the tales through their telling by the *brigata*, the party of young, noble Florentines fleeing the plague of 1348. Indeed, the three *novelle* of the Eighth Day are tied through Dioneo back to one of the most dramatic moments in the *Decameron*, Licisca's outburst at the start of the Sixth Day.[1] I argue in this chapter that this scene provided Chaucer with not only a powerful way to link a frame narrative to the tales in a collection but also the topics, gender and class, which he developed at the start of his literary pilgrimage. While he could have derived the idea of assigning stories to fictional narrators in order to shape their messages from many places including of course Boccaccio's use of Dioneo in the *Decameron*, Licisca's account of her friend's wedding night is a striking example of the kind of intertwining of a frame narrative into the themes of individual stories in a collection that becomes a defining feature of the *Canterbury Tales*. It is, then, specifically relevant for my argument that an early example of this strategy is the Miller's drunken insist-

---

[1] The idea for this chapter occurred to me while listening to R. W. Hanning's paper, "The Question of Women in the *Decameron*: A Boccaccian *disputatio ad utramque partem* (In Honor of Joan M. Ferrante)," delivered at the 46th International Congress on Medieval Studies, Kalamazoo (2011). I would like to thank Bob for sending me a copy of it. As mentioned in Chapter 1, in her discussion of "The Frame" (*S&A*, 1.1–22) Cooper discusses this scene as "an approximate parallel" for Chaucer's "interplay between the characters of his frame and their counterparts within the tales" (1.13).

ence that he be allowed to respond to the Knight. Chaucer's move beyond Boccaccio is to allow the Liciscas to keep talking, and so it supports my interpretation that prominent, indeed chief, among these voices is the Wife of Bath's.

Discussions of gender and class are widespread in medieval sources, and yet they are joined in Licisca's outburst in a way that allowed Chaucer to see beyond his thinking on women apparent in *Troilus and Criseyde* and the *Legend of Good Women*:[2] conflicts between the sexes need to be considered in the wider context of inequalities between the upper and lower classes. Licisca is sent back to the kitchen by another woman, who holds power over the company on this day, yet only after her explanation of the situation has seemingly won a male adherent. Chaucer addressed these class- and gender-conflicts in the pairings of the Knight and Miller, and the Man of Law and Wife of Bath, the sets of tales that vied to open the collection and so indicate, I argue, his thinking as he began his work. In each case his method reveals a further dependence on the *Decameron* because he turned to Boccaccio's collection to construct a story that would respond to one he had already written. These narrative strategies, ideas, and stories could, of course, have come from separate places. Their appearance, however, together in one work with a dramatic moment that holds them together provides another indication of the depth of Chaucer's dependence on the *Decameron*. Licisca showed Chaucer how to write.

Licisca

As the *brigata* gathers on the Sixth Day, they are disturbed by a commotion coming from the kitchen. When the combatants are fetched to explain the

---

[2] Among much important scholarship on Chaucer's writing on women, I would draw attention first to Jill Mann's *Feminizing Chaucer* (1991; repr. Cambridge: D. S. Brewer, 2002), from which I have learned much. In contrast to Mann, who sees related themes about women spanning Chaucer's career, I am arguing that the *Canterbury Tales* marks a new beginning in his thinking. I have also been influenced by Kara A. Doyle, partic-ularly by her essay "Criseyde Reading, Reading Crisyde," in *New Perspectives on Criseyde*, ed. Cindy L. Vitto and Marcia Smith Marzec (Ashville: Pegasus Press, 2004), pp. 75–110, but also by her comments, one of which was that my thesis perpetuates the "escape narrative" argued against by Susan Schibanoff in *Chaucer's Queer Poetics: Rereading the Dream Trio* (Toronto: University of Toronto Press, 2006), esp. pp. 3–14. While acknowledging that the French and Italian literary traditions prior to Chaucer overlap in significant ways and that there are almost certainly more continuities than differences in Chaucer's own career, I would still claim that Boccaccio's use of *fabliaux* (broadly defined) in a high literary context, the *Decameron*, and more specifically his one example of a lower-class voice, Licisca's, in this work had a profound effect on his writing.

quarrel, Licisca insists on speaking first, puts down Tindaro, and then turns to the queen:

> "Madonna, costui mi vuol far conoscere la moglie di Sicofante e, né più né meno come se io con lei usata non fossi, mi vuol dare a vedere che la notte prima che Sicofante giacque con lei messer Mazza entrasse in Monte Nero per forza e con ispargimento di sangue; e io dico che non è vero, anzi v'entrò pacefìcamente e con gran piacer di quei d'entro. E è ben sí bestia costui, che egli si crede troppo bene che le giovani sieno sí sciocche, che elle stieno a perdere il tempo loro stando alla bada del padre e de' fratelli, che delle sette volte le sei soprastanno tre o quarto anni più che non debbono a maritarle. Frate, bene starebbono se elle s'indugiasser tanto! Alla fé di Cristo, ché debbo sapere quello che io mi dico quando io giuro: io non ho vicina che pulcella ne sia andata a marito, e anche delle maritate so io ben quante e quali beffe elle fanno a' mariti: e questo pecorone mi vuol far conoscer le femine, come se io fossi nata ieri!" (6, *Introduzione*, 8–10)

> ("Madam, this fellow thinks he knows Sicofante's wife better than I do. I've known her for years, and yet he has the audacity to try and convince me that on the first night Sicofante slept with her, John Thomas had to force an entry into Castel Dusk, shedding blood in the process; but I say it is not true, on the contrary he made his way in with the greatest ease, to the general pleasure of the garrison. The man is such a natural idiot that he firmly believes young girls are foolish enough to squander their opportunities whilst they are waiting for their fathers and brothers to marry them off, which in nine cases out of ten takes them three or four years longer than it should. God in Heaven, they'd be in a pretty plight if they waited all that long! I swear to Christ (which means that I know what I'm saying) that not a single one of the girls from my district went to her husband a virgin; and as for the married ones, I could tell you a thing or two about the clever tricks they play upon their husbands. Yet this great oaf tries to teach me about women, as though I were born yesterday"; McWilliam, p. 445).

The debate here concerns the conflicts between men and women. The moment, however, also pits the upper-class story tellers against their servants. When Dioneo pronounces Licisca right, her triumphant speech to Tindaro is cut short by Elissa:

> e, se non fosse che la reina con un mal viso le 'mpose silenzio e comandolle che più parola né romor facesse se esser non volesse scopata e lei e Tindaro mandò via, niuna altra cosa avrebbero avuta a fare in tutto quel giorno che attendere a lei. (6, *Introduzione*, 15)

> (but for the fact that the queen sternly commanded her to be silent, told her not to shout or argue any more unless she wanted to be whipped, and sent her back to the kitchen with Tindaro, there would have been nothing else to do for the rest of the day but listen to her prattle; McWilliam, p. 446)

The scene, then, dramatically links issues of gender and class.

Given the widely divergent interpretations of the *Decameron* that one finds in contemporary scholarship,[3] it would seem rash, to say the least, to claim that Chaucer must have understood this scene in a particular way. For Giuseppe Mazzotta it is part of the linguistic play that Boccaccio valorizes throughout the work and reinforces Dioneo's place "on the side of transgression."[4] In contrast, Janet Levarie Smarr links it to the authorial interruption in the Introduction to the Fourth Day, which includes the incomplete story of the "goslings" (a poor Florentine widower has tried to protect his son from the heartbreak of love by shielding him from women only to find that once the boy sees them nature proves stronger than all his efforts), to argue that "Boccaccio's solution is neither monkishness nor licentiousness but marriage."[5] Whether one understands the *Decameron* as espousing libertine or socially conservative views on women, the scene, placed at its mid-point, is a powerful statement on the theme of female sexuality, a topic which runs through the *Decameron*, but which is addressed in the *cornice* by a lower-class woman only here.

What is striking, I would argue, about the outburst is the speed with which Licisca, as both a servant and a woman, is silenced even as her performance ripples out into the text. Although she and Tindaro might appear not even to have existed prior to their emergence from the kitchen, Boccaccio had introduced them at the beginning of the *Decameron* when Pampinea, the first queen, summons the women's four maidservants and the three servants of the men to assign them new responsibilities. All are named and indeed each is identified as serving a specific member of the *brigata*. Licisca, Filomena's maidservant, is to help Pampinea's servant, Misia, "full-time" (McWilliam, p. 21; "continue," 1, *Introduzione*, 100)[6] in the kitchens. Because the other two male servants will have more extensive responsibilities (Dioneo's Parmeno

---

3   Marilyn Migiel, for example, views her interpretation, which stresses the ways "the presumed benefits to women are compromised" in the work, as opposed to the "unified reading" advanced by Franco Fido and other "Italian males working within Italian critical traditions"; *The Rhetoric of the* Decameron (Toronto: University of Toronto Press, 2003), pp. 160–61. See also the range of essays in *Boccaccio and Feminist Criticism*, ed. Thomas C. Stillinger and F. Regina Psaki (Chapel Hill: Annali Italianistica, 2006); and Valerio Ferme, *Women, Enjoyment, and the Defense of Virtue in Boccaccio's* Decameron (New York: Palgrave MacMillan, 2015).

4   Giuseppe Mazzotta, *The World at Play in Boccaccio's* Decameron (Princeton: Princeton University Press, 1986), pp. 232–33, and 264–65. See also Teodolinda Barolini, "Le parole son femmine e i fatti sono maschi: Toward a Sexual Poetics of the *Decameron* (*Decameron* 2.9, 2.10, 5.10)," *Studi sul Boccaccio* 21 (1993), pp. 175–97, repr. in *Dante and the Origins of Italian Literary Culture* (New York: Fordham University Press, 2006), pp. 281–303.

5   Janet Levarie Smarr, *Boccaccio and Fiammetta: The Narrator as Lover* (Urbana: University of Illinois Press, 1986), p. 177.

6   Branca glosses this word, "di continuo, in permanenza"; p. 44, note 6.

will be the steward for the group and Panfilo's Sirisco will serve under him as "buyer and treasurer," [McWilliam, p. 21; "spenditore e tesoriere," 1, *Introduzione*, 99]), Tindaro is to look after all three gentlemen. Pampinea does not pause to see if these new arrangements are acceptable to her friends and social equals, much less those below her, instead ending with a final command to the servants:

> "E ciascun generalmente, per quanto egli avrà cara la nostra grazia, vogliamo e comandiamo che si guardi, dove che egli vada, onde che egli torni, che egli oda o vegga, niuna novella altra che lieta ci rechi di fuori." (1, *Introduzione*, 101)

> ("And unless they wish to incur our royal displeasure, we desire and command that each and every one of the servants should take good care, no matter what they should hear or observe in their comings and goings, to bring us no tidings of the world outside these walls unless they are tidings of happiness," McWilliam p. 21.)

While this command reinforces the Introduction's emphasis on escaping plague-ridden Florence, it may also look forward specifically to the Introduction to the Sixth Day.

An attentive reader connecting the two moments would be struck by at least two questions. Who has power here? A female ruler establishes a new order for the servants, and yet it is clearly one in which the men dominate: Parmeno is placed in control of the household and Misia and Licisca are to cook what Sirisco buys for them. This arrangement, moreover, explains Licisca's presence in the kitchen, but leaves Tindaro's place there ambiguous. He is not put in a position of power over the women and so there may well be boundaries that he should not cross. A second question, however, raises a topic even more central to the work: is Sicofante's wedding night news ("novella"), and if so is it happy ("lieta")?[7] What is, in other words, the relationship of the pleasurable phantasy world of the *brigata* to the real world they have left behind?

As provocative as these questions are, Boccaccio did little more with the servants as named individuals to explore them. In the Introduction, following

---

[7] *Novella* is not defined in TLIO. It is used in the sense of "a story" in *Il Novellino*, written in the thirteenth century; see for example *novelle* 21 and 89, as well as the title given to the collection of 85 *novelle*, many of which correspond to those in *Il Novellino*, found in Florence, Biblioteca nazionale, Panciatichiano-Palatino 32: "libro di novelle e di bel parlar gentile"; see Joseph P. Consoli, ed., The Novellino *or* One Hundred Ancient Tales*: An Edition and Translation based on the 1525 Gualteruzzi editio princeps*, Garland Library of Medieval Literature 105A (New York: Garland, 1997), pp. xi–xii, 42–43, and 116–17. See also the Introduzione in the edition of Quondam, Fiorilla and Alfano, esp. pp. 5–22, although the use of *novella* considered here is not discussed.

Pampinea's instructions, the aristocratic men and women return to the house after a stroll in the gardens "to find that Parmeno had made a zealous beginning to his duties" (McWilliam, p. 22; "trovarono Parmeno studiosamente aver dato principio al suo uficio," 1, *Introduzione*, 104) by preparing an elegant meal; and they are then seated where "Parmeno had assigned them" (McWilliam, p. 22; "secondo il giudicio di Parmeno," 1, *Introduzione*, 104). Although he is identified twice here, Parmeno's name then drops from the text even in the Introduction to the Sixth Day when, as he is sent to fetch Licisca and Tindaro, he is called "il siniscalco" (6, *Introduzione*, 5). Boccaccio again toys with the theme in the Introduction to the Seventh Day, whose stories (as we shall see further in a moment) are linked in theme to Licisca's outburst, when the scene shifts to the *Valle delle Donne*:

> Ogni stella era già delle parti d'oriente fuggita, se non quella sola la qual noi chiamiamo Lucifero che ancora luceva nella biancheggiante aurora, quando il siniscalco levatosi con una gran salmeria n'andò nella Valle delle Donne per quivi disporre ogni cosa secundo l'ordine e il comandamento avuto dal suo signore. (7, *Introduzione*, 2)

> (Every star had vanished from the eastern heavens, excepting that alone which we call Lucifer, which was still glowing in the whitening dawn, when the steward arose and made his way with a large baggage-train to the Valley of the Ladies, there to arrange everything in accordance with his master's orders and instructions; McWilliam, p. 484.)

Both the morning-star and the valley are given proper names, and yet, even as he works tirelessly to see to the *brigata*'s comfort, Parmeno remains simply the steward. It is then probably not mere coincidence that he appears without a name for a final time in the Conclusion of the work: "e come il nuovo giorno apparve, levati, avendo già il siniscalco via ogni lor cosa mandata" (10, *Conclusione*, 16; "next morning they arose at the crack of dawn, by which time all their baggage had been sent on ahead by the steward," McWilliam, p. 797). Similarly, Tindaro is named twice more: in the Conclusion to the Sixth Day Dioneo sends him to get his "cornamusa" (6, *Conclusione*, 48) so Dioneo can provide music for dancing, and in the Conclusion to the Seventh Day the *brigata* again dances "quando al suono della cornamusa di Tindaro e quando d'altri suon carolando" (7, *Conclusione*, 8; "accompanied sometimes by Tindaro on the bagpipe and sometimes by the music of other instruments," cf. McWilliam p. 549). He too blends back into the harmony of the *brigata*'s existence. The point seems to be that from the perspective of class conflict, Licisca's outburst happens only once and then is quickly contained.

As already noted in Chapter 2, issues related to gender are pervasive throughout the *Decameron*, but the immediate context of Licisca's outburst silences her suggestion that women do, and by implication should, have control of their sexuality. The queen of the day, Elissa, immediately turns the problem of judging Licisca's claim over to Dioneo, who rather than waiting as he has been asked to the end of the day to pronounce "the last word" (McWilliam, p. 445; "sentenzia finale," 6, *Introduzione*, 12) on the subject, responds immediately. Even though his verdict seems at first to support Licisca, the situation becomes more complex when in the Conclusion to the Sixth Day Elissa appoints him the next ruler and he in turn recalls Licisca in establishing the theme for their stories:

> "Valorose donne, in diverse maniere ci s'è della umana industria e de' casi varii ragionato tanto, che, se donna Licisca non fosse poco avanti qui venuta, la quale con le sue parole m'ha trovata materia a' futuri ragionamenti di domane, io dubito che io non avessi gran pezza penato a trovar tema da ragionare. Ella, come voi udiste, disse che vicina non aveva che pulcella ne fosse andata a marito e sogiunse che ben sapeva quante e quali beffe le maritate ancora facessero a' mariti. Ma lasciando stare la prima parte, che è opera fanciullesca, reputo che la seconda debbia esser piacevole a ragionarne, e perciò voglio che domane si dica, poi che donna Licisca data ce n'ha cagione, *delle beffe le quali o per amore o per salvamento di loro le donne hanno già fatte a' lor mariti, senza essersene essi o avveduti o no.*" (6, *Conclusione*, 4–6)

> ('Worthy ladies, our discussions have ranged so widely over the field of human endeavor, and touched upon such a variety of incidents, that if Mistress Licisca had not come here a short while ago and said something which offered me a subject for our deliberations on the morrow, I suspect I should have had a hard job to find a suitable theme. As you will have heard, she told us that none of the girls in her neighbourhood had gone to her husband a virgin; and she added that she knew all about the many clever tricks played by married women on their husbands. But leaving aside the first part, which even a child could have told you, I reckon that the second would make an agreeable subject for discussion; and hence taking our cue from Mistress Licisca, I should like us to talk tomorrow about *the tricks which, either in the cause of love or for motives of self-preservation, women have played upon their husbands, irrespective of whether or not they were found out,*" McWilliam, p. 478).

While this speech recalls much of what Licisca has said, there are several changes that suggest its tone, indicated by the repeated reference to her as a "donna," is not one of respect.[8]

Absent from Dioneo's remarks are Licisca's comments that relate sex before marriage to a rebellion against the control men exert over women. As

---

8   Branca comments on the phrase, "con rispetto caricaturato come nella VI 4,9 n."; p. 775, note 2.

Robert Hanning noted in a paper delivered at Kalamazoo in 2011,[9] Licisca's "mini-allegory of the sex-act initiating marriage" replaces the male perspective of "a violent, bloodletting invasion" with a female one depicting a "royal entry in which messer Mazza is welcomed by the inhabitants," making the experience "much less a paradigmatic instance of male power imposed on, or aggression against, the female body." In this context her noting that fathers and brothers take three to four years longer than they should to arrange marriages for the women under their charge further challenges this system. Her outrage at Tindaro expresses the frustration of women controlled by men.

In contrast Dioneo transforms this moral outrage into moral superiority. In his mouth her appeal to her own experience ("io non ho vicina che pulcella ne sia andata a marito") becomes an occasion to mock the morals of lower class women ("disse che vicina non aveva che pulcella ne fosse andata a marito"), a fact so banal that it is an "opera fanciullesca," not worthy of further discussion. Moreover, by separating this claim from the statement that married women play tricks ("beffe") on their husbands, he replaces Licisca's ongoing rebellion with the suggestion that all women after marriage (when there should be no need to seek pleasure elsewhere) prove deceitful. The question as he frames it is whether the "valorose donne," the women of the *brigata*, are really any different from "donna Licisca." Moreover, when some of the women ("alcuna delle donne," 6, *Conclusione*, 7) object to using the tricks women play on their husbands as the topic for the day, Dioneo refuses to relent, offering several arguments that all return to a core theme of the *Decameron*: because the women are themselves all chaste, they cannot be faulted for telling morally questionable stories.[10] While Boccaccio might have intended Licisca's outburst to be liberating for women, here Dioneo appropriates her words for his own end, a defense of artistic freedom that, like chastity, must be imposed on women.

Boccaccio carried Licisca's challenge to male authority one step further by linking it to events connected with the *Valle delle Donne*, and yet even here the effect, however provocative the scene itself may be, is to silence her voice. After the women have agreed to his plan and Dioneo has given the members of the *brigata* permission to do what they please until dinner, Elissa takes

---

[9] The following remarks draw on ideas presented by Professor Hanning; see note 1 above.

[10] One of Dioneo's arguments seems both manipulative and insulting: "'e a dirvi il vero, chi sapesse che voi vi cessaste da queste ciance ragionare alcuna volta forse suspicherebbe che voi in ciò foste colpevoli, e per ciò ragionare non ne voleste'" (6, *Conclusione*, 13; "'but the real point is this, that if anyone were to discover that you had refrained at any time from discussing these little peccadilloes, he might well suspect that you had a guilty conscience about them, and that this was why you were so reluctant to talk about them,'" McWilliam p. 479). Similar is the Pardoner's claim that sinners should not offer to his relics; the *Pardoner's Prologue*, VI, 377–88, and see the note for other possible sources of this idea.

her female friends to a place nearby unknown to the others; they do not tell the men, who are playing dice, where they are going. Boccaccio's elaborate description of the valley is itself, as critics have noted,[11] distinctly feminine, and the women's activity more than mildly suggestive: after making certain that no one can observe them, they undress ("spogliarono") and swim in the lake, whose water "concealed their chaste white bodies no better than a thin sheet of glass would conceal a pink rose" (McWilliam, p. 481; "non altramenti li lor corpi candidi nascondeva che farebbe una vermiglia rosa un sottil vetro," 6, *Conclusione*, 30). Their actions are then linked back to the topic of the next day's stories, and so to Licisca's outburst, when on their return Pampinea tells Dioneo, "'oggi vi pure abbiam noi ingannati'" (6, *Conclusione*, 33; "we have stolen a march upon you today," McWilliam, p. 481).[12] Dioneo responds: "'e come?...cominciate voi prima a far de' fatti che a dir delle parole?'" (6, *Conclusione*, 34; "'What?...Do you mean to say you have begun to do these things even before you talk about them?'" McWilliam, p. 481). The rebellion, however, is immediately contained. Pampinea answers in the affirmative, but prefaces this with "signor nostro" (6, *Conclusione*, 35; "your majesty," McWilliam, p. 481); the men immediately travel to the valley, where they too swim in the lake; and Dioneo orders the next day's stories to be told there. While scholars disagree on whether these *novelle* support or undercut the idea of women's authority,[13] there is very little that suggests the women carry their rebellion further. Some of them surmise from the song that Filomena sings at the end of the day that she is involved in "some new and exciting love" (McWilliam, p. 550; "nuovo e piacevole amore," 7, *Conclusione*, 15), but it is never confirmed. Instead, because attention then turns to Filomena's decision to suspend the storytelling for Friday and Saturday so all can "meditate upon the things that were done on those two days for the salvation of our souls" (McWilliam, p. 550; "a memoria riducendoci che in cosí fatti giorni per la salute delle nostre anime adivenne," 7, *Conclusione*, 17), the remark seems as likely to call attention to the women's sinful nature, whatever their specific sins may be. In any case the next queen, Lauretta, decides not to reverse Dioneo's topic by commanding stories told about the tricks played on wives by their husbands, but instead broadens it to "the tricks that people in general, men and women alike, are forever playing upon one

---

[11] See in particular, Thomas C. Stillinger, "The Language of Gardens: Boccaccio's 'Valle delle Donne,'" originally published in *Traditio* 29 (1983), pp. 301–21, and repr. in *Boccaccio and Feminist Criticism*, ed. Stillinger and F. Regina Psaki (Chapel Hill: Annali d'italianistica, Studi e testi 8, 2006), pp. 105–27. Neal McTighe has connected the Valley to Kristeva's concept of a pre-symbolic space where meaning is generated; "Generating Feminine Discourse in Boccaccio's *Decameron*: The 'Valle delle Donne' as Julia Kristeva's Chora," *Romance Notes* 47 (2006), pp. 41–48.

[12] More literally, "today we too have deceived you"; Branca comments that the unusual syntax is more common in Boccaccio's time; p. 781, note 4.

[13] See, for example, McTighe, "Generating," and Migiel, *Retoric*, pp. 76–80.

another" (McWilliam, p. 548; "di quelle beffe che tutto il giorno o donna a uomo o uomo a donna o l'uno uomo all'altro si fanno," 7, *Conclusione*, 4).[14] Licisca's challenge to male authority has become no more than the occasion to tell amusing stories.

Licisca as Source

Since Chaucer did not retell the story of Sicofante's wife, place in his frame an incident in which servants are called before their masters to be reprimanded, nor echo any of Boccaccio's specific language from the Introduction to the Sixth Day, a conventional argument about a source relationship is not possible here.[15] If, however, one considers both the framing and the content of two sets of tales—the one originally written for the Wife of Bath (placed first here because I will argue Chaucer focused initially on her), the *Shipman's Tale*, and the first assigned to the Man of Law, *Melibee*, as well as the *Knight's Tale* and the *Miller's Tale*—a pattern emerges that is complex enough to point to Licisca's outburst as the main source for Chaucer's thinking as he developed his initial ideas for the *Canterbury Tales*.

Recognizing that Licisca's story of her friend's wedding night is similar to the *novelle* told by upper-class members of the *brigata* and different because of its narrator, Chaucer started (perhaps even before he settled on the idea of a pilgrimage to Canterbury) by pairing tellers whose social status would place their views in conflict: a Man of Law would oppose a Wife of Bath and a Knight a Miller. His decision, as can be seen in the *Introduction to the Man of Law's Tale*,[16] to begin with the first pair indicates that the opposing views of men and women would, as one would expect from the cause of Licisca's outburst, be his opening topic. With Prudence, its wise yet submissive female character, the already-written *Melibee* appeared an appropriate story for the Man of Law, one that would set up the Wife of Bath's response about a very different kind of woman, the merchant's wife in the *Shipman's Tale*, who had been drawn from the *Decameron* 8.10. At the same time, Chaucer began exploring the second issue, class, in the same way, opposing the drafted *Knight's Tale*, which affirms a social hierarchy founded on the divine order of the universe, to the *Miller's Tale*, again constructed from Boccaccio's collection precisely to challenge the Knight's conservative views. Learning ulti-

---

[14] While not literal, the translation renders the meaning accurately.
[15] See Chapter 1 for discussion of the problems surrounding this issue.
[16] I agree, therefore, with Carleton Brown, who argued that Chaucer planned to begin the tale-telling with the Man of Law; "The Man of Law's Head-link and the Prologue of the *Canterbury Tales*," *Studies in Philology* 34 (1937), pp. 8–35. I do not of course agree with his belief that the *fabliaux* are later (p. 28).

mately from Licisca, Chaucer investigated how class broadens the discussion of gender.

Two details,[17] which are in turn both related to my larger argument about Licisca's significance, in the *Introduction to the Man of Law's Tale*, support the claim that at one point Chaucer planned to open the storytelling with not the Knight and the Miller but rather the Man of Law and the Wife of Bath: the Host sets the day and time and the Man of Law reviews Chaucer's own works. As it stands, this Introduction is too abrupt to begin a frame narrative for an entire collection:

> Oure Hooste saugh wel that the brighte sonne
> The ark of his artificial day hath ronne
> The ferthe part, and half an houre and moore,
> And though he were nat depe ystert in loore,
> He wiste it was the eightetethe day
> Of Aprill, that is messager to May;
> And saugh wel that the shadwe of every tree
> Was as in lengthe the same quantitee
> That was the body erect that caused it.
> And therfore by the shadwe he took his wit
> That Phebus, which that shoon so clere and brighte,
> Degrees was five and fourty clombe on highte,
> And for that day, as in that latitude,
> It was ten of the clokke, he gan conclude,
> And sodeynly he plighte his hors aboute. (II, 1–15)

It is not clear, for example, who "oure Hooste" is or when, as we learn later, the Man of Law "submytted" to his "juggement" (II, 35–36); Chaucer would have had to fill in these and other details most likely before, but perhaps after, the stories themselves began. The elaborate use, however, of Nicholas of Lynn's *Kalendarium*, completed in 1386,[18] to establish that it is precisely ten o'clock on 18 April suggests that the moment marks an important stage in the collection. Indeed, Chaucer might have recalled the Introduction to the First Day of the *Decameron*, where Boccaccio not only set the year, 1348, but specified that the women and men meet on a Tuesday (1, *Introduzione*, 49), leave Florence at dawn on the following day (1, *Introduzione*, 89), and then begin their storytelling shortly after nones ("nona," 1, *Introduzione*, 109; the ninth hour after dawn and part of the Divine Office, so corresponding to 3 pm), when Pampinea awakes them from a rest. In any case the Host's remarks

---

17 Both are discussed by Brown, "Man of Law," p. 25, who adds a third, the exhortation against idleness, which he shows is closely paralleled near the beginning of the *Roman de la Rose*.

18 *The Kalendarium of Nicholas of Lynn*, ed. Sigmund Eisner (Athens: University of Georgia Press, 1980); for a discussion of Chaucer's use of this work, see pp. 29–34.

seem even more likely to precede the first story since Chaucer introduced his last story, the Parson's,[19] in a similar way:

> By that the Maunciple hadde his tale al ended,
> The sonne fro the south lyne was descended
> So lowe that he nas nat, to my sighte,
> Degreës nyne and twenty as in highte.
> Foure of the clokke it was tho, as I gesse,
> For ellevene foot, or litel moore or lesse,
> My shadwe was at thilke tyme, as there,
> Of swiche feet as my lengthe parted were
> In sixe feet equal of proporcioun. (X, 1–9)

Again using the *Kalendarium*, the narrator calculates from the length of a shadow that it is four o'clock. Taken together, these passages appear to mark his opening and closing stories of the *Canterbury Tales*.

A discrepancy, however, in these temporal settings is also worth considering since it, when related to the *General Prologue*, points to Chaucer's reordering of the opening of the *Canterbury Tales*. A shadow is, at this latitude, eleven times one-sixth of the height of an object that casts it, as specified in the *Parson's Prologue*, on either 16 or 17 April,[20] a day or two before the date in the *Introduction to the Man of Law's Tale*. While it is possible that Chaucer did not expect his audience to recognize this problem, it shows instead, I would argue, that by the time he composed the less specific temporal setting of the opening lines of the *General Prologue* ("the yonge sonne / Hath in the Ram his half cours yronne"; I, 7–8; and so sometime before 11 April),[21] he had already decided that the Knight and the Miller would begin the stories, rendering the opening of the *Introduction to the Man of Law's Tale* unnecessary, and so slated to be cancelled. [22] In contrast, it is difficult to imagine that he would specify 18 April as the date of the *Introduction to the Man of Law's Tale* after writing the *General Prologue*.

The temporal setting in the *Introduction* is, moreover, linked to Licisca's outburst since it leads the Host to digress on the evils of wasting time, which he concludes by comparing it to a woman's loss of her virginity. Like the

---

[19] The Host's comment, "'Lordynges everichoon, / Now lakketh us no tales mo than oon'" (X, 15–16), establishes the *Parson's Tale* as the last.

[20] I follow Siegfried Wenzel's note in the *Riverside Chaucer*, ed. Benson, p. 955; Eisner writes that "the passage can apply only to 17 April or earlier"; *Kalendarium*, ed. Eisner, p. 33.

[21] See Benson's note in the *Riverside Chaucer*, ed. Benson, p. 799.

[22] This explanation does not remove the problem that, since the sun passed through Aries from 12 March to 11 April, even assuming the phrase "hath in the Ram his half cours yronne" refers to the second half of the sun's course, the journey to Canterbury (some sixty miles) would have taken at least five days.

stream "that turneth nevere agayn" (II, 23), but unlike goods that "may recovered be" (II, 27), time,

> "...wol nat come agayn, withouten drede,
> Namoore than wole Malkynes maydenhede,
> Whan she hath lost it in hir wantownesse." (II, 29–31)

As Patricia J. Eberle notes, the reference to "Malkynes maydenhede" joins "several proverbial elements":

> Malkin, a diminutive of Maud (ME Malde, Lat. Matilda), was often used for a woman of the lower classes (NPT VII.3384) or of loose morals (MED *s.v. malkin*). In this sense, Malkin's maidenhead, as used in PPA 1.157–58, is proverbial for something 'no man desirith' (see Whiting M511). Here, however, the reference is to the proverb that virginity, once lost, cannot be recovered (Whiting, M20, citing Conf. Aman. 5.5646–49 and 5.6208–11).[23]

Like Dioneo, the Host here suggests that lower-class women do not value virginity, pronouncing a first male view on Licisca's topic.

The Man of Law's review of Chaucer's works, which in itself suggests an opening by recalling a similar list in the *Prologue* to the *Legend of Good Women* (F 417–30) and anticipating one in the *Retraction* (X, 1085–88), introduces a different kind of question about chronology because it leads to references to the stories "Canacee" (II, 78) and "Tyro Appollonius" (II, 81), both included in the *Confessio Amantis*, completed in 1390.[24] Even if, however, these references are to Gower's collection (as I believe they are and discuss in more detail in Chapter 5),[25] they need not date the *Introduction to the Man of Law's Tale* to a period after Chaucer's initial work on the *Canterbury Tales*. While one might want to argue that he conceived of his collection only following the completion of Gower's,[26] I would favor the view articulated by Eberle that, because the two poets had been on friendly terms since at least 1378, "Chaucer would not have needed to wait until the first complete version of the *Confessio* was issued to know about the planned inclusion of Apollonius," its final work, or indeed Canace. In any case by identifying Chaucer's subject as "loveris" (II, 53), who may be either male or female,[27]

---

[23] *Riverside Chaucer*, ed. Benson, p. 854.

[24] I would like to thank Will Robins for pointing out this problem to me.

[25] Writing in the notes to the *Riverside Chaucer*, ed. Benson, Eberle casts some doubt on a direct relationship by commenting that both stories were available in other versions" (p. 856). Since the two appear in the *Confessio Amantis*, a reference to Gower seems more likely.

[26] Derek Pearsall notes that "the chief basis" for assigning the beginning of the *Canterbury Tales* to 1387 "is that it is the first year when he is not known to have been engaged on another major work"; *Life*, p. 227.

[27] See the *MED, s.v.*

the Man of Law points to the relationship between men and women as central to Chaucer's work:

> "But natheless, certeyn,
> I kan right now no thrifty tale seyn
> That Chaucer, thogh he kan but lewedly
> On metres and on rymyng craftily,
> Hath seyd hem in swich Englissh as he kan
> Of olde tyme, as knoweth many a man;
> And if he have noght seyd hem, leve brother,
> In o book, he hath seyd hem in another.
> For he hath toold of loveris up and doun
> Mo than Ovide made of mencioun
> In his Episteles, that been ful olde." (II, 45–55)

The comparison to Ovid's *Heroides*, fifteen letters by women to their male lovers, emphasizes this subject as does his following reference to the *Book of the Duchess*, considered Chaucer's first major poem, as "of Ceys and Alcione" (II, 57): the story of the Black Knight's grief is subsumed into the opening story, which focuses instead on a wife's grief for her dead husband. Similarly, placing Cupid in the title of the work, "the Seintes Legende of Cupide" (II, 61), that we conventionally call the *Legend of Good Women*, calls more attention to Chaucer as a love poet than does his other way of referring to this collection, "the book of the XXV. Ladies" (X, 1085), found in the *Retraction*. The following list allows him to name sixteen women (nine of whom have stories that appear in *Legend of Good Women*) and three "false" men, "Enee," "Demophon," and "Jason" (the "dreynte Leandre" is the only exception). The overall impression of this review, summed up in a last line that is addressed to women as a group, is that Chaucer has written favorably about them: "'Youre wifhod he comendeth with the beste!'" (II, 76). While the Man of Law asserts there is nothing left to say on this subject, the review provides the context for a new approach, which will include the voice of a lower class woman who will challenge male assumptions about female virtue.

The choice of *Melibee* for the Man of Law also shows Licisca's influence since the story concerns a strong, female character, Prudence, yet one who remains completely subservient to her husband and so invites a response from a female teller. Written before Chaucer began work on the *Canterbury Tales* and then assigned to the Man of Law,[28] *Melibee* may have appeared an

---

[28] See Cooper, *Canterbury Tales*, pp. 311–12, who notes that the omission of a comment in Chaucer's source, which laments the fate of a land ruled by a child and so which "would hardly have been tactful" from "1372, if not earlier," dates the translation to before the *Canterbury Tales* period. She also links additions about a "wilde hert" to Richard's assumption a "badge of the white hart" in 1390. I would suggest that this date indicates when he revised the work for Fragment VII, the "Literary Fragment." The Man of Law's comment that he will "speke in prose" (II, 96) has led many to

appropriate way to begin the discussion because it is itself a debate between a husband and a wife, yet one in which the expected gender roles are reversed. This reversal occurs near the work's beginning after Melibee has returned home to find his wife has been beaten and his daughter wounded "with fyve mortal woundes" (II, 971):

> This noble wyf Prudence remembred hire upon the sentence of Ovide, in his book that cleped is the Remedie of Love, where as he seith,/ "He is a fool that destourbeth the mooder to wepen in the deeth of hire child til she have wept hir fille as for a certein tyme,/ and thanne shal man doon his diligence with amyable wordes hire to reconforte, and preyen hire of hir wepyng for to stynte." (VII, 976–78)

Here the wife turns to Ovid, a reference that fits in smoothly with the review of Chaucer's works in the *Introduction*, to find how a man should deal with a grief-stricken woman—though in her case how she should deal with her husband. This pattern holds throughout the rest of the work, in which Prudence is the voice of reason and moral authority.[29] While she instructs Melibee, however, she remains subservient to him, addressing him, for example, in a passage immediately following the one just quoted, "'Allas, my lord'" (VII, 980). Even in the end as Melibee prepares to follow her advice and forgive his enemies, the story implies that her wisdom comes from God, whom he thanks for having given him such a wife:

> Whanne Melibee hadde herd the grete skiles and resouns of dame Prudence, and hire wise informaciouns and techynges, / his herte gan enclyne to the wil of his wif, considerynge hir trewe entente, / and conformed hym anon and assented fully to werken after hir conseil, / and thonked God, of whom procedeth al vertu and alle goodnesse, that hym sente a wyf of so greet discrecioun. (VII, 1870–73)

In this patriarchal world Prudence is not thanked and does not speak again.[30]

The *Shipman's Tale*, which was written for the Wife of Bath,[31] extends Licisca's challenge to male authority by using a woman in control of her own

---

the conclusion that *Melibee* would follow; see Brown, "Man of Law's Head-link," pp. 17–19, for other reasons.

[29] Cooper calls attention to "a number of oddities" that Chaucer inherited from his source, the most surprising of which is the suggestion that one should make peace with "the flessh, the feend, and the world" (VII, 1421) and yet she comments that "it is easy to overstate the case for allegory"; *Canterbury Tales*, p. 317.

[30] For an opposing interpretation of this passage, see Mann, *Feminizing*, p. 98.

[31] In the cancelled *Epilogue of the Man of Law's Tale*, the pilgrim insisting on telling the next tale comments, "'My joly body schal a tale telle'" (II, 1185), which sets up the wife's offer to her husband at the end of the *Shipman's Tale*: "'Ye shal my joly body have to wedde'" (VII, 423). This echo, combined with other evidence (see Cooper, *Canterbury Tales*, p. 278), establishes that Chaucer originally intended the Wife of Bath to respond to the Man of Law.

sexuality to point to the economic basis of marriage. Here slightly more than a quarter of the story (89–208) is devoted to the negotiations of the wife of a merchant with one of his close friends, a monk, to exchange sex for one hundred francs. Unlike Boccaccio's three *novelle*, however, which all end, as one would expect in stories about the "lover's gift regained," by focusing on the male lover's success at the expense of the woman, Chaucer concluded with an argument between the husband and wife, which appropriately takes place in bed. As in *Melibee*, the husband gets the last word, and yet here it is no more than an admonition to his wife, and, as the audience knows, means more than he thinks:

> "Now wyf," he seyde, "and I foryeve it thee;
> But, by thy lyf, ne be namoore so large.
> Keep bet thy good, this yeve I thee in charge." (VII, 430–32)[32]

The merchant both forgives the return of the hundred francs and acknowledges that it was hers because he asks her to be more thrifty in the future. Aware of the entire story, however, the audience may hear in "good" not just "wealth" but also "virtue,"[33] which reduces him to asking his wife, even as he does not realize it, to be more faithful. Rather than making him look weak, however, this remark recalls the wife's claim that she has in fact spent the money well, on clothes for his "honour" (VII, 418–22), which echoes the remarks at the opening of the tale about the expense, benefits, and dangers of having a beautiful wife (VII, 3–19). The theme of a woman's use of her goods, including clothing, for economic advantage appears, as we have seen in Chapter 2, prominently in 8.10, where a courtesan in Palermo convinces a Florentine merchant of her wealth through, in part, an elaborate display of her wealth. By associating this theme, however, not with the lovers but with the husband and wife, Chaucer investigated the economics of marriage summed up in the punning on "wedde" (VII, 423) near the tale's end.

Licisca's rebellion remains most clear in the tale's final couplet. After the husband's request, the teller, originally the Wife of Bath, turns to the audience:

---

[32] The variant readings *my* and *oure* in line 432 call attention to the central economic issue of the tale: to whom did the "hundred frankes" belong? "Thy," the reading of Hengwrt and so presumably what Chaucer wrote, is a surprising acknowledgement by the merchant that they were, indeed, the wife's. As such they would correspond to the money that Jancofiore controls in 8.10 and would support a radical reading of the tale: women need control over their money. The reading of Ellesmere, "oure," weakens this statement, but at least implies that money in marriage should be shared. The "my" of other manuscripts (see *The Text of the* Canterbury Tales *Studied on the Basis of All Known Manuscripts*, John M. Manly and Edith Rickert, 8 vols. (Chicago: University of Chicago Press, 1940), 4/2.123) returns to the situation depicted in the tale and in line with the assumptions Chaucer sought to challenge: the merchant controls all the finances.

[33] *MED, s.v.*, meanings 11 and 1.

> Thus endeth my tale, and God us sende
> Taillynge ynough unto oure lyves ende. Amen. (VII, 433–34)

This mock prayer, with its accompanying "Amen" in the Ellesmere manuscript, parodies the end of *Melibee*, where the main character pardons his enemies and then explains his reason:

> "Wherfore I receyve yow to my grace/ and foryeve yow outrely alle the offenses, injuries, and wronges that ye have doon agayn me and myne,/ to this effect and to this ende, that God of his endelees mercy/ wole at the tyme of oure diynge foryeven us oure giltes that we han trespassed to hym in this wrecched world./ For doutelees, if we be sory and repentant of the synnes and giltes which we han trespassed in the sighte of oure Lord God,/ he is so free and so merciable/ that he wole foryeven us oure giltes/ and bryngen us to the blisse that nevere hath ende." Amen. (VII, 1881–87)

Risking the loss of eternal salvation, the teller of the *Shipman's Tale* endorses the life of the courtesan where sex and money are freely, if under different names, exchanged.

For his second pair, the Knight and the Miller, Chaucer again had an already-written story, "al the love of Palamon and Arcite" (*Legend of Good Women*, F 420), that would open a discussion of the outburst's other theme, class, and he turned once more, as the following chapter shows in more detail, to the *Decameron* for a response that would challenge the Knight's aristocratic perspective. By adding a philosophical underpinning drawn from the *Consolation of Philosophy*, he had used Boccaccio's *Teseida* to reflect profoundly on the order of the universe.[34] Told by the Knight, however, it also becomes a conservative defense of the existing social hierarchy in which Theseus's authority simply reflects the divine plan. In this context Arcite's rise to prominence, for example, after his return to Athens takes on added significance. Dressed as "a povre laborer" (I, 1409), he performs menial tasks ("to drugge and drawe," I, 1416) in Emily's household without being recognized even as all appreciate his abilities:

> A yeer or two he was in this servyse,
> Page of the chambre of Emelye the brighte,
> And Philostrate he seyde that he highte.
> But half so wel biloved a man as he
> Ne was ther nevere in court of his degree;
> He was so gentil of condicioun
> That thurghout al the court was his renoun.
> They seyden that it were a charitee

---

[34] This theme has been discussed in many places; let me note here Robert W. Hanning, "'The Struggle between Noble Designs and Chaos': The Literary Tradition of Chaucer's Knight's Tale," *Literary Review* 23 (1980), pp. 519–41.

That Theseus wolde enhauncen his degree,
And putten hym in worshipful servyse,
Ther as he myghte his vertu excercise. (I, 1426–36)

Chaucer here expanded Boccaccio's much simpler statement that because Arcita serves Teseo and his court so well, Teseo makes him "in tutto suo sergiente" ("his sergeant in charge of everything")[35] into a reflection on the inherent qualities of the upper class,[36] a theme Chaucer then emphasized at the start of the *Prologue to the Miller's Tale*:

Whan that the Knyght had thus his tale ytoold,
In al the route nas ther yong ne oold
That he ne seyde it was a noble storie
And worthy for to drawen to memorie,
And namely the gentils everichon. (I, 3109–13)

The aristocratic bias of the story reflects the views of aristocrats.

The *Miller's Tale* itself challenges the assumptions about class implied in the *Knight's Tale* by depicting a society in which social hierarchies seem not to matter and by mocking the Knight's certainties about divine and human order. Its opening lines confuse such distinctions by introducing John, "a riche gnof" (I, 3187), who has economic power over his social superior, Nicholas, "a poure scoler" (I, 3190), who boards and lodges with him. Similarly, at the tale's end the neighbors, who rush in to see John after he has fallen, are "bothe smale and grete" (I, 3826), which here seems to specify not lower- and upper-class but "everyone."[37] A distinction between groups appears briefly at the conclusion of the opening description of Alison when the Miller remarks that someone of lower status can only attain by marriage what a lord can simply do:

She was a prymerole, a piggesnye,
For any lord to leggen in his bedde,
Or yet for any good yeman to wedde. (I, 3268–70)

This comment, however, hardly fits the tale since Nicholas is less a lord than John a "good yeman." Indeed, it seems no more than a joke at, of course, the woman's expense, except that it calls attention by contrast to Alison's more active role in the story. Similarly, differences in class could explain why by cuckolding and then, with Alison, silencing John at the tale's end, Nicholas has, as J. A. W. Bennett puts it, "the last laugh": here we may have, to quote

---

[35] Quoted from *S&A*, 2.151.
[36] In keeping with the proper progression of a knight's development, Theseus makes Arcite a "squier" (I, 1440), a further step toward his regaining his full stature by the tale's end.
[37] See the *MED*, *s.v.v.* and the gloss in the *Riverside Chaucer*, ed. Benson, p. 76.

Bennett again, the "triumph of gown over town."[38] The Miller's own summing up, however, indicates that all have been humiliated:

> Thus swyved was this carpenteris wyf,
> For al his kepyng and his jalousye,
> And Absolon hath kist hir nether ye,
> And Nicholas is scalded in the towte. (I, 3850–53)

Nicholas is as much laughed at as laughing.

This blurring of social distinctions through laughter reverses a premise of the *Decameron* in which the breakdown in society caused by the plague becomes a reason to tell amusing stories. While Chaucer need not have learned from Boccaccio that laughter dissolves social hierarchies, he might well have been struck by the odd description of the effect of Licisca's words on the women: "facevan le donne sí gran risa, che tutti i denti si sarebbero loro potuti trarre" (6, *Introduzione*, 11; "the ladies were laughing so hardily that you could have pulled all their teeth out," p. 445). Even as they dismiss their social inferior, their own dignity comes under question. In contrast as the *Reeve's Prologue* indicates, Chaucer's laughter is more inclusive, excluding only the Reeve:

> Whan folk hadde laughen at this nyce cas
> Of Absolon and hende Nicholas,
> Diverse folk diversely they seyde,
> But for the moore part they loughe and pleyde.
> Ne at this tale I saugh no man hym greve,
> But it were oonly Osewold the Reve. (I, 3855–60)[39]

The Reeve feels attacked as an individual (and on a personal matter, his wife's fidelity) identified by his profession—he like John in the *Miller's Tale* is a carpenter. A division remains, but not one based on class.

The second way that the *Miller's Tale* questions the Knight's assumptions about class, by mocking any certain knowledge of the divine plan, is drawn from *Decameron* 3.4. Here a monk, Dom Felice, pretends to know a strict penitential exercise that will allow one of his acquaintances, known as Friar Puccio because of his devotion to religion, "to achieve saintliness" (McWilliam, p. 217; "di divenir santo," 3.4, 12): he must, along with following other instructions, stand all night in an upstairs bedroom gazing on the heavens

---

[38]   J. A. W. Bennett, *Chaucer at Oxford and at Cambridge* (Toronto: University of Toronto Press, 1974), p. 56.

[39]   N. S. Thompson discusses the close correspondence of "Diverse folk diversely they seyde" to Boccaccio's "diversi cose diversamente parlando" (4.7, 5; "ranging widely over diverse subjects," McWilliam, p. 378); *Chaucer, Boccaccio, and the Debate of Love: A Comparative Study of* The Decameron *and* The Canterbury Tales (Oxford: Clarendon Press, 1996), pp. 18–19. See also Cooper, "Frame," *S&A*, 1.11–12.

with his arms outstretched and reciting three hundred paternosters and three hundred Hail Marys. As in the *Miller's Tale*, the real reason for the plan is Dom Felice's desire to sleep with Friar Puccio's wife. In Chaucer's tale Nicholas's plan also relies on special religious knowledge, derived specifically from his study of astrology:

> "Now John," quod Nicholas, "I wol nat lye;
> I have yfounde in myn astrologye,
> As I have looked in the moone bright,
> That now a Monday next, at quarter nyght,
> Shal falle a reyn, and that so wilde and wood
> That half so greet was nevere Noes flood.
> This world," he seyde, "in lasse than an hour
> Shal al be dreynt, so hidous is the shour.
> Thus shal mankynde drenche, and lese hir lyf." (I, 3513–21)

Here the reader sees a particular example of Nicholas's use of astrology mentioned at the tale's beginning: he may know "a certeyn of conclusiouns" (I, 3193) if asked "in certein houres" (I, 3195), but the information he gives will be made up to achieve the result he wants. It is, however, not just Nicholas's claims that should be doubted, as a couplet in the *Prologue* makes clear:

> An housbonde shal nat been inquisityf
> Of Goddes pryvetee, nor of his wyf. (I, 3163–64)

By stressing that God's plan is unknowable,[40] the *Miller's Tale* implies that the Knight's divine plan reflects little more than self-interest. It is to this point that I turn in the next chapter.

---

[40] See Frederick M. Biggs and Laura Howes, "Theophany in the 'Miller's Tale,'" *Medium Ævum* 65 (1996), pp. 269–79.

4

Friar Puccio's Penance:
Upending the Knight's Order

As Chapters 2 and 3 have argued, in turning to Jancofiore to inform his portrayal of the wife in the *Shipman's Tale* (and thereby beginning that of the Wife of Bath), Chaucer sought a direct contrast to Boccaccio's conventional view of the place of women in society. The case of the *Miller's Tale*, as the last chapter has suggested, is more complicated. Here there is no comparable character who opposes Boccaccio's aristocratic bias that Chaucer had identified by assigning his adaptation of the *Teseida* to the Knight. While suggestive, the conflict between John, a rich middle-class tradesman, and Nicholas, a student and so likely to be of higher social standing even if "poure" (I, 3190), does not play out along class lines, nor do any of the other characters—most importantly Alison and Absolon, but also Gerveys, Robyn, Gille, the cloisterer, who informs Absolon that John is likely to be away, nor the "neighebores, bothe smale and grete" (I, 3826), who pour into the "hostelrye" (I, 3203) at the tale's conclusion and then laugh at John's "fantasye" (I, 3840)—resolve this issue. Instead, Chaucer began his response on the topic of social hierarchies in a more open-ended way, here by allowing a middle-class pilgrim to respond to the *Knight's Tale* with a narrative in which class seems not to matter.

One of the sources Chaucer probably used, Guérin's *De Berangier au lonc cul*, does indeed explicitly, if not very profoundly, concern class, as does a second, *Decameron* 7.2, the story of Peronella and her lover, whom she hides in a tub. Chaucer, however, chose not to emphasize those parts of these narratives in his tale. Instead he turned to *Decameron* 3.4, Dom Felice's seduction of Monna Isabetta, to question the Knight's certainties about divine and human order which see power flowing down from the top. Moreover, he suffused his tale with a sense of the value of the secular world. By using two of Boccaccio's *novelle* and the technique of combining separate narrative motifs that he had learned from 8.10, Chaucer caught an enduring strength of the *Decameron*, its depiction of a wide range of human experience in this world.

In identifying *De Berangier au lonc cul* and *Decameron* 7.2 and 3.4 as sources for the *Miller's Tale*, the previous paragraph has set aside an obvious problem: its relationship to the very similar Middle Dutch *boerde*, *Heile van*

Beersele. In his chapter on the *Miller's Tale* in the 1941 *Sources and Analogues* Stith Thompson refers to this work to support his argument for a lost French *fabliau*, itself a reflection of an oral tradition, that was the common source for it and Chaucer's tale.[1] He asserts, then, that the two earliest literary versions are analogues, dependent on a lost work that contained the flood, the misdirected kiss, and the branding. As discussed in Chapter 1, his analysis reflects the Finnish historical-geographical school of folklore, which is no longer uncritically accepted and yet which may still be useful, as in the case of the Lover's Gift Regained, in analyzing particular popular traditions. Recognizing Thompson's argument about Chaucer's indebtedness to folklore but arguing largely from the surviving textual evidence, Peter G. Beidler writing in the new *Sources and Analogues* reframes the questions by considering *Heile van Beersele* to be if not Chaucer's actual source, "the closest we have to it," in his terminology, "a hard analogue with near source status" (*S&A*, 1.249). One of his criteria for determining a "hard analogue," that the work "is old enough in its extant form that Chaucer could have known it,"[2] calls attention to evidence that is potentially devastating to my view that the direction of influence runs in the other direction, that is from the *Miller's Tale* to *Heile van Beersele.* If the one manuscript, Brussels, Koninklijke Bibliotheek, II, 1171, in which the *boerde* survives is older than Chaucer's tale, Beidler is correct, and other potential sources become largely irrelevant for my main argument about Chaucer's use of the *Decameron.*

   This chapter, then, turns first to the manuscript of *Heile van Beersele* to show that while it might be earlier than the *Miller's Tale*, its date cannot be conclusively determined. More compelling, I then argue, is the literary evidence of the tubs in the two tales, which not only cause narrative problems within *Heile van Beersele* but also draw attention to the interior space necessary for the story to work. Because some middle-class dwellings in Oxford were built to accommodate the academic functions of the fledgling colleges, John's "hostelrye," unlike a prostitute's room on Cow Gate Street in Antwerp, would have had a hall. Moreover, by descending directly from the *Miller's Tale*, *Heile van Beersele* not only fails to provide evidence for an earlier popular narrative, but also casts doubt on the ability of the later analogues to do so because they too may derive, directly or indirectly, from Chaucer's tale. A full examination of this topic must await further research into the use of sources by each of the early modern authors involved, but two points can be made. Because these later versions appear in the literate context of renaissance humanism created in part by the success of the *Decameron*, a knowledge of Chaucer's work, while as yet undocumented, is possible. More

---

[1]   Thompson, "The Miller's Tale," pp. 106–23. The relevance of *Heile* to the *Miller's Tale* was first discussed by A. J. Barnouw, "Chaucer's 'Milleres Tale,'" *Modern Language Review* 7 (1912), pp. 145–48.

[2]   Beidler sets out this system in "New Terminology."

specifically the unlikeliness of the narrative having originated in popular tradition is again shown by their difficulty in handling tubs in the rafters. Chaucer, it appears, wrote a "popular" tale from separate sources including two of the *Decameron's novelle*, 7.2 and 3.4, a narrative that has both inspired and fooled later generations.

The Manuscript of Heile van Beersele

Heile van Beersele has been discovered in a single manuscript, previously in the collection of Thomas Phillipps, but acquired in 1888 by the Koninklijke Bibliotheek in Brussels, where it is catalogued as II, 1171.[3] *Heile van Beersele's* rubric begins on line 15 of the second column on folio 330r (Fig. 1) and it ends on line 6 of the first column of 331v, making it the third of the five short texts that conclude the volume of 332 folios. As it now stands, the manuscript, which contains texts in Middle Dutch, is made up of two distinct parts, the work of two scribes whose efforts have been irregularly bound together: one copied the first part of Jacob van Maerlant's *Spiegel Historiael*, a translation of Vincent of Beauvais's *Speculum historiale*,[4] as well as *Van den VII vroeden van binnen Rome*, a version of the *Seven Sages of Rome* (fols. 1–32v and 81r–284r);[5] the other, part of Hein van Aken's *Die Rose*, a translation of the *Roman de la Rose*,[6] and five shorter texts (fols. 33r–80r

3   On the history of the manuscript, see A. N. L. Munby, *The Dispersal of the Phillipps Library*, Phillipps Studies 5 (Cambridge: Cambridge University Press, 1960), pp. 28–30; and Jan Deschamps, "De Catalogus van de Middelnederlandse Handschriften van de Koninklijke Bibliotheek van België," *De Gulden Passer* 39 (1961), pp. 258–73. It has not yet been described by Deschamps and Herman Mulder in the *Inventaris van de Middelnederlandse handschriften van de Koninklijke Bibliotheek van België* (Brussels: Koninklijke Bibliotheek van België, 1998–).
4   *Jacob van Maerlant's* Spiegel historiael..., ed. M. de Vries and E. Verwijs, 4 vols. (Leiden: Brill, 1863–79). See Jos A. A. M. Biemans, *Onsen Speghele Ystoriale in Vlaemsche...*, 2 vols. (Louvain: Peeters, 1997); and J. van Mierlo's chapter on Jacob van Maerlant in the *Geschiedenis van de letterkunde der Nederlanden*, ed. Frank Baur, et al. (Brussels: Standaard, 1937–51), 1.286–303.
5   Ed. K. Stallaert, *Van den VII Vroeden van binnen Rome* (Gent: Siffer, 1889). See Jos A. A. M. Biemans, "Op zoek naar contouren van het onzichtbare: die miniaturen in Hs. Brussel, KB, II 1171," *De nieuwe taalgids*, 87 (1994), pp. 217–30; G. P. M. Knuvelder, *Handboek tot de Geschiedenis der Nederlandse Letterkunde*, 4 vols. ('s-Hertogenbosch: Malmberg, 1971–78), 1.222–23; and Hans R. Runte, J. Keith Wikeley, and Anthony J. Farrell, *The Seven Sages of Rome and the Book of Sinbad: An Analytical Bibliography* (New York: Garland, 1984), pp. 33–35.
6   Die Rose *van Heinric van Aken*, ed. Eelco Verwijs ('s-Gravenhage: Martinus Nijhoff, 1868). See also, J. van Mierlo, *De Middelnederlandsche letterkunde van omstreeks 1300 tot de Renaissance* (Brussels: Standaard, 1940), 16–26; and D. E. van der Poel, *De Vlaamse Rose en* Die Rose *van Heinric*, Middeleeuwse Studies en Bronnen 13 (Hilversum: Verloren, 1989).

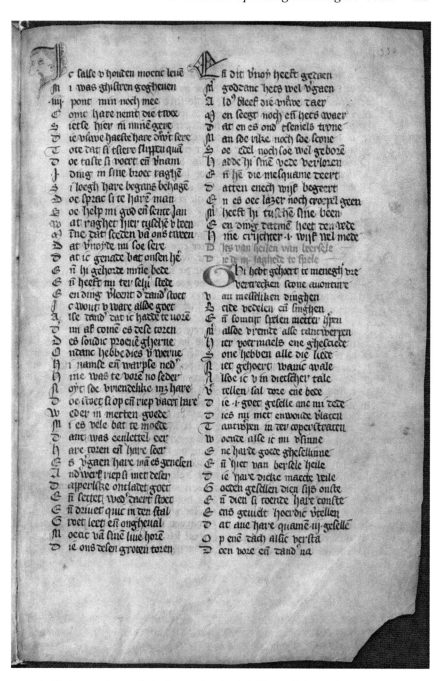

1. *Heile van Beersele* in Brussels, Koninklijke Bibliotheek van België,
MS II, 1171, fol. 330ʳ.

and 285r–332v).[7] W. E. Hegman, who has reconstructed the later history of the manuscript from its sale in Brussels in 1614 and through the collections of Hieronymus Winghius, a canon at Doornik (Tournai), the Doornik Cathedral Library, Adam Clarke, and Thomas Thorpe before it reached Phillipps, suggests that the two parts may have been written at the same scriptorium.[8] He dates both hands to the second half of the fourteenth century.[9] J. P. Gumbert, who has examined plates of the relevant folios, considers the manuscript to be more likely from the first half, or at most the middle, of the fourteenth century, than from its final quarter.[10] In his chapter Beidler includes the views of Geert Claassens:

> There are surely no indications to date it into the fifteenth century—it's clear-cut fourteenth century—and some indications to place it around 1350. I think that a dating of around 1350–75 is rather safe. There are no indications that would justify a dating before 1350, but the use of the so-called "tongue-e" at the end of the line, in combination with the sporadic use of small letters in the capital column, make a dating in the third quarter of the fourteenth century plausible. Until further evidence turns up, I would accept such a dating. (*S&A* 2.263)

Citing the opinion of J. A. A. M. Biemans, Bart Besamusca dates both parts of the manuscript to "the first half of the fourteenth century."[11] While there

---

7 In addition to *Heile*, there are two other *boerden*: *Dits vanden vesscher van Parijs* (fol. 328v–30r) and *Vander vrouwen die boven haren man minde* (332r–v); both are edited by C. Kruyskamp, *Middelnederlandse Boerden* ('s-Gravenhage: Martinus Nijhoff, 1957), pp. 100–08 and 115–18. The two other texts are *Vander wiue wonderlijcheit* (327r–8v; ed. K. Stallaert in *Dietsche Warande*, NS [3rd ser.] 2 [1889], pp. 158–71) and *Van dinghen die selden ghescien* (331v–2r; ed. J. F. Willems in *Belgisch Museum*, 10 [1846], pp. 118–20).

8 W. E. Hegman, "Het Cheltenhamse *Rose*-Handschrift," *Spiegel der Letteren*, 30 (1988), pp. 67–71. See also Biemans, *Onsen Speghele*, 2.429–31.

9 Hegman, "Cheltenhamse," p. 69. See also Biemans, *Onsen Speghele*, although his concern is primarily with the first part of the manuscript; after describing the contents of the second, he comments, "Dit tweede handschrift blijft hier verder grotendeels buiten beschouwing" (2.427; "the second hand remains here for the rest largely outside the investigation"). Because, however, he supports the possibility that the two parts were together from the beginning, and even suggests that they were written for the same individual, his revised date of the first script to the first half of the fourteenth century might imply that the second is from this same time; see 2.426–32. I would like to thank J. P. Gumbert for calling my attention to this work and its significance. On 18 October 2002, Albert Derolez wrote to me: "it is virtually impossible to come to a conclusion: the manuscript is probably second half of the fourteenth century, but the first half cannot be excluded; whether earlier or later than 1387 is impossible to say. 'Ca. 1400' looks too late to me."

10 E-mail, 5 November 2002.

11 Bart Besamusca, "The Manuscript Context of the Middle Dutch Fabliaux," in *"Li premerains vers": Essays in Honor of Keith Busby*, ed. Catherine M. Jones and Logan E. Whalen (Amsterdam: Rodopi, 2011), p. 31, note 14.

is some variation here, the consensus of these authorities would place the manuscript before Chaucer began working on the *Canterbury Tales*, usually considered to be around 1387.[12]

While a date for this manuscript earlier than the composition of the *Miller's Tale* may be more likely on paleographical grounds, it is not certain. Scholars have discovered no external evidence, such as a colophon, that would fix its time of writing precisely, and, moreover, it is always possible that a scribe trained in, say, the 1360's might still be writing the same way decades later. I would note that its script, Textualis Libraria, is similar to two dated manuscripts from the 1360's: Brussels, Koninklijke Bibliotheek, 3067–73, which contains the Middle Dutch *Treatise on the Ten Commandments*, from 1361;[13] and Ghent, Bibliotheek van de Universiteit 942, a Dutch translation of Albert of Brescia's *De amore et dilectione Dei et proximi et aliarum rerum*, from 1367.[14] A similar hand also appears in Brussels, Koninklijke Bibliotheek, 1805–08, a Dutch translation of Gregory the Great's *Dialogi*, from 1395.[15] Indeed dated examples from 1444 (Brussels, Koninklijke Bibliotheek, 19607)[16] and 1453 (The Hague, Museum Meermanno-Westreenianum, 10 C 19 (187)[17] show that some features of this earlier tradition survive into the fifteenth century.

The date of the manuscript indicates of course only by what point a text must have been written, and the manuscript context of *Heile van Beersele* suggests that this is not the author's original: the scribe treats it as he does the other items in the codex, almost certainly copying it from an exemplar. On the other hand, the dates of its texts are also often useful for paleographers in determining the age of a manuscript. It is generally agreed that Chaucer wrote the *Miller's Tale*, unlike the *Knight's Tale*, for the collection; less certain, however, is the tendency, summarized by Douglas Gray, to place it and the *Reeve's Tale* "in the later years" of this work because of their "sophisticated adaptation" to its frame-story.[18] Robert D. French has suggested that Chaucer

---

[12] See Pearsall, *Life of Geoffrey Chaucer*, pp. 226–27; and Benson, *Riverside Chaucer*, p. 3.

[13] Reproduced by Albert Derolez, *The Palaeography of Gothic Manuscript Books from the Twelfth to the Early Sixteenth Century* (Cambridge: Cambridge University Press, 2003), plate 31.

[14] François Masai and Martin Wittek, *Manuscrits datés conservés en Belgique. Tome I: 819–1400*, (Brussels: E. Story-Scientia, 1968), p. 40 and plate 169.

[15] Masai and Wittek, *Manuscrits datés. I*, p. 51 and plate 214.

[16] François Masai and Martin Wittek, *Manuscrits datés conservés en Belgique. Tome III: 1441–1460*, (Brussels: E. Story-Scientia, 1978), p. 26 and plate 456.

[17] G. I. Lieftinck, *Manuscrits datés conservés dans les Pays-Bas. Vol. 1: Les manuscrits d'origine étrangère (816–c. 1550)*, (Amsterdam: North Holland Pub. Co., 1964), p. 55 (item 128) and plate 154.

[18] Douglas Gray, "The Miller's Prologue and Tale," in the *Riverside Chaucer*, ed. Benson, p. 841. See also Cooper, *Canterbury Tales*, pp. 94–95; Pearsall, *Life of Geoffrey Chaucer*, pp. 226–27; and Thomas W. Ross, *The Miller's Tale*, A Variorum Edition of

would have begun writing the *Miller's Tale* as soon as he decided to use the *Knight's Tale* as his first story.[19] In Chapter 3 I have gone further, arguing that it and the *Shipman's Tale* stand at the beginning of his work on the collection; Chapter 5 argues that this initial stage of the project was before 1390. If *Heile van Beersele* is, then, an adaptation of the *Miller's Tale*, Brussels, Koninklijke Bibliotheek, II, 1171 may be dated to the last thirteen years of the fourteenth century.

Tubs in Two Tales

The contemporary *Miller's Tale* and *Heile van Beersele* are so similar that it might be possible to argue the direction of transmission either way. The main difference between them, as many have noted in considering more generally the relation of the tale to the *fabliau* tradition,[20] is Chaucer's portrayal of his main characters: Alison, John, Nicholas, and Absolon are all more developed than Heile and her three lovers, Willem Hoeft,[21] a priest, and a smith named Hugh. Considering the characters also reveals that Chaucer created a more complex narrative than necessary by using two, Nicholas and Absolon, to perform roles occupied by the priest in *Heile van Beersele*; Nicholas introduces the story of the flood, but it is Absolon who carries the tale's anticlerical themes. Similarly, unlike *Heile van Beersele*, in which the third lover is a smith, Chaucer used a final character, Gervase, to loan Absolon the hot "kultour" (I, 3776) needed in the branding, and contrasted him, as Thomas W. Ross notes, to the "vague cloisterer" from whom Absolon has attempted to learn John's whereabouts (I, 3657–70).[22] He also included a maid for Alison, Gille, and a servant for John, who shares the Miller's name, Robyn; both are sent to London and so are not involved in the tale's conclusion.[23]

---

the Works of Geoffrey Chaucer 2.3 (Norman: University of Oklahoma Press, 1983), pp. 6–7.

[19] Robert D. French, *A Chaucer Handbook*, 2nd edn (New York: Appleton-Century-Crofts, 1947), 393.

[20] See Ross, *Miller's Tale*, pp. 8–9. Bennett considers the descriptions of Absolon and Alison to reveal "how ill the label of 'fabliau' befits this tale"; *Chaucer at Oxford*, p. 42.

[21] His profession, a miller ("een moeldre"; 36), may reflect that of the teller of *Miller's Tale*. Quotations of from Beidler's edition in *S&A*, 2.266–75; the accompanying translation is by Henk Aertsen.

[22] See Ross's note on line 3761, *Miller's Tale*, pp. 232–33.

[23] Ross comments that "Nicholas appeals to John's snobbery (God does not deign to save mere knaves and wenches like Robyn and Gille) and at the same time arranges for the two inconvenient witnesses to be absent during the flood and the lovemaking"; *Miller's Tale*, p. 201. John's decision to send them to London (I, 3631) may show both his good nature in trying to save them, and his stupidity in believing that he can do so by getting them out of Oxford, allowing the detail to resonate with his desire to save Alison (I, 3522–24).

The four main characters, then, are more developed and are surrounded by other people. These differences, however, by themselves prove little about the direction of transmission because Chaucer could have embellished a simpler story or the author of *Heile van Beersele* could have simplified Chaucer's.

The clearest indication that the story originated with Chaucer is how plausible the three tubs tied in the roof appear in the *Miller's Tale* in contrast to how unlikely even a single one seems in *Heile van Beersele*.[24] Securing a tub capable of holding an adult in the rafters of a house would be a job for a carpenter, and indeed the Miller describes John's efforts to do so:

> He gooth and geteth hym a knedyng trogh,
> And after that a tubbe and a kymelyn,
> And pryvely he sente hem to his in,
> And heng hem in the roof in pryvetee.
> His owene hand he made laddres thre,
> To clymben by the ronges and the stalkes
> Unto the tubbes hangynge in the balkes,
> And hem vitailled, bothe trogh and tubbe,
> With breed, and chese, and good ale in a jubbe,
> Suffisynge right ynogh as for a day. (I, 3620–29)

This hard labor then causes him to fall asleep almost as soon as he gets into his tub:

> The dede sleep, for wery bisynesse,
> Fil on this carpenter right, as I gesse,
> Aboute corfew-tyme, or litel moore;
> For travaille of his goost he groneth soore,
> And eft he routeth, for his heed myslay. (I, 3643–47)

While Chaucer's narrative moves these objects with apparent ease, it also reminds us that John expends considerable energy in doing so. *Heile van Beersele* provides no such explanation. When Willem asks where to hide after Heile has decided to let her second lover, the priest, enter, she tells him:

> Heile seide, "daer boven hangt .i. bac,
> Dies ic hier voermaels ghemac
> Hadde te menegen stonden;
> Ane die haenbalke es hi gebonden
> Met enen vasten zele wel.
> Daer sidi bat dan ighering el." (67–72)

> (Heile said, "Up there hangs a trough
> Which I have found convenient here

---

24 Without elaborating, Thompson characterizes the flood episode in *Heile* as "garbled"; "Miller's Tale," p. 112.

> On many previous occasions;
> To the crossbeam it is securely tied
> With a strong rope.
> There you will be better off than anywhere else.")

The vague phrase, "which I have found convenient here / On many previous occasions," indicates the author's difficulty in accounting for this detail. The falling tub, moreover, is essential to the plot since it is the mechanism that powers the story's conclusion;[25] without it, the misdirected kiss and the branding would not engage the flood.[26]

Audiences have probably paid less attention to the oddity of the tub in *Heile van Beersele* because its descent is just one of three outrageous events that conclude the story: the misdirected kiss and the branding demand equal if not greater notice. The difference between them is however significant. As is well-recognized,[27] the aim of the *fabliau* is to amuse through its shocking subject matter (sex and excrement) and its transgressive vocabulary, but John Hines also notes in the genre "a number of prominent characteristics that can be called 'realistic'": "the *fabliaux* present a consistent world of characters and events, a world that in terms of motivation and execution of actions, of

---

[25] Chaucer might have been thinking about clocks, as this part of the tale contains several references to time (see I, 3516, 3645, 3654–55, 3675, and 3687). He established the theme in the comment that Nicholas is able to foretell the future "in certein houres" (I, 3195), although the use of "certein" in a previous line ("and koude a certeyn of conclusiouns," I, 3193), undercuts both comments—Nicholas predicts what he wants whenever it is useful to him. The point is to contrast the comedy of human time with the perfect movement of the spheres in the *Knight's Tale*. On the development of clocks, see Silvio A. Bedini, "Clocks and Reckoning of Time," *DMA*, 3.457–64; and Lynn Thorndike, *A History of Magic and Experimental Science*, 8 vols. (New York: Macmillan, 1923–58), 3.388–92. For the changes in society brought about by this new technology, see Jacques Le Goff, "Labor Time in the 'Crisis' of the Four-teenth Century: From Medieval Time to Modern Time," in *Time, Work, and Culture in the Middle Ages*, trans. Arthur Goldhammer (Chicago: University of Chicago Press, 1980), pp. 43–52. The detail further ties the tale to Oxford through Merton scholars; see Bennett, *Chaucer at Oxford*, p. 59. Pearsall comments that Nicholas "was surely named after his illustrious predecessor in the science of the stars," Nicholas of Lynn; *Life of Geoffrey Chaucer*, pp. 218, 336, and note 32. His calendar was discussed in the previous chapter. On Chaucer's use elsewhere of such technical information, see Joseph E. Grennen, "Calculating the Reeve and His Camera Obscura," *Journal of Medieval and Renaissance Studies* 14 (1984), pp. 245–59; and "Science and Sensi-bility in Chaucer's Clerk," *Chaucer Review* 6 (1971), pp. 81–93.

[26] In his note on John's sudden awakening from his slumber (3815), Ross writes that "Tillyard...speaks for all readers when he exclaims about this line, 'The surprise, the sudden union of the two themes is sublime'"; *Miller's Tale*, p. 242, citing E. M. W. Tillyard, *Poetry Direct and Oblique*, rev. edn (London: Chatto & Windus, 1945), p. 90.

[27] See Charles Muscatine, *The Old French Fabliaux* (New Haven: Yale University Press, 1986), pp. 105–51; and Erik Hertog, *Chaucer's Fabliaux as Analogues*, Mediaevalia Lovaniensia I/XIX (Leuven: Leuven University Press, 1991), p. 2.

the basic set of relationships noted above, is very much a human world."[28] Although obviously not common occurrences, putting a bare bottom out a window and having it branded with a hot iron are actions readily enough imagined, requiring only a breach of decorum and a particularly malicious sense of revenge. In contrast it seems unlikely for a *fabliau* to hinge on the presence of a tub, fortuitously hanging in the rafters, that is large enough and sufficiently secure for a person to hide in.[29] Nor will this problem disappear by claiming that the author of *Heile van Beersele* has distorted his source on this point: one would still need to get the tub up into the roof. The most likely explanation for Heile's tub is that it comes directly from Chaucer's story.

In contrast, the one major narrative inconsistency in the *Miller's Tale*, the delay of Nicholas and Alison in achieving their goal, does not involve a similar violation of these conventions of realism, but rather shows Chaucer playing with the generic expectations of the *fabliau*. The opening scene, in which Nicholas and Alison have ample time to talk and which concludes with Nicholas having "thakked hire aboute the lendes weel" (I, 3304),[30] makes the entire flood story unnecessary: at the moment, John is away at Oseneye (I, 3274), and apparently Gille and Robyn, too, are engaged elsewhere. The lovers have no need to wait. Alison's explanation of why they must, "'Myn housbonde is so ful of jalousie'" (I, 3294), seems at first plausible both because it echoes the Miller's earlier description of John, "Jalous he was, and heeld hire narwe in cage" (I, 3224), and because the situation is common in similar stories.[31] Chaucer, however, undercut this convention by failing to show us John's jealousy even when, for example, he is awoken by Absolon's singing under his window (I, 3364–69). Nicholas's elaborate plot is remarkable precisely because there is no need for it, and its complexity seems certain to draw attention to the lovers rather than keeping their affair secret, as Alison requests (I, 3295). In any case there can be little doubt that Chaucer could have motivated the delay more convincingly had he wished to by making John appear more jealous.

---

[28] John Hines, *The Fabliau in English* (London: Longman, 1993), p. 13. See also, however, Bloch's critique of this approach; *Scandal of the Fabliaux*, pp. 4–7, 53–58, and 109.

[29] I discuss below the extract from Apuleius's *Metamorphoses* printed by Benson and Andersson (*Literary Context*, pp. 6–8) as well as Boccaccio's retelling of this story. Tubs also figure in *De Cuvier* and *De .II. Changeors*; *French Fabliau*, ed. Eichmann and DuVal, 2.142–45 and 2.197–207. A husband uses a tub in *Des Tresces* to capture his wife's lover, and the wife gives her beaten husband a bath at the end of *De la Borgoise d'Orliens*; *Cuckolds, Clerics, & Countrymen: Medieval French Fabliaux*, trans. John DuVal; introductions, texts and notes, Raymond Eichmann (Fayetteville: University of Arkansas Press, 1982), pp. 69 and 85.

[30] As Ross's notes indicate, the phrase "rage and pleye" (I, 3273) as well as Nicholas's opening gestures (I, 3276 and 3279) and first speeches (I, 3277–8 and 3279–80) have possible sexual connotations; *Miller's Tale*, pp. 153–55.

[31] See Nykrog, *Fabliaux*, pp. 187–92.

Moreover, unlike the tubs, which suggest the direction of transmission was from the *Miller's Tale* to *Heile van Beersele*, the delay at the beginning of Chaucer's tale cannot be explained by its reliance on the Middle Dutch version since in *Heile van Beersele* there is no such delay. On the day that Heile learns of the men's interest, she devises a way to satisfy them all that very night (21–46). This opening, however, presents its own difficulty since it seems unlikely that a prostitute would make such appointments and then prove so incapable of fulfilling them. That Heile is a prostitute, indeed an experienced one, is clear from the first description of her:

> T'Antwerpen in der Coperstraten
> Woende, alse ic mi versinne,
> Ene harde goede ghesellinne
> Ende hiet van Bersele Heile,
> Die hare dicke maecte veile
> Goeden gesellen dien sijs onste,
> Ende dien si toende hare conste. (14–20)

> (In Antwerp in the Cow Gate Street
> Lived, as I understand,
> A very frivolous woman
> Named Heile of Beersele,
> Who often offered herself for sale
> To good fellows whom she favored
> And to whom she showed her skill.)

She does plan to have the three arrive at different times—the first in the evening, the second at the "slaepclocke" (40; "evening bell"), and the third at the "diefclocke" (43; "night bell")—but then makes no effort to be rid of one before the next arrives. This problem of timing is central to the story since, to work, it must gather the three men around the woman at the same moment. Once Chaucer had introduced the decision of Nicholas and Alison to wait, he was able to develop the other parts of the plot, including Absolon's wooing as well as John's procuring of the tubs. Although *Heile van Beersele* may begin more plausibly than the *Miller's Tale*, its opening causes problems later, again indicating that the direction of transmission is more likely to have been from England to the Low Countries.

Some further narrative inconsistencies in *Heile van Beersele* return us to the tubs. In the *Miller's Tale*, it is clear why John does not realize what is happening on the final night: his intelligence is so limited that he has believed Nicholas's impossible story about a second flood, and his hard work to prepare for it leaves him so exhausted that he then sleeps through most of the night, waking only when Nicholas cries for water after his branding (I, 3816–18). The logic in *Heile van Beersele* is less clear. It seems initially unlikely that Willem Hoeft, the first client, would believe Heile's explanation of the priest's arrival: "'Hi soude mi over thoeft lesen / Ende beteren mi dat mi deert'" (62–63; "'He would say a prayer over my head / And cure me from what ails me'"). The problem increases, however, when, in the tub, he hears and believes the priest's odd sermon—another unmotivated detail in *Heile van Beersele* clearly set up in the *Miller's Tale*[32]—following his love-making with Heile:

> Oec soe seidi dit bat voert,
> Dat die tijt noch soude comen
> Dat God die werelt soude doemen,
> Beide met watre ende met viere;
> Ende dat soude wesen sciere,
> Dat al die werelt verdrinken soude,
> Grote ende clene, jonge ende oude. (80–86)

> (He also added
> That the time was about to come
> When God would destroy the world,
> Both with water and with fire;
> And that it was to happen soon,
> That all the world would be drowned,
> The great and the small, young and old.)

It seems incredible that Willem would not hear what the two have been doing or the following exchange with the smith, which then leads to the branding.

A related problem is the distance of the tubs from their respective floors, a detail important not only for the drama of the end of the story but also for the explanation of why the first lover is unaware of what is happening below. In the *Miller's Tale*, the three are apparently a long way up: Nicholas tells John, "'Thanne shaltow hange hem in the roof ful hye'" (I, 3565), and, as already noted, John makes ladders to reach them, which Nicholas and Alison then use (I, 3648). Equally relevant, however, are the Miller's other remarks about John's house, which have been placed in context by J. A. W. Bennett.[33] The opening lines of the tale make it clear that it is a substantial structure, and by calling it a "hostelrye" or "in" (I, 3203 and 3622) Chaucer implied, as Bennett explains, "that it was large enough to be rented as an academic hall or a grammar hall—for houses were taken for such purposes by the year; most halls were originally private houses, as the name Peter*house* reminds us" (p. 31).[34] This is of course only one detail of many that situate the

---

[32] Chaucer prepares for the flood story from the opening description of Nicholas's ability to prophesy the weather (I, 3190–98).

[33] Bennett, *Chaucer at Oxford*, 26–57.

[34] The hall is a prominent feature of the domestic architecture of the wealthy throughout the medieval period in England; see Margaret Wood, *The English Medieval House* (London: Phoenix House, 1965); Eric Mercer, *English Vernacular Houses: A Study of Traditional Farmhouses and Cottages* (London: H.M. Stationery Office, 1975); John Schofield, *Medieval London Houses* (New Haven: Yale University Press, 1994);

story; and yet for my argument, it is the most important.[35] Chaucer's Oxford provides the physical space for the tub to fall.

In contrast the Antwerp of *Heile van Beersele* offers only a good example of why this narrative is so difficult to set. As was mentioned at the beginning of Chapter 2, short comic tales like this one often take place in unspecified locations, making the opening passage, quoted above, which identifies not only the city but the Cow Gate Street on which Heile lives, distinctive. The name itself has caused some confusion. The 1941 *Sources and Analogues* translated "in der Coperstraten" as "in the Market Street," apparently understanding it as related to Middle Dutch "copen" ("to buy") and "coper" ("a buyer"),[36] although the compound itself is not common, suggesting first to speakers of Modern Dutch "Copper-street."[37] The correct identification was made by Kruyskamp:

> De naam van deze straat, eig. Koepoortstraat, wordt nog thans in de Antw. volkstaal uitgesproken als Koeperstraat. Het is niet bekend dat deze straat een buurt van Venusdierkens geweest zou zijn.[38]

> (The name of this street, actually Koepoortstraat, is these days still pronounced as Koeperstraat in the Antwerp dialect. It is not known that this street would have been a neighborhood of prostitutes).

Unlikely, then, are associations of Heile with a thriving commercial center. Instead, the name may lead to a more general understanding of domestic architecture and prostitution.

Coperstrate takes us back to Antwerp as it was in the late Middle Ages, before the remarkable expansion during the sixteenth century that led to its becoming one of the greatest commercial centers of western Europe.[39] Canals, built around the turn of the twelfth century, connecting natural water courses and offering some protection to the growing town, were crossed by bridges, one of which was called the "Koepoortbrug," the "Cow-gate-bridge";

P. S. Barnwell and A. T. Adams, *The House Within: Interpreting Medieval Houses in Kent* (London: H.M. Stationery Office, 1994); and Anthony Emery, *Greater Medieval Houses of England and Wales*, 2 vols. (Cambridge: Cambridge University Press, 1996–2006).

35   For discussions of the tale's many Oxford allusions, see Bennett's chapter, "Town and Gown" in *Chaucer at Oxford*, pp. 26–57; and Cooper, *Canterbury Tales*, pp. 98–99.

36   Jan de Vries, *Nederlands Etymologisch Wordenboek* (Leiden: Brill, 1963–71), *s.v.*

37   I would like to thank Peter Calliauw for his help on this problem.

38   Kruyskamp, *Middelnederlandse Boerden*, pp. 109 and 127.

39   See the essays, several of which will be mentioned in following notes, in *Antwerp: Twelve Centuries of History and Culture*, ed. Karel van Isacker and Raymond van Uytven (Antwerp: Fonds Mercator, 1986); and L. Voet, G. Asaert, H. Soly, A. Verhulst, F. de Nave, and J. van Roey, *De Stad Antwerpen van de Romeinse Tijd tot de 17de EEUW: Topografische studie rond het plan van Virgilius Bononiensis, 1565* (Brussels: Gemeentekrediet van België, 1978).

thirteenth-century sources identify a "Coperstrate,"[40] in all likelihood the street running from the eastern end of the main market (or the short street coming out of this end of the market) north to the bridge. Between roughly 1200 and 1410, Antwerp expanded four more times,[41] with Coperstrate leading to the "Paardemarkt" ("Horse Market," established in 1298), which in turn led to the "Rodepoort" ("Royal Gate"), one of the main gates built into the last medieval walls of the city.[42] These expansions reflect the growing importance of Antwerp due to its fairs and its involvement in the wool and cloth industries.[43] Gustaaf Asaert's assessment of the aldermen's registers of 1394–95 leads him to conclude that the city's 20,000 inhabitants lived mainly in houses, which account for 81% of the structures, the others being mostly farms (5%) or one-room hovels (13%).[44] Much of the land enclosed by final expansions of the walls remained open, however, allowing for the dramatic increase in population during the fifteenth and sixteenth centuries.[45]

While full information about Coperstrate is difficult to obtain, as one of the older streets near the main market it was almost certainly built up with houses. These were probably not guild houses since Asaert suggests that they were concentrated north and west of the market.[46] The early map of the city (Fig. 2), included by Louis van Caukercken in his *Kronijk* written at the

---

[40] Also spelled as "Coeporte," "Coporte," "Cuperstrate," and "Coeperstrate"; see F. Prims, "Onze plaats- et straatnamen in de XIIIde eeuw," *Antwerpsch Achievenblad*, 2nd ser., 2 (1927), pp. 89–115. See also R. Vande Weghe, *Geschiedenis van de Antwerpse straatnamen* (Antwerp: Mercurius, 1977), p. 266.

[41] See the plans in Gustaaf Asaert, "De Late Middeleeuwen," in Voet *et. al.*, *Stad Antwerpen*, pp. 44, 48, 50, and 52.

[42] Apparently Coperstrate ended at Koepoortbrug, although a plan of Antwerp published by Joan Blaeu in the seventeenth century places it on the north side of the bridge; I have consulted this and other early maps and views of Antwerp in the eighteenth-century collection of Christoffel Beudeker, now preserved in twenty-four volumes in the Map Collection of the British Library, Antwerp being in volume 15 (C.9.e.4). The maps and views have been identified in pencil; that referred to here is 26a. On this collection, see Anna E. C. Simoni, "Terra Incognita: the Beudeker Collection in the Map Library of the British Library," *The British Library Journal* 11 (1985), pp. 143–75. A plan by J. Deur names the street north of the Koepoortbrug as "Clapdorp," which leads to the "Marché aux Chavaux"; Plan de la Ville et Citadelle d'Anvers (Amsterdam, 1720), British Library Maps 31145.(28), identified in the catalogue as post-1701.

[43] Bruges remained the dominant center during this time and Antwerp had to compete with other smaller cities as well; see R. Van Uytven, "The Port on the Rhine and Regional Market with International Fairs," in van Isacker and van Uytven, *Antwerp*, pp. 50–55.

[44] Gustaaf Asaert, "The City of Antwerp in the Middle Ages," in van Isacker and van Uytven, eds., *Antwerp*, p. 49.

[45] The census of 1568 establishes that there were around 100,000 inhabitants of the city; see H. Soly, "The Growth of the Metropolis," in van Isacker and van Uytven, *Antwerp*, pp. 84–92.

[46] Asaert, "City," p. 41.

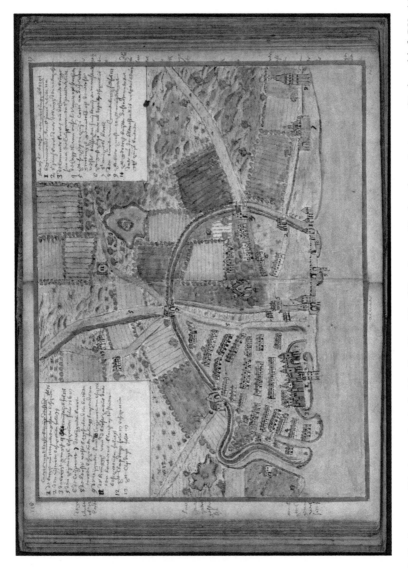

2. Early map of Antwerp included in the *Kronijk* of Louis van Caukercken, Antwerp, Stadsarchief, PK. 116. The covered "coypoort" (6) is at 10 o'clock.

end of the seventeenth century,[47] that identifies "de coypoort" (item 6 in the legend) as a covered bridge over the canal, shows four sets of buildings in two rows leading toward the center of town. All appear to be relatively modest one- or two-story structures, the same impression created by the map of Hans Liefrinck and Lambert van Noort (1569; Fig. 3),[48] although that of Joris Hoefnagel (1580; Fig. 4) indicates more substantial two- or three-story buildings.[49]

These general comments and plans may be augmented by local documents. Several records from the beginning of the fourteenth century indicate that some properties on the street were being developed at this time.[50] On 25 September 1305, Seger Kersmaker's ("candle-maker") bought "een erf" ("a premise") from St. Bernard's Abbey (6.37); a year later (13 August 1306), it was identified as a "huus" ("house") in another document that concerns a "hofstad" ("farm") between Seger's house and that of Willem Vlas (6.41). On 27 April 1307, Petrus Winne de Cupere ("the cooper") obtained "een eigendom" ("a property") again from St. Bernard's Abbey (6:169).[51] Entries in the *Clementijnboeck*, a register begun in 1383 to contain the laws and ordinances of the city but serving also as a record of administrative decisions and legal judgments,[52] reveal something about the street's residents at the end of the century. One dated 18 June and 5 July 1389 describes the sentence imposed on Willeme van den Hoghenhuys, "den maerscalc in de Coeperstrate" ("the farrier in Coperstrate"), and Willeme Bornecolven, "de veruwere" ("the dyer"), because they had assaulted Gielise, "den borduerwerkere, ende syn wyf, wonachtich in de Coeperstrate" ("the embroiderer and his wife dwelling in Coperstrate") within her own house ("binnen haers selfs huyse," 25.184). Among a group of adulterous women all sentenced on 1 July 1392 is Katline, who had drawn Verdackere, "den hoedemakere in de Coeperstrate" ("the hood maker in Coperstrate") away from his wife (25.258). Another entry, dated only 1404, records the sentence of Reynken,

---

47 Antwerp, Stadsarchief, PK 116. The map appears between pp. 116 and 117. The chronicle is available online at the FelixArchief.be; the map is image 85. I would like to thank Inge Schoups and Martine Reusen for information about this map and for arranging for its reproduction.

48 British Library, Maps 31145.(4).

49 British Library, Maps 31145.(1); also included in Beudeker (see note 42 above), 28.

50 Floris Prims, "Antwerpsche Akten uit den tijd van Hertog Jan II (1294–1312)," *Antwerpsch Archievenblad*, 2nd ser., 5 (1930), pp. 33–77 and 100–23; and 6 (1931) pp. 27–62 and 151–93. References are to the volume of the journal and page.

51 See also 27 January 1308, although this "half huis" is "buiten" ("outside") the bridge (5.75).

52 The volume, covering the years 1288–1414, was edited by Frans Jozef Van den Branden in *Antwerpsch Archievenblad*, 25 (1888), pp. 101–465 and 26 (1889), pp. 1–136. Both are available online at the FelixArchief, *inventarisnummer* 2162#25 and 2162#26. For an index, see "Naamregister op het Clementynboek," *Antwerpsch Archievenblad*, 2nd ser., 5 (1930), pp. 124–59.

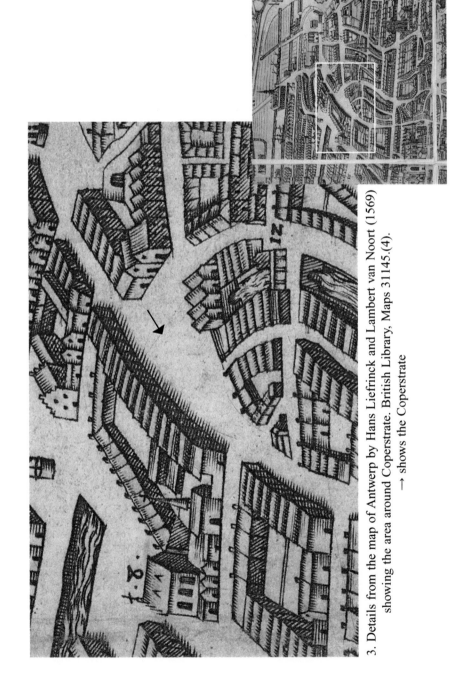

3. Details from the map of Antwerp by Hans Liefrinck and Lambert van Noort (1569) showing the area around Coperstrate. British Library, Maps 31145.(4).
→ shows the Coperstrate

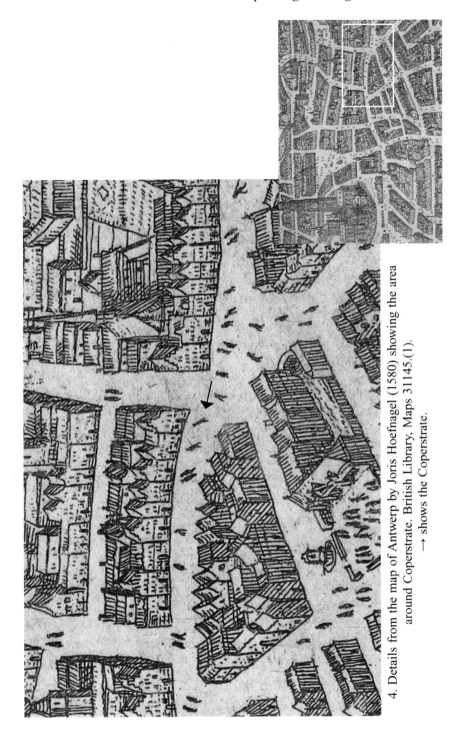

4. Details from the map of Antwerp by Joris Hoefnagel (1580) showing the area around Coperstrate. British Library, Maps 31145.(1). → shows the Coperstrate.

"de tymmerman in de Coeperstrate" ("the carpenter in Coperstrate") and his wife for the disturbance they have caused (25.421). While the overlap of some of these professions with characters from the *Miller's Tale* is, of course, mere chance, the occupations of the residents both at the beginning and the end of the century suggest a middle-class street. The legal fight over "one-sixth of a half house" ("sestendeele vander helft van eenen huyse ghestaen in de Coepoirstrate," 27.1–2) recorded in the *Oudt Register, mette Berderen (1336–1439)*, a continuation of *Clementynboek*,[53] may serve as a reminder that more than one family would probably occupy each structure.[54]

While there is, to my knowledge, no evidence connecting Coperstrate with prostitutes, it would not be unreasonable to imagine one living there; the real question is what kind of space she might have been expected to occupy. An ordinance of 31 May 1403 in the *Clementijnboek* allows "alle vroukene van stade, die opembaerlic int boerdeel zitten" ("all women of the town who openly sit in the brothel") to continue using the squares and yards previously taken, specifically naming "Guldenenberch," "Caudenberch," and "Boxstege," as well as the outermost grounds of the town, but forbidding them in other areas (25.399). It also mentions prostitutes dwelling in "a house or room" ("eenige huyse of cameren"). The mention of a brothel is interesting since here one might imagine a large common room, although its desertion except for Heile and her lovers would then be difficult to explain; in any case, Heile apparently lives alone.[55] Thus while the later, stunning views of Antwerp, such as that of Claes Janszoon Visscher (1652; Fig. 5),[56] depicting the commercial height of the city,[57] might suggest spaces large enough to

[53] *Antwerpsch Archievenblad*, 26.414–72; 27.1–472; 28.1–472; and 29.1–261. An index appears in *Antwerpsche Archievenblad*, 2nd ser., 5 (1930), pp. 167–241.

[54] For a discussion of domestic architecture during the medieval period, see Dominique Barthémy and Philippe Contamine, "The Use of Private Space," in *A History of Private Life. II. Revelations of the Medieval World*, ed. Georges Duby, trans. Arthur Goldhammer (Cambridge, MA: Harvard University Press, 1988), pp. 430–31 and 460–70. See also Jean Chapelot and Robert Fossier, *The Village and the House in the Middle Ages*, trans. Henry Cleere (Berkeley: University of California Press, 1985); and Jacques Heers, *La Ville au Moyen ge en Occident: paysages, pouvoirs et conflits* (Paris: Fayard, 1990).

[55] See Leah Otis, "Prostitution," in *DMA*, 10.154–55; and her *Prostitution in Medieval Society: The History of an Urban Institution in Languedoc* (Chicago: University of Chicago Press, 1985). See also Jacques Rossiaud, *Medieval Prostitution*, trans. Lydia G. Cochrane (Oxford: Blackwell, 1988); Ruth Mazo Karras, *Common Women: Prostitution and Sexuality in Medieval England* (New York: Oxford University Press, 1996); and Lorcin, *Façons*, pp. 51–57.

[56] Detail taken from Beudeker (see note 44 above) 30. As the British Library catalogue records, this print is 7' x 1' 4½" (approximately 2.1m x 0.4m). Coperstrate runs parallel to the river behind "De Borch kerck."

[57] The Scheldt was closed in 1648 to shipping, leading to Amsterdam and Rotterdam becoming the main ports in the region. Antwerp's second "Golden Age" was in the 1860s.

5. Detail from a view of Antwerp by Claes Janszoon Visscher, 1562. British Library, Maps C.9.e.4, 30.

have a tub hanging in the rafters but temporarily used by a prostitute, the late fourteenth- or early fifteenth-century reality makes this possibility much less likely. Unlike John's "hostelrye," Heile's dwelling probably did not have a ground floor that would have been open to the rafters.

Tubs in Other Tales

The insight that a hanging tub large enough to hold a person fits ill into Heile's domestic space on Cow Gate Street in Antwerp has implications for our understanding of the other proposed analogues to the *Miller's Tale*. In addition to *Heile van Beersele* there are six that require attention here.[58] The first five are similar to Chaucer's tale because they contain, with one exception, all three parts of the plot (the flood, the misdirected kiss, and the branding): Masuccio Salernitano's *Viola e li suoi amanti* (1476); Hans Sachs's *Der Schmit im Pachdrog* (1537); Valentin Schumann's *Ein andere Hystoria, von einem Kauffmann, der forchte sich vor dem Jüngsten Tage* (1559); Kaspar Cropacius's *Fabula de sacerdote et simplici rustico* (1581); and an untitled story in an anonymous collection, *Lyrum Larum sue Nugae Venales Joco Seriae; Das ist, Lustig in Ehren kan niemandt nit weren* (?1680). Because each includes distinctive features, it is of course possible that they are part of an older popular tradition also represented in the *Miller's Tale*. Their late dates, however, make this explanation even initially less likely than that they descended ultimately from Chaucer's work through perhaps complicated lines of transmission, which might include oral retellings. The sixth, the bowdlerized version *Die Sündfluth* (1845), is clearly related to the others, retaining for example the cry for water, and yet it has reduced the story to three characters, a farmer, his wife, and a smith. Testing the thesis that all of the other analogues that have been proposed are from the *Miller's Tale* would involve not only a comparison of their narratives but also an analysis of their authors' source habits and so must await the work of others. The seven—including *Heile van Beersele*—closest analogues, however, suggest strongly that Chaucer created a tale that became remarkably popular.

The relationship of the *Miller's Tale* to the earliest of these analogues, Masuccio Salernitano's *Viola e li suoi amanti*,[59] is, for my argument, a fortui-

---

58   The first four works considered here are included in Thompson, "Miller's Tale" and/ or Benson and Andersson, *Literary Context*, pp. 3–77, both of which consider other analogues as well. Erik Hertog discusses these four and *Heile van Beersele*; see *Chaucer's Fabliaux*, pp. 106–21. Richard Daniels also considers the analogues that I discuss here, with the exception of *Viola e li suoi amanti* and *Die Sündfluth*; see "Textual Pleasure in the *Miller's Tale*," in *The Performance of Middle English Culture: Essays on Chaucer and the Drama in Honor of Martin Stevens*, ed. James J. Paxson, Lawrence M. Clopper, and Sylvia Tomasch (Cambridge: D. S. Brewer, 1998), pp. 111–23.

59   Quotations are from Benson and Andersson, *Literary Context*, pp. 26–37.

tous place to begin because it involves the main issues under discussion. To my knowledge, no one has argued that Masuccio knew Chaucer's works,[60] and yet the two stories are similar and different in significant ways. Unlike Heile, Viola is married, indeed to a "lignaiuolo" (a "wood-worker," pp. 28–29),[61] a detail that resonates more strongly with Chaucer's tale because it plays no further role in the plot. Instead, however, of involving a husband, the plot revolves around three lovers, a Genoese merchant, a friar, and a smith, each of whom she has promised to satisfy as soon as her husband spends a night away from home. The merchant is told to come first, the friar after 11 o'clock, and the smith at dawn. The merchant proves slow, requiring not just the inducements of a downstairs meal, but also comforts of the upstairs bedroom. When the friar arrives early, Viola sends her first lover out of her bedroom window to wait in an "arvarello de erbicciole" ("box for plants," pp. 32–33).[62] He then witnesses the second couple's continuing activities after Viola, having satisfied the friar's desires once downstairs, is unable to induce him to leave. Arriving at dawn, the smith kisses the friar's arse, realizes what he has done and so returns with a hot spit. In the ensuing commotion, which wakes the neighbors, the merchant finally decides to jump off the window ledge, breaking his leg. The *novella* concludes with the smith conveying the friar to his convent and the merchant to his house, returning to Viola's house to enjoy the merchant's meal and Viola's attentions, and then beginning his day at the forge.

Remaining within the assumptions of the Finnish historical-geographical school of folklore, one might consider *Viola e li suoi amanti* as representing the stage in the development of tale type 1361 before the prediction of the flood was added, and yet because there is no other evidence for such a version, and since Masuccio wrote between fifty and a hundred years after Chaucer's death, this possibility seems less likely than that he adapted the narrative of the *Miller's Tale*. The collection in which it was published indicates a literate source for the *novella*.[63] Indeed Masuccio, or to use his given

---

[60] Heffernan discusses both a brief Italian biography of Chaucer, which appeared in 1647, and Stefano Surigone's *Epitaphium Galfridi Chaucer*, which appeared in Caxton's 1478 edition of the *Boece*, as exceptions to the general consensus that Chaucer was virtually unknown in Italy until the nineteenth century; see *Comedy in Chaucer and Boccaccio*, pp. 1–13.

[61] That his trade is making wooden shoes decreases but does not negate this similarity.

[62] The meaning of the phrase "arvarello de erbicciole" is clear even though the first word is, apparently, rare. A. Mauro prints "arbaretto de erbecciole"; see *Il Novellino* (Bari: Laterza, 1940), p. 253. Citing only this occurrence, *arbarétto* is defined as "barattolo, vaso, cassetta" in Salvatore Battaglia, *Grande dizionario della lingua italiana*, 21 vols., "Indice degli autori citati," and "Supplemento," 2004 (Turin:Unione Tipografico-Editrice Torinese, 1961–2004), *s.v.* If Masucccio did indeed create a word here, it is perhaps further evidence that he was translating from another source.

[63] In the dedication to Ippolita Sforza, daughter of the Duke of Milan, Masuccio imagined his work taking its place in her "sublime e gloriosa biblioteca"; Masuccio,

name, Tommaso Guardati, provides a good example of the literate circles in which *novelle* circulated following the success of the *Decameron*.[64] Born to noble parents—his father was secretary to Raimondello Orsini, prince of Salerno, and his mother the daughter of Tommaso Mariconda, a knight in the service of Margherita di Durazzo, regent of Naples—Masuccio himself became secretary to Roberto Sanseverino, then prince of Salerno. His *novelle*, written during the 1450s, were each dedicated to a member of the nobility or an intellectual in the court of the King of Naples. That the *Decameron* was the inspiration for his work may be inferred from a comment in the opening of the third part of his collection in which he claimed to have imitated Boccaccio's "ornatissimo idioma e stile,"[65] and in the structure of his work, which contains fifty stories divided into five sections. Discovering the sources of his individual narratives, however, has so far proved more difficult. Letizia Panizza relates his second *novella*, in which a friar seduces a nun by convincing her that God wants her to bear the Fifth Evangelist, to Friar Alberto's similar use of the claim that the angel Gabriel is in love with a lady to achieve a similar end (*Decameron* 4.2).[66] Similarly, Emilio Pasquini also compares Masuccio's fourth *novella*, which recounts how Friar Girolamo of Spoleto deceives the people of Sorrentino with a bone that he claims is the arm of Saint Mark, with Boccaccio's story of Friar Cipollo, who intends to use one of Gabriel's feathers for a similar purpose (*Decameron* 6.10).[67] If these source relationships are correct, Boccaccio's method of freely adapting short narratives for new purposes had indeed found another follower. In this literate context, *Viola e li suoi amanti* appears to be a surprisingly close reworking of Chaucer's story.

As a retelling of the *Miller's Tale*, Masuccio's *novella* can make us aware of particular features of the original. The most significant change is the omission of the flood motif, which both serves in Chaucer's tale as the means to remove the husband, and then re-enters the story unexpectedly at its end. That Masuccio (or an intermediate) considered these details unnecessary or perhaps unworkable indicates how extraordinary the *Miller's Tale* is. While

---

Novellino, p. 3. See also Judith Bryce, "'Fa finire uno bello studio et dice volere studiare.' Ippolita Sforza and her Books," *Bibliothèque d'Humanisme et Renaissance* 64 (2002), pp. 55–69.

[64] See Emilio Pasquini, "Letteratura popolareggiante, comica e giocosa, lirica minore e narrativa in volgare del Quattrocento," in *Storia della letteratura italiana*, 14 vols., ed. Enrico Malato (Rome: Salerno, 1995–2005), 3.803–911; and Letizia Panizza, "The Quattrocento," in *The Cambridge History of Italian Literature*, ed. Peter Brand and Lino Pertile (Cambridge: Cambridge University Press, 1996), pp. 154–58.

[65] Masuccio, *Novellino*, p. 180.

[66] Panizza, "Quattrocento," p. 155. See also Pasquini, "Letteratura," 3.886.

[67] Pasquini, "Letteratura," 3.886. He also compares Masuccio's ninth *novella* with *Decameron* 3.8.

not finding an effective substitute for the shot-window,[68] Masuccio did work effectively with the problem of domestic space by having the merchant provide a meal to be consumed downstairs, and so providing Viola some justification in believing she could satisfy the friar quickly without the merchant becoming aware of what she was doing. Her plan fails, leaving the humiliated merchant to watch the long second act. These changes, then, draw our attention to the distinctive setting of a hall within a house necessary for Chaucer's tale. The most revealing detail in *Viola e li suoi amanti*, however, is the "arvarello," the flowerbox outside Viola's window where the merchant is to sit, a remnant, I would suggest, of the tubs.

With its tub in the roof, Hans Sachs's *Der Schmit im Pachdrog*, published sixty-one years after *Il Novellino* appeared in print, might seem to provide stronger evidence for a popular version of a narrative known to Chaucer.[69] Here again, however, there is both internal and external evidence that suggests this work also derived from the *Miller's Tale*. Although asserting that there is "no direct link between Chaucer and any of the other early analogues," Erik Hertog lists five "details [in Sachs's narrative] that are remarkably similar to Chaucer's" and so indicate "a special relation";[70] I note these in the following summary by providing the corresponding phrases from the *Miller's Tale*. In order to sleep with the wife of a smith, a priest follows his sermon by predicting "ein grose wasser gûes" (8; "a great water downpour"), exhorting his listeners to flee to the mountains. Instead, the smith hangs his "pachtrog" (14; modern German "backtrog" [kneading tub]; compare Chaucer's "knedyng trogh" I, 3548, cf. 3564 and 3620) under his roof and retires to it. Thinking he has gone, his wife sends for the priest, and their night together begins. The smith's apprentice, with whom the wife too is involved, also recognizes the opportunity and so knocks at her "kamertuer" (28; "chamber door"). She responds: "'Ge nûr von mir weg, allers dropfen'" (30; "'Go away from me, you fool'"; compare "'Go fro the wyndow, Jakke fool,'" I, 3708). When he asks for a kiss, we learn that the "kamer" has "ein fensterlein" (33; "a little window"; compare "shot-window," I, 3358 and 3695), out of which the priest puts his arse. When the apprentice returns a second time with a hot iron rod, the priest repeats the action, and "den schmidknecht anplies" (44; "passes wind on the apprentice"; compare "leet fle a fart," I, 3806). The result is the same, with the priest's cry for water waking the smith, who cuts

---

[68]   As he pretends to try to open the door, the friar says to the smith, "'Anima mia, baciami un tratto per questa fessura che è bene larga'" ("'My love, give me a little kiss through this crack, which is large enough,'" pp. 34–35). Chaucer's night is "derk…as pich, or as the cole" (I, 3731), which explains why Absolon does not see what he kisses; Masuccio apparently found this detail unconvincing.

[69]   Quotations are from Benson and Andersson, *Literary Context*, pp. 60–63, by line numbers.

[70]   Hertog, *Chaucer's Fabliaux*, p. 107, note 13.

the ropes holding his trough and so falls to the ground "als schlueg ins haus der dünder" (50; "as if thunder had struck in the house," a detail that Hertog compares to the description of the fart in the *Miller's Tale*, I, 3807). Not only are these stories very similar, but they also contain evidence of verbal borrowings.

The sheer volume of Sachs's writing presents a daunting problem to source-scholars: in his *Summa al meiner gedicht*, he described, for example, gathering his work into thirty-four volumes.[71] Even without a full accounting of all his works, scholars recognize that this enormous output was based on his re-use of earlier stories.[72] Prominent among his sources are the Bible, the classics, and Boccaccio; to date, Chaucer has not figured on this list. There is, however, a second instance where one of Sachs's works, *Der Dot im Stock* (1555; *Death in the Tree Trunk*) has been recognized as related to one of the *Canterbury Tales*, the Pardoner's.[73] Because scholars have, however, approached this question looking only for evidence of Chaucer's use of popular material, the possibility that Sachs drew his play directly from Chaucer's collection remains largely unexplored.[74] And yet, as Walter Morris Hart has detailed,[75] *Der Dot im Stock* follows Chaucer's version closely, indeed more closely than any other with the possible exception of an Italian play, *Rappresentazione di Sant'Antonio*.[76] Chaucer, it appears to me, is Sachs's source.

Before leaving *Der Schmit im Pachdrog*, let me note two odd features that again point to the distinctive quality of Chaucer's narrative. It is not immediately apparent why, having been told to flee to the mountains to avoid a flood, the smith would decide to hang a kneading trough in his ceiling. Sachs attempts to gloss over this question by connecting his house "an dem pach" (11; "on the brook"; modern German *Bach*) with "sein pachtrog" (14). Rather than explaining it, this pun calls attention to an unlikely situation. Also revealing is the insistence on the wife's "kamer," with apparently both a door and window to the outside, since the apprentice wishes to enter through

71 See lines 157 ff.; see *Meistergesänge, Faftnachtspiel, Schwänke*, ed. Eugen Geiger (Stuttgart: Rhilipp Reclam, 1973), p. 7; and Joachim G. Bopeckh, Günter Albrecht, Kurt B ttcher, Klaus Gysi, and Paul Günter Kron, *Geschichte der deutschen Literatur von 1480 bis 1600* (Berlin: Volk un Wissen Volkseigener Verlag, 1961), pp. 434–35.

72 See Helen Watanabe-O'Kelly, "The Early Modern Period (1450–1720)," in *The Cambridge History of German Literature*, ed. Watanabe-O'Kelly (Cambridge: Cambridge University Press, 1997), p. 112; and Bopeckh, et al., *Geschichte*, p. 436.

73 An extract appears in Frederick Tupper, "The Pardoner's Tale," in *Sources and Analogues*, ed. Bryan and Dempster, pp. 429–36.

74 See Chapter 1 for the suggestion that Chaucer created this story.

75 Walter Morris Hart, "The *Pardoner's Tale* and *Der Dot im Stock*," *Modern Philology* 9 (1922), pp. 17–22. Hart does not consider Chaucer to be Sachs's source, but rather assumes that both worked from a common lost text.

76 Hamel prints the relevant passages in "The Pardoner's Tale," *S&A*, 1.294–313.

one and kiss through the other. While one could construct an imaginative floor plan that would satisfy the narrative, I would argue that it leaves the impression of an author aware of the difficulty of placing the husband in his tub and the lovers in their bed within the same house.

The final three analogues and the much later bowdlerized version may be dealt with more briefly. Son of a Leipzig printer and bookseller of the same name, Valentin Schumann worked (except for a year fighting against the Turks) for various printers in southern Germany, leaving behind a single volume, *Nachtbüchlein*, containing fifty-one short narratives.[77] The second work in the collection, *Ein Andere Hystria, von einem Kauffmann, der forchte sich vor dem Jüngsten Tag*,[78] offers the most extreme solution presented by the tubs: here they are removed from the house, becoming instead a boat, which when completed, the merchant hoists up and suspends awaiting the flood. When he cuts it down at the end of the story, "der kauffman halber tod auss dem schiff in sein hauss wurd tragen" ("the merchant, half dead, was taken out of the boat and into the house," pp. 66–67). Born in Pilsen where he later held the office of Syndicus, Kaspar Cropacius was one of the many poets laureate of the Holy Roman Empire.[79] A single volume of poems, *Cropacii Poemata*, was published two years after his death in 1580.[80] The pastoral setting of his *Fabula de sacerdote et simplici rustico* justifies the description of "a mean raft (42; "exiguam...ratem"), yet makes its placement "in the lofty roof of his house" (43); "Sublimique domus in culmine") appear even more odd.[81] When it falls, the craft crashes not onto a dirt floor, but "in silices" (82; "onto the rocks"). The chronologically last of the five analogues, an untitled story in the anonymous collection of amusing anecdotes and riddles, *Lyrum Larum*,[82] and the bowdlerized version, *Die Sünd-*

---

[77] The 1559 edition can be found online at http://books.google.com/books?id=apxQ AAAAcAAJ&printsec=frontcover&source=gbs_ge_summary_r&cad=0#v=onepage& q&f=false/. See also Bopeckh, et al., *Geschichte*, pp. 407–08.

[78] Quotations are from Benson and Andersson, *Literary Context*, pp. 64–67.

[79] See John L. Flood, *Poets Laureate in the Holy Roman Empire: A Bio-bibliography*, 4 vols. (Berlin: Walter de Gruyter, 2006). The introduction provides much information about the tradition in which these authors wrote.

[80] The 1580 edition is available online at http://books.google.com/books?id=Vh9XA AAAAcAAJ&pg=PP16&dq=cropacii+poemata&hl=en&sa=X&ei=wvopU8StCebN0g HNtYGwAg&ved=0CC8Q6AEwAA#v=onepage&q=cropacii%20poemata&f=false/.

[81] Quotations are from Benson and Andersson, *Literary Context*, pp. 72–77, by line number. They translate "a tiny craft" and "to the rooftop of his house."

[82] The British Library has two editions of the work. The one printed in 1680 identifies the place of publication as "Fridlibii" and the publisher "Typis et sumptibus Sociorum Narre"; it has 369 items. See http://www.muenchener-digitalisierungszentrum.de/index.html?c=autoren_index&projekt=&ordnung=alpha&ab=Flavigny,%20 Louise%20Mathilde%20de&suchbegriff=&kl=&l=en/. The other of 1700 does not identify a publisher or place of publication and has 361 items. Item 279 is the one that concerns us here. In the version online, it appears on 119 (misnumbered in the edition

fluth, provide some evidence that the story circulated in an oral form; yet both are long after Chaucer's day and their ultimate sources are more likely to have been one of the literate versions already discussed. Each calls attention to the difficulty of placing a tub in the rafters. In the seventeenth-century tale, the peasant ties his "Teichtrog" ("dough-trough") "oben im Haus an den Giebel" ("up in the house in the gable"),[83] while in the nineteenth-century one, the farmer and his helper raise the "Backtrog" ("kneading trough") by winding it "um zwei Hahnenbalken" ("around two rooster-poles").[84]

Taken as a group, these analogues point strongly toward Chaucer's author-ship of a story that was then retold in many later forms. Inconsistences abound in the descriptions of the tubs that become a boat in Schumann's retelling and a planter in Masuccio's. Normal domestic spaces simply do not provide the room necessary for the *Miller's Tale*. These analogues attest instead to the popularity of Chaucer's creation.

Peronella, Berangier and Punishment according to the Joints of the Body

The question of the actual sources of the *Miller's Tale* leads first to the narra-tive technique which Chaucer learned from watching Boccaccio reset the Lover's Gift Regained in three distinct places, Varlungo, Milan, and Naples, because his tale sprang from a recognition of the humorous possibilities offered by the story of Peronella, *Decameron* 7.2, which Boccaccio had taken largely from Apuleius's *Metamorphoses* (VIII.v–vii).[85] Chaucer saw a more outrageous conclusion possible in Oxford where there was domestic space to wind three tubs into the rafters. He was drawn to this idea since it

---

as 199)–20. The story was identified and printed by Reinhold Kohler, "Nochmals zu Chaucer's The Miller's Tale," *Anglia* 2 (1879), pp. 135–36.

[83] Kohler, "Nochmals," p. 135.

[84] Karl Müllenhof, *Sagen Märchen un Lieder der Herzogtümer Schleswig, Holstein und Lauenburg* (Kiel: Schwerssche, 1845), p. 589.

[85] See Lee, *Decameron*, p. 186. The extract is printed by Benson and Andersson, *Literary Context*, pp. 6–9. It seems unlikely that Chaucer knew the earlier work. Neither Bruce Harbert nor Richard L. Hoffman mentions Apuleius; see "Chaucer and the Latin Clas-sics," *Geoffrey Chaucer*, ed. Derek Brewer, Writers and their Background (London: Bell, 1974), pp. 137–53, and "The Influence of the Classics on Chaucer," *Companion to Chaucer Studies*, ed. Beryl Rowland, rev. edn (New York: Oxford University Press, 1979), pp. 185–201. His works, however, became more widely known in the mid-fourteenth century; see Carl C. Schlam, "Apuleius in the Middle Ages," *The Classics in the Middle Ages*, ed. Aldo S. Bernardo and Saul Levin, Medieval & Renaissance Texts & Studies 69 (Binghamton: Center for Medieval and Early Renaissance Studies, 1990), pp. 363–69. See also, D. S. Robertson, "The Manuscripts of the *Metamorposes* of Apuleius," *Classical Quarterly* 18 (1924), pp. 27–42 and 85–99; and P. K. Marshall, "Apuleius," *Texts and Transmission: A Survey of the Latin Classics*, ed. L. D. Reynolds (Oxford: Clarendon Press, 1983), pp. 15–16.

would provide a visual challenge to the Knight's belief in a divinely ordered, hierarchical universe: the tubs are a parody of the Boethian "faire cheyne of love" (I, 2988) that Theseus expounds at the end of the *Knight's Tale*. Chaucer developed this response to the Knight most consistently by turning to *Decameron* 3.4, the story of Friar Puccio, which with its elaborate ruse to allow the priest to sleep with Monna Isabetta also provided him with a means to move the tubs into the rafters. Before considering 3.4, however, I would like to discuss here not only 7.2 but also Guérin's *De Berangier au lonc cul*, and an eschatological motif, punishment according to the joints of the body, since these combine to form the mechanism that brings one of the tubs crashing to the floor. They also show Chaucer moving the emphasis of the tale away from directly challenging contemporary social hierarchies and toward his more general themes of judgment and misjudgment.

Boccaccio located Apuleius's Milesian story in an "out of the way" (McWilliam, p. 491; "molto solitaria," 7.2, 9) part of Naples called Avorio, made the husband a bricklayer, identified his wife as Peronella, and both named her lover Giannello Scrignario and suggested some class distinction between them by describing him as "un giovane de' leggiadri" (7.2, 8; a "gallant, dandy").[86] Otherwise, the two narratives are very similar.[87] In both when the lovers are interrupted one morning by the husband's unexpected return, the women hide the men in in a *dolium* (Apuleius) or a *doglio* (Boccaccio), large earthenware vessels used by the Romans and later Italians for storing and transporting liquids.[88] On learning that their husbands are accompanied by potential buyers of these now hiding places, both immediately claim that they have already found others willing to pay more for them. The husbands get into the tubs to clean them. Apuleius continued:

> At vero adulter bellissimus ille pusio inclinatam dolio pronam uxorem fabri superincurvatus secure dedolabat. Ast illa capite in dolium demisso maritum suum astu meretricio tractabat ludicre. Hoc et illud et aliud et rursus aliud purgandum demonstrat digito suo, donec utroque opere perfecto....
>
> (Meanwhile, the dashing lover-boy stretched the worker's wife on the tub and, throwing himself upon her, fearlessly gave her a barrel of fun. And she put her head down into the tub and played a whore's trick on her husband;

---

[86] Translating Branca's note, p. 799, note 7.

[87] See, however, Forni's analysis of Boccaccio's changes in the description of the tub, which is in Apuleius old and cracked, but in 7.2 sound although encrusted with the dried dregs of wine. Forni comments, "Giannello is a wit: deceiving the husband is not sufficient for him, he must also mock him in the presence of his wife with a covert accusation of neglecting his sexual duties," *Adventures in Speech*, p. 73.

[88] See *Paulys Real-Encyclopädie der classischen Altertumswissenschaft*, 2nd edn, ed. Georg Wissowa, vol. 5 (Stuttgart: J. B. Metzler, 1905), *s.v.*; and *Der neue Pauly, Enzyklopädie der Antike*, ed. Hubert Cancik and Helmuth Schneider, vol. 3 (Stuttgart: J. B. Metzler, 1997), *s.v.*

she pointed here and there, indicating this place and that which needed cleaning, until both jobs were finished.)[89]

Boccaccio preserved this scene, but is more explicit about the act itself:

> E mentre che cosí stava e al marito insegnava e ricordava, Giannello, il quale appieno non aveva quella mattina il suo disidero ancor fornito quando il marito venne, veggendo che come volea non potea, s'argomentò di fornirlo come potesse; e a lei accostatosi, che tutta chiusa teneva la bocca del doglio, e in quella guisa che negli ampi campi gli sfrenati cavalli e d'amor caldi le cavalle di Partia assaliscono, a effetto recò il giovinil desiderio; il quale quasi in un medesimo punto ebbe perfezione e fu raso il doglio, e egli scostatosi e la Peronella tratto il capo del doglio e il marito uscitone fuori. (7.2, 33–34)

> (While she was busy instructing and directing her husband in this fashion, Giannello, who had not fully gratified his desires that morning before the husband arrived, seeing that he couldn't do it in the way he wished, contrived to bring it off as best he could. So he went up to Peronella, who was completely blocking up the mouth of the tub, and in the manner of a wild and hot-blooded stallion mounting a Parthian mare in the open fields, he satisfied his young man's passion, which no sooner reached fulfilment than the scraping of the tub was completed, whereupon he stood back, Peronella withdrew her head from the tub, and the husband clambered out; McWilliam, p. 494).

That the position here is itself mildly scandalous is made clear at the beginning of the following tale: "non seppe sí Filostrato parlare obscuro delle cavalle partice, che l'avedute donne non ne ridessono, sembiante faccendo di rider d'altro" (7.3, 2; "Filostrato's reference to the Parthian mare was not so abstruse as to prevent the alert young ladies from grasping its meaning and having a good laugh, albeit they pretended to be laughing for another reason," McWilliam, p. 495). This allusion to the "Parthian mare" calls attention to the part of the woman's anatomy placed out the window in the *Miller's Tale*,[90] linking it to *De Berangier au lonc cul*. In any case the tubs in the *Metamorphoses* and the *Decameron* remain securely on the ground until the husbands carry them home for the lovers. Winding them into the roof belongs to Chaucer.[91]

---

[89] Benson and Andersson, *Literary Context*, pp. 8–9.

[90] The metaphor might also be the source for the descriptions of Alison as a "colt" (I, 3263 and 3282).

[91] I have suggested elsewhere that *Le Chevalier à la corbeille* ("The Knight in the Basket"), one of the four *fabliaux* in the Harley Manuscript (London, British Library, Harley 2253), offers another source for this motif; see Frederick M. Biggs, "A Bared Bottom and a Basket: A New Analogue and a New Source for the *Miller's Tale*," *Notes and Queries* n.s. 56 (2009), pp. 340–41.

Long recognized as an analogue to the *Miller's Tale*, *De Berangier au lonc cul* is likely to be the source for the misdirected kiss since it is rare to find stories of women exposing themselves in this way. Indeed, the only other example I know is the Anglo-Norman *fabliau*, *La Gageure* ("The Wager"), found in the Harley Manuscript (London, British Library, Harley 2253; c. 1340), which is less close to the *Miller's Tale* not only because of its "violent" misogyny but also because it lacks the confusion, shared by Chaucer's tale and *De Berangier au lonc cul*, over just what has been kissed.[92] It is also revealing that in all six of the analogues to the *Miller's Tale* discussed earlier, the priest performs this action twice, revealing not that they come from a source independent of Chaucer's tale, but rather that the genre as a whole is anti-clerical and that these later authors considered it unlikely for a woman to behave as "Berangier" and Alison do.

The misdirected kiss is of course misdirected only from the perspective of the one kissing. In *De Berangier au lonc cul*, Guérin used it explicitly to humiliate a lower-class character, supporting the aristocratic wife's actions. The son of a "usurier riche et conblé" (17; "a rich and prosperous usurer"),[93] marries the daughter of a nobleman, who has fallen into debt to his father. The narrator comments:

> Ainsi bons lignaiges aville,
> Et li chastelain et li conte
> Declinent tuit et vont à honte;
> Se marient bas por avoir,
> Si en doivent grant honte avoir,
> Et grant domaige si ont il;
> Li chevalier mauvais et vill
> Et coart issent de tel gent,
> Qui covoitent or et argent
> Plus qu'il ne font chevalerie;
> Ainsi est noblece perie. (24–34)

> (Thus good heritage is abased,
> And noblemen and counts
> All decline and come to shame.
> Those who marry beneath themselves for money
> Ought to be ashamed of it,
> And great harm they have from it.
> Evil and lowborn knights
> And cowards issue from such folk,

---

92 See Biggs, "Bared Bottom." The characterization of this *fabliau* is that of Carter Revard who edited and translated it in the "Four Fabliaux from London, British Library MS Harley 2253, Translated into English Verse," *Chaucer Review* 40 (2005), pp. 111–40.

93 I follow the text and translation in Benson and Andersson, *Literary Context*, pp. 10–25, by line numbers.

Who covet gold and silver
More than doing chivalrous deeds.
Thus does nobility perish.)

Made a knight by his father-in-law, the husband proves more interested in the comforts of his new position than in valorous deeds, and indeed when spurred into action by his wife's scorn, he rides out to the nearest forest to batter his own armor so he can pretend to have engaged in combat. His wife becomes suspicious and so arms herself as a knight and follows him. When she finds him again hacking at his shield with his sword, she demands to know why he is damaging her woods and mistreating his weapons. He responds that if he has harmed her in any way ("Se ge vos ai de reins meffait," 211), he will make it up with "avoir et deniers" (214; "riches and money"). Instead, she offers him a choice:

"Comment que vos jostez à moi
Et ge vos creant et octroi,
Se vos cheez, ja n'i faudrez,
Maintenant la teste perdrez
Que ja de vos n'aurai pitié;
Ou ge descendrai jus à pié,
Si me prenrai à abaissier;
Vos me venroiz el cul baisier,
Trés el milieu se vos volez." (219–27)

(Either you joust with me—
And I swear to you and guarantee,
If you fall, without fail
Straightway you lose your head,
For I will have no pity on you—
Or I will dismount on foot,
And I will bend over
And you will come and kiss my arse,
Exactly in the middle, if you please.)

He chooses the second option, but before following through on it, he discovers an anatomical puzzle referred to in the *fabliau's* title:

Et cil regarde la crevace;
Du cul et du con, li resanble
Que trestot li tenist ensanble.
A lui meïsme pense et dit
Que onques si lonc cul ne vit... (242–46)

(And he looked at the crevice
Of the arse and the quim, and it seemed
To him that it was all one.
He thinks and says to himself
That he has never before seen so long an arse.)

De Berangier au lonc cul concludes with the wife riding home, sending for a lover, and then, when her husband finds them in bed, telling him that if he acts against her she will complain to his dear friend, "mesire Berangier / Au lonc cul" (290–91; "Lord Bérenger / Of the Long Arse"). Before its closing moral, the story provides a final reference to class: "Et cele fait sa volenté / Qui ne fu sote ne vilaine" (296–97; "And she did what she pleased / She who was neither foolish nor lowborn").

Chaucer adapted this well-directed kiss,[94] which Guérin had used to assert the superiority of the upper class, both to provoke the response that would conclude his story and develop themes of judgment and misjudgment as they pertain to an individual, a community, and, finally, God. The last first. Like the husband in *De Berangier au lonc cul*, Absolon too is unsure what he has just done:

> Abak he stirte, and thoughte it was amys,
> For wel he wiste a womman hath no berd.
> He felte a thyng al rough and long yherd,
> And seyde, "Fy! allas! what have I do?" (I, 3736–39)

Alison finds the situation funny—"'Tehee!' quod she, and clapte the wyndow to" (I, 3740) as does Nicholas:

> "A berd! A berd!" quod hende Nicholas,
> "By Goddes corpus, this goth faire and weel." (I, 3742–43)

Obviously, the scene is humorous and yet Chaucer engaged it in the main themes of his narrative by anticipating it in a complicated pun on "pryvitee" in the tale's prologue. In order to annoy the Reeve, the Miller announces that his story will be about a member of the Reeve's profession, a carpenter, who is deceived by a clerk. The Reeve objects:

> "Stynt thy clappe!
> Lat be thy lewed dronken harlotrye.
> It is a synne and eek a greet folye
> To apeyren any man, or hym defame,
> And eek to bryngen wyves in swich fame.
> Thou mayst ynogh of othere thynges seyn." (I, 3144–48)

---

[94] Schumann's version may retain an echo of Chaucer's use of this motif in the final prayer, "Ich wolte, das es allen also gienge, die den frommen männern ire weyber nicht wolten mit friden lassen, sondern tag und nacht mit bitt und geschenck nachlauffen, wie der schmid, und ihn die frawen liessen in hindern kussen" ("I wish that everyone would fare this way, who refuses to leave the wives of good men alone and day and night pursues them with prayers and presents, like the smith, and the women would let them kiss their arse," Benson and Andersson, *Literary Context*, pp. 66–67).

The Miller's complex response leads to a pun that associates God's secrets with a wife's genitalia:

> "Leve brother Osewold,
> Who hath no wyf, he is no cokewold.
> But I sey nat therfore that thou art oon;
> Ther been ful goode wyves many oon,
> And evere a thousand goode ayeyns oon badde.
> That knowestow wel thyself, but if thou madde.
> Why artow angry with my tale now?
> I have a wyf, pardee, as wel as thow;
> Yet nolde I, for the oxen in my plogh,
> Take upon me moore than ynogh,
> As demen of myself that I were oon;
> I wold bileve wel that I am noon.
> An housbonde shal nat been inquisityf
> Of Goddes pryvetee, nor of his wyf.
> So he may fynde Goddes foyson there,
> Of the remenant nedeth nat enquere." (I, 3151–66)

By linking God's plan, which will not be fully known until the Last Judgment,[95] with a woman's "privates," Chaucer used the Miller to challenge the Knight's certainty about the existence of "the faire cheyne of love" (I, 2988), a divine order that favors those at the top.

As we will see when we turn in a moment to the flood, the themes of judgment and misjudgment remain central to the *Miller's Tale*. Here let me note that Absolon's form of revenge, the branding, links its concluding actions to the eschatological motif of punishment according to the joints of the body. Thomas J. Farrell points out that the phrase "poetic justice," invoked by earlier critics "was first used about seventeenth-century neoclassical tragedy, and can be applied to medieval texts only anachronistically."[96] One feature, however, of the *Visio Pauli* which Theodore Silverstein suggests is then widely dissem-

---

95 I Corinthians 13:9–12: "For we know in part and we prophesy in part. But when that which is perfect is come, that which is in part shall be done away.... We see now through a glass in a dark manner; but then face to face." Laura Howes and I have argued that through this association of ideas Chaucer invoked another biblical story, God's revelation of his "posteriora" ("back parts") to Moses in Exodus 23:23; see "Theophany in the Miller's Tale," *Medium Ævum* 65 (1996), pp. 269–79; see also Louise M. Bishop "'Of Goddes pryvetee nor of his wyf': The Confusion of Orifices in 'The Miller's Tale," *Texas Studies in Language and Literature* 44 (2002), pp. 231–46. Commentary tradition on the passage in Exodus distinguishes between knowing God through faith, as we can in this world, and through reason, possible only in the next.

96 Thomas J. Farrell, "Privacy and the Boundaries of Fabliau in the *Miller's Tale*," *ELH* 56 (1989), p. 778.

inated is the "appropriateness of punishment to sin."[97] The example that he uses to illustrate this point—sinners immersed in a "fiery stream, each to the depth that accords with the nature of his transgression"—includes one group particularly relevant to the *Miller's Tale*. The archangel Michael explains to Paul that those immersed to the navel (*umbilicum*), "sunt fornicatores et adulterantes, qui postea non recordantur venir ad penitenciam" ("are the fornicators and adulterers who did not afterwards seek penance").[98] Similarly, in John Audelay's version, written before 1426, when Paul sees sinners hanging on burning trees—

> Sum be þe hed, sum be þe tungus treuly,
> Sum be þe fyt, sum be þe hond,
> Sum be þe membirs of here body,
> Þat þai han sunnyd within herthe leuand

—Michael explains:

> Þese greuyn God ful greuously
> With al þe lymys of here body,
> In lechory, slouþ, and glotone,
> And dyed in det and dedle syn.[99]

These examples indicate that Nicholas's burn "amydde the ers" (I, 3810) is generally appropriate for fornication. Because, however, the correlation in the *Visio* between sin and punishment is far from exact, it is possible that the placement of Absolon's stroke is appropriate for another reason. The contrast between the fart and the question which it answers—Absolon's 'Spek, sweete bryd, I noot nat where thou art' (I, 3805)—recalls the discrepancy between Nicholas's crude actions and his learning epitomized in the couplet,

> As clerkes ben ful subtile and ful queynte;
> And prively he caughte hire by the queynte.... (I, 3275–76)

The fart itself, then, may serve as a mocking reminder of his pretended higher knowledge,[100] making his *ars* a fitting body part for punishment. The

---

97 Theodore Silverstein, *Visio Sancti Pauli: The History of the Apocalypse in Latin together with Nine Texts*, Studies and Documents 4 (London: Christophers, 1935), p. 12.

98 *Visio S. Pauli*, ed. Herman Brandes (Halle: M. Niemeyer, 1885), p. 76. This is a version of Redaction IV, which was widely disseminated in the later Middle Ages. For other redactions, see Theodore Silverstein and Anthony Hilhorst, eds., *Apocalypse of Paul: A New Critical Edition of Three Long Latin Versions*, Cahiers d'orientalisme 21 (Geneva: Cramer, 1997).

99 "Poem 16," *The Poems of John Audelay*, ed. Ella Keats Whiting, Early English Texts Society, Original Series 184 (London: Oxford University Press, 1931), p. 112.

100 For a similar use, see the *Summoner's Tale*, and the analysis in Cooper, *Structure*, p. 132.

precisely appropriate nature of the penalty that Nicholas pays encourages the reader to believe that some just judge is at work.

Any sense of justice in Nicholas's punishment, however, is overwhelmed by questions about the fates of the other characters. At first the idea of a correlation between sin and punishment seems to explain John's broken arm (I, 3829): he has held his wife "narwe in cage" (I, 3224). Yet the religious context forces us to consider whether John's jealousy really is a sin, a doubt Chaucer increased by developing his character beyond that of the stock figure in a *fabliau*. Similarly, there seems little theological significance in Absolon's punishment, even though it corresponds to his squeamish nature (I, 3337). It is, however, Alison who presents the most obvious problem to the possibility of justice, since she remains unpunished even though she performs the same actions as Nicholas.[101] While failing to resolve the question, an eschatological perspective nevertheless focuses attention on the theme of judgment and misjudgment. Moreover, by combining *De Berangier au lonc cul* with the motif of punishment according to the joints of the body, Chaucer brought the flood story to a dramatic conclusion.

Decameron *3.4: Narrative Borrowings*

From the opening description of Nicholas's predicting the weather (I, 3190–98) to the concluding laughter of the neighbors at John's "fantasye" (I, 3840), the flood plays a prominent role in the *Miller's Tale*, and while the Bible itself and its reworking in the Corpus Christi plays are obviously sources for this material,[102] Chaucer's decision to have his character exploit religion to gain sexual pleasure is distinctive enough to deserve further attention. *Decameron* 3.4, which has been considered an analogue for the tale,[103] provides

---

[101] For other interpretations, see Peter G. Beidler, "Art and Scatology in the *Miller's Tale*," *Chaucer Review* 12 (1977), pp. 90–102, repr. in Beidler, *Chaucer's Canterbury Comedies*, pp. 1–16; Elaine Tuttle Hansen, *Chaucer and the Fictions of Gender* (Berkeley: University of California Press, 1992), pp. 234–35; and Derek Pearsall, *The Canterbury Tales* (London: Routledge, 1985), p. 178.

[102] See Míceál F. Vaughan, "Chaucer's Imaginative One-Day Flood," *Philological Quarterly* 60 (1981), pp. 117–23; V. A. Kolve, *Chaucer and the Imagery of Narrative, the First Five Canterbury Tales* (Stanford: Stanford University Press, 1984), pp. 197–216; and Sandra Pierson Prior, "Parodying Typology and the Mystery Plays in The Miller's Tale," *Journal of Medieval and Renaissance Studies* 16 (1986), pp. 57–71.

[103] Richard Stephen Guerin provides reviews the evidence in his doctoral thesis *The Canterbury Tales* and *Il Decamerone* (University of Colorado, 1966), 16–17. Heffernan writes, "even a casual reading of *Decameron* 3, 4 reveals that Chaucer picked up important cues from Boccaccio that helped him shape the scene of the lovers' arrangements for the tryst in *The Miller's Tale*"; "Chaucer's *Miller's Tale*," p. 319. N. S. Thompson comments, "what links the two narratives is the motif of a secret knowledge of salvation that the scholar imparts (in Boccaccio, the attainment of a paradise and in Chaucer,

not only this general idea but also parallels for the way Chaucer structures his narrative.[104] Although there are differences, both stories introduce the lovers' schemes in similar ways, depict responses from the wives when they learn from their husbands about the plans, and culminate in descriptions of significant nights when the lovers enjoy each other's company virtually in the presence of the husbands. While these similarities may be mere coincidences, it seems more likely that Chaucer was drawn to the spatial challenge that Boccaccio's narrative presented—how can lovers be together when husbands are so close?—because it mirrored the problem he had found in the story of Peronella.

The narrative element that connects *Decameron* 3.4 most closely to the *Miller's Tale* is that both introduce the schemes that control the action through long speeches in which the lovers, Dom Felice and Nicholas, hoodwink the husbands, Puccio di Rinieri (referred to as Friar Puccio because he has become a lay member of the Franciscans) and John, by seeming to take them into their confidence, pretending to reveal secrets to them, and swearing them to secrecy. In 3.4, Dom Felice immediately announces the confidential nature of his information and insists that he will only reveal it if Friar Puccio promises not to tell others:

> "Io ho già assai volte compreso, fra Puccio, che tutto il tuo disidero è di divenir santo; alla qual cosa mi par che tu vadi per una lunga via, là dove ce n'è una ch'è molto corta, la quale il Papa e gli altri suoi maggior prelati, che la sanno e usano, non vogliono che ella si mostri; per ciò che l'ordine chericato, che il più di limosine vive, incontanente sarebbe disfatto, sí come quello al quale più i secolari né con limosine né con altro attenderebbono. Ma per ciò che tu se' mio amico e haimi onorato molto, dove io credessi che tu a niuna persona del mondo l'appalesassi e volessila seguire, io la t'insegnerei." (3.4, 12–13)

> ("It has been obvious to me for some time, Friar Puccio, that your one overriding ambition in life is to achieve saintliness, but you appear to be approaching it in a roundabout way, whereas there is a much more direct route which is known to the Pope and his chief prelates, who although they use it themselves, have no desire to publicize its existence. For if the secret were to leak out, the clergy, who live for the most part on the proceeds of charity, would immediately disintegrate, because the lay public would no longer give them their support, whether by way of almsgiving or in any

---

salvation from the Flood) as the basis of a scheme for getting the husband apart so that the two lovers may enjoy each other intimately almost under the husband's nose"; "Local Histories: Characteristic Worlds in the *Decameron* and the *Canterbury Tales*," in *Decameron*, ed. Koff and Schildgen, p. 95.

[104] Lee notes that "no source seems to have been discovered for this story"; *Decameron*, p. 75. It is the sole item listed by Thompson under K1514.2, "husband duped into doing penance while rascal enjoys the wife," in the *Motif-Index*.

other form. However, you are a friend of mine and you have been very good to me, and if I could be certain that you would not reveal it to another living soul, and that you wanted to give it a trial, I would tell you how it is done," McWilliam, p. 259).

Even though there is no exact match in the Italian for McWilliam's "secret," the context makes it clear that this "way" ("via") to achieve salvation is known only to the highest church officials, "il Papa e gli altri suoi maggior prelati," and that they guard it carefully. Friar Puccio will not only save his soul, but also enter an exclusive group, which includes his teacher, if he agrees not to reveal it.

Nicholas is at least as direct in bringing John into his plan, even if his claims are less believable because they are more extreme. His first words to John, following his provocative "'Allas! / Shal al the world be lost eftsoones now?'" (I, 3488–89) as he pretends to awake from his trance at John's entrance, are designed to tie the two together:

> "… Fecche me drynke,
> And after wol I speke in pryvetee
> Of certeyn thyng that toucheth me and thee.
> I wol telle it noon oother man, certeyn." (I, 3492–95)

Nicholas does not, of course, need anything to drink; we have already been told that he has provided himself with "Bothe mete and drynke for a day or tweye" (I, 3411). While it may make him appear more spiritual in John's eyes if he seems to have been fasting for several days, it also binds the two together in fellowship, recalling Dom Felice's practice of dining at Friar Puccio's house (3.4, 8); Nicholas continues to speak only after "ech of hem had dronke his part" (I, 3498). Moreover, in the lines quoted above, Nicholas ties John to him with his assertions that this matter "toucheth me and thee" and that he "wol telle it noon oother man."[105] Yet also significant here is that he introduces the idea of secrets and secrecy in the phrase "in pryvetee," a central theme, as we have already seen in the discussion of the misdirected kiss, of the tale as a whole.

The secret that Nicholas then offers to reveal to John, which does not concern just his spiritual salvation but should involve the saving of mankind, is known not exclusively to the most important Church officials but only to God himself, and Nicholas. He makes the point at the beginning of his speech, linking his own instruction ("conseil")[106] to God's:

> "John, myn hooste, lief and deere,
> Thou shalt upon thy trouthe swere me heere

---

[105] See also I, 3501, quoted below.
[106] *MED, s.v.*, cites I, 3503 under meaning 8, "A secret, private matter(s), a secret plan."

> That to no wight thou shalt this conseil wreye,
> For it is Cristes conseil that I seye...." (I, 3501–04)

He invokes this point again when he commands John not to tell his servant, and states that he may not save Alison's maid—the point being that John should not tell, nor can Nicholas save, either—because he will not reveal God's secrets:

> "But Robyn may nat wite of this, thy knave,
> Ne eek thy mayde Gille I may nat save;
> Axe nat why, for though thou aske me,
> I wol nat tellen Goddes pryvetee." (I, 3555–58)

Finally, near the end of his speech he adds that the three of them must not speak but rather pray when they are in the tubs, "For it is Goddes owene heeste deere" (I, 3588).[107] While these claims are, of course, absurd, Nicholas uses them to achieve the same end that Dom Felice has in Boccaccio's story.

Another detail that Chaucer has preserved from Dom Felice's speech should also be noted: as in 3.4, Nicholas forbids intercourse between John and Alison.[108] In the *Decameron* this injunction, which makes little sense because Friar Puccio is not interested in sex, is part of the penitential exercise:

> "e appresso questo gli conviene cominciare un digiuno e una abstinenzia grandissima, la quale convien che duri quaranta dí, ne' quali, non che da altra femina ma da toccare la propria tua moglie ti conviene astenere." (3.4, 16)

> ("and next he must start to fast and practise a most rigorous form of abstinence, this to continue for forty days, during which you must abstain, not only from the company of other women, but even from touching your own wife," McWilliam, p. 218).

Chaucer preserves this point, perhaps because it will make it easier for Alison not to be observed by John when she descends from her tub to be with Nicholas:

> "Thy wyf and thou moote hange fer atwynne,
> For that bitwixe yow shal be no synne,
> Namoore in lookyng than ther shal in deede.' (I, 3589–91)

---

[107] Recalling, as Heffernan notes ("Chaucer's *Miller's Tale*," p. 321), Friar Puccio's penance.

[108] See Heffernan, "Chaucer's *Miller's Tale*," p. 320; and Daniel P. Poteet II, "Avoiding Women in Times of Affliction: An Analogue for the 'Miller's Tale,' A 3589–91," *Notes and Queries* n.s. 19 (1972), pp. 89–90.

In both stories, however, this detail does little more than remind the audience, at the expense of the husbands, of the lovers' intentions.

Moreover, in both stories the husbands immediately tell their wives, although here too Chaucer develops the point to emphasize John's stupidity.[109] As already noted, Dom Felice asserts that he will only reveal this way to gain salvation if Friar Puccio swears he will not show it to others, and Panfilo, the teller of 3.4, continues:

> Frate Puccio, divenuto disideroso di questa cosa, prima cominciò a pregare con grandissima instanzia che gliele insegnasse e poi a giurare che mai, se non quanto gli piacesse, a alcun nol direbbe.... (3.4, 14)

> (Being anxious to learn all about it, Friar Puccio began by earnestly begging Dom Felice to teach him the secret, then he swore that he would never, without Dom Felice's express permission, breathe a word about it to anyone...; McWilliam, p. 218).

John, too, promises he will not reveal what Nicholas tells him:

> "Nay, Crist forbede it, for his hooly blood!"
> Quod tho this sely man, "I nam no labbe,
> Ne, though I seye, I nam nat lief to gabbe.
> Sey what thou wolt, I shal it nevere telle
> To child ne wyf, by hym that harwed helle!" (I, 3508–12)

In spite of his oaths, the rhyme of "labbe" ("one who cannot keep a secret, a blabbermouth") with "gabbe" ("to speak foolishly, talk nonsense; also talk indiscreetly") undercuts this speech and suggests that "sely" here probably means "foolish" or "gullible" rather than "spiritually favored."[110] More striking, however, is John's use of the word "wyf," although by also mentioning a "child," something he does not have, he suggests that he is not specifically thinking of Alison.

In any case while Friar Puccio receives permission to tell his wife, Monna Isabetta, John does not. As Panfilo tells his story, "e da lui partitosi e andatosene a casa, ordinatamente, con sua licenzia perciò, alla moglie disse ogni cosa" (3.4, 22; "after leaving Dom Felice he went straight home, where, having obtained the monk's permission beforehand, he explained everything to his wife in minute detail," McWilliam, p. 219). In the *Miller's Tale* John too goes directly to his wife, but here there is no indication that Nicholas has told him he may speak to her:

> This sely carpenter goth forth his wey.
> Ful ofte he seide "Allas and weylawey,"
> And to his wyf he tolde his pryvetee....(I, 3601–03)

---

[109] See Guerin, *Canterbury Tales*, pp. 20–21.
[110] *MED, s.vv.*

The characterization of John again as "sely" links this passage to the earlier one, but more important is that here the secret ("pryvetee") has become his own: he is not aware that it might have any larger meaning. John breaks his promise because he has understood it, as the empty phrases "allas and weylawey" indicate, only in the most superficial way.

Equally significant are the ways the wives respond: Chaucer uses this scene, as Boccaccio has, to show the woman's intelligence, but modifies it to suggest that Nicholas and Alison have already discussed the plan. In the *Decameron*, Monna Isabetta is apparently learning about the scheme for the first time, but quickly understands it and shapes a place for herself within it:

> La donna intese troppo bene, per lo star fermo infino a matutino senza muoversi, ciò che il monaco voleva dire; per che, parendole assai buon modo, disse che di questo e d'ogni altro bene che egli per l'anima sua faceva ella era contenta, e che, acciò che Idio gli facesse la sua penitenzia profittevole, ella voleva con essolui digiunare ma fare altro no. (3.4, 22)

> (The lady grasped the monk's intentions all too clearly, particularly when she heard about the business of standing still without moving a muscle until matins. Thinking it an excellent arrangement, she told her husband that she heartily approved of the idea, and also of any other measures he took for the good of his soul, adding that in order to persuade God to make his penance profitable she would join him in fasting, but there she would draw the line; McWilliam, p. 219).

Monna Isabetta thinks quickly here, anticipating Alison's tricking of Absolon at the end of the *Miller's Tale*, and decides immediately to fit in with this scheme, joining with the fasting, which sets up the joke at the conclusion of this story, but nothing else. Moreover, she incites her husband to undertake the program even as she reveals that she understands his weakness: she will fast "acciò che Idio gli facesse *la sua* penitenzia profittevole." Friar Puccio's concern is only with his own salvation.

Alison's response shows that she knows John's weakness as well. When she hears his story,

> ...she ferde as she wolde deye,
> And seyde, "Allas! go forth thy wey anon,
> Help us to scape, or we been dede echon!
> I am thy trewe, verray wedded wyf;
> Go, deere spouse, and help to save oure lyf." (I, 3606–10)

It is Alison's death that most concerns John when Nicholas tells him of the flood: "'Allas, my wyf! / And shal she drenche? Allas, myn Alisoun!'" (I, 3522–23); and one might hear Alison mocking John in her "Allas!" In any case she stresses her role as John's wife in the phrases "trewe, verray wedded wyf" and "deere spouse," and so her concluding "oure lyf" sounds like an affirmation of their life together, until of course one remembers that Nicholas will also be saved.

The suggestion at this point in the *Miller's Tale* that Alison already knows of Nicholas's scheme before John tells her—"And she was war, and knew it bet than he" (I, 3604)—draws attention to another change that Chaucer has made in his source: the reason why the lovers must come up with their elaborate plots in the first place. *Decameron* 3.4 addresses this problem directly:

> Ma quantunque bene la trovasse disposta a dover dare all'opera compimento, non si poteva trovar modo, per ciò che costei in niun luogo del mondo si voleva fidare a esser col monaco se non in casa sua; e in casa sua non si potea però che fra Puccio non andava mai fuor della terra; di che il monaco avea gran malinconia. (3.4, 11)

> (But although he found her very willing to give effect to his proposals, it was impossible to do so because she would not risk an assignation with the monk in any other place except her own house, and her own house was ruled out because Friar Puccio never went away from the town, all of which made the monk very disconsolate; McWilliam, p. 217).

While the Miller's claims that John was "jealous" and held Alison "narwe in cage" (I, 3224) allude to a similar explanation, it quickly becomes apparent that neither is true, and indeed that John is often away from his house where both Nicholas and Alison reside. The lack of any need for Nicholas's elaborate scheme to fool John is perhaps the most glaring inconsistency in Chaucer's tale, suggesting that he inherited it—at first surprisingly, but ultimately to good effect—from this source.

It is more difficult to see Chaucer's use of *Decameron* 3.4 in the conclusion of the *Miller's Tale* since he complicates the story by including a second lover, Absolon, as well as the details of the misdirected kiss and the branding. Even here, however, we can perceive the influence of 3.4, not only in the emphasis on the intelligence of the women but also in the question of domestic space. Panfilo's story culminates not on the first occasion when Dom Felice and Monna Isabetta enjoy the success of the scheme,[111] but rather on a later one when Friar Puccio is disturbed from his penance by "alcuno dimenamento di palco" (3.4, 24; "a certain amount of vibration in the floorboards," McWilliam, p. 220) and so asks Monna Isabetta what is going on. The following exchange emphasizes her quick wit:

---

[111] The two stories also differ in that Nicholas's plan is designed to permit the lovers to be together only once while Dom Felice's makes this possible as long as Friar Puccio's penance lasts. Indeed, Panfilo concludes by remarking that his lovers continue meeting even after the penance has ended. Chaucer raises this possibility by describing John's public humiliation at the end of the tale, but leaves it unresolved.

La donna, che motteggevole era molto, forse cavalcando allora la bestia di san Benedetto o vero di san Giovanni Gualberto, rispose: "Gnaffé, marito mio, io mi dimeno quanto io posso."

Disse allora frate Puccio: "Come ti dimeni? che vuol dir questo dimenare?"

La donna ridendo (e di buon'aria e valente donna era e forse avendo cagion di ridere) rispose: "Come non sapete voi quello che questo vuol dire? Ora io ve l'ho udito dire mille volte: 'Chi la sera non cena, tutta notte si dimena.'" (3.4, 25–27)

(His wife, who had a talent for repartee, and who at that moment was possibly riding bareback astride the nag of St. Benedict or St. John Gualbert, replied: "Heaven help me, dear husband, I am shaking like mad."

"Shaking?" said Friar Puccio. "What is the meaning of all this shaking?"

His wife shrieked with laughter, for she was a lively, energetic sort of woman, and besides, she was probably laughing for a good reason. "What?" she replied. "You don't know its meaning? Haven't I heard you saying, hundreds of times: 'He that supper doth not take, in his bed all night will shake?'" McWilliam, p. 220).

Although it may be absurd to look for a source for laughter, we may hear an echo of Monna Isabetta in Alison's "'Tehee!'" (I, 3740) as she shuts the window on Absolon.[112] She has just told Nicholas, "'thou shalt laughen al thy fille'" (I, 3722) and the laughter of the "folk" (I, 3840) when they survey the entire scene also suggests that of the *Decameron*'s female story-tellers at Panfilo's account (3.5, 2). Chaucer has caught the lighthearted tone of this *novella*, and it is finally the woman who turns the scheme to her own pleasure.

This ending, however, also calls attention to the amusing challenge of *Decameron* 3.4, the proximity of the lovers to the husband. Boccaccio leads into the exchange quoted above with the comment that "era il luogo, il quale frate Puccio aveva alla sua penitenzia eletto, allato alla camera nella quale giaceva la donna, né da altro era da quella diviso che da un sottilissimo muro" (3.4, 24; "the place where Friar Puccio had elected to do his penance was adjacent to the room where the lady slept, from which it was separated only by a very thin wall," McWilliam, p. 220); and following their near discovery, the lovers engage in their activity "in altra parte della casa" (3.4, 30; "in another part of the house," McWilliam, p. 221). The limited space in houses makes this story all the more remarkable, returning us again to Chaucer's Oxford setting.

---

[112] N. S. Thompson also notes that this "humorous exchange with her husband on the other side of the bedroom wall . . . parallels Alison's ready repartee with Absolon," "Local Histories," p. 97.

Decameron *3.4: Religion*

Decameron 3.4 is also likely to be a source rather than an analogue for the *Miller's Tale* because we can see Chaucer developing its religious content for a specific purpose: to force his audience to question their certainty about their judgments of the characters, particularly John, and, more surprisingly, of the significance of the world in which they live. Simply by transforming the penitential exercise of 3.4 into a prediction of a second Flood, he made the theme of judgment more prominent, since Noah's flood was often associated typologically with the Last Judgment.[113] This theme dominates the end of the tale, as is apparent even to those, such as Seth Lerer, who view its particular details as lost in the carnivalesque laughter of the "folk" (I, 3826–49) and so consider the tale as a whole to be essentially secular.[114] Yet within the laughter, the Miller's perspective remains distinct, condemning John as the jealous husband of the *fabliaux* tradition: 'Thus swyved was this carpenteris wyf, / For al his kepyng and his jalousye' (I, 3850–51). That Chaucer expected his audience to question this view seems evident, as has already been mentioned, from John's lack of jealousy throughout the story and, most clearly, from the way he is introduced, which differs significantly from the opening description of Friar Puccio in *Decameron* 3.4. The result of this questioning, however, is not to turn the tale into one with a clear moral, but rather to open the possibility that the physical world may have more spiritual significance than we assume, a theme, too, that Chaucer could have borrowed, if to a different end, from Boccaccio's *novella*.

Both *Decameron* 3.4 and the *Miller's Tale* begin with descriptions of the husbands, even agreeing on the detail that they both are prosperous ("ricco," 3.4, 4; and "riche," I, 3188). Panfilo's version, however, moves toward its important concluding detail—Friar Puccio is quite possibly a member in a confraternity of flagellants:

---

[113] The Flood is compared to the Second Coming in Matthew 24:38–9 (cf. Luke 17:26–7) and to the fire of Judgment in 2 Peter 3:6–7. See also Jack P. Lewis, *A Study of the Interpretation of Noah and the Flood in Jewish and Christian Literature* (Leiden: Brill, 1968), pp. 169–73; Biggs and Howes, "Theophany," p. 278, note 18; and Daniel Anlezark, *Water and Fire: The Myth of the Flood in Anglo-Saxon England* (Manchester: Manchester University Press, 2006), pp. 21–43 and 73–84.

[114] "The brilliance of the *Miller's Tale* rests precisely in this confusion of scatology and eschatology. All the apocalyptic imagery of flood and fire, hell mouth and horror, finds itself reduced to farts and private parts. And the proper response to such theatricalized mockery and play is the laughter of the group. The townsfolk's response to John the Carpenter's experience may well model our own, as we are invited to laugh at this fantasy (I, 3840)"; Seth Lerer, *The Yale Companion to Chaucer* (New Haven: Yale University Press, 2006), p. 252. This Bakhtinian reading of the tale is anticipated by Alfred David, who indeed quotes Bakhtin; *The Strumpet Muse: Art and Morals in Chaucer's Poetry* (Bloomington: Indiana University Press, 1976), pp. 92–107. See also Pearsall, *Canterbury Tales*, pp. 179–80.

Secondo che io udi' già dire, vicino di San Brancazio stette un buono uomo
e ricco, il quale fu chiamato Puccio di Rinieri, che poi essendo tutto dato
allo spirito si fece bizzoco di quegli di san Francesco e fu chiamato frate
Puccio; e seguendo questa sua vita spirituale, per ciò che altra famiglia non
avea che una donna e una fante, né per questo a alcuna arte attender gli
bisognava, usava molto la chiesa. E per ciò che uomo idiota era e di grossa
pasta, diceva suoi paternostri, andava alle prediche, stava alle messe, né
mai falliva che alle laude che cantavano i secolari esso non fosse, e digiu-
nava e disciplinavasi, e bucinavasi che egli era degli scopatori. (3.4, 4–5)

(Close beside the Church of San Pancrazio, or so I have been told, there
once lived a prosperous, law-abiding citizen called Puccio di Rinieri, who
was totally absorbed in affairs of the spirit, and on reaching a certain age,
became a tertiary in the Franciscan Order, assuming the name of Friar
Puccio. In pursuit of these spiritual interests of his, since the other members
of his household consisted solely of a wife and maidservant, which relieved
him of the necessity of practising a profession, he attended church with
unfailing regularity. Being a simple, well-intentioned soul, he recited his
paternosters, attended sermons, went to mass, and turned up infallibly
whenever lauds were being sung by the lay-members. Moreover, he prac-
tised fasting and other forms of self-discipline, and it was rumoured that
he was a member of the flagellants; McWilliam, p. 216).

As Gordon Leff notes at the beginning of his discussion of the movement,
which originated in Perugia in 1260, "flagellation as such was neither new
nor heretical,"[115] and when Clement VI banned it in 1351, following a widespread outbreak in response to the Plague, his attention was apparently
directed mainly toward Germany and the Low Countries where the distur-
bances had been most violent.[116] Yet Clement VI's bull, *Inter sollicitudines*,
condemns more widely the "prophana multitudo simplicium hominum, qui
se Flagellantes appellant"[117] ("the ungodly multitude of simple men, who

[115] Gordon Leff, *Heresy in the Later Middle Ages: The Relation of Heterodoxy to Dissent
c. 1250–c. 1450*, 2 vols. (Manchester: University of Manchester Press, 1967), 2.485.
[116] See Richard Kieckhefer, "Radical Tendencies in the Flagellant Movement of the
Mid-Fourteenth Century," *Journal of Medieval and Renaissance Studies*, 4 (1974), pp.
157–76; and John Henderson, "The Flagellant Movement and Flagellant Confraternities in Central Italy 1260–1400," in *Religious Motivation: Biographical and Sociological Problems for the Church Historian*, ed. Derek Baker, Studies in Church History 15
(Oxford: Blackwell, 1978), pp. 147–60. Henderson discusses flagellation in Florence
in the fourteenth and fifteenth centuries in *Piety and Charity in Late Medieval Florence*
(Oxford: Clarendon Press, 1994); see especially pp. 113–54.
[117] *Corpus documentorum Inquisitionis haereticae pravitatis Neerlandicae*, ed. Paul
Fredericq, 4 vols. (Ghent: Martinus Nijhoff, 1889–1900), 1.200. See Leff, *Heresy*, p.
485. Chaucer may also have been influenced in his decision to change Friar Puccio's
private penance to an apocalyptic second flood by the Flagellants' "letter from heaven,"
published on Christmas Day 1348, that announced God would destroy the world unless
Christians stopped sinning; see Leff, *Heresy*, p. 488.

call themselves Flagellants"), and Boccaccio's construction, "bucinavasi che egli era degli scopatori," suggests that what Friar Puccio is doing is wrong.[118] In contrast, then, to V. A. Kolve, who sees the *novella* as moving "toward a moment of greater thematic tension" than the *Miller's Tale* because Friar Puccio "practices genuine devotion" in one room while Monna Isabetta and Dom Felice engage in fornication in another,[119] I would argue that this opening might well influence a reading of the story: Dom Felice's scheme not only exploits Friar Puccio's weakness but also points out his sin, and so Friar Puccio deserves to live in ignorance of his wife's and his friend's dishonesty toward him.

Apparently recognizing that Boccaccio's initial characterization of the husband could change, upon reflection, the sense of his *novella*'s conclusion, Chaucer too began his tale with a significant piece of information, yet one that does not lead to a single conclusion but rather invokes such different possible interpretations that it makes us aware of the difficulty of passing any judgment at all on John. His opening lines conclude with the assertion that John is a carpenter:

> Whilom ther was dwellynge at Oxenford
> A riche gnof, that gestes heeld to bord,
> And of his craft he was a carpenter. (I, 3187–89)

This profession is significant for the story, explaining John's absences at Oseney and his ability both to hang tubs in the rafters and to construct ladders to reach them. It also, however, has meaning outside of the story for the Miller, who tells his tale to anger the Reeve, a carpenter (I, 614 and I, 3913–15) who, apparently, fears being cuckolded (I, 3151–53). From the Miller's perspective, John deserves his punishment, much as Friar Puccio does, because he is a stock character from the *fabliaux* tradition, the foolish old man who has married a much younger wife (I, 3221–32). Since the tale itself, however, provides no indication that John is jealous and instead emphasizes his love for Alison, John's profession assumes meaning on a level not available to the Miller: he invokes not only Noah, builder of the Ark, but also Joseph, who in the popular tradition of the Corpus Christi plays fears Mary's pregnancy proves him a cuckold. As Hanning has noted, Chaucer sets up this possibility in the Miller's description of his tale as "a legend and a lyf, / Bothe of a carpenter and of his wyf" (I, 3141–42).[120] While neither Flood nor

---

[118] Heffernan comments, "Boccaccio even suggests that limited intelligence caused Puccio to become a religious fanatic,"; "Chaucer's *Miller's Tale*," p. 320.

[119] *Chaucer and the Imagery of Narrative*, 211. Kolve concedes that Friar Puccio's "is imprudent and excessive," but argues that "he seeks an end that, in other medieval contexts, might be affirmed" (p. 211).

[120] Robert W. Hanning, "'Parlous Play': Diabolic Comedy in Chaucer's *Canterbury Tales*," in *Chaucer's Humor: Critical Essays*, ed. Jean E. Jost, Garland Studies in Humor 5

Incarnation occurs in the tale, to consider it devoid of religious significance is to read it only as the Miller does.

Rather than offering a simple moral message such as, as has been suggested, the punishment of the sins of lechery, avarice and pride,[121] the *Miller's Tale*, in part through the character of John, directs our attention to the possibility of a spiritual dimension in this world, a theme Chaucer might well have found in the controlling joke of *Decameron* 3.4. Panfilo introduces the *novella* with the comment, "madonna, assai persone sono che, mentre che essi si sforzano d'andarne in Paradiso, senza avvedersene vi mandano altrui" (3.4, 3; "madam, many are those who, whilst they are busy making strenuous efforts to get to Paradise, unwittingly send some other person there in their stead," McWilliam, p. 216). He returns to this idea in the conclusion, where he notes that Monna Isabetta often tells Dom Felice during their times together, "'tu fai fare la penitenzia a frate Puccio, per la quale noi abbiamo guadagnato il Paradiso'" (3.4, 31; "'you make Friar Puccio do penance, but we are the ones who go to Paradise,'" McWilliam, p. 221). For Kolve, this is a "bedroom compliment,"[122] one that does not undercut the unarticulated yet still present moral perspective of the story. What may have caught Chaucer's attention, however, is the suggestion that physical activity, either penance or sex, is the means to gain the reward of a paradise in this world. While Boccaccio might expect readers to draw Kolve's further contrast between Friar Puccio's actions and those of Dom Felice and Monna Isabetta, his narrator, Panfilo, does not.

Similarly, it is being saved in this world that Chaucer emphasized in his discussion of a second flood, the more dramatic religious theme that he substitutes for Boccaccio's concern with penance as a way to achieve personal salvation in heaven. Nicholas's description of the approaching catastrophe to John reiterates the false prophecy that he has allowed him to overhear (I, 3488–89 quoted above) since it concerns only the destruction of mankind, not any moral reasons for this punishment or any suggestion of its place in a larger plan of salvation:[123]

(New York: Garland, 1994), p. 303. See further, as Hanning notes, Prior, "Parodying Typology," p. 61 and note 10.

[121] For example, D. W. Robertson claims that "the theme of the three temptations, or of the three basic sins to which these temptations appeal, appears as a framework for the Miller's Tale"; *A Preface to Chaucer: Studies in Medieval Perspectives* (Princeton: Princeton University Press, 1962), p. 382; see also Whitney F. Bolton, "The 'Miller's Tale': An Interpretation," *Mediaeval Studies* 24 (1962), pp. 83–94; and Paul A. Olson, "Poetic Justice in the *Miller's Tale*," *Modern Language Quarterly* 24 (1963), pp. 227–36. Pearsall dismisses these interpretations; *Canterbury Tales*, p. 179.

[122] *Chaucer*, p. 211.

[123] Kolve's discussion of the Corpus Christi plays demonstrates that these issues would have been readily apparent to a medieval audience; *Chaucer*, pp. 198–216.

> "Now John," quod Nicholas, "I wol nat lye;
> I have yfounde in myn astrologye,
> As I have looked in the moone bright,
> That now a Monday next, at quarter nyght,
> Shal falle a reyn, and that so wilde and wood
> That half so greet was nevere Noes flood.
> This world," he seyde, "in lasse than an hour
> Shal al be dreynt, so hidous is the shour.
> Thus shal mankynde drenche, and lese hir lyfe." (I, 3513–21)

John's response (I, 3522–23, quoted above) shows his concern only for Alison's physical survival. Indeed, the only suggestion of any spiritual significance for this event is Nicholas's remark that, although he does not know God's reason, John should be content "to han as greet a grace as Noe hadde" (I, 3560), which echoes Genesis 6:8, "Noe vero invenit gratiam coram Domino" ("But Noah found grace before the Lord"). Even here, however, Nicholas follows this comment with the promise: "'Thy wyf shal I wel saven, out of doute'" (I, 3561), a theme which he develops in his vivid account of their life first during and then after the Flood:

> "Thanne shaltou swymme as myrie, I undertake,
> As dooth the white doke after hire drake.
> Thanne wol I clepe, 'How, Alison! How, John!
> Be myrie, for the flood wol passe anon.'
> And thou wolt seyn, 'Hayl, maister Nicholay!
> Good morwe, I se thee wel, for it is day.'
> And thanne shul we be lordes al oure lyf
> Of al the world, as Noe and his wyf.'" (I, 3575–82)

Their reward will be not eternal salvation but sovereignty in this world and so "grace" appears to mean no more than "help from God in a secular matter."[124]

Although this emphasis on the purely physical nature of this flood reflects John's limited understanding of religious matters, the amount and kind of information Chaucer included about him gives him and the world in which he lives their own spiritual weight.[125] Of John's ignorance of religious matters there can be no doubt.[126] It is, for example, striking that Nicholas threatens

---

[124] *MED, s.v.*, definition 2.

[125] In contrast, Kolve argues that John's inability to place the flood in even the most apparent biblical context justifies his punishment: "complacent in his certainty that men 'sholde nat knowe of Goddes pryvetee' (3454), he forgets they need some candid sense of their own," *Chaucer*, p. 210.

[126] Alan J Fletcher explains many of the expressions that characterize John's belief; "The Faith of a Simple Man: Carpenter John's Creed in the *Miller's Tale*," *Medium Ævum* 61 (1992), pp. 96–105. While Fletcher is inclined to see Chaucer satirizing John through these descriptions, I would suggest that they might be read more positively.

him with the loss not of salvation but rather of his reason if he betrays him:[127]

> "And if thou telle it man, thou art forlore
> For this vengeaunce thou shalt han therfore,
> That if thou wreye me, thou shalt be wood." (I, 3505–07)

Moreover, immediately before this conversation, John has mixed charms with prayers when he attempts to awake Nicholas from his trance:

> Therwith the nyght-spel seyde he anon-rightes
> On foure halves of the hous aboute,
> And on the thresshfold of the dore withoute:
> "Jhesu Crist and Seinte Benedight,
> Blesse this hous from every wikked wight,
> For nyghtes verye, the white *pater-noster*!
> Where wentestow, Seinte Petres soster?" (I, 3480–86)

Yet in spite of this confusion and his desire to save Nicholas "from elves and fro wightes" (I, 3479), his initial appeal to him is particularly apt and contrasts his simple faith with Nicholas's pretended knowledge of spiritual secrets:

> "What! Nicholay! What, how! What, looke adoun!
> Awak, and thenk on Cristes passioun!" (I, 3477–78)

Douglas Gray comments in the *Riverside Chaucer* that "the recalling of Christ's passion is a traditional remedy against despair,"[128] and yet equally striking is the command that Nicholas change the direction of his gaze, away from hidden spiritual matters to God's revealed presence in this world, a theme Chaucer had set up with John's reflection on "another clerk" who was so intent "upon the sterres" that "he was in a marle-pit yfalle" (I, 3457–60).[129]

It is finally the specificity of John's Oxford that Chaucer used to question any simple judgment of this character and his world.[130] John's work for the

---

[127] Kisha Tracy has pointed out to me that this passage recalls John's fear that Nicholas has fallen "in some woodnesse" (I, 3452) and so may play on a particular weakness in his character.

[128] Gray, "Miller's," p. 846. See also Fletcher, "Faith," p. 101 and note 33; and Biggs and Howes, "Theophany," p. 271 and note 12.

[129] In contrast to Nicholas, John's devotion is genuine: see Heffernan's comparison ("Chaucer's *Miller's Tale*," p. 321) between Friar Puccio's prayers and the *Paternoster* begun by Nicholas as the three settle down in their tubs (I, 3638) and Ross, who calls attention to the words "devocioun," "biddeth," and "prayere" in the following lines (I, 3640–41) and comments "of the three, apparently only John is devout enough to pray," *Miller's Tale*, p. 213.

[130] Although he reaches a different conclusion, Bennett provides, it should be noted, much of the information on which the following remarks are based; *Chaucer at Oxford*.

Augustinian abbey of Oseney, which stands in stark contrast to Nicholas's exploitation of his university connections, Absolon's abuse of his ecclesiastical privileges, and Friar Puccio's self-serving religious practices, is carefully, if obliquely, detailed. Situated just outside the city walls, the abbey would, in J. A. W. Bennett's phrases, "catch the traveller's eye" with "its vast array of buildings," more notable even than the "noble Norman tower" of Saint Frideswide's monastery within.[131] John is at the abbey when Nicholas first approaches Alison (I, 3274), and again when Nicholas prepares to fool him with his trance (I, 3400); yet it is the scene in which the cloisterer responds to Absolon that reveals more about his work:

> This parissh clerk, this amorous Absolon,
> That is for love alwey so wo bigon,
> Upon the Monday was at Oseneye
> With compaignye, hym to disporte and pleye,
> And axed upon cas a cloisterer
> Ful prively after John the carpenter;
> And he drough hym apart out of the chirche,
> And seyde, "I noot; I saugh hym heere nat wirche
> Syn Saterday; I trowe that he be went
> For tymber, ther oure abbot hath hym sent;
> For he is wont for tymber for to go
> And dwellen at the grange a day or two...." (I, 3657–68)

The contrast with Absolon, who travels with friends "to disporte and pleye" is clear, and is strengthened if, as Bennett writes, "Oseney probably means Oseney Mead or Bulstake Mead—a name that itself suggests the sport of bull-baiting."[132] John is clearly known to the cloisterer for his work, and indeed is held in such esteem by the abbot that he trusts him to travel to outlying buildings to select timber.[133] It is this willingness to work, which is emphasized in the tale by his fatigue after making the ladders and hanging the tubs,[134] that sets him apart from Nicholas, who lives "After his freendes fyndyng and his rente" (I, 3219),[135] and from Friar Puccio, whose wealth, as the introductory passage quoted above reveals, allows him to attend a seemingly endless series of services since he does not need to follow any profession.

Helen Cooper speaks for many when she identifies the "firm grounding in fourteenth-century Oxford" as "one of the things that makes the Miller's

---

[131] Bennett, *Chaucer at Oxford*, p. 24.
[132] Bennett, *Chaucer at Oxford*, p. 54.
[133] Bennett, *Chaucer at Oxford*, p. 30.
[134] Cooper suggests that making tubs "would have been joiner's work," *Canterbury Tales*, p. 99; Bennett notes that "carpenters often made similar objects," *Chaucer at Oxford*, p. 30. Perhaps Chaucer acknowledged that there would not have been time to make them.
[135] See Ross, *Miller's Tale*, p. 138.

Tale unique."[136] Let me recall just one more example, the oaths, since they too may suggest Chaucer's use and development of *Decameron* 3.4. Panfilo's ribald comment, quoted earlier, that on the night in question Monna Isabetta "was riding bareback astride the nag of St. Benedict or St. John Gualbert" becomes more meaningful when we know that her lover is not just a monk, and so under the order of St. Benedict,[137] but one associated with the monastery of San Pancrazio, which at the time was under the control of the Vallombrosan order,[138] founded by the local Florentine saint, John Gualbert.[139] Similarly John, as he attempts to waken Nicholas from his trance, appeals to St. Frideswide (I, 3449), who as Cooper notes was "the most notable local saint"[140] and the founder of the Oxford monastery dedicated to her,[141] which was, like Oseney, under the control of Augustinian canons in the fourteenth century.[142] If Chaucer was aware of Boccaccio's use of a local tradition, he removed the satire from his, and instead surrounded it with two more oaths by John, both invoking "Seint Thomas" (I, 3425 and 3461). Since Alison has previously sworn "by Seint Thomas of Kent" (I, 3291), it seems likely that John also calls on Thomas Becket, whose shrine is the destination of the Canterbury pilgrims, and yet who as Bennett notes also had a significant local presence: "Oxford had a parish of St. Thomas, a St. Thomas Hall, a fraternity of St. Thomas with a private chapel at St. Mary's, the university church, and an annual gathering for Mass on St. Thomas's day, followed by a dinner; the fraternity's chantry priest, who acted as gospeller to the vicar of the parish, said Mass daily between five and six a.m., so that travellers and scholars could attend before beginning their day."[143] Alison's oath, promising to commit adultery, should warn against taking all references to spiritual matters as necessarily devout, a point that is again apparent in the conflicting interpretations of Gerveys's swearing "by seinte Neot" (I, 3771): Angus MacDonald associates it with Neot's chastising Alfred for his carnal desires,[144] while Mary Richards links it to the saint's habit of praying

---

[136] Cooper, *Canterbury Tales*, p. 99.

[137] Boccaccio makes similar jokes, as Branca points out, in 1.4 and 3.8; *Decameron*, p. 366.

[138] See Walter Paatz and Elizabeth Paatz, *Die Kirchen von Florenz, ein kunstgeschichtliches Handbuch*, 6 vols. (Frankfurt am Main: V. Klostermann, 1952–55), 4.565.

[139] See Kennerly M. Woody, "John Gualberti, St.," in *DMA* 7.123; and Anna Benvenuti, "San Giovanni Gualberto e Firenze," *I Vallombrosani nella società italiana dei secoli XI e XII*, ed. Giordano Monzio Compagnoni, Archivio Vallombrosano 2 (Vallombrosa: Edizioni Vallombrosa, 1995), pp. 83–112.

[140] Cooper, *Canterbury Tales*, p. 98.

[141] See John Blair, "Frithuswith," in the *Oxford Dictionary of National Biography*, 61 vols. (Oxford: Oxford University Press, 2004), 21.50–51.

[142] See David Knowles and R. Neville Hadcock, *Medieval Religious Houses, England and Wales* (New York: St. Martin's Press, 1971), pp. 169–70.

[143] *Chaucer at Oxford*, p. 15.

[144] Angus MacDonald, "Absolon and St. Neot," *Neophilologus*, 48 (1964), pp. 235–37.

early in the day.[145] Related to the present argument, however, is Ruth H. Cline's discussion of fourteenth-century traditions connecting St. Neot to the founding of Oxford University, and more specifically to New College.[146] Simply by invoking saints connected to Oxford, Chaucer strengthens the possibility that this world has greater religious significance than expected, although exactly what that significance is remains difficult to judge.

Apology and Judgment

While scholars have found the possible influence of other *novelle* in the *Miller's Tale*, it is Chaucer's borrowing from Boccaccio's *Conclusione dell'autore* in his "apology" at the end of the *Miller's Prologue* (I, 3167–86) that best supports the argument advanced here because it shows his interest in the themes of judgment and misjudgment. As has been noted,[147] he closely followed Boccaccio's claim—"ma io non pote' né doveva scrivere se non le raccontate, e per ciò esse che le dissero le dovevan dir belle e io l'avrei scritte belle" (16; "but I could only transcribe the stories as they were actually told, which means that if the ladies who told them had told them better, I should have written them better," McWilliam, p. 800)—that he should be excused for some of the stories since he merely reports what he has heard:

> And therfore every gentil wight I preye,
> For Goddes love, demeth nat that I seye
> Of yvel entente, but for I moot reherce
> Hir tales alle, be they bettre or werse,
> Or elles falsen som of my mateere. (I, 3171–75)

---

[145] Mary Richards, "The *Miller's Tale*: 'By Seinte Note,'" *Chaucer Review* 9 (1975), pp. 212–14. On the texts she cites, see also her "The Medieval Hagiography of St. Neot," *Analecta Bollandiana* 99 (1981), pp. 259–78.

[146] Ruth H. Cline, "Three Notes on *The Miller's Tale*," *Huntington Library Quarterly* 26 (1963), pp. 131–35. See also Edmund Reiss, "Daun Gerveys in the *Miller's Tale*," *Papers in Language and Literature* 6 (1970), pp. 115–24; and James Ortego, "Gerveys Joins the Fun: A Note on *Viritoot* in the *Miller's Tale*," *Chaucer Review* 37 (2003), pp. 275–79.

[147] The resemblance between the two passages was noted by Robert K. Root, "Chaucer and the *Decameron*," *Englische Studien* 44 (1912), pp. 1–7, and discussed more fully by Hubertis M. Cummings, *The Indebtedness of Chaucer's Works to the Italian Works of Boccaccio* (1916; repr. New York: AMS Press, 1967), pp. 177–78. See also Donald McGrady, "Chaucer and the *Decameron* Reconsidered," *Chaucer Review* 12 (1977), p. 2; Pearsall, *Canterbury Tales*, pp. 36–37; Beidler, "Just Say Yes," pp. 33–34; and Heffernan, "Chaucer's *Miller's Tale*," p. 314. Not recognizing the specific borrowing, Alastair Minnis uses the passages to contrast Boccaccio's "avant-garde practice" with that of Chaucer, who appears "quite conservative"; *Medieval Theory of Authorship: Scholastic literary attitudes in the later Middle Ages*, 2nd edn with a new preface (Philadelphia: University of Pennsylvania Press, 2010), pp. 203–04.

However, while Boccaccio then in effect conceded he is the author ("ma se pur prosuppor si volesse che io fossi stato di quelle e lo 'nventore e lo scrittore, che non fui, dico..." 17; "but even if one could assume I was the inventor as well as the scribe of these stories [which is not the case], I still insist...; McWilliam, p. 800), Chaucer maintained the fiction and shifted the responsibility for choosing what they read to the audience:[148]

> And therfore, whoso list it nat yheere,
> Turne over the leef and chese another tale;
> For he shal fynde ynowe, grete and smale,
> Of storial thyng that toucheth gentillesse,
> And eek moralitee and hoolynesse.
> Blameth nat me if that ye chese amys. (I, 3176–81)

Boccaccio, too, noted that "tuttavia chi va tra queste leggendo, lasci star quelle che pungono e quelle che dilettano legga" (19); "and the fact remains that anyone perusing these tales is free to ignore the ones that give offence, and read only those that are pleasing," McWilliam, p. 801). His mechanism, however, for allowing the reader to decide, the summaries that precede each tale (19), differs sharply from Chaucer's:

> The Millere is a cherl; ye knowe wel this.
> So was the Reve eek and othere mo,
> And harlotrie they tolden bothe two. (I, 3182–84)

By asking his readers to judge the character of the teller and not just the moral worth of the story, Chaucer opened the possibility that narrators, including his own fictional persona, may misjudge their material. His "apology," then, is not only derived from the same source as the following tale, but also points to the theme he developed in it.

Following *Decameron* 7.2 and especially *De Berangier au lonc cul* Chaucer might have written a tale that confronted conflict between social classes more directly. He did not. Instead, he challenged the Knight's self-interested assumptions about class through a story that asks the audience to pay more attention to the world in which we live. It does so in part by presenting a Christianity where God is not the abstract first-mover of the universe, but rather present among his creation, born in a manger to a carpenter and his wife. The *Miller's Tale*, however, stops far short of affirming this theology. Instead, like the *Decameron* as a whole and 3.4, its main narrative remains secular, the story of Alison, John, and Nicholas and their tubs suspended precariously in Oxford.

---

[148] See Biggs and Howes, "Theophany," pp. 275–76.

5

The *Wife of Bath's Tale* and the *Tale of Florent*

When Chaucer returned to the Wife of Bath, the *Canterbury Tales* was already well in progress, with the pairing of the Knight and the Miller successfully opening the key argument that would guide the pilgrimage as a whole. The debate would be about not just the proper ordering of the secular world, Licisca's questioning of misogyny and class hierarchies, but also its relationship to the divine. The place of women in society would still play a major role in this discussion, but only as one of a number of topics because other pilgrims would introduce other themes. This change in plan allowed Chaucer to rethink his only secular female character and the tale she would tell. No longer would the Wife of Bath need to respond to a story told by an upperclass male pilgrim as he had originally thought when he paired her with the Man of Law. Instead, she could begin her own group of tales, which would concern marriage, making hers the starting point to which the discussion would need continually to return. But there was a problem. The *Shipman's Tale*, which he had written to call attention to the economic basis of marriage, instead appeared to condone the exchange of sex for money, and so was too immoral for this opening position. Chaucer needed a woman more powerful than even Jancofiore, the courtesan from Palermo in 8.10, and a target more central than the cheap husband of the *Shipman's Tale*.

Using the technique he had learned from watching Boccaccio transform the idea in the popular "Versus de mola piperis"—how does a lover obtain his lady's favors without payment?—into three radically different *novelle,* Chaucer discovered in a tradition associated with Irish kingship a woman who, by sleeping with a man, transforms not just herself but his entire kingdom. The Celtic sovereignty goddess, who lies behind the Loathly Lady story he created, offered him a more powerful woman indeed. Because his concern, however, was with not myths of kingship but rather the issue of contemporary middle-class marriage, he redirected the discussion toward his own day by turning to the widespread tradition of misogyny, which because of its prevalence in Church writings also allowed him to continue the Miller's questioning of religious certainty. Within it he identified an anti-feminist commonplace that fit neatly with the transformation of the loathly lady: if a beautiful woman is never chaste, then, a woman might ask, which would you prefer your wife to be: ugly and faithful or beautiful and unfaithful? An Arthurian setting with a quest to discover what women most desire and the topics of rape, marriage, and class then filled out the tale. Moreover, although the *Decameron* did not provide a narrative that served as the basis of his own (beyond, as I think likely, Gretchen Hendrick's insight that the effort in 3.9 that Gilette of Narbonne must exert in order to marry the man of her choice lies behind the tale),[1] the debate the Wife opened provoked three responses that Chaucer drew from this work: the tales of the Clerk, Merchant, and Franklin rely on 10.10, 7.9 (and 2.10), and 10.5. The *Wife of Bath's Tale* both shapes and is shaped by this decameronian context.

This introduction to the *Wife of Bath's Tale* has set aside, as did my first description of the *Miller's Tale*, other suggested sources and analogues, most significantly John Gower's *Tale of Florent*, but also the *Weddyng of Syr Gawen and Dame Ragnell* and the *Marriage of Sir Gawain*. The first is clearly the most important because it and the *Wife of Bath's Tale* were written at nearly the same time. The broad argument against a common source has already been presented in the Chapter 1: unlike the Lover's Gift Regained, which in the form exemplified by the "Versus de mola piperis" and *Decameron* 8.2 left evidence of oral transmission across a variety of cultures from the twelfth to the fifteenth centuries, the narrative that both Gower and Chaucer told—a knight whose life is in danger because of something he has done and so must discover what women most desire, encounters a loathly lady who helps him and in return demands he wed her; when she finds he is reluctant to consummate the marriage, she offers him a choice, which, when he allows her to decide, she resolves by becoming beautiful—is not even considered a tale type by Aarne and Thompson. Part of it is included by Thompson in the *Motif-Index* (D 732): "man disenchants loathsome woman by embracing her." Even this statement, however, both overlooks the other details these narratives share and calls attention to a telling difference between them, since it is in the *Tale of Florent* but not in the *Wife of Bath's Tale* that we learn of an initial enchantment. It is more likely that one of these authors borrowed from the other than that they developed such similar plots independently at almost exactly the same time. Similarly, the two later Middle English versions, *Dame Ragnell* and the *Marriage* are more likely to descend from Gower and Chaucer than to represent a popular tradition that is otherwise unattested.

Which, then, of the two, the *Wife of Bath's Tale* or the *Tale of Florent*, inspired the other? As the opening paragraphs of this chapter again indicate, the question is central to this book's main claims because it involves our understanding not only of Chaucer's use of sources but also the chronology of his work on the *Canterbury Tales*. If his tale is the earlier, then it is both a remarkable example of the creation of a new narrative by using the techniques he learned from his reading of the *Decameron* and a dramatic

---

[1]   Gretchen Hendrick developed the idea in her seminar paper, "*Decameron* 3.9 as a Source for the *Wife of Bath's Tale*," written for my graduate seminar on Chaucer in the fall of 2008. I use her ideas in this chapter with her permission.

confirmation that Licisca's outburst inspired much of his early work on the collection. That it could be is possible. Assuming that the generally accepted date, 1387, for the beginning of Chaucer's work on the *Canterbury Tales* is correct, there would have been as many as three years during which he could have written the *Wife of Bath's Tale* and Gower could have adapted it before issuing the first version of the *Confessio Amantis* in 1390. Although I would place other tales in this period, before writing his Loathly Lady story Chaucer must, in my view, have written only the tales of the Shipman, the Miller, and the Man of Law as well as at least the framing structure (but not necessarily all of the portraits) of the *General Prologue*; the others that figure in this equation, the *Knight's Tale* and *Melibee*, were both composed before he began the collection. The equivalent, then, of five tales in three years seems a modest rate of production for Chaucer. Moreover, it is reasonable to imagine that working from the *Wife of Bath's Tale*, Gower could have produced the *Tale of Florent* quickly and then inserted it into an appropriate place in his own largely completed work.

The work of this chapter is to show that these claims are likely. There is, it appears to me, no single detail such as the tubs in the *Miller's Tale* and *Heile van Beersele* that in itself proves that Chaucer wrote first. As several scholars have shown, both the *Wife of Bath's Tale* and the *Tale of Florent* are, for the most part, internally consistent, and so taken on their own either might be the original version. They do, however, present sharply different views on the issues they raise. Chaucer's tale challenges the assumption prevalent in the fourteenth century that men should exercise power over women, while Gower's teaches a lesson about male conduct within the conventions of courtly love. One, then, is radical, calling for an end to the abuse of women while the other is conservative, proposing no more than a modest refinement in the behavior of men. Recognizing this difference may refocus the discussion of sources. In contrast to my claim that Chaucer was strikingly original in his use of the materials from which he built his tales, it is widely recognized that Gower almost always relied on existing narratives for Genius's *exempla* in the *Confessio Amantis*, a fact that increases the likelihood that the *Tale of Florent* too had a direct source. More significant, however, is the nature of the material that Chaucer seems likely to have used. Because there is no reason to assume that a Loathly Lady tradition as posited by earlier scholars influenced by the Finnish historical-geographical school of folklore would have preserved earlier Celtic elements as it passed through some intermediate route into fourteenth-century England, it is probable that he turned to Irish materials: the *Wife of Bath's Tale* takes the woman's otherwise unexplained transformation from this tradition. That he did so is made more likely by the other Celtic elements in his story. Moreover, the misogyny that this powerful woman opposes is present only in the question that the Wife of Bath asks. While it remains possible that Gower constructed his narrative out of as yet unidentified sources, and that Chaucer then modified it by turning to Irish lore and a misogynist tradition, it is more likely that Chaucer created this narrative.

Same Story, Different Meaning

When looking back across hundreds of years at authors whose lives were shaped by experiences more similar to each other's than to our own, it is difficult to recognize a sharp contrast in their views, especially when the two particular stories under consideration are so similar in plot. However, scholars, particularly Derek Pearsall, R. F. Yeager, Peter G. Beidler, and James Dean, have identified significant differences in the themes of the *Tale of Florent* and the *Wife of Bath's Tale*, which indeed express larger concerns of the collections in which they appear. As Pearsall notes, throughout Gower's tale Florent "behaves with scrupulous honour and honesty combined with the most convincing humanity,"[2] allowing the narrative, as Beidler points out, to demonstrate "how a cautious and near-perfect knight *does* behave in a dangerous and hostile situation."[3] "Gower has Genius," according to Beidler, "tell the *Tale of Florent* as a means of transforming Amans, a character *outside* the tale, into a man worthy of a good woman's love" (p. 101).[4] Similarly, Dean writes that the tale "addresses issues of self-governance when one must adhere to one's word—maintain one's *trouthe*—under trying circumstances."[5] Whether one views the *Confessio Amantis* as about love, as Peter Nicholson does,[6] or governance, following Russell A. Peck,[7] the *Tale of*

---

2 Derek Pearsall, "Gower's Narrative Art," *PMLA* 81 (1966), pp. 475–84; repr. in *Gower's* Confessio Amantis*: A Critical Anthology*, ed. Peter Nicholson (Cambridge: D. S. Brewer, 1991), p. 80.

3 Peter G. Beidler, "Transformations in Gower's *Tale of Florent* and Chaucer's *Wife of Bath's Tale*," in *Chaucer and Gower: Difference, Mutuality, Exchange*, ELS Monograph Series 51, ed. R. F. Yeager (Victoria: English Literary Studies, 1991), p. 101.

4 Yeager considers the tale one of Gower's "'negative'" examples, "tales which demonstrate against a vice by showing its opposing virtue, or by presenting a character avoiding its pitfalls"; *John Gower's Poetic: The Search for a New Arion* (Cambridge: D. S. Brewer, 1990), pp. 136–37.

5 James Dean, "The Hag Transformed: 'The Tale of Florent,' Ethical Choice, and Female Desire in Late Medieval England," in *Approaches to Teaching the Poetry of John Gower*, ed. R. F. Yeager and Brian W. Gastle (New York: Modern Language Association of America, 2011), p. 143.

6 See Peter Nicholson, *Love and Ethics in Gower's* Confessio Amantis (Ann Arbor: University of Michigan Press, 2005).

7 See Russell A. Peck, *Kingship and Common Profit in Gower's* Confessio Amantis (Carbondale: Southern Illinois University Press, 1978) and "The Politics and Psychology of Governance in Gower: Ideas of Kingship and Real Kings," in *A Companion to Gower*, ed. Siân Echard (Cambridge: D. S. Brewer, 2004), pp. 215–38.

Florent fits firmly into its larger, conservative argument, a call for the reform of individuals but not of the institutions which control their lives.[8]

In contrast the immediate message of Chaucer's tale is radical: in Pearsall's wording, "it is not simply that the *Wife of Bath's Tale* proves that it is a good idea to concede sovereignty to women: the whole tale itself is a demonstration of women's inalienable right to that sovereignty, that there is really no alternative."[9] However, many readers, including Pearsall and Dean,[10] find it difficult to conclude that Chaucer wrote to support this view because the lack of evidence that the rapist Knight has indeed reformed makes the conclusion—his marriage to a beautiful woman—seem little more than the self-deluding fantasy of its immediate teller, the Wife of Bath.[11] While acknowledging this problem, I will focus on a more limited theme, and yet one that growing out of Licisca's outburst and fitting into the larger scheme of the *Canterbury Tales* indicates that Chaucer considered the Wife's claim seriously: in contrast to its beginning, the end of the *Wife of Bath's Tale* is dominated by female speech.

After an opening twenty-five-line aside to which we will return, the *Wife of Bath's Tale* begins with a remarkable sentence that carries the action from the initial rape through Arthur's granting power over the criminal's life to a woman, his queen, a progression that, indeed, expresses the theme of the tale. In doing so this sentence effectively contrasts the opening silence of the initial crime with both the immediate "clamour" it engenders and the more deliberate discussion between the royal partners. It calls attention, then, to each of these moments even as it moves without pause from one to the next. The first is central to the tale, breaking as it does the illusion of a conventional opening to an Arthurian romance with the unexpected rape:[12]

---

8   In contrast, Matthew W. Irvin finds in the tale greater ambiguity; see *The Poetic Voices of John Gower: Politics and Personae in the* Confessio Amantis (Cambridge: D.S. Brewer, 2014), pp. 98–113.

9   Pearsall, "Gower's Narrative Art," p. 80. As such it develops from Chaucer's transformation of 8.1, 8.2, and 8.10 into the *Shipman's Tale*.

10   See Pearsall, *Canterbury Tales*, p. 90; and Dean, "The Hag Transformed," p. 145.

11   Even Corinne Saunders, whose judicious study will inform the following paragraphs, concludes her discussion of this tale with the teller: "against medieval legal ambiguity, Chaucer pits the voice of woman—not the personal, emotional voice of the victim, but the more universal, rational and authoritative voice of the hag, a voice that, however, is mediated and itself undercut by his construction of the gat-toothed, red-stockinged Wife of Bath, born beneath both Mars and Venus"; *Rape and Ravishment in the Literature of Medieval England* (Cambridge: D. S. Brewer, 2001), p. 309.

12   On rape in romance, see Saunders's nuanced discussion, which, while oversimplifying, I will invoke here with a single sentence: "actual rape is found only on the margins of romance—in classical legend, in medieval chronicles, in Arthurian pseudo-history and in French non-romance—*pastourelles*, the *fabliau*-romance of *Renart* and the prose tale of the *La Fille du Comte de Ponthieu*, none of which have English counterparts," p. 187.

> And so bifel that this kyng Arthour
> Hadde in his hous a lusty bacheler,
> That on a day cam ridynge fro ryver,
> And happed that, allone as he was born,
> He saugh a mayde walkynge hym biforn,
> Of which mayde anon, maugree hir heed,
> By verray force, he rafte hire maydenhed.... (III, 882–88)

That this is rape is unquestionable. The knight acts "by verray force"; although we are not told how she resists, the woman, as "maugree hir heed" indicates, does not consent.[13] If there is speech, it has no positive result. Moreover, these lines sharply distinguish the classes of the two: the knight is, of course, aristocratic, a detail reinforced not only by his membership in King Arthur's court but also by his previous activity, hawking, which is expressed by the extended meaning of "ryver."[14] In contrast the woman is a peasant since she is both alone and walking.[15] One immediately imagines her need to be by the river: she is washing clothes or drawing water. The topic of *gentilesse*, which the hag develops in her long speech on the wedding bed, is motivated by this opening.

If the rape, while unexpected at the start of a romance, seems unfortunately likely to have occurred as well in Chaucer's day as any other, the following events are genuinely surprising, until we recognize that our surprise is the tale's point. This violation of a lower-class woman by a knight becomes through popular outrage a concern for the king himself and its legal consequence is death:

> For which oppressioun was swich clamour
> And swich pursute unto the kyng Arthour
> That dampned was this knyght for to be deed,
> By cours of lawe, and sholde han lost his heed—
> Paraventure swich was the statut tho.... (III, 889–93)

In her survey of rape in medieval English literature, Corinne Saunders provides ample evidence that in both thirteenth- and fourteenth-century England violence against women would have been considered a plea of the Crown and so "punishable only by death or loss of member."[16] She also notes, however, that from the end of the thirteenth century, when "cases of forcible coition" became "indistinguishable from those of abduction," with both referred to as *raptus* (p. 61), the emphasis in the courts shifted to abduc-

---

[13] The *MED* lists two nouns under 'hēd', one becoming Modern English "head," the other "heed."

[14] See the *MED*.

[15] See Bernard F. Huppé, "Rape and Woman's Sovereignty in the *Wife of Bath's Tale*," *Modern Language Notes* 63 (1948), pp. 378–81; and Saunders, *Rape*, p. 302 note 80.

[16] Saunders, *Rape*, p. 50.

tion, making it even less likely that the several examples she alludes to from the thirteenth century of lower-class women bringing suit against their superiors would have been surpassed by cases in Chaucer's day. Moreover, these thirteenth-century suits were dropped, leading Saunders to comment: "since it was the custom to try nobles by their peers, the difficulty of collecting a jury meant that appeals brought against noblemen rarely if ever came to trial" (p. 58). In spite of the claim, then, that the knight is "dampned by cours of lawe" and the passage's other legal language, the "paraventure" opens the way to questioning not only the existence of such a "statut" but also the events themselves: when was a lower-class women ever likely to have received such justice? A summary of laws concerning rape that appears in the thirteenth-century treatise attributed to Henry of Bracton is, then, a possible source for positions taken in this passage:

> Raptus mulieris ne fiat defendit tam lex humana quam divina. Et sic fuit antiquitus observatum, quod si quis obiaverit mulieri vel alicubi invenerit, si sola vel socios habuerit cum pace dimittat eam, quam si per inhonestatem tetigerit, frangit edictum regis, et emendabit secundum iudicium comitatus. Si autem contra voluntatem eius iactet eam ad terram, forisfacit gratiam suam: quod si impudice discooperuerit eam et se super eam posuerit, omnium possessionum suarum incurrit damnum; quod si concubuerit cum ea, de vita et membris suis incurrit damnum. Adelstane.

> (Man-made as well as divine law forbid the rape of women. In ancient times the practice was as follows: if a man meets a woman or comes across her somewhere, whether she is alone or has companions, he is to let her go in peace; if he touches her indecorously he breaks the king's ordinance and shall give compensation in accordance with the judgement of the county court; if he throws her upon the ground against her will, he forfeits the king's grace; if he shamelessly disrobes her and places himself upon her, he incurs the loss of all his possessions; and if he lies with her, he incurs the loss of his life and members. Athelstan.)[17]

Strict punishment of this crime is an ideal, but its implementation seems to belong only to a confused and distant past.[18] In any case invoking as it does with the terms "clamour" and "pursute" the common law practice of "hue and cry,"[19] Chaucer's passage implies a noisier scene than the first.

In the third moment in this opening sentence the commotion returns to

---

[17] *Henry de Bracton: On the Laws and Customs of England* (De legibus et consuetudinibus Angliae), ed. George E. Woodbine, trans. and notes by Samuel E. Thorne, 4 vols. (Cambridge, MA: Harvard University Press, in ass. with Selden Society, 1968–77), vol. II, "De placitis coronae," pp. 414–15. This passage is quoted and discussed in Saunders, *Rape*, pp. 54–55.

[18] Saunders notes that Æthelstan "is a particular, though in this instance legendary, English law maker," p. 55.

[19] See Robert J. Blanch, "'Al was this land fulfild of fayerye': The Thematic Employment

order as power passes—through the assistance of her ladies and the action of the king—to the queen. Again, this turn of events seems somewhat illogical although less dramatically so than in the previous moment:

> But that the queene and other ladyes mo
> So longe preyeden the kyng of grace
> Til he his lyf hym graunted in the place,
> And yaf hym to the queene, al at hir wille,
> To chese wheither she wolde hym save or spille. (III, 894–98)

Since the knight is already condemned to death, why would these women intervene? The point here, however, and throughout the tale is both simple and strong: because the crime is rape, a clear abuse of male power in not considering a woman's right to decide in so personal a matter, the solution must be to empower the oppressed. Through speech the queen and her ladies gain that power.

The opening of the *Tale of Florent* is neither more nor less illogical; it simply conveys a different message. Like Chaucer's "lusty bacheler," Florent too is "wifles" (I, 1411), a first hint that this tale will also examine marriage. Rather than challenging this institution, however, Genius upholds it by describing a near perfect knight from whose actions Amans should learn. In addition to his high social standing as "nevoeu to th'emperour" (I, 1409), Florent's good qualities are immediately described: "a worthi knyght," "a courteour," and "a man that mochel myhte," he is "chivalerous," "amorous," and eager for fame (I, 1408–17). Even the parents of the knight he has slain are aware not only of the risk of taking vengeance on him because of his lineage but also of his "worthinesse / of knyhthod and of gentilesse" (I, 1435–39). Given these strengths, it seems somewhat odd that Florent would agree to the grandmother's scheme to lure him to his death by making him promise that he will consent to this punishment if he is unable to answer her question. Here, however, as at the two other key moments in the tale,[20] the knight receives full information before making his choice. The grandmother explains that he may avoid vengeance for his deed if he can answer her question and that he may have time to find the answer (I, 1455–71). When he asks what the question is, she tells him clearly ("what alle wommen most desire" (I, 1481);[21] it is only

---

of Force, Willfulness, and Legal Conventions in Chaucer's *Wife of Bath's Tale*," *Studia Neophilologica* 57 (1985), pp. 41–51.

20 The loathly lady announces that her payment for revealing the secret will be marriage before she reveals it and she becomes beautiful before he gives her power to decide whether she will be so by day or night.

21 The two works, *Hoe Walewein wilde weten vrowen gepens* and *Arthur and Gorlagon*, which were mentioned in Chapter 1 as analogues, differ significantly. In the former, Walewein, who is upset when it is suggested that Ydeine will not be faithful to him, asks the queen "Oft si iet wiste oppenbare / Wat gepense in vrouwen ware" (1479–80; "whether she had any clear knowledge / about the thoughts of women"); *Five Inter-*

then that we learn that "Florent this thing hath undertake" (I, 1485). As in the *Wife of Bath's Tale*, there is some legal language in this exchange—Florent, for example, asks for the question "under seales write" (I, 1474), and yet the entire scene is premised on him being a knight of integrity, one who when offered a challenge accepts. There is, then, no need for him to change at the end of the tale, just delay until the forces of good can return to their proper alignment. His obedience throughout is less a promise to the woman he weds than an affirmation of the institution of marriage, which in the scheme of the *Confessio Amantis* as a whole is an essential part of God's proper ordering of his world.

The first moment when the logic of the *Tale of Florent* comes close to breaking down in a way that might itself suggest that Gower's version was derived from Chaucer's—the grandmother's response to the knight's correct answer—again calls attention to the different commitments of the two tales to the theme of empowering women. It is set up by a telling detail. When Florent arrives at the castle, it is the lord with "his conseil" (I, 1631) who arrives first and who sends for the grandmother: her power exists within the context of his. In contrast, in the *Wife of Bath's Tale* the queen controls the moment and is attended only by women:

> Whan they be comen to the court, this knyght
> Seyde he had holde his day, as he hadde hight,
> And redy was his answere, as he sayde.
> Ful many a noble wyf, and many a mayde,
> And many a wydwe, for that they been wise,
> The queene hirself sittynge as a justise,

---

polated Romances from the Lancelot Compilation, ed. and trans. David F. Johnson and Geert H. M. Claassens, Dutch Romances 3 (Cambridge: D. S. Brewer, 2000), pp. 112–13. When told that "nobody may know it, / so varied is their thought" (1484–85), he sets out to find the answer. In *Arthur and Gorlagon*, the king begins a similar quest after having been told by the queen that "quippe agnoscas te nunquam ut ingenium mentemue femine comperisse" (16–17; "Indeed, you reveal that you have never understood the nature or mind of a woman"); *Latin Arthurian Literature*, ed. and trans. Mildred Leake Day, Arthurian Archives 11 (Cambridge: D. S. Brewer, 2005), pp. 208–09. Neither story offers a clear answer. In contrast, the questions in the *Wife of Bath's Tale* and the *Tale of Florent* are both direct, as opposed to implied, and are answered using the related terms "sovereynetee" (III, 1038) and "soverein" (I, 1609). *Hoe Walewein* is dated to before 1320 because of its inclusion in the *Lancelot Compilation*, preserved in The Hague, Koninklijke Bibliotheek, 129. A. 10, which contains a colophon ascribing ownership of the manuscript to and perhaps identifying its main scribe as Lodewijc van Velthem; see Johnson and Claassens, *Five Interpolated Romances*, pp. 3–5. Moreover, the text identifies itself as a translation from French (1613). *Arthur and Gorlagon* survives in Oxford, Bodleian Library, Rawlinson B 149, which is dated to the late fourteenth or early fifteenth century; see Day, *Latin Arthurian Literature*, p. 47. Day writes that "the slight evidence suggests a Welsh or possibly Breton author, and composition toward the end of the twelfth century" (p. 43).

> Assembled been, his answere for to heere,
> And afterward this knyght was bode appeere. (III, 1023–30)

After some delay, which I will turn to in a moment, the scene in the *Tale of Florent* ends abruptly; as soon as the grandmother hears the answer,

> Sche seide, "Ha! Treson! Wo thee be,
> That hast thus told the privité,
> Which alle wommen most desire!
> I wolde that thou were afire." (I, 1659–62)

The vehemence here calls attention to how awkwardly the question fits in this tale: the answer is known to half the population, who have agreed among themselves never to reveal it to the other half.

In contrast the *Wife of Bath's Tale* presents the knight's answer with a significant elaboration and then details a more nuanced response to it. When commanded to reveal "what thyng that worldly wommen loven best" (III, 1034), he responds,

> "My lige lady, generally," quod he,
> "Wommen desiren to have sovereynetee
> As wel over hir housbond as hir love,
> And for to been in maistrie hym above.
> This is youre mooste desir, thogh ye me kille.
> Dooth as yow list; I am heer at youre wille." (III, 1037–42)

Unlike this scene in the *Tale of Florent* where the question is referred to but not articulated, here it is both restated and then repeated in the answer. More significantly, the knight uses his answer to shape the queen's response: because all women want the power that she now has over him, by killing him she would prove indeed prove that he is right. The reaction to his statement is similarly revealing:

> In al the court ne was ther wyf, ne mayde,
> Ne wydwe that contraried that he sayde,
> But seyden he was worthy han his lyf. (III, 1044–46)

Rather than agreeing with the knight, the women cannot deny what he has said: in this particular case the answer saves his life. While it is not clear that the knight has understood his words since he may simply be repeating what the loathly lady has told him to say, the scene itself leads to the conclusion that if the question is rape, the answer is obvious: women need power.

In contrast Gower had shifted the focus of his tale away from the question of what women most desire to Florent's need to fulfil his obligations even before the knight returns to the court. At the end of their first exchange, the loathly lady agrees with his condition that if he does not use her advice, he need not marry her:

> "This covenant I wol allowe,"
> Sche seith; "if eny other thing
> Bot that thou hast of my techyng
> Fro deth this body mai respite,
> I woll thee of thi trowthe acquite,
> And elles be non other weie." (I, 1590–95)

She then reveals the answer, and yet ends her speech with more important information, the command that once he has saved his life, he must return to her:

> "And elles this schal be my lore,
> That thou schalt seie, upon this molde
> That alle wommen lievest wolde
> Be soverein of mannes love:
> For what womman is so above,
> Sche hath, as who seith, al hire wille;
> And elles may sche noght fulfille
> What thing hir were lievest have.
> With this answere thou schalt save
> Thiself, and other wise noght.
> And whan thou hast thin ende wroght,
> Com hier agein, thou shalt me finde,
> And let nothing out of thi minde." (I, 1606–18)

The knight does not comment on the answer, but instead focuses on his unappealing alternatives:

> He goth him forth with hevy chiere,
> As he that not in what manere
> He mai this worldes joie atteigne:
> For if he deie, he hath a peine,
> And if he live, he mot him binde
> To such on which of alle kinde
> Of wommen is th'unsemlieste.... (I, 1619–25)

Indeed, once in the court, he tries to avoid using her information:

> Florent seith al that evere he couthe,
> Bot such word cam ther non to mowthe,
> That he for gifte or for beheste
> Mihte eny wise his deth areste. (I, 1641–44)

It is only when pushed for his final answer that he "an hope cawht" (I, 1654) that her words might help. His relief, however, is momentary; following the grandmother's brief outburst, the focus returns to him:

> Bot natheles in such a plit
> Florent of his answere is quit:

And tho began his sorwe newe,
For he mot gon, or ben untrewe,
To hire which his trowthe hadde.
Bot he, which alle schame dradde,
Goth forth in stede of his penance,
And takth the fortune of his chance,
As he that was with trowthe affaited. (I, 1663–71)

In this tale, women's desires come far below the testing of Florent's "trowthe."

The contrasting moment in the *Wife of Bath's Tale*, which may echo *Decameron* 3.9, confirms the central place of rape in the discussion of the clear need to empower women. Boccaccio's *novella*, whose story is well known because Shakespeare adapted it in *All's Well that Ends Well*, reaches its dramatic conclusion when Gilette of Narbonne, who has earned the right to marry Bertrand of Roussillon by curing the King of France of a fistula but who then must obtain her husband's ring and have his child in her arms before he will live with her, arrives at his palace having fulfilled both conditions:

> "Signor mio, io sono la tua sventurata sposa, la quale, per lasciar te tornare e stare in casa tua, lungamente andata son tapinando. Io ti richeggio per Dio che le condizion postemi per li due cavalieri che io ti mandai, tu le mi osservi: e ecco nelle mie braccia non un sol figliuolo di te, ma due, e ecco qui il tuo anello. Tempo è adunque che io debba da te sí come moglie esser ricevuta secondo la tua promessa." (3.9, 58)

> ("My lord, behold your unfortunate bride, who has suffered the pangs of a long and bitter exile so that you could return and settle in your ancestral home. I now beseech you, in God's name, to observe the conditions you imposed upon me through the agency of those two knights I sent to you. Here in my arms I carry, not merely one of your children, but two; and here is your ring. So the time has come for you to honour your promise and accept me as your wife," McWilliam, p. 273).

Although many details differ, with its emphasis on honoring a promise this passage is at least a significant analogue for the *Wife of Bath's Tale*:[22]

> "Mercy," quod she, "my sovereyn lady queene!
> Er that youre court departe, do me right.
> I taughte this answere unto the knyght;
> For which he plighte me his trouthe there,
> The firste thyng that I wolde hym requere
> He wold it do, if it lay in his myghte.
> Bifore the court thanne preye I thee, sir knyght,"
> Quod she, "that thou me take unto thy wyf,
> For wel thou woost that I have kept thy lyf.
> If I seye fals, sey nay, upon thy fey!" (III, 1048–57)

---

[22] Hendrick made this point in "*Decameron* 3.9."

What makes this connection even stronger is the knight's claim that his reason for not wanting to marry the loathly lady is her social status: "Allas, that any of my nacioun / Sholde evere so foule disparaged be!" (III, 1068–69). The first meaning in the *Middle English Dictionary* for *disparagen* borrowed from Old French *desparagier*, is "to degrade socially (i.e. for marrying below rank or without proper ceremony."[23] When first told by the king that he is to marry his childhood friend, Gilette,

> Beltramo, il quale la conoscea e veduta l'avea, quantunque molto bella gli paresse, conoscendo lei non esser di legnaggio che alla sua nobiltà bene stesse, tutto sdegnoso disse: "Monsignore, dunque mi volete voi dar medica per mogliere? Già a Dio non piaccia che io sí fatta femina prenda giammai." (3.9, 22)

> (Bertrand knew the girl, and had thought her very beautiful on seeing her again. But knowing that her lineage was in no way suited to his own noble ancestry, he was highly indignant, and said: "But surely, sire, you would not want to marry me to a she-doctor. Heaven forbid that I should accept a woman of that sort for a wife," McWilliam, p. 267).

The knight in the *Wife of Bath's Tale* claims he acts for the same reason. That he is lying returns the story to his rape of a lower class woman at the tale's opening.

Chaucer confirms this focus on rape in lines that epitomize much of his thinking about the Wife of Bath: how would situations looks if the expected order were reversed? When in court the loathly lady tells him that he must marry her as he agreed in return for having taught him the correct answer,

> This knyght answerde, "Allas and weylawey!
> I woot right wel that swich was my biheste.
> For Goddes love, as chees a newe requeste!
> Take al my good and lat my body go." (III, 1058–61)

The rapist-knight suddenly discovers that his body is more precious to him than all his possessions. Although it may reveal nothing about which of the two tales influenced the other, the comparable passage in *Tale of Florent* confirms their different messages. When in their first exchange the loathly lady has told Florent what she will require in exchange for her information, he first refuses, but when she then points out that he will certainly die, the narrative continues:

> Florent behihte hire good ynowh
> Of lond, of rente, of park, of plowh,
> Bot al that compteth sche at noght.

---

[23] See the *MED, s.v.*

> Tho fell this knyht in mochel thoght,
> Now goth he forth, now comth agein,
> He wot noght what is best to sein,
> And thoghte, as he rod to and fro,
> That chese he mot on of the tuo,
> Or for to take hire to his wif
> Or elles for to lese his lif.
> And thanne he caste his avantage,
> That sche was of so gret an age,
> That sche mai live bot a while,
> And thoghte put hire in an ile,
> Wher that no man hire scholde knowe,
> Til sche with deth were overthrowe. (I, 1565–80)

In this negotiation Florent remains in control. He may offer a substantial part of his "land, income, game-preserve, and plowland";[24] it is, however, his decision to make. Moreover, his following reflection not only suggests a profound disrespect for the person offering him aid but also calls attention to the resources he has to make his problem disappear later. The tale does not question his power; it rewards him, as his place in society does, for using it well. In contrast, in presenting his knight's discovery that he cannot negotiate, Chaucer in the *Wife of Bath's Tale* reflects on the fate of women who must enter into marriage, which will, like rape, place them under the control of men.

The second place where the logic of *Florent* wavers in a way that suggests this narrative is derivative also occurs because of the emphasis in Gower's tale not on empowering women but rather upholding male "trowthe." The conclusions of the two stories are similar and contain striking minor differences: in the *Tale of Florent*, the loathly lady transforms herself before she asks her question; her question is whether he would like her to be fair by day and foul by night or foul by day and fair by night; and, once he has turned over power to her, she reveals that the problem has gone away because in doing so he has fulfilled the condition her stepmother created when transforming her into her previously hideous shape. One might ask how this loathly lady is able to become beautiful before her stepmother's condition is met, and yet more telling is the exchange that leads up to the final events. In Gower's tale the issue of female sovereignty has receded so far into the background that there is no reason for the knight to raise it, except that it is part of the tale Gower knew.

The final scene in the *Tale of Florent* begins in a way that is consistent with Gower's emphasis on fulfilling obligations.[25] Naked in their wedding bed, yet

---

24 Peck's gloss on the line.
25 See Yeager's analysis of I, 1774–1800, which examines "Florent's mental conflict"; *John Gower's Poetic*, pp. 123–24.

with her husband's back turned toward her, the loathly lady insists that he fulfil his promise:

> Bot evere in on sche spak and preide,
> And bad him thenke on that he seide,
> When that he tok hire by the hond. (I, 1795–97)

Although the decision is difficult, Florent again does, as he has throughout the tale, what is expected of him:

> He herde and understod the bond,
> How he was set to his penance,
> And, as it were a man in trance,
> He torneth him al sodeinly.... (I, 1798–1801)

Confronted by a beautiful woman and yet another unappealing choice, Florent, after some delay and again being forced to decide, acts unexpectedly: he turns the decision over to someone else. This development is effective in Gower's tale, demonstrating as it does his central theme of the need for obedience in love, and yet the knight goes beyond what the situation requires:

> He seide: "O ye, my lyves hele,
> Sey what you list in my querele,
> I not what ansuere I schal give:
> Bot evere whil that I may live,
> I wol that ye be my maistresse,
> For I can noght miselve gesse
> Which is the beste unto my chois.
> Thus grante I yow myn hole vois,
> Ches for ous bothen, I you preie;
> And what as evere that ye seie,
> Right as ye wole so wol I." (I, 1821–31)

As the opening and close of this speech make clear, Florent does not know how to resolve this particular problem; what is gratuitous is that he renounces all control of future decisions, making her his "maistresse" (I, 1825). It is this larger issue of "sovereignty" that provides the solution to the loathly lady's condition and is then trivialized in the resolution of the tale:

> "Mi lord," sche seide, "grant merci,
> For of this word that ye now sein,
> That ye have mad me soverein,
> Mi destiné is overpassed...." (I, 1832–35)

She explains:

> "The kinges dowhter of Cizile
> I am, and fell bot siththe awhile,

As I was with my fader late,
That my stepmoder for an hate,
Which toward me sche hath begonne,
Forschop me, til I hadde wonne
The love and sovereineté
Of what knyht that in his degré
Alle othre passeth of good name." (I, 1841–49)

Without Florent's unmotivated renunciation of power, the spell would not have been broken. Moreover, the issue arises only because a stepmother "for an hate" uses it to torment her stepdaughter. Indeed, Amans's summation of the tale, focusing as it does solely on the man, indicates that female sovereignty functions as a minor plot device:

Thei live longe and wel thei ferde,
And clerkes that this chance herde
Thei writen it in evidence
To teche how that obedience
Mai wel fortune a man to love
And sette him in his lust above,
As it befell unto this knyht. (I, 1855–61)

While the phrase "and sette him in his lust above" may mean, as it is partially glossed in Peck's edition, "and placed him 'in a state of prosperity,'" it still draws attention to the conventional, patriarchal theme of the tale as a whole. Women need only limited power, in this case to overcome the evil designs of another woman.

In contrast Chaucer's conclusion focuses on the theme of female sovereignty that dominates the tale by transforming a misogynistic commonplace into a challenge to male authority. Here too the married couple hold their decisive conversation in their wedding bed, the husband unwilling to consummate the marriage. Yet the loathly lady's opening questions are more pointed, recalling as they do the rape at the start of the story:

His olde wyf lay smylynge everemo,
And seyde, "O deere housbonde, benedicitee!
Fareth every knyght thus with his wyf as ye?
Is this the lawe of kyng Arthures hous?
Is every knyght of his so dangerous?" (III, 1086–90)

The phrase "of kyng Arthures hous" recalls the story's opening couplet: "And so bifel that this kyng Arthour / Hadde in his hous a lusty bacheler" (III, 883–84). Moreover, although here its first meaning is probably "national custom" or "usual mode of behavior,"[26] "lawe" also echoes the immediate

---

[26] See *MED laue*, meaning 9.

consequence of the rape: "That dampned was this knyght for to be deed, / By cours of lawe, and sholde han lost his heed" (III, 891–92). The loathly lady's real taunt, however, is in "dangerous," which suggests first, as Jill Mann glosses it in her edition, that he is "hard to please" because of his refusal to consummate their marriage.[27] Because it also means "domineering, overbearing," it too recalls the opening rape.[28] Its force, however, is in the root, *daunger* which in romance refers specifically "the resistance offered to a lover by his ladylove."[29] Once again the conventional gender roles are reversed.

The knight's actual response, which is not to the following plea that he tell the loathly lady what she has done wrong, but rather to her suggestion that she could "amend" the situation if she understood it, introduces the topic, her appearance, that it turn leads to her manipulation of the misogynistic tradition behind the choice she offers. The knight claims that she cannot because she is the problem:

> "Amended?" quod this knyght, "Allas, nay, nay!
> It wol nat been amended nevere mo.
> Thou art so loothly, and so oold also,
> And therto comen of so lough a kynde,
> That litel wonder is thogh I walwe and wynde.
> So wolde God myn herte wolde breste!' (III, 1098–103)

Although apparently not intending to do so, he again recalls the opening rape by asserting that the third, and therefore most important reason, or so he claims, for his failure to consummate his marriage is her lower class status. It is this topic that the loathly lady treats first, and at greatest length,[30] before turning at the end of her speech to the real reason for his behavior:

> "Now ther ye seye that I am foul and old,
> Than drede you noght to been a cokewold;
> For filthe and eelde, also moot I thee,
> Been grete wardeyns upon chastitee.
> But nathelees, syn I knowe youre delit,
> I shal fulfille youre worldly appetit.
> Chese now," quod she, "oon of thise thynges tweye:
> To han me foul and old til that I deye,

---

27 Mann, *Canterbury Tales*, p. 249.
28 *MED daungerous*, meaning 1.
29 *MED daunger*, meaning 4.
30 As Gretchen Hendrick noted in her paper, the discussion of money in this speech, a topic not introduced by the knight, again makes *Decameron* 3.9 a significant analogue for the *Wife of Bath's Tale*. The *novella* is resolved when Gilette fools her husband into believing that he is sleeping with a noble but poor woman with whom he is infatuated when in fact he is sleeping with her.

And be to yow a trewe, humble wyf,
And nevere yow displese in al my lyf,
Or elles ye wol han me yong and fair,
And take youre aventure of the repair
That shal be to youre hous by cause of me,
Or in som oother place, may wel be.
Now chese yourselven, whether that yow liketh." (III, 1213–27)

As Margaret Schlauch has pointed out,[31] behind this question is a wide-spread misogynist tradition that the Wife of Bath herself echoes in the *Prologue to the Wife of Bath's Tale*:

And if that she be fair, thou verray knave,
Thou seyst that every holour wol hire have;
She may no while in chastitee abyde,
That is assailled upon ech a syde. (III, 253–56)

Because it is by denigrating women that men seek to control them, Chaucer has again reversed the situation, allowing the loathly lady to express this theme in a way that lets her gain power over her husband. Forced to answer which choice he would prefer, the knight cannot decide.

His only recourse in this situation is to place himself under her control, a decision that the loathly lady then extends to their relationship as a whole. His words suggest, if not a change of heart, at least a recognition of his new position:

"My lady and my love, and wyf so deere,
I put me in youre wise governance;
Cheseth youreself which may be moost plesance
And moost honour to yow and me also.
I do no fors the wheither of the two,
For as yow liketh, it suffiseth me." (III, 1230–35)

It is for her to desire, for him merely to be satisfied with her pleasure. Yet she pushes further, and he agrees this particular reassignment power will hold throughout their marriage:

"Thanne have I gete of yow maistrie," quod she,
"Syn I may chese and governe as me lest?"
"Ye, certes, wyf," quod he, "I holde it best." (III, 1236–38)

Unlike the *Tale of Florent* where the issue of sovereignty re-emerges unexpectedly and is then trivialized, the *Wife of Bath's Tale* makes it central throughout.

---

[31] Margaret Schlauch, "The Marital Dilemma in the Wife of Bath's Tale," *PMLA* 61 (1946), pp. 416–30.

As noted above, however, many readers find the subsequent lines of the *Wife of Bath's Tale* unsatisfying because they undercut this feminist message. The loathly lady announces that she will be "bothe fair and good," becoming so immediately, leaving one to wonder if the knight really deserves such a wife. With the concluding couplet of the story, these doubts increase: "And she obeyed hym in every thyng / That myghte doon hym plesance or likyng" (III, 1255–56). After what has just happened, it seems incomprehensible that the emphasis should be on the obedience of the wife. These lines may indeed indicate that Chaucer's own views were more conventional than the argument his Wife of Bath makes. Yet they have the immediate effect of forcing the audience first to consider her perspective, as indeed the following lines do as well:

> And thus they lyve unto hir lyves ende
> In parfit joye; and Jhesu Crist us sende
> Housbondes meeke, yonge, and fressh abedde,
> And grace t'overbyde hem that we wedde;
> And eek I praye Jhesu shorte hir lyves
> That noght wol be governed by hir wyves;
> And olde and angry nygardes of dispence,
> God sende hem soone verray pestilence! (III, 1257–64)

Here we are fully back into the mind of the character we have met in the *Wife of Bath's Prologue*,[32] hearing not only references to her life and her views on her experiences of marriage, but indeed her own distinctive phrases. What Chaucer has accomplished, then, is to allow the voice of the maiden silenced in the opening rape to be heard with increasing force—in the words of the queen, in the speech of the loathly lady on her wedding bed, and in the Wife of Bath's complex, even contradictory views on marriage. The conversation has not ended: men—the Friar, Summoner, Clerk, Merchant, and Franklin— will all have a chance to speak. They will, however, be responding. Licisca's right to be heard is secure.

Gower's Use of Sources

Although Russell A. Peck's insight that Gower's "folkloric instinct" both "makes his tales so different from their sources" and "sets him apart from Chaucer" is, I believe, correct,[33] in itself it does not offer a compelling reason to view the *Tale of Florent* as likely to have been the source of the *Wife of Bath's Tale*. As discussed in Chapter 1, the assumption that this "instinct" would have placed Gower in contact with a body of narratives, including

---

[32] It appears likely to me that the prologue was written after the tale.
[33] *Confessio Amantis*, 3.9.

in this case the Irish tale of a sovereignty goddess who is renewed when she sleeps with a new king, which grew larger as it was passed through the generations of particular groups and migrated to others, is no longer accepted by scholars of folklore. To claim more specifically, as a modern folklorist might expect, that Gower regularly drew his material from oral performances would contradict what he explicitly stated about his practice in writing the tales in the *Confessio Amantis* and what scholars have established about their sources. Indeed only one, the *Tale of Three Questions*, would appear to provide compelling evidence for an ambitious use of popular material similar to the *Tale of Florent*. Even here, there is a written tradition on which Gower, as he himself said, most likely drew. Moreover, although Peck writes of the "'Irishness'" of the *Tale of Florent*, this tale does not include any of the Celtic elements found in the *Wife of Bath's Tale*. A final piece of evidence that argues against the priority of the *Tale of Florent*, although speculative, is potentially too significant to ignore: Gower may have revised the way he introduced it in order to make it appear that he had a source other than the *Wife of Bath's Tale*: if so, it would point to this controversy as a cause for the long-discussed although often discredited falling-out between the two poets.

It is instructive to place Peck's specific claim about Gower's possible use of folklore in the *Tale of Florent* into the context of his more general remarks on the topic in the introduction to the third volume of his edition of the *Confessio Amantis*. Here he alludes to Gower's consistent efforts to adapt a wide variety of stories to his own agenda, one which he associated with popular views: "like the good folklorist, Gower listens to what he thinks the voice of the people might be, the voice of the common people and their common law, a voice 'which mai noght lie' (Prol. 124), simply because it is the authentic thing itself, that bundle of shared values beyond the individual, the voice of God—*vox populi, vox dei*" (3.8).[34] Eliding this "good folklorist" with the "good historian" who "recognizes that even the most objective historicizations are relative to the goals and predilections" of their authors,[35] Peck widens his view to include not just the writing of narratives but the ordering of society:

---

[34] Gower, I would argue, expressed this idea in some cases to shift responsibility for his criticisms away from himself. For example, as he began his critique of the three estates in the prologue to book 3 of the *Vox Clamantis*, he wrote: "A me non ipso loquor hec, set que michi plebis / Vox dedit, et sortem plangit vbique malam: / Vt loquitur vulgus loquor, et scribendo loquelam / Plango, quod est sanctus nullus vt ante status" (11–14; "I am not speaking of these things on my own part; rather the voice of the people has reported them to me, and it complains of their adverse fate at every hand; I speak as the masses speak, and even as I write I lament over what I say, namely, that no estate is pious as in days gone by," Stockton, p. 113). See also the conclusion to the work, book 7 chapter 25.

[35] On Gower's willingness to rewrite history to fit his own views, see A. G. Rigg and Edward S. Moore's analysis of the *Conica Tripertita*, which they label "the first and

Gower knows that history is culturally produced; but, at the same time, especially from his folklorist view, he insists that there *are* universals, and that they are *not* confined to issues of religion, faith or aesthetics. Within his political vision law supplies humankind with what for him are the universals necessary if life is to be orderly—divine law, to be sure, and natural law, too, but also the very human common law. Good laws sustain good lore. (3.8)

Gower's "folkloric instinct," then, does not, according to Peck, refer to his gathering and analyzing of the stories of his own or other communities in order to understand their particular points of view, but rather his certainty that his beliefs expressed traditional values that should be preserved. Whether Gower was correct in claiming that most of his contemporaries thought as he did is not of course the subject of this study. On the other hand it makes it likely that, as a challenge to the order of society and specifically the institution of marriage,[36] the *Wife of Bath's Tale* would have appeared to him in need of a major revision.

That Gower consistently turned to written sources rather than to oral traditions in writing his tales is evident from many passages in the *Confessio Amantis*. To understand them, however, it is necessary to consider how they fit into his practice throughout his writings of illustrating his main points with *exempla*, the brief narratives most characteristically defined by their use in sermons from the twelfth to the fifteenth century.[37] Like the medieval preacher whose main concern was the salvation of those he addressed, Gower too focused on contemporary problems, the reform of society and, for him, the often related theme of the proper expression of love through marriage.[38] This focus meant that he was deeply concerned with the happenings of his own day: the opening book of the *Vox Clamantis*, which recounts the revolt of 1381, and the *Cronica Tripetita*, which discusses more broadly Richard II's failed reign, are only the most obvious examples of his interest in current events. After an elaborate description of the Vices and Virtues, the *Mirour*

---

perhaps most overt piece of Lancastrian propaganda"; "The Latin Works: Politics, Lament and Praise," in Echard, *Companion to Gower*, p. 159.

36　The need for men to govern their wives is the refrain of the conclusion of the discussion of matrimony in the *Mirour de l'Omme*, 17593–748. On the topic of marriage in general, see Yeager's discussion, with which he concludes *John Gower's Poetic* (pp. 244–79). In presenting marriage as "an ideal image of sanctified harmony," Gower disregarded the systemic abuse against which Chaucer wrote.

37　See Claude Bremond and Jacques Le Goff, *L'"Exemplum,"* Typologie des sources du Moyen Âge occidental 40 (Turnhout: Brepols, 1996). The online *Thesaurus Exemplorum Medii Aevi* is now the essential resource for searching this material. The similarity of the *Mirour de l'omme* to contemporary preaching is noted by G. R. Owst, *Literature and the Pulpit in Medieval England* (Cambridge: Cambridge University Press, 1933), pp. 230–31.

38　See Yeager's analysis of the *Mirrour de l'omme* in "John Gower's French," *Companion to Gower*, ed. Echard, pp. 143–44.

de l'omme (1–18372), the first of his three major works and the one with the most direct bearing on the question of the priority of the *Tale of Florent*, turns to the reform of the Three Estates and indeed of the narrator himself (18373–27360) before offering its solution, praying to the Virgin Mary and Jesus, whose lives are retold (27361–9945).[39] Gower's focus in this work, then, is on England in his own time. Moreover, scholars are increasingly appreciative of the author's originality in composing it. Yeager, for example, notes not only "the magnitude of its vision" but also "the creative eclecticism with which Gower approached his sources in order to achieve it."[40] The imagination that conceived the *Mirour de l'omme* could certainly have composed the *Tale of Florent*. It is worth pointing out, however, that the main sources that Gower turned to in writing this French work are literary, as Yeager's summary indicates: "allegory from *psychomachiae* and the Sins traditions, microcosmic Man and *momento mori* from moral philosophy, social critique from estates satire, and (most importantly, perhaps) the promise of compassionate rescue offered to 'l'omme pecchour' by the Virgin's reassuringly human biography."[41] All of these point to Gower's extensive reading rather than to an engagement with oral traditions.

In the context of this use of the literary past to define the perspective from which to critique the present, it is not surprising to find Gower in the *Mirour de l'omme* also employing specific *exempla* to illustrate his points. Here, in contrast to the tales that Genius tells Amans in *Confessio Amantis*, he placed these *essamples*, which are drawn as in contemporary sermons from a wide range of largely literary sources including the Bible, saints' lives, moralized natural history, classical Latin literature, medieval writings in both Latin and French and, one must assume, the non-literary experience of the author himself,[42] into the text in ways that cause little interruption to the developing argument, even if, at times, in their plenitude they appear to become the argument itself. For example, in criticizing the practices of monks, Gower referred to three well-known stories:

> Homme fait saint lieu, mais lieu par droit
> Ne fait saint homme en nul endroit;
> Ce piert d'essamples, car je lis
> Qe Lucifer du ciel chaoit
> En la presence u dieus estoit;
> Si fist Adans de paradis;
> Auci d'encoste dieu le fitz

---

39 According to Macaulay, "a few leaves are lost at the end of the manuscript," 1.334.
40 Yeager, "John Gower's French," p. 141.
41 See also Macaulay, 1.xlvii.
42 More work remains to be done on identifying Gower's sources. The notes in Macaulay and Troendle, while helpful, have only begun the process. See Macaulay's list of "interesting details about general society, especially in the city of London," 1.lxvi–lxvii.

> Judas perist, q'estoit malditz:
> Par quoy chascun bien savoir doit
> Qe par l'abit que moigne ont prise
> Ne par le cloistre u sont assis
> Ne serront seint, si plus n'y soit. (21097–108)

(Man makes a place holy, but a place does not make a man holy at all. This is clear from examples, for I read that Lucifer (who was in God's presence) fell from Heaven; and so did Adam from Paradise. And so did cursed Judas, who was beside God the Son, perish. Whereby everyone must know well that monks will not be holy unless it be from something more than the habit they have taken or the cloister in which they dwell; Wilson, p. 282).

The references here are indeed so brief that they may appear to be merely "examples" in our modern sense of the word, which was also current in the fourteenth century, rather than the *exempla* of medieval preachers, which are distinguished by their narrative form.[43] *Essample*, however, is used so frequently in the *Mirour de l'omme* that it appears that Gower did not distinguish between references to stories or, more broadly, the moralized lore from many places that could be turned into narratives, and the stories themselves.[44] Typical, then, is its first use in connection with a story from 4 Kings 20:12–19 which Gower introduced to illustrate Hypocrisy, one of the five daughters of Pride:

> Roys Ezechie, truis lisant,
> Par cause qu'il fuist demostrant
> Le tresor q'ot el temple dieu
> As messagiers du Babilant,
> Par le prophete devinant
> Par force apres luy fuist tollu.
> Par ceste essample est entendu
> Que le tresor q'om ad reçu,
> Quel est a l'alme partenant,
> Ne soit apertement veeu
> Au siecle; car tout ert perdu,
> Si l'en s'en vait glorifiant. (1081–92)

---

[43] Bremond and Le Goff begin their discussion of *exempla* by quoting Frederick Crane's claim that it is at times difficult to distinguish the general meaning of "example" from the technical "illustrative story" in ecclesiastical writings of this period; *L'"Exemplum,"* p. 25.

[44] *Essample* and the related *essemplerie* are used in connection with *exempla* from the Bible throughout the work; see, for example, 1657, 2173, 2459, 2662, 10310, 10322, 10345, 10465, 10478.... For examples from saints' lives, see 12586 and 15769. Many *exempla* from natural history are attributed to Solinus (see Macaulay, 1.lvii and his notes to 1849, 2101, 3747...); see 19910 for the use of *essample* in connection with this kind of material. The term appears to be used less often in connection with secular literature; see, however, 16673 ("essamplaire") and 23907.

(Of King Ezecias, I find written that because he showed the treasure which the temple of God held to the messengers of Babylon, according to the divination of the prophet, it was taken by force after his reign. By this example it is to be understood that the treasure that man has received, which belongs to the soul, should not be openly seen by the world; for everything will be lost if he goes around boasting of it; Wilson, p. 282).[45]

While there is some narrative here, Gower omitted much of the detail given in the Bible, including, for example, the dialogue between Ezechias and Isaias. The emphasis of the *Mirour de l'omme* is on the moral rather than on the story itself.

The dramatic change in the *Confessio Amantis* is Genius's expansion of *exempla*, some of which are still drawn from the sources used in the earlier work but many more of which derive specifically from the classical tradition, into the around 150 longer tales that have dominated critical attention to the work.[46] The eleven specific *exempla* identified by Macaulay as carried over into the new work, which will again become significant when we turn to the likely sources of the *Tale of the Three Questions*, suggest that Genius's tales are both longer and more likely to be secular. Four are only slightly longer. The accounts of Socrates's patience, which also appears in the *Wife of Bath's Prologue* (III, 727–32), is told in twenty-four lines in the *Mirour de l'Omme* (4165–88) and in sixty in the *Confessio Amantis* (III, 639–98). The twelve lines about "Phirin" (18301–12), a Roman noble who, according to the cited Valerius Maximus ("Valeire dist," 18302), mutilated his body in order to avoid the attention of women, become fifteen in the *Confessio Amantis* (V, 6370–84). The discussion of the emperor Valerian (17089–100), who valued his virginity over his other accomplishments, roughly doubles in length (V, 6395–416), and fifteen lines (19981–20004) about king Codrus of Athens, again explicitly taken from Valerius and describing the king's willingness to die in battle when told he must do so to save his people, is recounted the second time in nineteen (VII, 3181–99). In the other cases, the differences in length are more pronounced: the Sirens (10909–20: I, 481–529, or 12/49), Nebuchadnezzar's Punishment (21079–96: I, 2785–3042, or 18/258),[47] the Travelers and the Angel (3234–38: II, 291–364, or 5/74), Lucius and the

---

[45] In his translation, Wilson renders "essample" as "parable"; I have also changed his spelling of the king's name.

[46] Peck begins the Introduction to the first volume of his edition by calling attention to Gower's role as a "maker of tales," 1.1.

[47] A missing leaf from the one manuscript of the *Mirour de l'omme* may have contained more material about Nebuchadnezzar; a more accurate comparison here might be between lines 21985–96 of the *Mirour de l'omme* with book 1 lines 2961–98 of the *Confessio Amantis*, the descriptions of Nebuchadnezzar living like a beast.

Statue of Apollo (7093–128: V, *7105–207, or 35/102),[48] Dives and Lazarus (7969–92: VI, 986–1109, or 24/124), the King, Wine, Women and Truth (22765–800: VII, 1783–899, or 36/117), and Tobias and Sara (17417–24: VII, 5313–65, or 8/53). It should also be noted that only four of these *exempla* are originally from the Bible, indicative of the greater shift in the tales toward classical sources.

These eleven examples also show the difficulty of establishing what parts of the *Confessio Amantis* should be considered "tales."[49] The term refers primarily of course to the long narratives that Genius introduces into the text in order to illustrate his moral points and, indeed, "tale" appears in this context many times in the work.[50] Questions, however, quickly arise: how long and how narrative must a tale be, and must it be identified as an *ensample*? Genius uses this term in introducing the material about "Phyryns" (V, 6371), and his discussion of Valerian ends with a single verse directed at Amans: "Lo nou, my sone, avise thee" (V, 6417). Both stories, however, are placed by Peck under the heading *Virginity*, making them formally distinct in his edition from, say, the *Tale of Codrus*, which is introduced in the text by naming its source, but not by identifying it as an *ensample*. The problem is further complicated by the "tales" of Nebuchadnezzar and Arion in the *Prologue*, which are told before Genius appears. My point in raising this issue is not to offer a precise count,[51] but rather to observe that Gower, like the preachers of his day, thought in *exempla*. The insight that led to the "middel weie" (*Prologue*, 17) of the *Confessio Amantis*, was his recognition that, in a form expanded well beyond what an actual sermon could bear, these *ensamples*/tales could reach a much wider audience.

In the *Prologue* to the *Confessio Amantis* Gower reflected specifically on this new way of writing. In describing a literary production from written sources, it uses a construction, "essampled of," which anticipates Genius's specific use of *exempla*:

> Of hem that writen ous tofore
> The bokes duelle, and we therfore
> Ben tawht of that was write tho:
> Forthi good is that we also
> In oure tyme among ous hiere

---

48 Following the practice of Macaulay in his edition, an asterisk before a line number refers to a passage in the first or second recension of the work, but omitted from Gower's final revision. Peck usually does not include these passages.

49 In the Introduction to volume 1 of his edition, Peck writes of "hundreds of tales" presented in the work; 1.15.

50 See *A Concordance to John Gower's Confessio Amantis*, ed. J. D. Pickles and J. L. Dawson (Cambridge: D. S. Brewer, 1987).

51 Nicholson provides a detailed explanation of his claim that the work contains 150 tales; see *Love and Ethics*, pp. 77 and 410–11, note 3.

Do wryte of newe som matiere,
Essampled of these olde wyse,
So that it myhte in such a wyse,
Whan we ben dede and elleswhere,
Beleve to the worldes eere
In tyme comende after this. (*Prologue*, 1–11)

From the evidence cited in the *Middle English Dictionary*, it appears that the verb *ensaumplen* had only recently been derived from its related noun: the first two appearances are in Wycliffite tracts from the 1380s, in which the verb means "to be a model of" and is used of Christ who "koude ensaumple kynghod and presthod" and whose life "was þe beste, þat shulde ensaumple alle oþir."[52] The chronologically next five examples, four of which—but not the one just quoted—are all from the *Confessio Amantis*. In three, *ensaumplen*, used reflexively, can be translated "to learn from (an example), be warned (by the fate of someone)." It appears dramatically at the conclusion of the epitaph written on the tomb of Iphis and Araxarathen (IV, 3684); Genius employs it to sum up the *Tale of Adrian and Bardus* (V, 5159); and in the *Counsel of Balaam*, which is based loosely on Numbers 22–25, the "Hebreus" learn not to sin with the "paien" women who have been sent among them once Phinees has slain an offending couple (VII, 4441). All of the examples of this construction, which is restricted to the *Confessio Amantis*, are a natural extension of Gower's use of *exempla*.

The final occurrence of *ensaumplen*, in the 1393 revision that adapts the *Prologue* for Henry Bolingbroke, again invokes the verb in the context of writing the *Confessio Amantis*. After contrasting the current times with the past, Gower continued:

And natheles be daies olde,
Whan that the bokes weren levere,
Wrytinge was beloved evere
Of hem that weren vertuous;
For hier in erthe amonges ous,
If no man write hou that it stode,
The pris of hem that weren goode
Scholde, as who seith, a gret partie
Be lost; so for to magnifie
The worthi princes that tho were,
The bokes schewen hiere and there,
Wherof the world ensampled is;
And tho that deden thanne amis
Thurgh tirannie and crualté
Right as thei stoden in degré,
So was the wrytinge of here werk. (*Prologue*, 36–51)

---

[52] Listed under (d) in the *MED, s.v.*

Although the *Middle English Dictionary* records this example under the same definition provided for the Wycliffite passages, it appears to be more similar to Gower's earlier use in the *Prologue*: the world is provided with examples (of good behavior) by ("wherof"; see *MED* 22a) the "worthi princes," whose deeds are recorded in "bokes." To return, then, to the first example, the "matiere" (*Prologue*, 6), which will be renewed in the *Confessio Amantis*, will be illustrated by "ensamples" taken from "these olde wyse." Peck glosses the final word as "wise [men/books]," but only "bokes" have been mentioned.[53] In these passages, then, Gower stated that sources for his tales were written.

This same point, which is reinforced at the beginnings of many of the tales, is further supported the scholarship on their actual sources. The first, the *Tale of Acteon*, is indeed typical. Genius announces that he will tell "a tale" (I, 330) that will teach Amans "thin yhe for to kepe and warde" (I, 331). The tale begins,

> "Ovide telleth in his bok
> Ensample touchende of mislok,
> And seith hou whilom ther was on,
> A worthi lord, which Acteon
> Was hote...." (I, 333–37)

Macaulay notes that the narrative is from Ovid's *Metamorphoses* III, 130–259. Eugen Stollreither adds that it is one of twenty-nine tales drawn from this source.[54] Nicholson comments that "Gower follows Ovid's version closely";[55] without disagreeing, Peck discusses significant differences between the two (1.260). While there is certainly still much to learn about the precise versions of the narratives that Gower turned to, I would consider only five of the around 150 tales, other than the *Tale of Florent*, as still lacking an identified written source.[56] Of these, three concern historical figures, Galba and Vitel-

---

53   Were it not for the following line, "wyse" here could also mean "a characteristic or customary manner" or "a way of proceeding or accomplishing something"; see *MED* 2a. See, however, Peck's discussion of *rime riche* here, which suggests that Gower intended a close connection between the ideas. In attributing this way of writing to earlier writers, he might have been thinking specifically of the *Preface* to book 1 of Valerius Maximus's *Factorum et dictorum memorabilium libri nouem*; see *Valerius Maximus. Memorable Doings and Sayings*, 2 vols., ed. and trans. D. R. Shackleton Bailey (Cambridge, MA: Harvard University Press, 2000), 1.12–13.

54   Eugen Stollriether, *Quellen-Nachweise zu John Gowers* Confessio Amantis. *T. 1* (Munich: Kastner & Lossen, 1901), pp. 34–35.

55   Nicholson, *Annotated Index*, p. 110.

56   Most of the sources for Gower's tales can be discovered by consulting the notes in the editions of Macaulay and Peck and the references in Nicholson's *Annotated Index*. New discoveries are still being made. Because it concerns a tale like *Florent*, significant for my argument is James T. Bratcher's identification of the likely source for *Tale of Rosiphelee*; see "The Function of the Jeweled Bridle in Gower's 'Tale of Rosiphelee,'" *Chaucer Review* 40 (2005), pp. 107–10.

lius (VI, 537–95), Nero (VI, 1151–227) and Caesar (VII, 2449–86), and so there appears to be little reason to assume that Gower created new tales about them from oral traditions. The other two, however, are relevant, although in one case, the *Tale of the Mountain and the Mouse*, the source has merely remained unrecorded. In the other, the sources of *Tale of Three Questions*, have been presented in a way that overlooks the written traditions from which Gower most likely worked.

The source of the *Tale of the Mountain and the Mouse* has been left unrecorded because it differs from those of the other tales and so may serve as a reminder of how few of the Genius's "ensaumples" were drawn from popular traditions. After noting that a king should not reveal his thoughts, Genius continues,

> For if a king schal upon gesse
> Withoute verrai cause drede,
> He mai be lich to that I rede;
> And thogh that it be lich a fable,
> Th'ensample is good and resonable. (VII, 3548–52)

The source is indeed one of the Aesopic fables,[57] the mountain in labor, which Gower might have read and, of course, heard, in many different versions. The one in the *Novus Aesopus* of Alexander Neckam appears to be as close as any to his tale:

> Cum gemitu magno Mons prægnans parturiebat,
>   Mugitu magnum exuberans tonitrum.
> Vicinos omnes timor ingens excruciabat
>   Auxilii nullus consiliive locus.
> Dicebant: Terram cum Mons hic occupet istam,
>   Quid faciet partus illius immodicus?
> Illius subito cumulus nos obruet ingens,
>   Membraque non minimo pondere nostra teret.
> Murem post multas peperit Mons ille querelas;
>   In risum versus sic fuit ille metus.
> Dicitur elatis istud qui maxima jactant,
>   Cum se facturos vix modicum faciunt.[58]

(With great groaning the pregnant mountain was giving birth, surpassing with its sound great thundering. Enormous fear tormented all the neighbors; there was no place of help or counsel. They said: since this mountain fills that land, what will its unbridled offspring do? Its huge mass will

[57] In using this term, I follow Mann, *From Aesop to Reynard*, pp. 2–4.
[58] Léopold Hervieux, *Les fabulistes latins depuis le siècle d'Auguste jusqu'à la fin du moyen âge*, 5 vols. (Paris: Firmin-Didot, 1893–99), 2.411. See also the edition of Giovanni Garbugino, *Fabulisti latini medievali* 2 (Genoa: Università degli studi di Genova, Dipartimento di archeologia, filologia classica e loro tradizioni, 1984).

quickly cover us and with its not lesser weight it will grind our limbs. After much wailing, the mountain gave birth to a mouse. Fear was thus turned to laughter. This is said about the mighty who boast about doing great things but do barely a small one.)

Gower changed the moral and some details. The basic narrative, however, had been in writing since Phaedrus composed his Aesopic fables in the first half of the first century AD and had been rewritten many times. As Gower's "I rede" indicates, there is much evidence which associates even this popular material with literate rather than oral traditions.

James T. Bratcher has filled one of the last gaps in the scholarship on the sources of the tales in the *Confessio Amantis* by identifying *King John and the Bishop* and Folktale Type 875, the Clever Peasant Girl, as analogues for the *Tale of Three Questions*.[59] His decision, however, to discuss these traditions by referring to a seventeenth-century ballad and a *märchen* published in German in the nineteenth century creates the impression that Gower worked from oral traditions.[60] Instead, the suggestions themselves point to the kind of source that Gower claimed to have used when Genius states that the tale is from "a cronique" (I, 3059; see also I, 3388), indeed one likely to have been associated with Spain since he identifies the main characters as king "Alphonse," his knight as "Danz Petro," and the knight's wise daughter as "Peronelle." As Francis J. Child's note mentions, the written record for the tale type found in *King John and the Bishop*, goes back at least as far as the late ninth-century *Futūḥ Miṣr* (*The Conquests of Egypt*) by Ibn 'Abd al-Ḥakam.[61] Here a king, who "grudged his vezīrs their pay," threatens to kill them in a month unless they can answer three questions: "What is the number of the stars in the heavens?"; "What sum of money does the sun earn daily by his labor for each human being?"; and "What does God almighty do, every day?" (pp. 211–12). Unable to do so, they are aided by a potter who has one of them take up his work, and who receives from them clothing and a horse similar to their own. The potter also arranges to aid the son of a previous king

---

59   James T. Bratcher, "Gower and Child, No. 45, 'King John and the Bishop,'" *Notes and Queries* n.s. 48 (2001), pp. 14–15; and "Gower's 'Tale of Three Questions' and 'The Clever Peasant Girl' Folktale," *Notes and Queries* n.s. 53 (2006), pp. 409–10.

60   This is not, it appears, Bratcher's intention.

61   Francis James Child, *The English and Scottish Popular Ballad*, ed. Helen Child Sargent and George Lyman Kittredge (Boston, MA: Houghton Mifflin, 1904), p. 78 (item 45). The text was edited by Charles Torrey, *The History of the Conquest of Egypt, North Africa, and Spain, Known as the* Futuh Misr *of Ibn 'Abd Al-Hakam* (1922; repr. New York: AMS Press, 1980). Torrey published the Arabic and a translation of the passage under consideration here in "The Egyptian Prototype of 'King John and the Abbot,'" *Journal of the American Oriental Society* 20 (1899), pp. 211–14. See also, Christopher James Wright, "Ibn 'Abd al-Hakam's *Futuh Misr*: An Analysis of the Text and New Insights into the Islamic Conquest of Egypt," diss. University of California, Santa Barbara, 2006.

by getting the current ruler outside of the city. In the guise of a vezīr, he then approaches the king, answers the first two questions, and promises to show him the answer to the third on the following day. Taking him out of the city, the potter explains what God does every day:

> "he humbles men, and exalts men, and ends the life of men. To illustrate this: here is one of your own vezīrs sitting down to work in a potter's kiln; while I, a poor potter, am mounted on one of the royal beasts, and wear the garments of the court. And further, such a one (naming the rival prince) has just barred the gates of Memphis against you!" (p. 214)

The deposed king spends the rest of his days sitting by the gate of the city, "raving and drivelling" (p. 214). While there are many differences between the stories told by Ibn 'Abd al-Ḥakam and Gower, their essential similarities are clear: using apparently unsolvable riddles, kings threaten counsellors with death; and the counsellors are then aided by individuals of lower social standing. Moreover, the riddles themselves are related, most obviously in the themes of God's humbling of the powerful (Ibn 'Abd al-Ḥakam), and the value of humility and the worthlessness of pride (Gower), but also in the first questions concerning man's relationship to the earth.

This same story, although in version less close to the *Tale of Three Questions*, circulated in the West in the thirteenth and fourteenth century.[62] It appears in a collection of *exempla* compiled by Stephen of Bourbon:

> Legitur quod quidam rex, habens in terra sua quemdam divitem sapientem, non inveniens occasionem quomodo ejus pecuniam extorqueret, quesivit ab eo tres questiones, quas nisi solveret, multam pecuniam ei daret; que videbantur insolubiles. Prima fuit ubi erat medium terre, quasi centrum; alia, quot modii aque erant in mari; tercia quam magna erat misericordia Dei. Cum autem, die assignata, coram regis curia a carcere duceretur, in quo detinebatur ut se redimeret, nisi dictas questiones solveret, de consilio cujusdam philosophi dicti *Auxilium miserorum*, assumpto baculo, in terra infixit, dicens: "Hic est centrum terre et medium; improba si potes. Si vis ut mesurem modios maris, retine fluvia et aquas alias, ne subintrent illud, quousque mensuraverim, et tibi dicam numerum modiorum. Terciam solvere potero si tradideris mihi vestes tuas et solium ad hoc judicium faciendum." Quo facto, cum esset in sublimi solio in apparatu regio, ait: "Audite et videte sublimitatem misericordie Dei, quia parum ante eram servus, modo subito factus sum quasi rex; ante pauper, modo quasi dives; ante in imo, modo in alto; ante in cathenis et carcere, modo quasi in libertate; etc." Sic centrum misericordie Die est ubique in presenti vita; misericordie ejus non est numerus; sublimitas et universitas ejus est quod de

62 Walter Anderson provides a detailed study of the tradition; *Kaiser und Abt: Die Geschichte eines Schwanks*, FFC 42 (Helsinki: Suomalainen Tiedeakatemia, 1923).

carcere et vinculis peccatorum, per penitenciam modicam, venit peccator ad regnum celorum.[63]

(One reads that a certain king, having in his country a certain wealthy and wise subject and not finding a way to extort his money, asked him three questions, which seemed insoluble: unless he was able to solve them, he would have to give him much money. The first was, Where is the center or mid-point of the earth? The second, How many units of water are there in the sea? The third, How great is God's mercy? On the appointed day, he was brought before the court of the king from the prison in which he had been held and from which he would have to buy his way out unless he could answer the questions he had been asked. Following the advice of a certain philosopher called "the Help of the Wretched" and taking up a staff, he thrust it into the ground saying, "Here is the center and middle of the earth; prove it false if you can. If you wish that I measure the units of the sea, hold back, until I have measured them, the rivers and streams lest they steal into it, and I will tell you the number of units. I will be able to solve the third if you will give me your robes and your throne to pronounce this judgment." This having been done, when he was on the high throne in royal magnificence, he said: "Hear and see the height of the mercy of God: before I was a slave, suddenly I have become like a king; before I was a pauper, now like a rich man; before below, now on high; before in chains and prison, now free, etc." So the center of God's mercy is every place in this present life; his mercy is not numbered; and his height and wholeness is that from the prison and chains of sin, the sinner comes through penance to the kingdom of heaven.)

Here the role of the advisor to the oppressed subject is reduced, the question about the earth is changed so that it no longer concerns what is produced, and the theme of humility disappears. It demonstrates, however, the circulation of the narrative in Western, Latin sources.

Although it has been published only from a source translated into Catalan in 1451, a third example of the story of a king using insoluble riddles to extort his advisors is significant for our understanding of the sources of the *Tale of Three Questions*, because it both appears in the kind of text—a chronicle—that Gower claimed to have used, and develops the narrative in ways similar to the *Tale of Three Questions*. A section of the work known as either the *Genesi de Scriptura* or the *Compendi historial de la Biblia* turns to the narrative in a section on the Roman emperors and the conversion of Constantine.[64] After introducing Nero as responsible for the martyrdoms of

---

[63]   A. Lecoy de la Marche, *Anecdotes historiques,* légendes et apologues (Paris: Librairie Renouard, 1877), pp. 81–82. See the *Thesaurus Exemplorum Medii Aevi* (ThEMA), http://lodel.ehess.fr/gahom/thema/ for more information.

[64]   *Genesi de Scriptura trelladat del provençal a la llengua catalana per Mossen Guillem Serra en l'any M.CCCCLI*, ed. Miquel Victoria Amer (Barcelona: A. Verdaguer, 1873); the tale of Nero and Seneca appears on pp. 277–81.

Peter and Paul and for burning the body of John the Baptist, it moves to a full account of the emperor's killing of Seneca, focusing immediately on not the advisors but their helper, the "mestre ten saui" (p. 277; "teacher of the wise"). The questions the king poses, which are similar to those in the other narratives (What does God in heaven do? How many day's journeys ["jornadas"; p. 277] does the sun go in a day? What is my value?), appear in an exchange in which Seneca does not take part. Instead, he learns of it far from Rome: "Senecha era en Spanya e guarda e viu en les esteles, e conech per la gran sciencia qui en ell era que lemperador volia ociure .iii. homens a tort bons" (pp. 277–78; "Seneca was in Spain; he looked and saw in the stars, and knew through the great learning that he had that the emperor wished wrongly to kill three men"). He returns to Italy disguised as a beggar and provides the answers to the advisors. The story ends differently from the other versions: suspecting that the advisors have been helped, Nero recognizes and confronts Seneca, and then, seeing the great honor paid to him by the Romans, becomes angry and kills him. With this abrupt conclusion, the chronicle shifts to the next emperor.

While the story's conclusion differs greatly from the one in the *Tale of the Three Questions*, simply its retelling within a chronicle helps to locate Gower's version. There is, indeed an historical context that explains why this story was retold about Seneca and Nero. Seneca the Younger, born in Cordoba, was Nero's tutor and then advisor during the first eight years of his reign. Although he had retired and was travelling outside of Rome, he killed himself, according to Tacitus's retelling of the events in *Annales* XV.lx–lxiv, on Nero's command following the failed attempt of Gaius Calpurnius Piso to assassinate the emperor.[65] These events are reinterpreted in the *Primera Crónica General de España*, written for Alfonso X, king of Castile (1252–84). In this account, Nero meets Seneca and his nephew, Lucan, at a gathering of wise advisors in Cordoba following a failed uprising and takes both back to Rome. Seneca becomes Nero's advisor, with good effect, until he is converted by St. Paul; Nero then commands his death and the death of Lucan.[66] It is Nero's reputation that dictates the ending of the story in the *Genesi de Scriptura*. However, the emphasis on advising rulers, with its counterpart, the wisdom of the rulers themselves, may also have contributed to the unidentified version that served as Gower's direct source, or the *Tale of Three Questions* itself, if an intermediary did not exist. One need look no further than the journey of the Queen of Sheba to Solomon's court "to test him with

---

[65] *Tacitus V, the Annals, books XIII–XVI*, trans. John Jackson (Cambridge, MA: Harvard University Press, 1937), pp. 310–19.

[66] *Primera Crónica General de España*, 2 vols., ed. Ramón Menéndez Pidal, Fuentes Cronísticas de la Historia de España 1 (Madrid: Editorial Gredos, 1977–8), 1.124. See also, Feliciano Delgado Léon, "Séneca en la Edad Media español," *Boletín de la Real Academia de Córdoba* 127 (1994), pp. 415–32.

hard questions" (1 Kings 10:1) to recall that riddling competitions were often associated with wise rulers.[67] Alfonso X, known to modern historians as "el sabio," is praised for his learning in the preface to the *Primera Crónica*:

> Si capis, Hesperia, que dat tibi dona sophia
> Regis, splendescet tibi fama decus quoque crescet.
> Rex, decus Hesperie thesaurus philosophie,
> Dogma dat hyspanis; capiant bona, dent loca uanis. (1.2)

(O Spain, if you take the gifts that the wisdom of the king gives you, you will shine forth, and you will grow in fame and beauty. The king, who is the ornament of Spain and the treasure of philosophy, gives instruction to the Spanish people. Let good men take what is good, and leave what is vain to those who are vain.)[68]

A reimagining of the narrative with Alfonso X as a protagonist would almost certainly lead to a different outcome.

It is, however, the new emphasis on the other main character that opens the way to the narrative that Gower or, as seems more likely, his direct source told. In Ibn 'Abd al-Ḥakam's version, it is not the potter, but rather another prince who takes power, and in Stephen of Bourbon's *exemplum* this role is reduced to a single phrase. In contrast, although doomed, Seneca is a worthy rival to Nero, and as such this story is ready to encompass another, a tale first recorded in the *Book of Delight*, by a late twelfth-, or perhaps early thirteenth-century Jewish physician who lived part of his life in Barcelona, Joseph ben Meir Ibn Zabara. Indeed, in the introduction to the 1932 translation of this work by Moses Hadas, Merriam Sherwood makes the connection between one of its stories and the *Tale of Three Questions*.[69] The story concerns a king who asks his eunuch to find a wise man to interpret his dream in which "an ape of Yeman" had leapt upon "the necks of his wives and concubines" (p. 72). During his journey, the eunuch meets a countryman, to whom he says a number of bewildering things, beginning with "Peace to thee, thou worker of earth, who art thyself earth and yet eat earth" (p. 72), before the countryman takes him back to his house, where his wise young daughter explains the eunuch's cryptic comments, and so reveals her wisdom. The eunuch tells her

---

[67] See the chapter "Riddle Tales from Literary Sources" by Christine Goldberg in *Turandot's Sisters: A Study of the Folktale AT 851*, Routledge Library of Editions: Folklore 16 (London: Routledge, 1993), pp. 13–41.

[68] Translated by Joseph F. O'Callaghan, *The Learned King: The Reign of Alfonso X of Castile* (Philadelphia: University of Pennsylvania Press, 1993), p. 270. For assessments of the king's reputation, see also Robert I. Burns, "Epilogue: Apotheosis," in *The Worlds of Alfonso the Learned and James the Conqueror: Intellect and Force in the Middle Ages*, ed. Burns (Princeton: Princeton University Press, 1985), pp. 203–10.

[69] Joseph ben Meir Ibn Zabara, *The Book of Delight*, trans. Moses Hadas, intro. by Merriam Sherwood (New York: Columbia University Press, 1932), p. 17.

the king's dream, which she says she will explain only in the royal presence. Brought before the king and then taken into a private chamber, the wise daughter at first refuses to interpret the dream but then does, leading to the conclusion of the story:

> "My lord king, search among thy wives and maidservants and concubines, and thou wilt find amongst them a man clothed in their habit. He doth come in unto them and lie with them, and he is the ape whom thou sawest leaping upon their necks in thy dream." So the king searched among his wives and concubines and found among them a handsome youth, comely in form and features, from his shoulder and upwards taller than the crowd; before his countenance gold or silver would be dimmed. The king seized him and butchered him before their eyes and cast his blood in their faces; thereafter he slew them all. And he took the maiden to wife and put the crown royal upon her head, and vowed a vow that never as long as she lived would another woman lie in his bosom, but she alone would be his portion and his lot. (pp. 75–76)

Here, then, is the rest of Gower's tale, which develops a similar plot concerning a king and riddles with a wise daughter, who aids her father and marries the king.

Again, a collection of Latin *exempla*, in this case a work known as the *Compilatio singularis exemplorum*,[70] helps bridge the gap between in this case a Hebrew work and the Latin West. In an *exemplum* given the title "Das schlaue Mädchen" by its editor, the king of Sheba—the story ends by identifying his wise wife as the Queen who visits Solomon—hears a voice that tells him a monkey is sleeping with his wife. After killing all the monkeys in his land to no effect, the king explains the situation to a loyal retainer who responds: "si fraus est aliqua ex parte regine, per aliam mulierem melius inueniretur; et ego iam diu est uidi quandam puellam nobilem sapientissimam: si placet, ego ibo et eam adducam" (p. 4; "if there is deceit on the queen's part, it will be discovered more easily by another woman; I have seen for a long time a certain most wise, noble girl; if you would like, I will go and bring her to you"). The middle part of the story is more complicated: the king's minister first meets the girl's fiancé, bewildering him with riddling statements that the woman herself untangles at a feast after which the fiancé is told: "meliori marito dabitur quam vos sitis" (p. 6; "she will be given a better husband than you are"). Taken to court, the girl lives with the queen for three days and then arranges for a public stripping of her lover, who has been disguised as a woman. The conclusion, however, is swift: "rex autem statim iusticiam fecit de mecho ac mecha et videns sapienciam puelle accepit

---

[70] Alfons Hilka, ed., *Neue Beiträge zur Erzählungsliteratur des Mittelalters (Die Compilatio singularis exemplorum der Hs. Tours 486, ergänzt durch eine Schwesterhandschrift Bern 679)* (Breslau: Grass, Barth & Comp., 1913), pp. 4–6.

eam in vxorem" (p. 6; "the king exercised judgment on the adulterers and, seeing the wisdom of the girl married her"). Although too late to be sources for Gower, two more versions of the story suggest its presence in the Iberian peninsula: Giovanni Sercambi retold it, in *Novella V,* of "lo re Gostanzo di Portogallo,"[71] and a Provencal collection that dates to the fifteenth century begins, "Alphons estoit ung noble roy."[72]

While it is of course possible the Gower combined these two narratives to write the *Tale of Three Questions,* his use of the riddles about pride and humility in the *Mirour de l'omme* (1376–79) provides further indication that he found them already joined in his immediate source.[73] In the earlier French work, he concluded the section on Humility, which focuses first on her five daughters who combat the five daughters of Pride, with a discussion of the virtue herself:

> Quoy plus coustoit et meinz valoit,
> Et plus valoit et meinz coustoit,
> Jadis uns sages demanda:
> Et uns autres luy respondoit,
> Q'orguil plus couste en son endroit,
> Et sur tout autre meinz valdra;
> Mais cil q'umblesce gardera
> Meinz couste et plus proufitera
> Au corps et alme, quelque soit.
> Dont m'est avis que cil serra
> Malvois marchant q'achatera
> Le peiour, qant eslire doit. (12601–12)

(A wise man asked long ago, "what cost the most and was of least value, and what was of most value that cost the least." Another answered him, "Pride cost the most in itself and will be of less value than anything else; but the one who will keep humility spent the least and will profit most in body and soul, whatever happens." Therefore in my opinion he will be a bad merchant who buys the worse when he must choose; Wilson, p. 172).

As Macaulay points out in the introduction to his edition,[74] Gower included more than forty proverbs in the *Mirour;* the lack of a similar list of riddles suggests that these are rarer. There is little reason, then, to assume that he

---

[71] Giovanni Sercambi, *Novelle: nuovo testo critico con studio introduttivo et note,* revised edn, 2 vols., ed. Giovanni Sinicropi, Filologia. Testi e studi 5 (Florence: Le Lettere, 1995), 1.95. On the date of this work, see Sinicropi's introduction, 1.9–32.

[72] "Du Roy Alphons, qui fut trompé par le malice de sa femme," chapter 8 in E. Langlois, *Nouvelles françaises inédites du quinzième siècle* (Paris: Honoré Champion, 1908), p. 46.

[73] See *Complete Works,* ed. Macaulay, 1.xliii. Macaulay noted the correspondence between the passages.

[74] 1.lviii–lx.

drew on oral tradition for the two above. In contrast, the lines imply that they were already embedded in a narrative: "a wise man asked...another answered." Because we know that Gower re-used eleven *exempla* from the *Mirour* in writing the *Confessio Amantis*, it appears that here too he returned to a story that he had alluded to in the earlier work. To do so, of course, it would have had to have been one that he had not written but read. While we may not have the immediate source of the *Tale of Three Questions*, the evidence points to its existence and so removes the most compelling support for the claim that Gower used similar oral materials in constructing the *Tale of Florent*.

The Chaucer–Gower Quarrel and the Date of the Wife of Bath's Tale

The claim that Chaucer created the *Wife of Bath's Tale* to embody what he saw as Licisca's challenge to the patriarchal assumptions of his society only to have it rewritten by Gower to express traditional views on the subject of marriage provides a new starting pointing for understanding the now usually discounted theory of a falling-out between these two authors.[75] That they were friends through the completion of *Troilus and Criseyde*, usually dated to the mid-1380s, is demonstrated by the opening of the penultimate stanza of the work:

> O moral Gower, this book I directe
> To the and to the, philosophical Strode,
> To vouchen sauf, ther nede is, to correcte,
> Of youre benignites and zeles goode. (V, 1856–59)

Evidence for an end to their mutual esteem is found in the change in the way Gower introduced the *Tale of Florent*. In the first version of the *Confessio Amantis*, dated to 1390 and distinguished from the later recensions by three passages—the account of the poem's beginning in a meeting on the Thames with Richard II (*Prologue*, *24–93), Venus's address to Chaucer (VIII, *2941–57), and, finally, a Latin prayer for Richard (beginning after line *2970 of book VIII) that leads into a commendation of the king and a dedication of

---

[75] See in particular Andy Galloway, "Gower's Quarrel with Chaucer and the Origins of Bourgeois Didacticism in Fourteenth-Century London Poetry," in *Calliope's Classroom: Didactic Poetry from Antiquity to the Renaissance*, ed. Annette Harder, A. A. MacDonald and G. J. Reinink (Paris: Peeters, 2007), pp. 245–68. Rather than an actually falling out, Galloway interprets the evidence as a literary debate over personal and political power in society. Moreover, his characterization of the views of these authors differs from those presented in this study.

the work to him (VIII, *2971–3053)[76]—Genius turns from discussing the need for "obedience in love" to the story by commenting, "And in ensample of þis matiere / A tale I fynde as þou schalt hiere."[77] While Gower often used "tale" to introduce his *exempla*, here it could refer to his actual source, one of the *Canterbury Tales*. Gower presumably believed that his retelling would please his friend.

That it did not is suggested by one of the two pieces of evidence adduced by Thomas Tyrwhitt when he first proposed that the authors quarreled, the possible reference to Gower in "the reflection upon those who relate such stories as those of *Canace*, or of *Apollonius Tyrius*" in the *Introduction to the Man of Law's Tale*:[78]

> But certainly no word ne writeth he
> Of thilke wikke ensample of Canacee,
> That loved hir owene brother synfully—
> Of swiche cursed stories I sey fy!—
> Or ellis of Tyro Appollonius,
> How that the cursed kyng Antiochus
> Birafte his doghter of hir maydenhede,
> That is so horrible a tale for to rede,
> Whan he hir threw upon the pavement.
> And therfore he, of ful avysement,
> Nolde nevere write in none of his sermons
> Of swiche unkynde abhomynacions,
> Ne I wol noon reherce, if that I may. (II, 77–89)

While "ensample" appears often in the *Canterbury Tales*, its use here in the context of two of the tales—one of which occupies most of book VIII—in the *Confessio Amantis* makes it all but certain that this passage was, to use Tyrwhitt's words, "leveled at" Gower. The point of attack, Gower's moral blindness to rape, which is explicitly described, even in cases of incest, continues the argument central to the *Wife of Bath's Tale*. The full force of the passage, however, relies on recognizing the bond that it establishes between the two men by associating the Man of Law with Gower and the fictional author Chaucer with the real one: both retell stories about violence against women, feigning moral outrage but perpetuating their oppression. As writing and rape blend, the final clause, "if that I may," becomes the most damning.

---

[76] John H. Fisher explains Macaulay's division of the manuscripts into the three recensions; see *John Gower: Moral Philosopher and Friend of Chaucer* (New York: New York University Press, 1964), pp. 8–12 and 116–27. For more recent views, see note 79 below.

[77] Peck records this reading in his textual notes, 1.305.

[78] Thomas Tywhitt, *The Canterbury Tales of Chaucer, to which are added an essay upon his language and versification and an introductory discourse, together with notes and a glossary* (London: T. Payne, 1775–78), 4.147–48.

Gower, the narrator of the *Canterbury Tales*, and the Man of Law have the power to treat the stories of others and women honestly, but they do not. For this, the *Wife of Bath's Tale* and its author condemn them.

This criticism of Gower sharpens when one recalls the passage praising Chaucer at the conclusion of the 1390 version of the *Confessio Amantis*. Venus's final words to Amans concern him:

> "And gret wel Chaucer whan ye mete,
> As mi disciple and mi poete:
> For in the floures of his youthe
> In sondri wise, as he wel couthe,
> Of Ditees and of songes glade,
> The whiche he for mi sake made,
> The lond fulfild is overal:
> Wherof to him in special
> Above alle othre I am most holde.
> For thi now in hise daies olde
> Thow schalt him telle this message,
> That he upon his latere age,
> To sette an ende of alle his werk,
> As he which is myn owne clerk,
> Do make his testament of love,
> As thou hast do thi schrifte above,
> So that mi court it mai recorde." (VIII, *2941–57)

Having read and then rewritten the *Wife of Bath's Tale*, Gower's response was to lecture Chaucer on the need to return to more conventional love poetry, the kind of work that Gower found appropriate to his own views. Moreover, the decision to delete this passage becomes more pointed when placed in the context of another change, which because it seems so unnecessary repays close attention, in the 1392 recension of the *Confessio Amantis*, the new introduction to the *Tale of Florent*:

> Wherof, if that thee list to wite
> In a cronique as it is write,
> A gret ensample thou myht fynde,
> Which now is come to my mynde. (I, 1403–06)

By substituting "cronique" for "tale," Gower tried to hide his real source.[79] The quarrel, as discussed in Chapter 1, continued in the vehemence of

---

[79] Thomas Hahn characterizes the change as from a "popular tale" to a "literate narrative"; Peter Nicholson places it in the context of Gower's other revisions; "Gower's Manuscript of the *Confessio Amantis*," in *The Medieval Python: The Purposive and Provocative Work of Terry Jones*, ed. R. F. Yeager and Toshiyuki Takamiya (New York: Palgrave Macmillan, 2012), pp. 75–86. See also Terry Jones, "Did John Gower Rededicate his 'Confessio Amantis' before Henry IV's Usurpation?" in *Middle English Texts*

Chaucer's denunciation of alchemy in the *Canon's Yeoman's Tale*, written at some time after the period that concerns us here.

The initial chronology of the quarrel has clear implications for understanding the origin of the *Canterbury Tales*. The publication of the first version of the *Confessio Amantis* in 1390 means that the *Wife of Bath's Tale* must have been written long enough before this date for Gower to have used it to compose the *Tale of Florent*. It also establishes that Gower did not know of Chaucer's displeasure with what he had done because it concludes with remarks that, while intended to praise him, made matters worse. He certainly knew it by the time of the third recension of the work, around 1392. That Gower did not immediately make these revisions in the second recension might suggest that he was unaware of Chaucer's reaction at this time. On the other hand it is not necessary to conclude that Chaucer's response in the *Introduction to the Man of Law's Tale* and more generally in his writing of his own tale about Custance needed to await the publication of the *Confessio Amantis* in 1390. It seems likely that the two authors would have read each other's work in draft. In any case dating the *Wife of Bath's Tale* to before 1390 supports the central claims of this book, that Licisca's rebellion began the *Canterbury Tales*.

Making the Wife of Bath's Tale

The *Tale of Three Questions*, discussed in the previous section to show that Gower worked from written rather than oral materials, may be used to restate my argument about the sources of the *Canterbury Tales* and, more specifically, to introduce those of the *Wife of Bath's Tale*. Because a narrative that combines the stories of Ibn 'Abd al-Ḥakam and Joseph ben Meir Ibn Zabara has not been found, it remains possible that it was Gower who joined them, and did so for a reason similar to what I am claiming about Chaucer: to exemplify the point that brings book I of the *Confessio Amantis* to a fitting close, the injunction to practice humility and avoid pride. And yet, Boccaccio's recasting of the "Versus de mola piperis" in three distinct economic settings so that the story itself became all but unrecognizable as it was retold is simply on a different scale from what Gower might have done. It was recognizing Boccaccio's technique that opened for Chaucer a new way to write, not to retell old stories but rather to use disparate materials to create new ones. The sources of the *Wife of Bath's Tale*, both dissimilar and unlikely, exemplify the very different starting points from which Chaucer worked. One is the Irish tradition of a sovereignty goddess who is transformed from being old and

in Transition: A Festschrift Dedicated to Toshiyuki Takamiya on his 70th Birthday, ed. Simon Horobin and Linne R. Mooney (York: York Medieval Press, 2014), pp. 40–74.

loathly through her union with a new king. The other is a ubiquitous anti-feminist theme, the claim that a beautiful woman is never chaste. From these two ideas Chaucer wrote a tale that, while appearing timeless, had a specific role to play in his collection.

Because the Finnish historical-geographical school of folklore discussed in Chapter 1 was dominant at the moment when in 1892 Whitley Stokes identified the Irish sovereignty legends as the ultimate source for what was perceived at the time to be a group of fourteenth- and fifteenth-century English loathly-lady stories and because the motif itself appears to be of great antiquity, scholars have focused on the possible routes of transmission for early Celtic material into late medieval England.[80] This transmission, it was believed, would also account for the change in the story's focus, from the rule of a country to dominance in a marriage. The lack of evidence for intermediary versions, and our changed understanding of oral culture, point to a different way to solve this problem: Chaucer encountered the legend directly or at some small remove from a speaker of Irish.

There is some circumstantial evidence suggesting that the issue of Irish sovereignty was topical in the 1380s. Although Ireland was not the focus of most English monarchs during the thirteenth and fourteenth centuries, it would have been at the center of court interest when on 12 October 1385 Richard II bestowed its land and lordship on Robert de Vere, Earl of Oxford, his favorite.[81] Within months the king received a request from a council held in Dublin late in 1385, but unaware of de Vere's appointment, that he come in person to Ireland. While it seems unlikely that de Vere, much less the king, intended to undertake this journey, de Vere was granted funds to maintain 500 men-at-arms and 1,000 archers in Ireland for two years. All changed in October 1386 when the Appellants seized power and in the following autumn defeated the force that de Vere had raised in Cheshire to restore Richard to power. The Merciless Parliament of 1388 then annulled his claim to the duchy. In this context stories about Irish sovereignty might indeed have been of interest in England. Moreover, although set in the perhaps fifth-century reigns of either Niall of the Nine Hostages or Lugaid mac Dáire, the legends to which Stokes referred are actually recorded in manuscripts of the twelfth

---

[80] See Maynadier, *Wife of Bath's Tale*; Eisner, *Tale of Wonder*; Bollard, "Sovereignty"; and Peck, "Folklore."

[81] See Nigel Saul, *Richard II* (New Haven: Yale University Press, 1997), pp. 270–75. The Irish perspective, or more accurately perspectives, on these events is more difficult to establish. A useful introduction to this problem is J. A. Watt's chapter, "Approaches to the History of Fourteenth-Century Ireland," in *A New History of Ireland. II. Medieval Ireland. 1169–1534*, ed. Art Cosgrove (Oxford: Clarendon Press, 1987), pp. 303–13. His following chapters, "Gaelic Polity and Cultural Identity" (pp. 314–51) and "The Anglo-Irish Colony under Strain, 1327–99" (pp. 352–96), also provide essential background to the proposal that a traditional Irish tale about sovereignty was told to Chaucer at this time.

through the fifteenth centuries. All contain the motif of a sudden and miraculous transformation of an old and ugly woman into a young beautiful one at the moment when she sleeps with a new king, who at this moment attains sovereignty over his land.

The prevalence of this motif in Irish sources, and its absence in other traditions, suggests that it resonated in this culture from an early date.[82] Indeed Amy Mulligen has argued that it was given new force through the inclusion of a Christian understanding of leprosy as the disease suffered by *caillech* in the prose *Echtra mac nEchach Muigmedóin*, composed in the eleventh century for Máel Sechnaill mac Domnaill, king of Ireland from 980 to 1002, when Brían Bóruma took power, and then again from 1014 to 1022: "a story that reinvigorates a divinely ordained, historical, and long-held claim to Ireland's kingship might have been seen as a necessary balm for the Uí Néill dynasty at this particularly turbulent period."[83] This prose tale is closely related to a metrical version of the story, the poetic *Echtra mac nEchach Muigmedóin*, attributed Cuán ua Lothcháin, court poet of Máel Sechnaill. The praise poem, which survives in two twelfth-century manuscripts, the Book of Leinster (Dublin, Trinity College, 1339)[84] and Oxford, Bodleian Library, Rawlinson B 502,[85] contains a series of tests that proclaim Níall Noígíallach, whose mother is a Scottish captive, the rightful successor to his father. A loathly lady appears in the narrative when he and his four stepbrothers find themselves in need of water; the first goes to a nearby stream:

---

[82] See in particular Proinsias Mac Cana, "Aspects of the Theme of King and Goddess in Irish Literature," Études Celtiques 7 (1955–6), pp. 76–114 and 356–413, and 8 (1958–9), pp. 59–65. Near the end of this study, he comments, "Irish poets down through the ages persisted in identifying the rightful king as the lawful husband of the territorial goddess, until finally in the eighteenth century the exiled Stuarts came to be regarded as the rightful spouses of Éire instead of those foreigners who then held her in thrall," p. 60.

[83] Amy C. Mulligan (published under Eichhorn-Mulligan), "The Anatomy of Power and the Miracle of Kingship: The Female Body of Sovereignty in a Medieval Irish Kingship Tale," *Speculum* 81 (2006), p. 1018. As an example of the motif of the sovereignty goddess, she also discusses the hag, Cailb, who asks Conaire Mór for a place to sleep, and by implication sex, at the beginning of the eleventh-century *Togail Bruidne Da Derga*; she cites the edition of Eleanor Knott (Dublin: Dublin Institute for Advanced Studies, 1936). By his not sleeping with her, "she remains an untransformed, threatening spectacle of female sexuality; and kingly power is stripped away," p. 1030. Nine manuscripts, dated from the early twelfth to the sixteenth centuries, contain the work or fragments from it; see CELT, the online resource for Irish history, literature, and politics, https://www.ucc.ie/celt/.

[84] The manuscript is dated to the second half of the twelfth century at CODECS, the online database and e-resources for Celtic Studies, http://www.vanhamel.nl/codecs/, where there is further bibliography.

[85] The manuscript is available on line at Early Manuscripts at Oxford University, http://image.ox.ac.uk/. It is dated here to the second quarter of the twelfth century. For further bibliography, see CODECS, http://vanhamel.nl/codecs/.

Écess óenmná ar a brú,   bél aicce i tallfad cú,
a curach fíacal 'moa cenn,   éitchi indát fúatha Hérenn. (35)[86]

(A seer, a single woman,[87] is on its bank; her mouth has room for a hound;
a coracle of teeth around her head;[88] [she is] uglier than all the spectres of
Ireland.)[89]

He and two more of his brothers refuse to kiss her; a fourth, who gives her
a hasty kiss, is promised a hasty visit to Tara. Finally, when Niall encounters the woman, whose ugliness is again described, she says that he will not
receive a drink unless he shares her bed ("cen chéim dó 'na comlepaid,"
47).[90] The following two stanzas make it clear that he does, after which the
woman is described: "cid cáem grían i cleith nime, áille níab na hingine"
(51; "though the sun in sky is lovely, more lovely is the splendor of the
girl").[91] The same narrative with some differing details appears in the prose
Echtra mac nEchach, and here, as Mulligen notes, the meaning of the transformation is made explicit when the woman states "Misi in Flaithius" (15;
"I am the Sovereignty"),[92] explaining further "acus amail adcondarcais misi
co granna connda aduathmar artús ⁊ alaind fadeoid, is amlaid sin in flaithius,
uair is annam fogabar he cen chatha ⁊ cen chongala, alaind maisech immorro
ria nech e fodeoid" (16; "and as you have seen me loathsome, houndlike,
fearsome first and beautiful afterwards, the sovereignty is like that, since
it is seldom gotten without battles and without conflict, yet before any it is
ultimately beautiful and of pleasing appearance").[93] This version survives in
two fourteenth-century manuscripts, the Book of Ballymote (Dublin, Royal
Irish Academy 23 P 12 (536) and the Yellow Book of Lecan (Dublin, Trinity
College 1318).[94]

---

[86] The text is both edited and translated by Maud Joynt, "Echtra mac Echdach
Mugmedóin," Ériu 4 (1919), pp. 91–111. I have, however, modified her translation.

[87] Under éices the *DIL* explains that "the word is cognate with (*do*)-écci and the original meaning is probably "seer" (see *éicse*), but though this would suit the context
in many exx. it is commonest in the general sense of "scholar, learned man, sage,
poet"; óenmná can be explained as a genitive of apposition: see Rudolf Thurneysen, *A
Grammar of Old Irish*, trans. D. A. Binchy and Osborn Bergin (Dublin: Dublin Institute for Advanced Studies, 1946), pp.158–59. The Book of Leinster reads "senmna,"
an old woman.

[88] The *DIL* refers to this description under *curach*.

[89] The line is glossed in the *DIL*, s.v. étig.

[90] Under *comlepaid* the *DIL* translates, "common bed; act of sharing a bed, cohabiting,
lying with."

[91] For "áille," the Book of Leinster reads "cóimiu." This line is cited in the *DIL s.v. níam*.

[92] The text is edited and translated by Whitley Stokes, "The Death of Crimthann Son of
Fidach, and the Adventures of the Sons of Eochaid Muigmedón," *Revue celtique* 24
(1903), pp. 172–207. The references are to his section numbers.

[93] The translation is by Mulligen, p. 1034.

[94] On the dates of these manuscripts, Mulligan cites two articles by Tomás Ó Conche-

The same story of Níall is told not in support of the Uí Néill dynasty, but rather of the O'Connors of Connacht at the end of the twelfth or the beginning of the thirteenth century. Indeed this poem's opening stanza makes this point:

> Tairnic in sel-sa ac Síl Néill
> mar do ordaig in flaith féin
> dá fuair in flaithes fuirmech
> Niall coscarach cathbuidnech. (1)

(Síl Néill's era has come to an end just as was ordained by the sovereignty itself for whom triumphant Niall of the battle hosts obtained firm rule.)[95]

Otherwise, the narrative is similar. The "fuath" (10; "spectre") is less ugly than old—her hand emaciated, her eyes watery, and her head bald—and her demand is explicit from the start: none will receive water "acht dul 'na caemtha i cétóir" (11; "unless first he lie with her"). Only Niall does, to discover beside him "ingin mongbuide macdacht" (29; "a golden-haired young maiden"), who informs him that she is the sovereignty ("in flaithes meise," 32). This poem survives in two manuscripts in the Royal Irish Academy in Dublin, D ii 1, the Book of C Mhaine, from the late fourteenth century,[96] and A v 2, from the seventeenth century.[97]

The further circulation of the motif is found in two more sources, the metrical *Dindsenchas*, a collection of history, law, and genealogy linked to famous places, and *Cóir Anmann*, a similar work organized around names; both associate it not with Niall but with Lugaid Loígde, a legendary high-king of Ireland in Munster. As Edward Gwynn notes, the version in the *Dindsenchas* probably derives from the poetic *Echtra mac nEchach*.[98] Here the entry on Carn Máil starts with a story about a different Lugaid and then shifts abruptly to the seven sons of Dáire, all named Lugaid on account of a prophecy that a son of this name will succeed to the throne, who are hunting:

> Mar robátar isin tig
> na fir thall ocon tenid

anainn, "The Book of Ballymote," *Celtica* 14 (1981), pp. 15–25; and "Scríobhaithe Leacáin Mhic Fhir Bhisigh," *Celtica* 19 (1987), pp. 141–75. The Yellow Book of Lecan is available online at Irish Script on Screen, http://isos.dias.ie/, where there is additional information and bibliography.

95 Brian Ó Cuiv, ed. and trans., "A Poem Composed for Croibhdhearg Ó Conchubhair," Ériu 34 (1983), pp. 157–74. References are to stanza numbers.

96 It is available online at Irish Script on Screen, http://isos.dias.ie/, where there is additional information and bibliography. See also CODECS, http://vanhamel.nl/.

97 Ó Cuiv, "Poem Composed," p. 158.

98 *The Metrical Dindsenchas. Part 4*, Royal Irish Academy, Todd Lecture Series 11, ed. and trans. Edward Gwynn (Dublin: Hodges, Figgis, & Co., 1924), p. 409. The text and translation appear on pp. 134–43; they are cited by line numbers.

> dosriacht caillech, gránda ind ail,
> is sí acgarb écosmail. (69–72)

(When the men were in the house sitting over by the fireside, there entered a hag, a loathly offense. She was hideous, unsightly.)

Her address to them is direct: "'Fóed nech úaib lemm innocht / nó eter choin is duine ndron roforníss uili m' óenor'" (102–04; "'One of you must sleep with me tonight, or I will devour you all, unaided, hound and strong man alike'"). However, although one steps forward and the woman becoming beautiful explains that she is the "flathius Alban is Hérend" (128; "the kingship of Alba and Erin"), she continues,

> "Duit rotócbus cend innocht,
> acht sain ní bia diar comrocc:
> mac bías ocut, óebdu de,
> issé mac las' fóim-se." (129–32)

("To thee have I revealed myself this night, yet nothing more shall come of our meeting; the son thou shalt have, he it is that I shall sleep with—happier fate.")

The metrical *Dindsenchas* survives in six manuscripts, three of which, the Book of Leinster, the Book of Ballymote, and the Book of Uí Mhaine, have already been mentioned. The other three are the Book of Lecan (Dublin, Royal Irish Academy, 23 P 2) from the late fourteenth to the early fifteenth century;[99] London, British Library, Egerton 1781, from the fifteenth century;[100] and London, British Library, Harley 5280, from the sixteenth century.[101]

Finally the motif appears in a more complex narrative setting in two of the three versions of *Cóir Anmann*.[102] It is introduced in the context of the same explanation as the one found in the metrical *Dindsenchas*: the five sons of Dáire are called Lugaid because of a prophecy that the one with this

---

[99] It is available online at Irish Script on Screen, http:isos.dias.ie/, where there is additional information and bibliography. See also CODECS, http://vanhamel.nl/.

[100] See CODECS, http://vanhamel.nl/.

[101] See the British Library's online catalogue of illuminated manuscripts http://bl.uk/catalogues/illuminatedmanuscripts/; and CODECS, http://vanhamel.nl/.

[102] The texts are edited and translated by Sharon Arbuthnot, *Cóir Anmann: A Late Middle Irish on Personal Names*, 2 vols., Irish Texts Society 59 and 60 (London: Irish Texts Society, 2005–06). She edits the "earliest version," which she dates to the late twelfth century (1.72), from the Book of Ballymote: my quotations are from it. She edits the "long version," which she dates to the first half of the thirteenth century (1.72), from Dublin, Trinity College, 1337. In the case of the story that concerns us here, these two are very similar. Her "short version" does not contain the story. It should be noted, however, that, following the story in the "earliest version," she edits another account of it from Edinburgh, the National Library of Scotland, Advocates 72.1.7: the details that concern us are all included, but the narrative has been shortened.

name would become king. This, however, is then complicated by a second prophecy, announced by a druid: "tiucfaid lægh [co] niam n-orda isan ænach... ⁊ in mac gebus in lægh, is e gebus [in rigi] dud t'éis" (1.102; "a fawn with golden sheen will come into the assembly, and the son who captures the fawn will take [the kingship] after you," 1.139). The fawn appears and eventually is captured by one of the brothers while another cuts it up. A sudden snow drives each of them in succession to seek shelter in a house which has "a huge fire, and food and ale in abundance, and silver dishes, and couches of white bronze," and a "caillech aduathmar" (1.102; "a terrible old woman," 1.139). She tells the first that he may have a bed "dia tis im coimle[b]aid inocht, ad fia" (1.102; "if you come and share my bed tonight, you will have it," 1.139). After he has refused, she says "ro teipis flaithius ⁊ rigi" (1.102; "you have forfeited sovereignty and kingship," 1.139). She asks the other brothers not that they sleep with her, but about what they have met; their answers become incorporated into their names. The last explains, "dorala dam laeg allaid, ⁊ aduadus m'aenur" (1.103; "I met a fawn and I ate it by myself," 1.140), becoming Lugaid of the Fawn. He then enters the house, and as the woman approaches the coach, "anddar leis ba grian ic turgabail i mís Mai soillsi a gnuisi. Ocus ba samulta leis a boladh fri lubgort cumra" (1.103; "he thought that the brightness of her face was the sun rising in the month of May. And her scent seemed to him like a fragrant herb-garden," 1.140). After they sleep together, she says, "maith do turus...ar is misi in Flatus ⁊ gebasu flatus Erenn" (1.103; "your journey has been profitable, for I am Sovereignty and you will take the sovereignty of Ireland," 1.140). The story concludes with the brothers' return to the assembly where they relate their adventure, after which everyone disperses. The earliest version of *Coir Anmann* survives in five manuscripts, three of which, the Book of Ballymote, the Book of Uí Mhaine, and the Book of Lecan, have already been mentioned. The other two, both in the National Library of Scotland in Edinburgh, Advocates 72.1.1 and 72.1.7, are from the fifteenth century. One of the three manuscripts of the long version, Dublin, Trinity College 1337, is from the sixteenth century. The other two, Dublin, Trinity College 1393 and Dublin, Royal Irish Academy 24 P 13, are from the seventeenth century.[103]

Although there is no surviving evidence of new versions of the Loathly Lady story being created in Ireland in the fourteenth century,[104] the manu-

---

103 See Arbuthnot, *Cóir Anmann*, 1.2–4.

104 There are some suggestions, however, that traditions of a *banais rige*, a marriage of a new king to the land, continued into the fourteenth century; see Watt, "Gaelic polity," p. 322 and Saul, *Richard II*, p. 271. In assessing the literary response to the Anglo-Norman invasion James Carney notes that "contrasted with the virtual absence of manuscripts in the period 1150–1350, the survival of a considerable number in the period 1370–1500 is suggestive of a literary revival that reached its peak in the early years of the fifteenth century"; "Literature in Irish, 1169–1534," in *New History of*

scripts indicate that a literate Irishman of Chaucer's day might well have been familiar with one or more of these versions, in addition to oral renderings of them or similar tales. Because we have no evidence that Chaucer read Irish, it seems likely that he encountered the motif in an oral setting. The detail that caught his attention was the otherwise unexplained transformation of an ugly old woman into a beautiful young one as she sleeps for the first time with a new man. Chaucer, however, transformed the point of the motif. As Mulligan points out, "despite the fact that the female hag does choose her kingly mate in the literary renderings of political empowerment, medieval Ireland was a patriarchal culture in which women held very little political power and historically had no role in determining who would be king."[105] In the Irish legends, then, the loathly lady represents the land, and the story is one of a new king taking control over her/it. Chaucer in contrast focused on the woman, who has the power to make her own decision and uses it to gain control in her marriage. The answer to rape as emblematic of women's unjust lack of control over their lives is to empower them.

The Loathly Lady narrative, however, is only one of the two main sources that Chaucer used to construct the *Wife of Bath's Tale*. The other is a well-known and, in one way, surprisingly related misogynist tradition: a beautiful woman is never faithful. As Margaret Schlauch has shown, it is this claim that underlies the woman's offer to her husband that brings the tale to a close:

> "Chese now," quod she, "oon of this thynges tweye;
> To han me foul and old til that I deye,
> And be to yow a trewe, humble wyf,
> And nevere yow displese in al my lyf,
> Or elles ye wol han me yong and fair,
> And take youre aventure of the repair
> That shal be to youre hous by cause of me,
> Or in som oother place, may wel be.
> Now chese yourselven, wheither that yow liketh." (III, 1219–27)

Schlauch writes, "fairy tales deal rarely with the alternative of chastity versus infidelity."[106] Implicit, however, in the story of the Irish sovereignty goddess is not only the simple attractiveness of youth and beauty but also the more complex issue of fidelity: the goddess remains faithful to the king as long as he is young and perfect but will inevitably find a new partner. There is, then, a lie in the woman's solution at the end of the *Wife of Bath's Tale*:

Ireland, ed. Cosgrove, p. 689. Many of the manuscripts that contain the narrative of the Irish sovereignty goddess are the ones to which he refers.

[105] Mulligan,"Anatomy of Power," p. 1015.

[106] Schlauch, "Marital Dilemma," pp. 417–18. As noted in Chapter 1 (pp. 49–52), this theme underlies the question of what women most desire.

> "Kys me," quod she, "we be no lenger wrothe,
> For, by my trouthe, I wol be to yow bothe—
> This is to seyn, ye, bothe fair and good.
> I prey to God that I moote sterven wood,
> But I to yow be also good and trewe
> As evere was wyf, syn that the world was newe.
> And but I be to-morn as fair to seene
> As any lady, emperice, or queene,
> That is bitwixe the est and eke the west,
> Dooth with my lyf and deth right as yow lest.
> Cast up the curtyn, looke how that it is." (III, 1239–49)

By linking this lie to the Church Chaucer both criticized the misogyny of his own society and left the way open for further debate on the secular theme.

While Schlauch's extensive survey of the theme points to a few secular examples, notably Eustache Deschamps's *Le Miroir de Mariage* and the continuation of the *Roman de la Rose* by Jean de Meun, most appear in religious writings. Although perhaps unknown to Chaucer because it was first published in 1406,[107] the *Miroir* provides a parallel for the idea behind the question:

> Se tu la prens, qu'elle soit belle,
> Tu n'aras jamais paix a elle,
> Car chascuns la couvoitera,
> Et dure chose a toy sera
> De garder ce que un chascun voite
> Et qu'il poursuit et qu'il couvoite,
> Car tu as contre toy cent oeulx,
> Et li desirs luxurieux
> Est toutes fois contre beauté,
> Qui es contraire au chasteté. (1625–34)
> ....
> S'il est qui preingne femme laide,
> Nulz homs n'ara sur elle envie;
> Et ou sera plus mortel vie
> Qu'a cellui qui possidera
> Ce que nulz avoir ne vourra,
> Que il possidera touz seulx. (1736–41)

---

[107] This argument was advanced by Zacharias P. Thundy, "Matheolus, Chaucer, and with Wife of Bath," in *Chaucerian Problems and Perspectives: Essays Presented to Paul E. Beichner, C.S.C.*, ed. Edward Vasta and Thundy (Notre Dame: University of Notre Dame Press, 1979), pp. 24–58. Citing his work in *S&A* (2.355), Hanna and Lawler comment, "since Deschamps clearly knew Chaucer's work we think it at least possible that Chaucer may have seen his through some private means, so that the 'publication' of the *Miroir* in 1406 is not an insuperable obstacle."

(If you marry somebody because she's pretty she'll never bring you peace because every man who comes along will want her, and it will be a hard thing for you to keep what every man wants and pursues and covets; you have a hundred eyes against you, and lecherous desire is always after beauty, which is contrary to chastity....If you marry an ugly woman no man will envy you—but what deadlier life is there than to have something that nobody else wants, and so have it all alone?)[108]

Even though he focused not on the chastity of an ugly wife, but her desire for "touz ceuz qui la voient" ("all who see her"), Jean de Meun had expressed a similar idea:

> S'el rest bele, tuit i aqueurent,
> tuit la porsivent, tuit l'anneurent,
> tuit i hurtent, tuit i travaillent,
> tuit i luitent, tuit i bataillent,
> tuit a li servir s'estudient,
> tuit li vont entor, tuit la prient,
> tuit i musent, tuit la covoitent,
> si l'ont en la fin, tant esploitent,
> car tour de toutes parz assise
> enviz eschape d'estre prise.
> S'el rest lede, el veust a touz plere.
> En conment porroit nus ce fere
> qu'il gart chose que tuit guerroient
> ou qui veust touz ceuz qui la voient? (8557–70)

(If she's pretty, they'll come running, chase her, seek to honor her, punch and wrestle each other for her, strain and battle over her, strive to serve her, surround her, woo her, hover near her, covet her—and in the end they will have her, they press her so, for a tower besieged on all sides will hardly escape being taken. If she's ugly, she will try to please them all. And how is somebody supposed to guard a thing that everybody is fighting over, or who wants all who see her?)[109]

As he acknowledged, the source for this passage is the *Liber de nuptiis* of Theophrastus, which survives because Jerome reproduced it in his *Adversus Jovinianum* (Hanna and Lawler add, "if he did not make it up"; *S&A* 2.353):

Pulchra cito adamatur, feda facile concupiscit. Difficile custoditur quod plures amant; molestum est possidere quod nemo habere dignetur. Minore tamen miseria deformis habetur quam formosa servatur. Nichil tutum est in

---

[108] The texts and translations for this and the following passages are from Hanna and Lawler's chapter on the *Wife of Bath's Prologue*, *S&A* 2.351–403; here 2.396–97. I retain their line numbers, which refer to either the editions from which they quote or their own lineation.

[109] *S&A* 2.366–68.

quo tocius populi vota suspirant. Alius forma, alius ingenio, alius facetiis, aliius liberalitate sollicitat. Aliquo modo expugnatur quod undique incessitur. (34–39)

(A beautiful wife will be quickly surrounded by lovers, an ugly one will have difficulty restraining her desires. What many love is hard to keep; to have what no one else wants is irksome. Still it is less painful to have an ugly wife than to keep a beauty. Nothing is safe that the whole population is longing and sighing for. One man tempts by his shape, another by his brains, another by his jokes, yet another by his generosity. What is attacked from all sides will fall, one way or another.) [110]

As Schlauch notes, a contrast between "pulchra" and "feda," which is clearly parallel with a complementary one, "impudica : pudica" in the immediately preceding passage "approaches" the wording of the *Wife of Bath's Tale*:

Verum quid prodest etiam diligens custodia, cum uxor impudica servari non possit, pudica non debeat? Infida enim custos est castitatis necessitas; et illa vere pudica dicenda est cui licuit peccare, si voluit. (31–34)

(But in truth what does even diligent watchfulness avail, since an immodest wife cannot be guarded, and a modest one should not be? Necessity is a faithless watchkeeper over chastity; and only a woman who could have sinned if she wanted to can truly be called modest.)

She details, moreover, similar ideas expressed in the writing of, among others, John of Salisbury, Alexander Neckam, and Innocent III. To these, as Lindy Brady has noted, may be added similar expressions gathered in the modern collections of proverbs. [111]

The misogyny inherent in the loathly lady's question ties the Wife of Bath's *Tale* closely to her *Prologue*. Just as the final phrases of the narrative, as noted above, take the reader back into the mind of the character, this technique of challenging the Church's teachings on women simply by having one of them express them in her own voice links the two parts of Chaucer's argument. Women must be heard.

The *Wife of Bath's Tale*, however, looks not only back toward its *Prologue*, but also ahead to the rest of the tales of the "Marriage Group," which include

---

[110] *S&A* 2.358–59.

[111] "Antifeminist Tradition," p. 163. Brady cites section 8.2, "Schönheit und Keuschheit finden sich selten vereint," in the *Thesaurus proverbiorum medii aevi. Lexikon der Sprichwörter des romanisch-germanischen Mittelalters*, 13 vols. and supplement, founded by Samuel Singer, ed. Kuratorium Singer (Berlin: De Gruyter, 1995–2002), 10.224–26; and items 8059, 13870, 26263, and 26335 in Hans Walther, *Proverbia sententiaeque Latinitatis Medii Aevi. Lateinische Sprichwörter und Sentenzen des Mittelalters*, 5 vols. (Göttingen: Vandenhoeck & Ruprecht, 1963–67). Brady notes that this idea appears in *Arthur and Gorlagon*, ed. Day, *Latin Arthurian Literature*, p. 214, lines 16–17.

three, those of the Clerk, the Merchant, and the Franklin, that have long been recognized as having analogues in the *Decameron*. In light of the argument of this book, all deserve renewed attention beyond simply noting here that they show Chaucer's decision not to resolve Licisca's challenge in the new story for the Wife of Bath, but rather to use it to open a debate. The placement of the *Clerk's Tale*, which draws on 10.10, the story of Griselda that concludes the *Decameron*, is particularly significant since it is merely the next statement, following the tales of the Friar and the Summoner, in the controversy. Its extreme views, made more prominent by following Petrarch's Latin rewriting of Boccaccio's story, ultimately do not contradict the Wife's but rather provide a clear example of the misogyny that surrounds her. By focusing on the last and most outrageous of Lydia's actions to prove her love for Pyrrhus, making love to him in a pear-tree in her husband's presence (7.9), the following *Merchant's Tale* then mocks the *Clerk's Tale* in much the same way that the *Miller's Tale* parodies the *Knight's Tale*, a connection made stronger by its new setting in Lombardy. It is, however, the *Franklin's Tale* with its transformation of the flowing garden in winter (10.5) into the removal of the rocks from the coast of Brittany which engages the *Wife of Bath's Tale* most closely. Tied to the first tale of the group by its genre, the Breton lay, it proposes not sovereignty in marriage, but equality. However, when decisions must be made at the tale's end, it is the men who do so, and the men who compete for the honor of being "mooste fre" (V, 1622). From the perspective of the *Wife of Bath's Tale*, its message too is flawed, and so the debate must continue, circling back to the Wife herself and, by implication, Licisca's challenge.[112]

---

[112] I am aware of but have not discussed the case of Cecily Chaumpaigne because the evidence appears to me to be much less conclusive than Chaucer's writings on this topic.

Conclusion

Identifying the dependence of the *Canterbury Tales* on the *Decameron* has led to insights into the origin of this great unfinished collection, Chaucer's methods of composition, and his views on two of the defining issues of his day, class and gender. Because *Decameron* 8.1, 8.2, and 8.10 all contributed to the *Shipman's Tale*, there can be no doubt that he had read Boccaccio's work attentively, perceiving in it something that has all but eluded modern critics: they tell the same story in three different economic settings. Moreover, the two main themes, the oppression of women and inequalities in class, of Licisca's outburst at the beginning of the Sixth Day and its dramatic effect on the following stories of the Seventh and Eighth Days provide a set of correspondences that point to the beginning of the *Canterbury Tales*. It would open with two pairs of tellers: a man of law opposing a secular woman and a knight opposing a miller. While the tales for the upper-class characters, *Melibee* and "al the love of Palamon and Arcite" (*Legend of Good Women*, F 420), had already been written, the two new ones were derived from the *Decameron*, the three *novelle* already mentioned from the Eighth Day for the first tale written for the Wife of Bath, and 3.4 and 7.2 for the *Miller's Tale*. While the first set of tales ran into trouble because the *Shipman's Tale* proved too ambiguous for the Wife of Bath, the combination of the Knight and Miller developed into the progression from the *General Prologue* to the fragmentary *Cook's Tale*, a reflection on the order of society. During this time, Chaucer also revised the other pair, finally deciding to allow the Wife of Bath to begin her own group of tales and writing a new story for her. Here his debt to the *Decameron* was primarily his use of Boccaccio's way of creating narratives from ideas, but Gower's almost immediate rewriting of this tale for inclusion in the first version of the *Confessio Amantis* offers further support for the claim that it was indeed Licisca's outburst that stands at the start of the *Canterbury Tales*.

Place may provide a way to sum up what Chaucer learned from Boccaccio about the relationship between stories and ideas. The meaning of the "Versus de mola piperis," whatever that might have been for these authors, changed simply by being set in the hamlet of Varlungo, the urban centre of Milan, and the international port of Palermo. Similarly the old market town of Saint-Denis, on the road from Paris to the new banking capital of Bruges, expressed the idea behind Chaucer's recombining of these *novelle*—there is continuity within this change that is also significant for understanding the economics of marriage. The sources of narratives need not be other narratives. They can be found in many different places. Oxford contributes much to the *Miller's Tale*, but central to my argument is that in John's "hostelrye" it offered the space needed to wind three tubs into the rafters of a hall. And Oxford's reputation for theological speculation allowed this simple act to comment with devastating effect on the Knight's complacent certainty about a divine order that favored the upper-class. The indeterminate Arthurian setting of the *Wife of Bath's Tale*, which both stands in contrast to and echoes the "halles, chambres, kitchenes, boures, / Citees, burghes, castels, hye toures, / Thropes, bernes, shipnes, dayeryes' (III, 869–71) blessed by the friars, challenges this line of thought. And yet may we not see a point, or many, in relocating the sovereignty of Ireland into the domestic setting of a new wife and her more common husband? How does the story look not from the place where he stands, but from hers? Moreover, simply by placing the entire setting in a pre-Christian past, Chaucer directed our attention to secular rather than religious answers to this question.

Would Chaucer have expected and, for my argument, needed his audience to recognize his sources? In some cases, such as the *Knight's Tale* and the *Nun's Priest's Tale*, the answer is clearly yes; in others such as *Thopas* and the *Squire's Tale*, maybe; because he invoked not particular texts, but rather the kinds of materials from which the story had been drawn. On the other hand, there is no evidence that at this time anyone in England, except perhaps Italian merchants in London, were reading the *Decameron*; it strains credulity to imagine that Chaucer expected his audience to recognize his use of these *novelle*. He could not, in other words, anticipate an enthusiastic reading of the *Shipman's Tale*, similar to Petrarch's rewriting of *Decameron* 10.10, based on an appreciation of his literary ingenuity. Similarly, it is difficult to imagine that, even with its Celtic trappings, the *Wife of Bath's Tale* would have led many to consider legends of Irish sovereignty. Like Boccaccio, Chaucer used his sources, whatever they were, to write engaging narratives.

A study of these sources from our perspective, however, reveals that, as in the case of the *Nun's Priest's Tale*, in writing the *Shipman's Tale* Chaucer worked not from a single narrative, but from several. Similarly, as in the cases of the *Cook's Tale*, the *Squire's Tale*, *Thopas*, the *Canon's Yeoman's Tale*, and perhaps the *Pardoner's Tale*, there is no single narrative that is the source for the tales of the Miller and the Wife of Bath. Chaucer's plots in these cases are his own. Moreover, tracing sources as we can solves old literary problems such as the debts of one author to another. The author of *Heile van Beersele* retold the *Miller's Tale*. Gower rewrote the *Wife of Bath's Tale* in the *Tale of Florent*. Chaucer read the *Decameron*. Most significantly, however, they give us insight into authors' reasons for writing, because they allow us to recognize the development of their ideas. Starting from Licisca's challenge to the gender and class structures of her day, Chaucer developed complex arguments of his own which, in my opinion, went beyond what Boccaccio intended to express. He challenged the oppression of women and the lower class in ways that his Italian source did not. And yet, at least in his early work on the *Canterbury Tales*, Chaucer like Boccaccio rejected religious truth as providing an answer to these secular concerns. There are other tales to follow and so more to say, but in my view, and as I hope I have shown above, the opening of the *Canterbury Tales* is from the *Decameron*.

Appendix

The Manuscripts of the "Versus de mola piperis"

The following list derives from two sources: Peter Nicholson, "The Medieval Tale of the Lover's Gift Regained," *Fabula: Journal of Folklore Studies* 21 (1980), pp. 200–22; and In Principio, the online *incipit* index of Latin texts made available by Brepols (accessed at the British Library, 29 December 2016). Each is identified following the date of the manuscript. References to online reproductions and additional bibliography are then mentioned.

1. Cambridge, Gonville and Caius College, 249, opening flyleaf: 15th century. Nicholson.
   See M. R. James, *A Descriptive Catalogue of the Manuscripts in the Library of Gonville and Caius College, vol. 1* (Cambridge: Cambridge University Press, 1907), pp. 300–05.

2. Cambridge, Trinity College, O. 2. 45, p. 16: 1273. Nicholson.
   See M. R. James, *The Western Manuscripts in the Library of Trinity College, Cambridge*, 4 vols. (Cambridge: Cambridge University Press, 1900–04), 3.150–60. The catalogue is available at http://sites.trin.cam.ac.uk/james/ .

3. Erlangen, Universitätsbibliothek, 281, fragment pasted to fol. 145v: 14th century. Nicholson.
   See Johann Conrad Irmischer, *Handschriften-Katalog der Königliche Universitäts-Bibliothek zu Erlangen* (Frankfurt a. M.: Heyder und Zimmer, 1852), p. 78.

4. Erlangen, Universitätsbibliothek, 393, inside front cover: 15th century. Nicholson.
   See Irmischer, *Handschriften-Katalog*, p. 112; and http://www.handschriftencensus.de/7110 .

5. Eton, Eton College, 125, fol. 167v: 13th century. In Principio.
   See N. R. Ker, *Medieval Manuscripts in British Libraries*, 5 vols. (Oxford, 1969–2002), 2.742–45; and M. R. James, *A Descriptive Catalogue of the Manuscripts in the Library of Eton College* (Cambridge: Cambridge University Press, 1895), pp. 56–57.

6. Heidelberg, Universitätsbibliothek, Heid. Hs. 46, fol. 132r: 18th century. Nicholson.

The poem is the first item in a part of the manuscript identified as "epigrammata quaedam vetusta ex codice V. C. Johannes Gerardi Vossii descripta." The manuscript is available online through http://www.ub.uni-heidelberg. de/helios/digi/digilit.html/ .

7. London, British Library, Harley 2851, fol. 130v: 2nd half of the 13th century. Nicholson.

A description can be found through http://www.bl.uk/catalogues/illuminatedmanuscripts/ . The contents have been most fully described by H. L. D. Ward, *Catalogue of Romances in the Department of Manuscripts in the British Museum*, 3 vols. (London: Printed by order of the Trustees, 1883–1910), 2.401, 669 and 748; and 3.503–09.

8. Lyon, Bibliothèque municipale, 784, fol. 116r: 15th century. In Principio.

The record in In Principio was submitted by the IRHT. See A. Molinier and F. Desvernay, *Catalogue général des manuscrits des bibliothèques publiques de France*, vol. 30 (Paris: E. Plon, Nourrit, 1900), pp. 212–14.

9. Naples, Biblioteca nazionale, IV. F. 19 (267), fol. 156r: 15th century. In Principio.

The record in In Principio was submitted by the Bibliothèque nationale de France. Because the manuscript contains Antonio Beccadelli's *Hermaphroditus*, it is included in Tlion, Tradizione della letteratura italiana online, http://tlion.sns.it .

10. Paris, Bibliothèque nationale de France, lat. 8320, fol. 86r, col. 2: 13th century. Nicholson.

A facsimile is available online at http://gallica.bnf.fr/ark:/12148/btv1b 10721145t . The manuscript is described and dated to the 11th, 14th, and 15th centuries at http://www.musmed.fr/CMN/FPnlat_online_5000.htm/ .

11. Paris, Bibliothèque nationale de France, lat. 16581, fol. 2v: 13th century. Nicholson.

See Léopold Delisle, *Inventaire des manuscrits de la Sorbonne conservés a la Bibliothèque impériale sous les numéros 15176–16718 du fonds latin* (Paris: Durand et Pedone-Lauriel, 1870), p. 67.

12. Sterzinger Miscellaneen-Handschrift: 14th century. Nicholson.
See Ingaz V. Zingerle, ed., *Bericht über die Sterzinger Miscellaneen-Handschrift* (Vienna: Gerold, 1867), p. 319.

13. St. Florian, Stiftsbibliothek, XI, 58, fol. 97r: 15th century. Nicholson.

The identification is made by Hans Walther, "Beiträge zur Kenntnis der mittellateinischen Literatur (aus Handschriften süddeutscher und österreichischer Bibliotheken)," *Zentralblatt für Bibliothekswesen* 49 (1932), p. 330. The catalogue for the library is available online at http://manuscripta.at/diglit/czerny_1871/0001 .

14. Vatican, Biblioteca Apostolica, Reg. lat. 1428, fols. 47v–51v: 15th century. In Principio.

The record on In Principio was submitted by the IRHT. It indicates that the poem is included among the poems of Aeneas Siluius Piccolomini, later Pope Pius II. A facsimile is available through http://www.mss.vatlib.it/ .

15. Vienna, Österreichische Nationalbibliothek, 3219, fol. 178v: 15th century. Nicholson.

The identification is made by Hans Walther, "Beiträge zur Kenntnis der mittellateinischen Literatur (aus Handschriften süddeutscher und österreichischer Bibliotheken)," *Zentralblatt für Bibliothekswesen* 49 (1932), p. 339. The manuscript is described online at http://manuscripta.at/m1/hs_detail.php?ID=7345/ .

Bibliography

Primary Sources

Manuscripts

Aberystwyth, National Library of Wales, Peniarth 392D.
Antwerp, Stadsarchief, PK 116.
Brussels, Koninklijke Bibliotheek, 1805–08.
Brussels, Koninklijke Bibliotheek, 3067–73.
Brussels, Koninklijke Bibliotheek, 19607.
Brussels, Koninklijke Bibliotheek, II, 1171.
Cambridge, Gonville and Caius College, 249 (277).
Cambridge, Trinity College, O. 2. 45.
Dublin, Royal Irish Academy, A v 2.
Dublin, Royal Irish Academy, D ii 1.
Dublin, Royal Irish Academy, 23 P 2.
Dublin, Royal Irish Academy, 23 P 12.
Dublin, Royal Irish Academy, 24 P 13.
Dublin, Trinity College, 1318.
Dublin, Trinity College, 1337.
Dublin, Trinity College, 1339.
Dublin, Trinity College, 1393.
Edinburgh, National Library of Scotland, Advocates 72. 1. 1.
Edinburgh, National Library of Scotland, Advocates 72. 1. 7.
Erlangen, Universitätsbibliothek, 281.
Erlangen, Universitätsbibliothek, 393.
Eton, Eton College, 125.
Ghent, Bibliotheek van de Universiteit, 942.
The Hague, Koninklijke Bibliotheek, 129. A. 10.
The Hague, Museum Meermanno-Westreenianum, 10 C 19 (187).
Heidelberg, Universitätsbibliothek, Heid. Hs. 46.
Kew, The National Archives, CP 40/ 519.
London, British Library, Egerton 843.
London, British Library, Egerton 1781.
London, British Library, Harley 2253.
London, British Library, Harley 2851.
London, British Library, Harley 5280.
London, British Library, Royal 17. B. 47.
Lyon, Bibliothèque municipale, 784.
Naples, Biblioteca nazionale, IV. F. 19 (267).
Oxford, Bodleian Library, Rawlinson B 149.
Oxford, Bodleian Library, Rawlinson B 502.

Paris, Bibliothèque nationale de France, italien 63
Paris, Bibliothèque nationale de France, lat. 8320.
Paris, Bibliothèque nationale de France, lat. 16581.
San Marino, Huntington Library, El 26 C 9.
St. Florian, Stiftsbibliothek, XI, 58.
Vatican, Biblioteca Apostolica, Reg. lat. 1428.
Vienna, Österreichische Nationalbibliothek, 3219.

Maps

Antwerp, Stadsarchief, PK 116: Early map of Antwerp in the *Kronijk* of Louis van Caukercken.
London, British Library, Maps C.9.e.4, 30: View of Antwerp by Claes Janszoon Visscher, 1562.
London, British Library, Maps 31145.(1): Map of Antwerp, Joris Hoefnagel, 1580.
London, British Library, Maps 31145.(4): Map of Antwerp, Hans Liefrinck and Lambert van Noort, 1569.
London, British Library, Maps 31145.(26a): Plan of Antwerp published by Joan Blaeu, 17th century.
London, British Library, Maps 31145.(28): "Plan de la Ville et Citadelle d'Anvers," J. Deur, after 1701.

Databases

Cetedoc: Christian Latin Texts. Brepols. Accessed at the British Library, 3 January 2017.
In Principio: Incipit Index to Latin Texts. Brepols. Accessed at the British Library, 3 January 2017.

Printed Books

Albertus Magnus. *Book of Minerals*. Translated by DorothyWyckoff. Oxford: Clarendon Press, 1967.
Alfred of Sareshel [Shareshill]. *De mineralibus*. Edited by E. J. Holmyard and D. C. Mandeville. In *Avicennae* De congelatione et conglutinatione lapidum, *being selections of the* Kitâ al-Shifâ'; *the Latin and Arabic texts*, pp. 45–55. Paris: Paul Geuthner, 1927.
Anonimalle Chronicle. Extract on the Peasant's Revolt, 1381. Translated in Myers, ed., *English Historical Documents*, 4.127–40.
Antwerpsche Akten. Edited by Floris Prims, "Antwerpsche Akten uit den tijd van Hertog Jan II (1294–1312)." *Antwerpsch Archievenblad*, 2nd ser., 5 (1930), pp. 33–77 and 100–23; and 6 (1931) pp. 27–62 and 151–93.
Antwerpsche Teksten. Edited by Floris Prims, "Antwerpsche Teksten uit den tijd van Hertog Jan III (1313–1355)." *Antwerpsch Archievenblad*, 2nd ser., 6 (1931), pp. 294–309; 7 (1932), pp. 71–76, 83–121, 161–210 and 266–88; and 8 (1933), pp. 39–76 and 142–57.
Apuleius. "De adulterio cuisdam pauperis fabula." Extract from the *Metamorphoses* (VIIII, 5–7). Edited and translated by Benson and Andersson. In *Literary Context*, pp. 6–9.

Aristotle. *Meteorologica*. Edited and translated by H. D. P. Lee. 2nd edn. Cambridge, MA: Harvard University Press, 1962.

Arnaldus de Villa Nova. *De lapide philosophorum*. Extract. In *S&A*, 2.738–40.

——. *Rosarium*. Extract. In *S&A*, 2.740.

Arthur and Gorlagon. Edited and translated in Mildred Leake Day, *Latin Arthurian Literature*, pp. 208–35. Arthurian Archives 11. Cambridge: D. S. Brewer, 2005.

Audelay, John. "Poem 16." Edited by Ella Keats Whiting. In *The Poems of John Audelay*, Early English Texts Society, Original Series 184, pp. 111–23. London: Oxford University Press, 1931.

Avicenna (Abū ʿAlī al-Ḥusayn ibn ʿAbd Allāh ibn Sīnā): see Alfred of Sareshel.

Biblia Sacra iuxta Vulgatam versionem. 5th edn. Edited by Roger Gryson and Robert Weber. Stuttgart: Deutsche Bibelgesellschaft, 2007.

Boccaccio, Giovanni. *Decameron*. Edited by Vittore Branca. Turin: Einaudi, 1980.

——. *Decameron*. Edited by Amedeo Quondam, Maurizio Fiorilla, and Giancarlo Alfano. 2013. 6th edn. Milan: BUR Classici, 2016.

——. *The Decameron*. Translated by G. H. McWilliam. 2nd edn. London: Penguin, 1995.

——. *Teseida*. Extract. In *S&A*, 2.136–214.

Bryan, W. F. and Germaine Dempster, eds. *Sources and Analogues of Chaucer's Canterbury Tales*. 1941. Reprinted, New York: Humanities Press, 1958.

"Carn Máil." Edited and translated by Edward Gwynn. *The Metrical Dindsenchas. Part 4*. Royal Irish Academy, Todd Lecture Series 11, pp. 134–43. Dublin: Hodges, Figgis, & Co., 1924.

Chaucer, Geoffrey. *The Book of the Duchess*. Edited by Benson. In *Riverside Chaucer*, pp. 329–46.

——. *The Canterbury Tales*. Edited by Benson. In *Riverside Chaucer*, pp. 23–328.

——. *The Legend of Good Women*. Edited by Benson. In *Riverside Chaucer*, pp. 587–630.

——. *Troilus and Criseyde*. Edited by Benson. In *Riverside Chaucer*, pp. 471–585.

Le Chevalier à la corbeille. Edited and translated by Revard. In "Four Fabliaux," pp. 117–23.

Clement VI. *Inter sollicitudines*. Edited by Paul Fredericq. In *Corpus documentorum Inquisitionis haereticae pravitatis Neerlandicae*, 4 vols., 1.199–201. Ghent: Martinus Nijhoff, 1889–1900.

Clementijnboeck: http://zoeken.felixarchief.be/zHome/Home.aspx?id_isad=177282. Reproduced from [Van den Branden, Frans Jozef Peter, ed.] "Clementynboeck 1288–1414." In *Antwerpsch Archievenblad*, 25 [1888], pp. 101–465 and 26 [1889], pp. 1–136.

Cóir Anmann. Edited by Sharon Arbuthnot. *Cóir Anmann: A Late Middle Irish on Personal Names*, 2 vols. Irish Texts Society 59 and 60. London: Irish Texts Society, 2005–06.

Compilatio singularis exemplorum. Edited by Alfons Hilka. *Neue Beiträge zur Erzählungsliteratur des Mittelalters (Die* Compilatio singularis exemplorum *der Hs. Tours 486, ergänzt durch eine Schwesterhandschrift Bern 679*. Breslau: Grass, Barth & Comp., 1913.

Les Coustumes, stylle et usaige de la court et chancellerye des foires de Cham-

paigne et de Brye. Edited by Félix Bourquelot. In *Étude sur les foires de Champagne: sur la nature, l'étendue et les règles du commerce qui s'y faisait aux XIIe, XIIIe et XIVe siècles*, Mémoires présentés par divers savants à l'Académie des Inscriptions et Belles-Lettres de l'Institut Impérial de France, 2nd ser., 5/2.325–71. Paris: L'Imprimerie impériale, 1865.

Cropacius, Kaspar. *Cropacii Poemata*. The 1580 edition is available online at http://books.google.com/books?id=Vh9XAAAAcAAJ&pg=PP16&dq=cropaci-i+poemata&hl=en&sa=X&ei=wvopU8StCebN0gHNtYGwAg&ved=0C-C8Q6AEwAA#v=onepage&q=cropacii%20poemata&f=false/ .

——. *Fabula de sacerdote et simplici rustico*. Edited and translated by Benson and Andersson. In *Literary Context*, pp. 72–77.

De Berangier au lonc cul: see Guérin.

De Cuvier. Edited and translated by Eichmann and DuVal. In *French Fabliau*, 2.142–49.

De .II. Changeors. Edited and translated by Eichmann and DuVal. In *French Fabliau*, 2.197–207.

De la Borgoise d'Orliens. Translated by DuVal and edited by Eichmann. In *Cuckolds*, pp. 80–86.

Deschamps, Eustache. *Le Miroir de Mariage*. Extract. In *S&A*, 2.394–403.

——. *Œuvres complètes*. 11 vols. Edited by Marquis de Queux de Saint-Hilaire and Gaston Reynaud. Société des anciens textes français. Paris: Firmin Didot & cie, 1878–1903.

Dindsenchas (metrical). see "Carn Máil."

Dits vanden vesscher van Parijs. Edited by Kruyskamp. In *Middelnederlandse Boerden*, pp. 100–08.

Durant. *Des .III. bocus menesterels*. Edited and translated by Eichmann and DuVal. In *French Fabliau*, 2.162–73.

"Du Roy Alphons, qui fut trompé par le malice de sa femme." Edited by E. Langlois. In *Nouvelles françaises inédites du quinzième siècle*, pp. 48–51 (chapter 8). Paris: Honoré Champion, 1908.

DuVal, John, trans., and Raymond Eichmann, ed., *Cuckolds, Clerics, & Countrymen: Medieval French Fabliaux*. Fayetteville: University of Arkansas Press, 1982.

Echtra mac Echdach nMugmedóin (poetic). Edited and translated by Maud Joynt. "Echtra mac Echdach Mugmedóin," *Ériu* 4 (1919), pp. 91–111.

Echtra mac Echdach nMugmedóin (prose). Edited and translated by Whitley Stokes. "The Death of Crimthann Son of Fidach, and the Adventures of the Sons of Eochaid Muigmedón," *Revue celtique* 24 (1903), pp. 172–207.

"Een boerman hadde eenen dommen sin." Edited by Dieuwke E. van der Poel, Dirk Geirnaert, Hermina Joldersma, Johan Oosterman, and Louis Peter Grijp. In *Het Antwerps Liedboek,*. 2 vols., 1.84–85. Tielt: Lannoo, 2004.

Eichmann, Raymond and John DuVal, eds., *The French Fabliau B.N. MS. 837*. 2 vols. Garland Library of Medieval Literature A/16, 17. New York: Garland, 1984–85.

Elegiac *Romulus*: see *Romulus*, Elegiac.

La Gageure. Edited and translated by Revard. In "Four Fabliaux," pp. 124–27.

Genesi de Scriptura (or *Compendi historial de la Biblia*). *Genesi de Scriptura trelladat del provençal a la llengua catalana per Mossen Guillem Serra en l'any M.CCCCLI*. Edited by Miquel Victoria Amer. Barcelona: A. Verdaguer, 1873.

Gerard of Cremona: see Pseudo-Razi.

Gesta romanorum. Edited by Hermann Oesterley. Berlin: Weidmannsche Buchhandlung, 1872.

——. Translated by Charles Swan. 1876. Reprinted New York: Dover Publications, 1959.

Girart d'Amiens. *Meliacin*. Extract. In *S&A*, 1.176–80.

Gower, John. *Confessio Amantis*. Edited by Russell A. Peck with Latin translations by Andrew Galloway. 3 vols., 2nd edn of vol. 1. TEAMS Middle English Texts Series. Kalamazoo: Medieval Institute Publications, 2003–06.

——. *Confessio Amantis*. Edited by G. C. Macaulay. *The Complete Works of John Gower. Vols. 2 and 3. The English Works*. Oxford: Clarendon Press, 1901.

——. *Mirour de l'omme*. Edited by G. C. Macaulay. *The Complete Works of John Gower. Vol. 1. The French Works*. Oxford: Clarendon Press, 1899.

——. *Mirour de l'omme (The Mirror of Mankind), by John Gower* Translated by William Burton Wilson; revised translation by Nancy Wilson Van Baak. East Lansing: Colleagues Press, 1992.

——.*Vox Clamantis*. Edited by G. C. Macaulay. *The Complete Works of John Gower. Vol. 4. The Latin Works*. Oxford: Clarendon Press, 1902.

——.*The Major Latin Works of John Gower:* The Voice of One Crying *and* The Tripartite Chronicle. Translated by Eric W. Stockton. Seattle: University of Washington Press, 1962.

Guérin. *De Berangier au lonc cul*. Edited and translated by Benson and Andersson. In *Literary Context*, pp. 10–25.

Guillaume de Lorris and Jean de Meun. *Roman de la Rose*. Edited by Félix Lecoy. *Le Roman de la Rose*, Les Classiques français du Moyen Âge, 92, 95, and 98. Paris: Champion, 1965–70.

——. Translated by Charles Dahlberg. *The Romance of the Rose*. 1971. Reprinted, Hanover: University Press of New England, 1986.

——. Extract. In *S&A*, 2.366–79.

Heile van Beersele. In *S&A*, 2.266–75.

Hein van Aken. *Die Rose*. Edited by Eelco Verwijs. Die Rose *van Heinric van Aken, met de fragmenten der tweede vertaling*, Van wege de Maatschappij der Nederlandsche Letterkunde te Leiden. 's-Gravenhage: Martinus Nijhoff, 1868.

Henry of Bracton. "De placitis coronae." Edited by George E. Woodbine. Translated by Samuel E. Thorne. In *Henry de Bracton: On the Laws and Customs of England (*De legibus et consuetudinibus Angliae*)*, 4 vols., 2.327–449. Cambridge, MA: Harvard University Press, in association with Selden Society, 1968–77.

Hervieux, Léopold (ed.). *Les fabulistes latins*. 5 vols., vols. 1–2 in 2nd edn. Paris: Librairie de Firmin-Didot et Cie, 1893–99.

Hoe Walewein wilde weten vrowen gepens. Edited and translated in David F. Johnson and Geert H. M. Claassens, *Five Interpolated Romances from the Lancelot Compilation*, pp. 112–31. Dutch Romances 3. Cambridge: D. S. Brewer, 2000.

Holcot, Robert. *Super sapientiam Salomonis*. Extracts. In *S&A*, 1.486–89.

Ibn 'Abd al-Ḥakam. *Futūḥ Miṣr (The Conquest of Egypt)*. Edited by Charles

Torrey. *The History of the Conquest of Egypt, North Africa, and Spain, Known as the* Futuh Misr *of Ibn 'Abd Al–Hakam.* 1922. Reprinted, New York: AMS Press, 1980.

——. Extract. Edited and translated by Charles Torrey. In "The Egyptian Prototype of 'King John and the Abbot,'" pp. 211–14. *Journal of the American Oriental Society* 20 (1899), pp. 209–16.

Ibn al-Jawzī, Abu al-Faraj. *Akhbār al-adhkiyā'.* Edited by Muhammad Mursī Khūlī. Cairo: Matābi' al-Ahrām al-Tijārīyah, 1970.

Ibn Zabara, Joseph ben Meir. *The Book of Delight.* Translated by Moses Hadas, with an introduction by Merriam Sherwood. New York: Columbia University Press, 1932.

"Increased severity against labourers at the parliament of Cambridge, 1388." In *English Historical Documents*, 4.1002–04. [From the continuation (1346–94) by the Monk of Westminster of Higden's *Polychronicon.*]

Isidore of Seville. *Etymologiarum sive Originum librii xx.* Edited by W. M. Lindsay. Oxford: Clarendon, 1911.

——. Translated by Stephen A. Barney, W. J. Lewis, J. A. Beach, and Oliver Berghof. *The* Etymologies *of Isidore of Seville.* Cambridge: Cambridge University Press, 2006.

Jacob van Maerlant. *Spiegel Historiael.* Edited by M. de Vries and E. Verwijs. *Jacob van Maerlant's Spiegel historiael, met de fragmenten der later toegevoegde gedeelten, bewerkt door Philip Utenbroeke en Lodewije van Velthem,* Van wege de Maatschappij der Nederlandsche Letterkunde te Leiden. 4 vols. Leiden: Brill, 1863–79.

Jacobus de Voragine. *Legenda aurea.* Extract. In *S&A*, 1.504–17.

Jerome. *Adversus Jovinianum.* Extract. In *S&A*, 2.361–67.

Juan Manuel. *El Conde Lucanor.* Extract. In *S&A*, 2.733–34.

Kruyskamp, C. *Middelnederlandse Boerden.* 's-Gravenhage: Martinus Nijhoff, 1957.

Llull, Raymond. *Arbor Scientiae.* Edited by Pere Villalba i Varneda. CCCM 180a. Turnhout: Brepols, 2000.

——. *Libre de Meravelles.* Extract. In *S&A*, 2.731–33.

Lyrum Larum sue Nugae Venales Joco Seriae; Das ist, Lustig in Ehren kan niemandt nit weren. The 1680 edition is available online at http://www.muenchener-digitalisierungszentrum.de/index.html?c=autoren_index&projekt=&ordnung=alpha&ab=Flavigny,%20Louise%20Mathilde%20de&such-begriff=&kl=&l=en .

Marie de France. "Le Coq et le renard." In *S&A*, 1.454–55.

The Marriage of Sir Gawain. In *S&A*, 2.442–48.

Masuccio Salernitano. *Il Novellino.* Edited by A. Mauro. Bari: Laterza, 1940.

——. *Viola e li suoi amanti.* Edited and translated by Benson and Andersson. In *Literary Context*, pp. 26–37.

Meliacin. Extract. In *S&A*, 2.176–81.

"Money, Money!" Edited by Rossell Hope Robbins. In *Historical Poems of the XIVth and XVth Centuries*, pp. 134–37. New York: Columbia University Press, 1959.

Myers, A. R. (ed.). *English Historical Documents. IV. 1327–1485.* London: Eyre & Spottiswoode, 1969.

Neckam, Alexander. *Novus Aesopus*. Edited by Hervieux. In *Les fabulistes latins, II. Phèdre et ses imitateurs*, pp. 392–416.

——. *Novus Aesopus*. Edited by Giovanni Garbugino. Fabulisti latini medievali 2. Genoa: Università di degli studi di Genova, Dipartimento di archeologia, filologia classica e loro tradizioni, 1984.

Nicholas of Lynn. *Kalendarium*. Edited by Sigmund Eisner. *Kalendarium, The Kalendarium of Nicholas of Lynn*. Athens: University of Georgia Press, 1980.

Nicholas Oresme. *De moneta*. Edited and translated by Charles Johnson. *The De Moneta of Nicholas Oresme and English Mint documents*. London: Nelson, 1956.

Il Novellino. Edited by Joseph P. Consoli. *The* Novellino *or* One Hundred Ancient Tales*: An Edition and Translation based on the 1525 Gualteruzzi editio princeps*. Garland Library of Medieval Literature 105A. New York: Garland, 1997.

Olympiodorus. *Commentaire à la minéralogie du livre III et au libre IV des* Météorologiques *d'Aristote*. Edited and translated by Cristina Viano. In *La matière des choses; le livre IV des* Météorologiques *d'Aristote et son interprétation par Olympiodore*, pp.210–375. Paris: Vrin, 2006.

Ordinance of Labourers (1349): see Statute of Labourers (1349).

Origen. *Contra Celsum*. Translated by Henry Chadwick. Cambridge: Cambridge University Press, 1953.

——. *Origenes Werke*, vol. 2. Edited by Paul Koetschau. Leipzig: Hinrichs, 1899.

Oudt Register, mette Berderen (1336–1439). *Antwerpsch Archievenblad*, 26.414–72; 27.1–472; 28.1–472; and 29.1–261; 27:1–2.

Ovid. *Heroides*. Edited by Grant Showerman. In *Ovid in Six Volumes: I* Heroides *and* Amores, 2nd edn, revised by G. P. Goold. Cambridge, MA: Harvard University Press, 1986.

——. *Metamorphoses*. Edited by R. J. Tarrant. Oxford: Clarendon Press, 2004.

Petrarca, Francesco. *Canzoniere*. Edited by Ugo Dotti. 2 vols. Rome: Donzelli, 1996.

——. *Historia Griseldis*. In *S&A* 1.109–129.

Petrus Alphonsi. *Disciplina clericalis*. Edited by Alfons Hilka and Werner S derhjelm. Acta Societatis Scientiarum Fennicae 38/4. Heidelberg: Carl Winter's Universitätsbuchhandlung, 1911.

——. *Disciplina clericalis/La Discipline de Clergie*. Edited and translated by Jacqueline Genot-Bismuth., Moïse le Séfarade, alias Pierre d'Alphonse. Paris: Editions de Paris, 2001.

——. *The* Disciplina clericalis *of Petrus Alfonsi*. Translated by P. R. Quarrie. Berkeley: University of California Press, 1977.

Plato. *Timaeus*. Translated by Donald J. Zeyl. Indianapolis: Hackett, 2000.

Pliny. *Natural History*. Edited and translated by H. Rackham. 10 volumes. Cambridge, MA: Harvard University Press, 1938–63.

Primera Crónica General de España. Edited by Ramón Menéndez Pidal. Fuentes Cronísticas de la Historia de España 1. 2 vols. Madrid: Editorial Gredos, 1977–78.

Proclus. *Commentary on Plato's* Timaeus. Volume 1. Translated by Harold Tarrant. Cambridge: Cambridge University Press, 2007.

Pseudo-Geber. (Paulus de Tarento's?). *Summa perfectionis*. Edited by William R. Newman. *The* Summa perfectionis *of Pseudo-Geber: A Critical Edition,*

Translation and Study. Leiden: Brill, 1991.

Pseudo-Razi. (Attributed to al-Rāzī, Abū Bakr Muḥammad ibn Zakariyyā' [Rhazes/Rasis]). *De aluminibus et salibus*. Translated by Gerard of Cremona. Edited by Robert Steele. In "Practical Chemistry in the Twelfth Century, Rasis *De aluminibus et salibus*. Translated by Gerard of Cremona," pp. 14–42. *Isis* 12 (1929), pp. 10–46.

Rappresentazione di Sant'Antonio. Extract. In *S&A*, 1.294–313.

Revard, Carter. "Four Fabliaux from London, British Library MS Harley 2253, Translated into English Verse." *Chaucer Review* 40 (2005), pp. 111–40.

Le Roman de Renart. Extract. In *S&A*, 1.456–75.

Le Roman de Renart le Contrefait. Extract. In *S&A*, 1.474–87.

Romulus, elegaic. Edited by Hervieux. In *Les fabulistes latins, II. Phèdre et ses anciens imitateurs*, pp. 316–51.

———. Edited by Paola Busdraghi. *L'Esopus attribuito a Gualtiero Anglico*. Favolisti latini medievali e umanistici 10. Genoa: Università degli studi di Genova, Dipartimento di archeologia, filologia classica e loro tradizioni, 2005.

Sachs, Hans. *Der Dot im Stock*. Extract. In Bryan and Dempster, *Sources and Analogues*, pp. 429–36.

———. *Meistergesänge, Faftnachtspiel, Schwänke*. Edited by Eugen Geiger. Stuttgart: Rhilipp Reclam, 1973.

———. *Der Schmit im Pachdrog*. Edited and translated by Benson and Andersson. In *Literary Context*, pp. 60–63.

Schumann, Valentin. *Nachtbüchlein*. The 1559 edition can be found online at http://books.google.com/books?id=apxQAAAAcAAJ&printsec=frontcover&-source=gbs_ge_summary_r&cad=0#v=onepage&q&f=false .

———. *Ein andere Hystoria, von einem Kauffmann, der forchte sich vor dem Jüngsten Tage*. Edited and translated by Benson and Andersson. In *Literary Context*, pp. 64–67.

Sercambi, Giovanni. "Novella V." Edited by Giovanni Sinicropi. In *Novelle: nuovo testo critico con studio introduttivo et note*, 2 vols., Filologia. Testi e studi 5, 1.95–116. Florence: Le Lettere, 1995.

"Das schlaue Mädchen." From the *Compelatio singularis exemplorum*. Edited by Alfons Hilka. In *Neue Beiträge zur Erzählungsliteratur des Mittelalters (Die Compilatio singularis exemplorum der Hs. Tours 486, ergänzt durch eine Schwesterhandschrift Bern 679)*, pp. 4–6. Breslau: Grass, Barth & Comp., 1913.

"Statute of Labourers, 1349." [Ordinance of Labourers, 1349.] In *Statutes of the Realm*, 1.307–09.

The Statutes of the Realm. Volume 1. S. I.: s. n., 1810.

"Statute the Second." [Statute of Labourers, 1351.] In *Statutes of the Realm*, 1.311–13.

Stephen of Bourbon. *Anecdotes historiques; légendes et apologues*. Edited by A. Lecoy de la Marche. Paris: Librairie Renouard, 1877.

Śukasaptati, textus ornatior. Edited by R. Schmidt. *Abhandlungen der Bayerischen Akademie der Wissenschaften* 21.2 (1898–99), pp. 317–416.

———. Translated by R. Schmidt. *Die Śukasaptati [textus ornatior] aus dem Sanskrit überetzt*. Stuttgart: W. Kohlhammer, 1899.

Śukasaptati, textus simplicior. Edited by R. Schmidt. *Abhandlungen für die*

Kunde des Morgenlandes 10.1 (Leipzig, 1893).

——. Translated by R. Schmidt. *Die Śukasaptati [textus simplicior]. Aus dem Sanskrit übersetzt.* Kiel: C. F. Haeseler, 1894.

——. *Shuka Saptati: Seventy Tales of the Parrot.* Translated by A. N. D. Haksar. New Delhi: HarperCollins, 2000.

"Die Sündfluth." Edited by Karl Müllenhof. In *Sagen Märchen un Lieder der Herzogtümer Schleswig, Holstein und Lauenburg*, pp. 589–90. Kiel: Schwerssche, 1845.

Tacitus. *Annales.* Translated by John Jackson. Cambridge, MA: Harvard University Press, 1937.

Tairnic in sel-sa ac Síl Néill. Edited and translated by Brian Ó Cuiv. "A Poem Composed for Croibhdhearg Ó Conchubhair," *Ériu* 34 (1983), pp. 157–74.

Theophrastus. *On Stones.* Edited by Earle R. Caley and John F. C. Richards. *Theophrastus on Stones: Introduction, Greek Text, English Translation, and Commentary.* Columbus: Ohio State University, 1956.

Togail Bruidne Da Derga. Edited and translated by Eleanor Knott. Dublin: Dublin Institute for Advanced Studies, 1936.

Des Tresces. Translated by DuVal, edited by Eichmann. In *Cuckolds*, pp. 66–76.

Valerius Maximus. *Factorum et dictorum memorabilium libri nouem. Memorable Doings and Sayings.* Edited and translated by D. R. Shackleton Bailey. 2 vols. Cambridge, MA: Harvard University Press, 2000.

Van den VII vroeden van binnen Rome. Edited by K. Stallaert. Ghent: Siffer, 1889.

Van dinghen die selden ghescien. Edited by J. F. Willems. *Belgisch Museum*, 10 [1846], pp. 118–20.

Vander vrouwen die boven haren man minde. Edited by Kruyskamp. In *Middelnederlandse Boerden*, pp. 115–18.

Vander wiue wonderlijcheit. Edited by K. Stallaert. *Dietsche Warande*, NS [3rd ser.] 2 [1889], pp. 158–71.

"Versus de mola piperis." Transcribed from Eton, Eton College 125.

Le Viandier of Taillevent: An Edition of All Extant Manuscripts. Edited by Terence Scully. Ottawa: University of Ottawa Press, 1988.

Vincent of Beauvais. *Speculum quadruplex sive Speculum maius.* 4 vols. Graz: Akademischen Druck- u. Verlagsanstalt, 1964–65.

Visio S. Pauli. Edited by Herman Brandes. Halle: M. Niemeyer, 1885.

——. Edited by Theodore Silverstein and Anthony Hilhorst. *Apocalypse of Paul: A New Critical Edition of Three Long Latin Versions.* Cahiers d'orientalisme 21. Geneva: Cramer, 1997.

The Weddyng of Syr Gawen and Dame Ragnell. In *S&A*, 2.420–41.

Secondary Sources

Aarne, Antti and Stith Thompson. *The Types of the Folktale: A Classification and Bibliography*, 2nd edn, FFC 184. Helsinki: Suomalainen Tiedeakatemia, Academia Scientiarum Fennica, 1961.

Aiken, Pauline. "Vincent of Beauvais and Chaucer's Knowledge of Alchemy."

Studies in Philology 41 (1944), pp. 371–89.

Anderson, Walter. *Kaiser und Abt: Die Geschichte eines Schwanks*. FFC 42. Helsinki: Suomalainen Tiedeakatemia, 1923.

Anlezark, Daniel. *Water and Fire: The Myth of the Flood in Anglo-Saxon England*. Manchester: Manchester University Press, 2006.

Armstrong, Lawrin. *Usury and Public Debt in Early Renaissance Florence: Lorenzo Ridolfi on the* Monte Commune. Texts and Studies 144. Toronto: Pontifical Institute of Mediaeval Studies, 2003.

Asaert, Gustaaf. "The City of Antwerp in the Middle Ages." In van Isacker and van Uytven, eds., *Antwerp*, pp. 38–49.

——. "De Late Middeleeuwen (ca. 1200–ca. 1500)." In Voet, et al., *Stad Antwerpen*, pp. 41–57.

Ashtiany, Julia, T. M. Johnstone, J. D. Latham, R. B. Serjeant, and Rex Smith, eds. *'Abbasid Belles-Lettres*. Cambridge History of Arabic Literature. Cambridge: Cambridge University Press, 1990.

Bailey, Mark. *The Decline of Serfdom in Late Medieval England: From Bondage to Freedom*. Woodbridge: Boydell and Brewer, 2014.

Barnwell, P. S. and A. T. Adams. *The House Within: Interpreting Medieval Houses in Kent*. London: H.M. Stationery Office, 1994.

Barolini, Teodolinda. "Le parole son femmine e i fatti sono maschi: Toward a Sexual Poetics of the *Decameron* (*Decameron* 2.9, 2.10, 5.10)." 1993. Reprinted in *Dante and the Origins of Italian Literary Culture*, pp. 281–303. New York: Fordham University Press, 2006.

Barthémy, Dominique and Philippe Contamine. "The Use of Private Space." In *A History of Private Life. II. Revelations of the Medieval World*, ed. Georges Duby, trans. Arthur Goldhammer, pp. 425–505. Cambridge, MA: Harvard University Press, 1988.

Battaglia, Salvatore. *Grande Dizionario della Lingua Italiana*, 21 vols., "Indice degli autori citati," and "Supplemento," 2004 (Turin: Unione Tipografico-Editrice Torinese, 1961–2004).

Baur, Frank, et al., eds. *Geschiedenis van de letterkunde der Nederlanden*. 7 vols. Brussels: Standaard, 1937–51.

Bedini, Silvio A. "Clocks and Reckoning of Time." In *DMA*, 3.457–64.

Beidler, Peter G. "Art and Scatology in the *Miller's Tale*." 1977. Reprinted in Beidler, *Chaucer's Canterbury Comedies*, pp. 1–16.

——. *Chaucer's Canterbury Comedies: Origins and Originality*. Seattle: Coffeetown Press, 2011.

——. "Chaucer's French Accent: Gardens and Sex-Talk in the *Shipman's Tale*." In Holley A. Crocker, ed., *Comic Provocations: Exposing the Corpus of Old French Fabliaux*, pp. 149–69. New York: Palgrave Macmillan, 2006.

——. "Just Say Yes, Chaucer Knew the *Decameron*: Or Bringing the *Shipman's Tale* Out of Limbo." In Koff and Schildgen, eds., *Decameron*, pp. 25–46. Reprinted in Beidler, *Chaucer's Canterbury Comedies*, pp. 161–90.

——. "The Miller's Tale." In Correale and Hamel, eds. *Sources and Analogues*, 2.249–75.

——. "New Terminology for Sources and Analogues." 2006. Reprinted in Beidler, *Chaucer's Canterbury Comedies*, pp. 29–36.

——. "Transformations in Gower's *Tale of Florent* and Chaucer's *Wife of Bath's*

Tale," In R. F. Yeager, ed., *Chaucer and Gower: Difference, Mutuality, Exchange*, ELS Monograph Series 51, pp. 100–14. Victoria: English Literary Studies, 1991.

Bennett, J. A. W. *Chaucer at Oxford and at Cambridge.* Toronto: University of Toronto Press, 1974.

Benson, Larry D. "General Prologue." In Benson, ed., *Riverside Chaucer*, pp. 797–98.

——. "The Order of the *Canterbury Tales.*" *Studies in the Age of Chaucer* 3 (1981), pp. 77–117.

——, ed., *The Riverside Chaucer*, 3ʳᵈ edn Boston: Houghton Mifflin, 1987.

Benson, Larry D. and Theodore M. Andersson, *The Literary Context of Chaucer's Fabliaux: Texts and Translations.* Indianapolis: Bobbs-Merrill, 1971.

Benvenuti, Anna. "San Giovanni Gualberto e Firenze." In Giordano Monzio Compagnoni, ed., *I Vallombrosani nella società italiana dei secoli XI e XII*, Archivio Vallombrosano 2, pp. 83–112. Vallombrosa: Edizioni Vallombrosa, 1995.

Besamusca, Bart. "The Manuscript Context of the Middle Dutch Fabliaux." In Catherine M. Jones and Logan E. Whalen, eds., *"Li premerains vers": Essays in Honor of Keith Busby*, pp. 29–45. Amsterdam: Rodopi, 2011.

Biemans, Jos A. A. M. *Onsen Speghele Ystoriale in Vlaemsche: Codicologisch onderzoek naar de overlevering van de* Spiegel historiael *van Jacob van Maerlant, Philip Utenbroeke en Lodewijk van Velthem, met een beschrijving van de handschriften en fragmenten.* 2 vols. Schrift en Schriftdragers in de Nederlanden in de Middeleeuwen 2. Louvain: Peeters, 1997.

——. "Op zoek naar contouren van het onzichtbare: die miniaturen in Hs. Brussel, KB, II 1171." *De nieuwe taalgids* 87 (1994), pp. 217–30.

Biggs, Frederick M. "A Bared Bottom and a Basket: A New Analogue and a New Source for the *Miller's Tale.*" *Notes and Queries* n.s. 56 (2009), pp. 340–41.

——. "The *Miller's Tale* and *Decameron* 3.4." *JEGP* 108 (2009), pp. 59–80.

——. "The *Miller's Tale* and *Heile van Beersele.*" *Review of English Studies* n.s. 56 (2005), pp. 497–523.

——. Review of Heffernan, *Comedy in Chaucer. JEGP* 110 (2011), pp. 409–11.

Biggs, Frederick M. and Laura Howes. "Theophany in the 'Miller's Tale.'" *Medium Ævum* 65 (1996), pp. 269–79.

Bishop, Louise M. "'Of Goddes pryvetee nor of his wyf': The Confusion of Orifices in 'The Miller's Tale." *Texas Studies in Language and Literature* 44 (2002), pp. 231–46

Blair, John. "Frithuswith." In *The Oxford Dictionary of National Biography*, 61 vols., 21.50–51. Oxford: Oxford University Press, 2004.

Blanch, Robert J. "'Al was this land fulfild of fayerye': The Thematic Employment of Force, Willfulness, and Legal Conventions in Chaucer's *Wife of Bath's Tale.*" *Studia Neophilologica* 57 (1985), pp. 41–51.

Bloch, Howard. *The Scandal of the Fabliaux.* Chicago: University of Chicago Press, 1986.

Boitani, Piero and Jill Mann, eds. *The Cambridge Companion to Chaucer.* Cambridge: Cambridge University Press, 2003.

Bollard, John K. "Sovereignty and the Loathly Lady Tale in English, Welsh and Irish." *Leeds Studies in English* 17 (1986), pp. 41–59.

Bolton, J. L. *The Medieval English Economy 1150–1500*. London: J. M. Dent, 1980.

Bolton, Whitney F. "The 'Miller's Tale': An Interpretation." *Mediaeval Studies* 24 (1962), pp. 83–94.

Bonner, Anthony. "Llull as Alchemist and Cabalist." In Bonner, ed., *Doctor Illuminatus: A Ramon Llull Reader*, with new introductions and new translation of *The Book of the Lover and the Beloved* by Eve Bonner, pp. 59–61 Princeton: Princeton University Press, 1993.

Bopeckh, Joachim G., Günter Albrecht, Kurt Böttcher, Klaus Gysi, and Paul Günter Kron, *Geschichte der deutschen Literatur von 1480 bis 1600*. Berlin: Volk un Wissen Volkseigener Verlag, 1961.

Brady, Lindy. "Antifeminist Tradition in *Arthur and Gorlagon* and the Quest to Understand Women." *Notes and Queries* n.s. 59 (2012), pp. 163–66.

——. "Feminine Desire and Conditional Misogyny in *Arthur and Gorlagon*." *Arthuriana* 24.3 (2014), pp. 24–25.

Branca, Vittore. *Boccaccio: The Man and His Works*. Translated by Richard Monges. New York: New York University Press, 1976.

Bratcher, James T. "The Function of the Jeweled Bridle in Gower's 'Tale of Rosiphelee.'" *Chaucer Review* 40 (2005), pp. 107–10.

——. "Gower and Child, No. 45, 'King John and the Bishop.'" *Notes and Queries* n.s. 48 (2001), pp. 14–15.

——. "Gower's 'Tale of Three Questions' and 'The Clever Peasant Girl' Folktale." *Notes and Queries* n.s. 53 (2006), pp. 409–10.

Bremond, Claude and Jacques Le Goff. *L'"Exemplum."* Typologie des sources du Moyen Âge occidental 40. Turnhout: Brepols, 1996.

Brewer, Derek, ed. *Medieval Comic Tales*, 2nd edn. Cambridge: D. S. Brewer, 1996.

Bridbury, A. R. "The Farming out of Manors." 1978. Reprinted in *The English Economy From Bede to the Reformation*, pp. 133–53. Woodbridge: Boydell Press, 1992.

Briggs, Chris. *Credit and Village Society in Fourteenth-Century England*. Oxford: Oxford University Press, 2009.

Britnell, Richard. *Britain and Ireland 1050–1530*. Economic and Social History of Britain. Oxford: Oxford University Press, 2004.

Brown, Carleton. "The Man of Law's Head-link and the Prologue of the Canterbury Tales." *Studies in Philology* 34 (1937), pp. 8–35.

Brundage, James A. "Usury." In *DMA*, 12.335–39.

Bryan, W. F. and Germaine Dempster, eds. *Sources and Analogues of Chaucer's Canterbury Tales*. 1941. Reprinted New York: Humanities Press, 1958.

Bryce, Judith. "'Fa finire uno bello studio et dice volere studiare.' Ippolita Sforza and her Books." *Bibliothèque d'Humanisme et Renaissance* 64 (2002), pp. 55–69.

Burns, Robert I. "Epilogue: Apotheosis." In Burns, ed., *The Worlds of Alfonso the Learned and James the Conqueror: Intellect and Force in the Middle Ages*, pp. 203–10. Princeton: Princeton University Press, 1985.

Burrow, J. A. and V. J. Scattergood. "The Shipman's Tale." In Benson, ed., *Riverside Chaucer*, pp. 910–13.

Butterfield, Ardis. *The Familiar Enemy: Chaucer, Language, and Nation in the*

Hundred Years War. Oxford: Oxford University Press, 2009.

———— . "France" In Fein and Raybin, eds., *Chaucer*, pp. 25–46.

Cahn, Kenneth S. ""Chaucer's Merchants and the Foreign Exchange: An Introduction to Medieval Finance." *Studies in the Age of Chaucer* 2 (1980), pp. 81–119.

Campion, Nicholas. *The Dawn of Astrology: A Cultural History of Western Astrology, Vol. 1: The Ancient and Classical Worlds*. London: Continuum, 2008.

Cancik, Hubert and Helmuth Schneider, eds., *Der neue Pauly, Enzyklopädie der Antike*. Vol. 3. Stuttgart: J. B. Metzler, 1997.

Carney, James. "Literature in Irish, 1169–1534." In Cosgrove, ed., *New History*, pp. 688–707.

Cavanaugh, Susan H. "The Nun's Priest's Prologue and Tale." In Benson, ed., *Riverside Chaucer*, pp. 935–41.

Chapelot, Jean and Robert Fossier. *The Village and the House in the Middle Ages*. Translated by Henry Cleere. Berkeley: University of California Press, 1985.

Charbonneau, Joanne A. "Sir Thopas." In Correale and Hamel, eds., *S&A*, 2.649–714.

Chatten, Nicola. "Fabliau. [Pl. fabliaux]." In Lindahl, McNamara, and Lindow, eds., *Medieval Folklore*, pp. 126–28.

Child, Francis James. *English and Scottish Popular Ballad*. Edited by Helen Child Sargent and George Lyman Kittredge. Boston: Houghton Mifflin, 1904.

Ciabattoni, Francesco and Pier Massimo Forni, eds. *The Decameron Third Day in Perspective*. Toronto: University of Toronto Press, 2014.

Clarke, K. P. *Chaucer and Italian Textuality*. Oxford: Oxford University Press, 2011.

Cline, Ruth H. "Three Notes on *The Miller's Tale*." *Huntington Library Quarterly* 26 (1963), pp. 131–35.

Coleman, William E. "Chaucer, the *Teseida*, and the Visconti Library at Pavia: A Hypothesis." *Medium Ævum* 51 (1982), pp. 92–101.

Collette, Carolyn P. and Vincent DiMarco. "The Canon's Yeoman's Tale." In Correale and Hamel, eds., *S&A*, 2.715–47.

Constable, Giles. *Three Studies in Medieval Religious and Social Thought*. Cambridge: Cambridge University Press, 1995.

Cooper, Helen. *The Canterbury Tales*. Oxford Guides to Chaucer, 2nd edn Oxford: Oxford University Press, 1996.

————. "The Frame." In Correale and Hamel, eds., *S&A*, 1.1–22.

————. *The Structure of the* Canterbury Tales. Athens: University of Georgia Press, 1983.

Copeland. Murray. "*The Shipman's Tale*: Chaucer and Boccaccio." *Medium Ævum* 35 (1966), pp. 11–28.

Correale, Robert M. with Mary Hamel, eds. *Sources and Analogues of the* Canterbury Tales, [*S&A*], 2 vols. Cambridge: D. S. Brewer, 2002 and 2005.

Cosgrove, Art, ed. *Medieval Ireland 1169–1534*. Volume 2 of *A New History of Ireland*. Oxford: Clarendon Press, 1987.

Crow, Martin M. and Clair C. Olson, *Chaucer Life-Records*. Oxford: Clarendon Press, 1966.

Cummings, Hubertis M. *The Indebtedness of Chaucer's Works to the Italian*

Works of Boccaccio. 1916. Reprinted New York: AMS Press, 1967.

Da Rold, Orietta. "Materials." In Gillespie and Wakelin, eds., *Production of Books*, pp. 12–33.

Daniels, Rhiannon. *Boccaccio and the Book: Production and Reading in Italy 1340–1520*. London: Modern Humanities Research Association and Maney Publishing, 2009.

Daniels, Richard. "Textual Pleasure in the *Miller's Tale*." In James J. Paxson, Lawrence M. Clopper, and Sylvia Tomasch, eds., *The Performance of Middle English Culture: Essays on Chaucer and the Drama in Honor of Martin Stevens*, pp. 111–23. Cambridge: D. S. Brewer, 1998.

David, Alfred. *The Strumpet Muse: Art and Morals in Chaucer's Poetry*. Bloomington: Indiana University Press, 1976.

De Roover, Raymond. *The Bruges Money Market around 1400*. Brussels: Paleis des Academiën, 1968.

——. *Money, Banking and Credit in Mediaeval Bruges: Italian Merchant-Bankers, Lombards, and Money-Changers. A Study in the Origins of Banking*. Cambridge, MA: Medieval Academy of America, 1948.

De Vries, Jan. *Nederlands Etymologisch Wordenboek*. Leiden: Brill, 1963–71.

Dean, James. "The Hag Transformed: 'The Tale of Florent,' Ethical Choice, and Female Desire in Late Medieval England." In R. F. Yeager and Brian W. Gastle, eds., *Approaches to Teaching the Poetry of John Gower*, pp. 143–58. New York: Modern Language Association of America, 2011.

Delgado Léon, Feliciano. "Séneca en la Edad Media español." *Boletín de la Real Academia de Córdoba* 127 (1994), pp. 415–32.

Delisle, Léopold. *Inventaire des manuscrits de la Sorbonne conservés a la Bibliothèque impériale sous les numéros 15176–16718 du fonds latin*. Paris: Durand et Pedone-Lauriel, 1870.

Derolez, Albert. *The Palaeography of Gothic Manuscript Books from the Twelfth to the Early Sixteenth Century*. Cambridge: Cambridge University Press, 2003.

Deschamps, Jan. "De Catalogus van de Middelnederlandse Handschriften van de Koninklijke Bibliotheek van België." *De Gulden Passer*, 39 (1961), pp. 258–73.

Deschamps, Jan and Herman Mulder. *Inventaris van de Middelnederlandse handschriften van de Koninklijke Bibliotheek van België*. Brussels: Koninklijke Bibliotheek van België, 1998– .

Diamond, Arlyn. "Introduction." In the "Colloquium: The Afterlife of Origins," pp. 217–20. *Studies in the Age of Chaucer* 28 (2006).

DiMarco, Vincent. "The Historical Basis of Chaucer's Squire Tale." 1989. Reprinted in Kathryn L. Lynch, ed., *Chaucer's Cultural Geography*, pp. 56–75. New York: Routledge, 2002.

——. "The Squire's Tale." In Correale and Hamel, eds., *S&A*, 1.169–209.

Doyle, Kara A. "Criseyde Reading, Reading Crisyde." In Cindy L. Vitto and Marcia Smith Marzec, eds., *New Perspectives on Criseyde*, pp. 75–110. Ashville: Pegasus Press, 2004.

Dundes, Alan. "From Etic to Emic Units in the Structural Study of Folktales." 1962. Reprinted with a postscript, "The Motif-Index and the Tale Type Index: A Critique," in Simon J. Bronner, ed., *The Meaning of Folklore: The Analytical Essays of Alan Dundes*, pp. 88–106. Logan: Utah State University Press, 2007.

Dyer, Christopher. *Making a Living in the Middle Ages: The People of Britain 850–1520*. New Economic History of Britain. New Haven: Yale University Press, 2002.

Eberle, Patricia J. "The Man of Law's Tale." In Benson, ed., *Riverside Chaucer*, pp. 854–63.

Echard, Siân, ed. *A Companion to Gower*. Cambridge: D. S. Brewer, 2004.

Edler, Florence. *Glossary of Mediaeval Terms of Business: Italian Series 1200–1600*. Cambridge, MA: Medieval Academy of America, 1934.

Edwards, Robert R. "Italy." In Fein and Raybin, eds., *Chaucer*, pp. 3–24.

Eichhorn-Mulligan, Amy C.: see Mulligan, Amy C.

Eisner, Martin. "The Tale of Ferondo's Purgatory (III.8)." In Ciabattoni and Forni, eds., *Decameron Third Day*, pp. 150–69.

Eisner, Sigmund. *A Tale of Wonder: A Source Study of* The Wife of Bath's Tale. Wexford: John English, 1957.

Ellis, Roger. "Translation." In Boitani and Mann, eds., *Cambridge Companion to Chaucer*, pp. 443–58.

el-Shamy, Hasan M. *Types of the Folktale in the Arab World: A Demographically Oriented Tale-Type Index*. Bloomington, IN: Indiana University Press, 2004.

Emery, Anthony. *Greater Medieval Houses of England and Wales*. 2 vols. Cambridge: Cambridge University Press, 1996–2006.

Farrell, Thomas J. "Privacy and the Boundaries of Fabliau in the *Miller's Tale*," *ELH* 56 (1989), pp. 773–95.

Fein, Susanna and David Raybin, eds. *Chaucer: Contemporary Approaches*. University Park: Pennsylvania State University Press, 2010.

——, ——, and Peter C. Braeger, eds. *Rebels and Rivals: The Contestive Spirit in* The Canterbury Tales. Studies in Medieval Culture 29. Kalamazoo: Medieval Institute Publications, 1991.

Ferme, Valerio. *Women, Enjoyment, and the Defense of Virtue in Boccaccio's Decameron*. New York: Palgrave MacMillan, 2015.

Field, P. J. C. "What Women Really Want: the Genesis of Chaucer's *Wife of Bath's Tale*." *Arthurian Literature* 27 (2010), pp. 59–85.

Fisher, John H. "Animadversions on the Text of Chaucer." *Speculum* 63 (1988), pp. 779–93.

——. *John Gower: Moral Philosopher and Friend of Chaucer* (New York: New York University Press, 1964

Fletcher, Alan J. "The Faith of a Simple Man: Carpenter John's Creed in the *Miller's Tale*," *Medium Ævum* 61 (1992), pp. 96–105.

Flood, John L. *Poets Laureate in the Holy Roman Empire: A Bio-bibliography*. 4 vols. Berlin: Walter de Gruyter, 2006.

Forbes, R. J. *Studies in Ancient Technology*, vol. 7. Leiden: Brill, 1963.

Forni, Pier Massimo. *Adventures in Speech: Rhetoric and Narration in Boccaccio's Decameron*. Philadelphia: University of Pennsylvania Press, 1996.

——. *Forme complesse nel Decameron*, Biblioteca di "Lettere italiane," Studi e Testi 42. Florence: Olschki, 1992.

——. "La realizzazione narrativa in Boccaccio." In Michelangelo Picone and Claude Cazalé Bérard, eds., *Gli zibaldoni di Boccaccio: memoria, scrittura, riscrittura*, pp. 415–23. Florence: F. Cesati, 1998.

Freedman, Paul. *Out of the East: Spices and the Medieval Imagination*. New

Haven: Yale University Press, 2008.

——. "Spices and Late-Medieval European Ideas of Scarcity and Value." *Speculum* 80 (2005), pp. 1209–27.

French, Robert D. *A Chaucer Handbook.* 2nd edn. New York: Appleton-Century-Crofts, 1947.

Furnivall, Frederick James, Edmund Brock, and W. A. Clouston, eds. *Originals and Analogues of Some of Chaucer's Canterbury Tales.* London: N. Trübner, 1872–88.

Galloway, Andy. "Gower's Quarrel with Chaucer and the Origins of Bourgeois Didacticism in Fourteenth-Century London Poetry." In Annette Harder, A. A. MacDonald, and G. J. Reinink, eds., *Calliope's Classroom: Didactic Poetry from Antiquity to the Renaissance*, pp. 245–68. Paris: Peeters, 2007.

Gaylord, Alan T. "*Sentence* and *Solaas* in Fragment VII of the *Canterbury Tales*: Harry Bailly as Horseback Editor." *PMLA* 82 (1967), pp. 226–35.

Gibbs, Laura. *Aesop's Fables.* Oxford: Oxford University Press, 2002.

Gillespie, Alexandra. "Bookbinding." In Gillespie and Wakelin, eds., *Production of Books*, pp. 150–72.

Gillespie, Alexandra, and Daniel Wakelin, eds. *The Production of Books in England 1350–1500.* Cambridge: Cambridge University Press, 2011.

Ginsberg, Warren. "'Gli scogli neri e il niente che c'è': Dorigen's Black Rocks and Chaucer's Translation of Italy." In Robert M. Stein and Sandra Pierson Prior, eds., *Reading Medieval Culture: Essays in Honor of Robert W. Hanning*, pp. 387–408. Notre Dame: University of Notre Dame Press, 2005.

——. *Tellers, Tales, & Translation in Chaucer's Canterbury Tales.* Oxford: Oxford University Press, 2015.

Goldberg, Christine. *Turandot's Sisters: A Study of the Folktale AT 851.* Routledge Library of Editions: Folklore 16. London: Routledge, 1993.

Gray, Douglas. "The Miller's Prologue and Tale." In Benson, ed., *Riverside Chaucer*, pp. 841–48.

Grennen, E. Joseph. "Calculating the Reeve and His Camera Obscura." *Journal of Medieval and Renaissance Studies* 14 (1984), pp. 245–59.

——. "The Canon's Yeoman and the Cosmic Furnace: Language and Meaning in the 'Canon's Yeoman's Tale.'" *Criticism* 4 (1962), pp. 225–40.

——. "The Canon's Yeoman's Alchemical Mass." *Studies in Philology* 62 (1965), pp. 546–60.

——. "Chaucer's Characterization of the Canon and his Yeoman." *Journal of the History of Ideas* 25 (1964), pp. 279–84.

——. "Saint Cecilia's 'Chemical Wedding': the Unity of the *Canterbury Tales* Fragment VIII." *JEGP* 65 (1966), pp. 466–88.

——. "Science and Sensibility in Chaucer's Clerk." *Chaucer Review* 6 (1971), pp. 81–93.

Guerin, Richard Stephen "*The Canterbury Tales* and *Il Decamerone*." PhD diss., University of Colorado, 1966.

——. "*The Shipman's Tale*: The Italian Analogues." *English Studies* 52 (1971), pp. 412–19.

Hahn, Thomas. "Old Wives' Tales and Masculine Intuition." In Hahn and Alan Lupack, eds, *Retelling Stories: Structure, Context, and Innovation in Traditional Narratives*, pp. 91–108. Woodbridge: Boydell and Brewer, 1997.

Halleux, Robert. *Les textes alchimiques*. Typologie des sources du Moyen Âge occidental 32. Turnhout: Brepols, 1979.

Hamel, Mary. "The Pardoner's Prologue and Tale." In Correale and Hamel, eds. *S&A*, 1.267–319.

Hanna, Ralph. "The Hengwrt Manuscript and the Canon of *The Canterbury Tales*." 1989. Reprinted in Hanna, *Pursuing History: Middle English Manuscripts and Their Texts*, pp. 140–55. Stanford: Stanford University Press, 1996.

Hanna, Ralph and Traugott Lawler. "The Wife of Bath's Prologue." In Correale and Hamel, eds. *S&A*, 2.351–403.

Hanning, Robert W. "Before Chaucer's *Shipman's Tale*: The Language of Place and the Place of Language in *Decameron* 8.1 and 8.2." In Laura L. Howes, ed., *Place, Space, and Landscape in Medieval Narrative*, pp. 181–96. Tennessee Studies in Literature 43. Knoxville: University of Tennessee Press, 2007.

——. "'Parlous Play': Diabolic Comedy in Chaucer's *Canterbury Tales*." In Jean E. Jost, ed., *Chaucer's Humor: Critical Essays*, Garland Studies in Humor 5, pp. 295–311. New York: Garland, 1994.

——. "'The Struggle between Noble Designs and Chaos': The Literary Tradition of Chaucer's Knight's Tale." *Literary Review* 23 (1980), pp. 519–41.

Hansen, Elaine Tuttle. *Chaucer and the Fictions of Gender*. Berkeley: University of California Press, 1992.

Harbert, Bruce. "Chaucer and the Latin Classics." In Derek Brewer, *Geoffrey Chaucer*, Writers and their Background, pp. 137–53. London: Bell, 1974.

Heers, Jacques. *La Ville au Moyen ge en Occident: paysages, pouvoirs et conflits*. Paris: Fayard, 1990.

Heffernan, Carol Falvo. *Comedy in Chaucer and Boccaccio*. Cambridge: D. S. Brewer, 2009.

——. "Chaucer's 'Shipman's Tale' and Boccaccio's *Decameron* VIII, i: Retelling a Story." In Keith Busby and Erik Kooper, eds., *Courtly Literature: Culture and Context*, pp. 261–70. Amsterdam: John Benjamins, 1990.

Hegman, W. E. "Het Cheltenhamse *Rose*-Handschrift." *Spiegel der Letteren* 30 (1988), pp. 67–71.

Helmholtz, R. H. "Usuy and the Medieval English Courts." *Speculum* 61 (1986), pp. 364–80.

Henderson, John. "The Flagellant Movement and Flagellant Confraternities in Central Italy 1260–1400." In Derek Baker, ed., *Religious Motivation: Biographical and Sociological Problems for the Church Historian*, Studies in Church History 15, pp. 147–60. Oxford: Blackwell, 1978.

——. *Piety and Charity in Late Medieval Florence*. Oxford: Clarendon Press, 1994.

Hertog, Erik. *Chaucer's Fabliaux as Analogues*. Mediaevalia Lovaniensia I/XIX. Leuven: Leuven University Press, 1991.

Hilary, Christine Ryan. "The Wife of Bath's Prologue and Tale." In Benson, ed., *Riverside Chaucer*, pp. 864–74.

Hines, John. *The Fabliau in English*. London: Longman, 1993.

Hoffman, Richard L. "The Influence of the Classics on Chaucer." In Beryl Rowland, ed., *Companion to Chaucer Studies*, pp. 185–201. New York: Oxford University Press, 1979.

Holmyard, John. *Alchemy*. Harmondsworth: Penguin, 1957.

Horobin, Simon. "Compiling the *Canterbury Tales* in Fifteenth-Century Manuscripts." *Chaucer Review* 47 (2013), pp. 372–89.

Howard, Donald R. *The Idea of the* Canterbury Tales. Berkeley: University of California Press, 1976.

Hulbert, James R. "The Nun's Priest's Tale." In Bryan and Dempster, eds., *Sources and Analogues*, pp. 645–63.

Huppé, Bernard F. "Rape and Woman's Sovereignty in the *Wife of Bath's Tale*." *Modern Language Notes* 63 (1948), pp. 378–81.

Irmischer, Johann Conrad. *Handschriften-Katalog der Königliche Universitäts-Bibliothek zu Erlangen*. Frankfurt a. M.: Heyder und Zimmer, 1852.

Irvin, Matthew W. *The Poetic Voices of John Gower: Politics and Personae in the* Confessio Amantis. Cambridge: D. S. Brewer, 2014.

James, M. R. *A Descriptive Catalogue of the Manuscripts in the Library of Eton College*. Cambridge: Cambridge University Press, 1895.

———. *The Western Manuscripts in the Library of Trinity College, Cambridge*. 4 vols. Cambridge: Cambridge University Press, 1900–04.

Johnson, David F. "Questing in the Middle Dutch *Lancelot Compilation*." In Norris J. Lacy, ed., *The Grail, the Quest and the World of Arthur*, pp. 92–108. Arthurian Studies 72. Cambridge: D. S. Brewer, 2008.

Jones, Terry. "Did John Gower Rededicate his 'Confessio Amantis' before Henry IV's Usurpation?" In *Middle English Texts in Transition: A Festschrift Dedicated to Toshiyuki Takamiya on his 70th Birthday*, ed. Simon Horobin and Linne R. Mooney, pp. 40–74. York: York Medieval Press, 2014.

Jordan, William Chester. Review of Shatzmiller, *Shylock Reconsidered*. In the *Jewish Quarterly Review* 82 (1991), pp. 221–23.

Karras, Ruth Mazo. *Common Women: Prostitution and Sexuality in Medieval England*. New York: Oxford Univeristy Press, 1996.

Kaske, R. E. *Medieval Christian Literary Imagery: A Guide to Interpretation*. Toronto Medieval Bibliographies 11. Toronto: University of Toronto Press, 1988.

Ker, N. R. *Medieval Manuscripts in British Libraries*. 5 vols. Oxford, 1969–2002.

Kermode, Frank. *The Sense of an Ending: Studies in the Theory of Fiction: With a new Epilogue*. New York: Oxford University Press, 2000.

Kieckhefer, Richard. "Radical Tendencies in the Flagellant Movement of the Mid-Fourteenth Century." *Journal of Medieval and Renaissance Studies* 4 (1974), pp. 157–76.

Knight, Stephen. Review of Correale and Hamel, eds., *Sources and Analogues*, vol. 1. In *Speculum* 79 (2004), pp. 1057–59.

Knowles, David and R. Neville Hadcock. *Medieval Religious Houses, England and Wales*. New York: St. Martin's Press, 1971.

Knuvelder, G. P. M. *Handboek tot de Geschiedenis der Nederlandse Letterkunde*. 4 vols. 's-Hertogenbosch: Malmberg, 1971–78.

Koff, Leonard Michael, and Brenda Deen Schildgen, eds. *The* Decameron *and the* Canterbury Tales*: New Essays on an Old Question*. Teaneck: Fairleigh Dickinson University Press, 2000.

Kolve, V. A. *Chaucer and the Imagery of Narrative, the First Five Canterbury Tales*. Stanford: Stanford University Press, 1984.

Koyama, Mark. "Evading the 'Taint of Usury': the Usury Prohibition as a Barrier to Entry." *Explorations in Economic History* 47 (2010), pp. 420–42.

Kruyskamp, C., ed. *Middelnederlandse Boerden*. 's-Gravenhage: Martinus Nijhoff, 1957.

Lacy, Norris. *Reading Fabliaux*. Birmingham: Suma Publications, 1999.

Lang, Andrew. *The Lilac Fairy Book*. London: Longmans, Green, 1910.

Langholm, Odd. *Economics in the Medieval Schools: Wealth, Exchange, Value, Money and Usury according to the Paris Theological Tradition, 1200–1350*. Studien und Texte zur Geistesgeschichte des Mittelalters 29. Leiden: Brill, 1992.

Langmuir, Gavin I. Review of Shatzmiller, *Shylock Reconsidered*. In the *Journal of Economic History* 50 (1990), pp. 715–17

Lavezzo, Kathy. "England." In Fein and Raybin, eds., *Chaucer*, pp. 47–64.

—— . "The Minster and the Privy: Rereading the *Prioress's Tale*." *PMLA* 126 (2011), pp. 363–82.

Lee, A. C. *The Decameron: Its Sources and Analogues*. 1909. Reprinted New York: Haskell House, 1966.

Leff, Gordon. *Heresy in the Later Middle Ages: The Relation of Heterodoxy to Dissent c. 1250–c. 1450*. 2 vols. Manchester: University of Manchester Press, 1967.

Le Goff, Jacques. "Labor Time in the 'Crisis' of the Fourteenth Century: From Medieval Time to Modern Time." In Le Goff, *Time, Work, & Culture in the Middle Ages*, trans. Arthur Goldhammer, pp. 43–52. Chicago: University of Chicago Press, 1980.

Lehmann, Paul, et al., eds. *Mittellateinisches Wörterbuch bis zum ausgehenden 13. Jahrhundert*. Munich: Beck, 1967– .

Lerer, Seth, ed. *The Yale Companion to Chaucer*. New Haven: Yale University Press, 2006.

Lettinck, Paul. *Aristotle's* Meteorology *and its Reception in the Arab World*. Leiden: Brill, 1999.

Lewis, Charlton T. and Charles Short. *A Latin Dictionary*. Oxford: Clarendon Press, 1969.

Lewis, Jack P. *A Study of the Interpretation of Noah and the Flood in Jewish and Christian Literature*. Leiden: Brill, 1968.

Liddell, Henry George, Robert Scott, Henry Stuart Jones, and Roderick McKenzie. *A Greek–English Lexicon*. Revised edn. Oxford: Clarendon Press, 1961.

Lieftinck, G. I. *Manuscrits datés conservés dans les Pays-Bas. Vol. 1: Les manuscrits d'origine étrangère (816–c. 1550)*. Amsterdam: North Holland Pub. Co., 1964.

Lindahl, Carl. "Folktale." In Lindahl, McNamara, and Lindow, eds., *Medieval Folklore*, pp. 142–48.

Lindahl, Carl, John McNamara, and John Lindow, eds. *Medieval Folklore: A Guide to Myths, Legends, Tales, Beliefs, and Customs*. Oxford: Oxford University Press, 2002.

Lodder, F. J. "Lachen om List en Lust. Studies over de middelnederlandse komische versvertellingen." PhD diss., Leiden University, 1997.

Lucas, Peter J. "Borrowing and Reference Access to Libraries in the Late Middle Ages." In Elisabeth Leedham-Green and Teresa Weber, eds., *The Cambridge History of Libraries in Britain and Ireland*, vol. 1, pp 242–62. Cambridge:

Cambridge University Press, 2006.

Lyall, R. J. "Materials: The Paper Revolution." In Jeremy Griffiths and Derek Pearsall, eds., *Book Production and Publishing in Britain 1375–1475*, pp. 11–29. Cambridge: Cambridge University Press, 1989.

Mac Cana, Proinsias. "Aspects of the Theme of King and Goddess in Irish Literature." Études Celtiques 7 (1955–6), pp. 76–114 and 356–413, and 8 (1958–9), pp. 59–65

MacDonald, Angus. "Absolon and St. Neot." *Neophilologus* 48 (1964), pp. 235–37

Manly, John M. and Edith Rickert. *The Text of the* Canterbury Tales *Studied on the Basis of All Known Manuscripts.* 8 vols. Chicago: University of Chicago Press, 1940.

Mann, Jill, ed. *The Canterbury Tales.* London: Penguin, 2005.

——. *Feminizing Chaucer.* 1991. Reprinted Woodbridge: D. S. Brewer, 2002.

——. *From Aesop to Reynard: Beast Literature in Medieval Britain.* Oxford: Oxford University Press, 2009.

Marshall, P. K. "Apuleius." In L. D. Reynolds, ed., *Texts and Transmission: A Survey of the Latin Classics*, pp. 15–16. Oxford: Clarendon Press, 1983.

Marzolph, Ulrich. *Arabia ridens. Die humoristische Kurzprosa der frühen abad-Literatur im internationalen Traditionsgeflecht.* 2 vols. Frankfurt am Main: Klostermann, 1992.

Masai, François and Martin Wittek. *Manuscrits datés conservés en Belgique. Tome I: 819–1400.* Brussels: E. Story-Scientia, 1968.

——. *Manuscrits datés conservés en Belgique, Tome III: 1441–1460.* Brussels: E. Story-Scientia, 1978.

Mazzotta, Giuseppe. *The World at Play in Boccaccio's* Decameron. Princeton: Princeton University Press, 1986.

Maynadier, G. H. *The* Wife of Bath's Tale*: Its Sources and Analogues.* London: Nutt, 1901.

McGrady, Donald. "Chaucer and the *Decameron* Reconsidered." *Chaucer Review* 12 (1977), pp. 1–26.

McNamara, John. "Exemplum [Pl. exempla]." In Lindahl, McNamara, and Lindow, eds., *Medieval Folklore*, pp. 122–24.

McTighe, Neal. "Generating Feminine Discourse in Boccaccio's *Decameron*: The "Valle delle Donne" as Julia Kristeva's Chora." *Romance Notes* 47 (2006), pp. 41–48.

McWilliam, G. H. "On Translating the *Decameron*." In H. C. Davis, D. G. Rees, J. M. Hatwell, and G. W. Slowey, eds., *Essays in Honour of John Humphreys Whitfield*, pp. 71–83. London: St George's Press, 1975.

Mercer, Eric. *English Vernacular Houses: A Study of Traditional Farmhouses and Cottages.* London: H.M. Stationery Office, 1975.

Migiel, Marilyn. *The Rhetoric of the* Decameron. Toronto: University of Toronto Press, 2003.

Minnis, Alastair. *Medieval Theory of Authorship: Scholastic literary attitudes in the later Middle Ages.* 2nd edn with a new preface. Philadelphia: University of Pennsylvania Press, 2010.

Miskimin, Harry A. *The Economy of Early Renaissance Europe 1300–1460.* Englewood Cliffs, NJ: Prentice Hall, 1969.

Molinier, A. and F. Desvernay. *Catalogue général des manuscrits des bibliothèques publiques de France*. Vol. 30. Paris: E. Plon, Nourrit, 1900,

Mooney, Linne R. "Chaucer's Scribe." *Speculum* 81 (2006), pp. 97–138.

Mulligan, Amy C. "The Anatomy of Power and the Miracle of Kingship: The Female Body of Sovereignty in a Medieval Irish Kingship Tale." *Speculum* 81 (2006), pp. 1014–54.

Munby, A. N. L. *The Dispersal of the Phillipps Library*. Phillipps Studies no. 5. Cambridge: Cambridge University Press, 1960.

Muscatine, Charles. *The Old French Fabliaux*. New Haven: Yale University Press, 1986.

Needham, Paul. "The Paper of English Incunabula." In Lotta Hellinga, ed., *The Catalogue of Books Printed in the XVth Century Now in the British Library*, BMC, Part XI, England, pp. 311–34. 't Goy-Houten: Hes & de Graaf, 2007.

Newman, William R. *The* Summa Perfectionis *of Pseudo-Geber: A Critical Edition, Translation and Study*. Collection de travaux de l'Académie internationale d'histoire des sciences 35. Leiden: Brill, 1991.

Nicholson, Peter. *An Annotated Index to the Commentary on Gower's* Confessio Amantis. Medieval & Renaissance Texts & Studies 62. Binghamton: Center for Medieval and Early Renaissance Studies, 1989.

——. "Gower's Manuscript of the Confessio Amantis." In *The Medieval Python: The Purposive and Provocative Work of Terry Jones*, ed. R. F. Yeager and Toshiyuki Takamiya, pp. 75–86. New York: Palgrave Macmillan, 2012.

——. *Love and Ethics in Gower's* Confessio Amantis. Ann Arbor: University of Michigan Press, 2005.

——. "The Medieval Tale of the Lover's Gift Regained." *Fabula: Journal of Folklore Studies* 21 (1980), pp. 200–22.

Noonan, John T. *The Scholastic Analysis of Usury*. Cambridge, MA: Harvard University Press, 1957.

Nykrog, Per. *Les Fabliaux: Nouvelle édition*. Geneva: Droz, 1973.

O'Callaghan, Joseph F. *The Learned King: The Reign of Alfonso X of Castile*. Philadelphia: University of Pennsylvania Press, 1993.

Ó Concheanainn, Tomás. "The Book of Ballymote." *Celtica* 14 (1981), pp. 15–25.

——. "Scríobhaithe Leacáin Mhic Fhir Bhisigh." *Celtica* 19 (1987), pp. 141–75.

Olson, Paul A. "Poetic Justice in the *Miller's Tale*." *Modern Language Quarterly* 24 (1963), pp. 227–36.

Ortego, James. "Gerveys Joins the Fun: A Note on *Viritoot* in the *Miller's Tale*." *Chaucer Review* 37 (2003), pp. 275–79.

Otis, Leah. "Prostitution." In *DMA*, 10.154–55.

——. *Prostitution in Medieval Society: The History of an Urban Institution in Languedoc*. Chicago: University of Chicago Press, 1985.

Owen, Charles A., Jr. "The Falcon's Complaint in the *Squire's Tale*." In Fein, Raybin, and Braerer, eds., *Rebels and Rivals*, pp. 173–88.

Owst, G. R. *Literature and the Pulpit in Medieval England*. Cambridge: Cambridge University Press, 1933.

Paatz, Walter and Elizabeth Paatz. *Die Kirchen von Florenz, ein kunstgeschichtliches Handbuch*. 6 vols. Frankfurt am Main: V. Klostermann, 1952–55.

Panizza, Letizia. "The Quattrocento." In Peter Brand and Lino Pertile, eds., *The Cambridge History of Italian Literature*, pp. 131–77. Cambridge: Cambridge

University Press, 1996.

Pasquini, Emilio. "Letteratura popolareggiante, comica e giocosa, lirica minore e narrativa in volgare del Quattrocento." In Enrico Malato, ed., *Storia della letteratura italiana*, 14 vols., 3.803–911. Rome: Salerno, 1995–2005.

Passmore, S. Elizabeth. "The Loathly Lady Transformed: A Literary and Cultural Analysis of the Medieval Irish and English Hag-Beauty Tales." PhD diss., University of Connecticut, 2004.

Passmore, S. Elizabeth and Susan Carter, eds. *The "Loathly Lady" Tales: Boundaries, Traditions, Motifs*, Studies in Medieval Culture 48. Kalamazoo: Medieval Institute Publications, 2007.

Patterson, Lee. "Perpetual Motion: Alchemy and the Technology of the Self." *Studies in the Age of Chaucer* 15 (1993), pp. 25–57

Pearsall, Derek. *The Canterbury Tales*. London: Routledge, 1985.

——. "Gower's Narrative Art." 1966. Reprinted in Peter Nicholson, ed., *Gower's* Confessio Amantis*: A Critical Anthology*, pp. 62–80. Cambridge: D. S. Brewer, 1991.

——. *The Life of Geoffrey Chaucer: A Critical Biography*. Oxford: Blackwell, 1992.

——, ed. *The Nun's Priest Tale*. Variorum Edition of the Works of Geoffrey Chaucer 2/9. Norman: University of Oklahoma Press, 1984.

Peck, Russell A. "Folklore and Powerful Women in Gower's 'Tale of Florent.'" In Passmore and Carter, eds., *The "Loathly Lady" Tales*, pp. 100–45.

——. *Kingship and Common Profit in Gower's* Confessio Amantis. Carbondale: Southern Illinois University Press, 1978.

——. "The Politics and Psychology of Governance in Gower: Ideas of Kingship and Real Kings." In Echard, ed., *Companion to Gower*, pp. 215–38.

Pellegrin, Elisabeth. *La Bibliothèque des Visconti et des Sforza, ducs de Milan, au XVe siècle*. Paris: C.N.R.S., 1955.

Pickles, J. D. and J. L. Dawson. *A Concordance to John Gower's* Confessio Amantis. Cambridge: D. S. Brewer, 1987.

Postan, M. M. "The Chronology of Labour Services." 1937. Reprinted in Postan, *Essays on Medieval Agriculture*, pp. 89–106.

——. *Essays on Medieval Agriculture and General Problems of the Medieval Economy*. Cambridge: Cambridge University Press, 1973.

——. "The Rise of a Money Economy." 1944. Reprinted in Postan, *Essays on Medieval Agriculture*, pp. 28–40.

Postan, M. M. and Edward Miller. *The Cambridge Economic History of Europe. Volume II. Trade and Industry in the Middle Ages*. 2nd edn. Cambridge: Cambridge University Press, 1987.

Poteet, Daniel P. "Avoiding Women in Times of Affliction: An Analogue for the *Miller's Tale*, A 3589–91." *Notes and Queries* n.s. 19 (1972), pp. 89–90.

Pratt, Robert A. "Chaucer and the Visconti Libraries." *English Literary History* 6 (1939), pp. 191–99.

——. "Some Latin Sources of the Nonnes Preest on Dreames." *Speculum* 52 (1977), pp. 538–70.

——. "Three Old French Sources of the Nonnes Preestes Tale." *Speculum* 47 (1972), pp. 422–44 and 646–68.

Prims, Floris. "Onze plaats- et straatnamen in de XIIIde eeuw." *Antwerpsch*

Achievenblad, 2ⁿᵈ ser., 2 (1927), pp. 89–115.

Prior, Sandra Pierson. "Parodying Typology and the Mystery Plays in *The Miller's Tale*." *Journal of Medieval and Renaissance Studies* 16 (1986), pp. 57–71.

Raftis, J. A. *The Estates of Ramsey Abbey*. Studies and Texts 3. Toronto: Pontifical Institute of Mediaeval Studies, 1957.

Raybin, David. "'And pave it al of silver and of gold': The Humane Artistry of the *Canon's Yeoman's Tale*." In Fein, Raybin, and Braeger, eds., *Rebels and Rivals*, pp. 189–212

Reames, Sherry L. "The Second Nun's Prologue and Tale." In Correale and Hamel, eds., *S&A*, 1.491–527.

Reiss, Edmund. "Daun Gerveys in the *Miller's Tale*." *Papers in Language and Literature* 6 (1970), pp. 115–24.

Revard, Carter. "Four Fabliaux from London, British Library MS Harley 2253, Translated into English Verse." *Chaucer Review* 40 (2005), 111–40.

Richards, Mary P. "The Medieval Hagiography of St. Neot." *Analecta Bollandiana* 99 (1981), pp. 259–78.

———. "The *Miller's Tale*: 'By Seinte Note.'" *Chaucer Review* 9 (1975), pp. 212–15.

Rigg, A. G. and Edward S. Moore. "The Latin Works: Politics, Lament and Praise." In Echard, ed., *Companion to Gower*, pp. 153–64.

Roberts, Jane. "On Giving Scribe B a Name and a Clutch of London Manuscripts from c. 1400." *Medium Ævum* 80 (2011), pp. 247–70.

Robertson, D. S. "The Manuscripts of the *Metamorphoses* of Apuleius." *Classical Quarterly* 18 (1924), pp. 27–42 and 85–99.

Robertson, D. W. *A Preface to Chaucer: Studies in Medieval Perspectives*. Princeton: Princeton University Press, 1962.

Robins, William. "The Case of the Court Entertainer: Popular Culture, Intertextual Dialogue, and the Early Circulation of Boccaccio's *Decameron*." *Speculum* 92 (2017), pp. 1–35.

Root, Robert K. "Chaucer and the *Decameron*." *Englische Studien* 44 (1912), pp. 1–7.

Ross, Thomas W. *The Miller's Tale*. A Variorum Edition of the Works of Geoffrey Chaucer 2/3. Norman: University of Oklahoma Press, 1983.

Rossiaud, Jacques. *Medieval Prostitution*. Translated by Lydia G. Cochrane. Oxford: Blackwell, 1988.

Rubio, Josep Enric. "Thought: The Art." In Alexander Fidora and Josep E. Rubio, eds., Robert D. Hughes, Anna A. Akasoy and Magnus Ryan, trans., *Raimundus Lullus: An Introduction to his Life, Works and Thought*, CCCM 214, pp. 243–97. Turnhout: Brepols, 2008.

Runte, Hans R., J. Keith Wikeley, and Anthony J. Farrell. *The Seven Sages of Rome and the Book of Sinbad: An Analytical Bibliography*. New York: Garland, 1984.

Saul, Nigel. *Richard II*. New Haven: Yale University Press, 1997.

Saunders, Corinne. *Rape and Ravishment in the Literature of Medieval England*. Cambridge: D. S. Brewer, 2001.

Scartz, Merlin. *A Medieval Critique of Anthropomorphism: Ibn al-Jawzī's Kitāb Akhbār aṣ-Ṣifāt*. Leiden: Brill, 2002.

Scattergood, John. "The Cook's Tale." In Correale and Hamel, eds. *S&A*, 1.75–86.

Schibanoff, Susan. *Chaucer's Queer Poetics: Rereading the Dream Trio*. Toronto: University of Toronto Press, 2006.

Schlam, Carl C. "Apuleius in the Middle Ages." In Aldo S. Bernardo and Saul Levin, eds., *The Classics in the Middle Ages*, Medieval & Renaissance Texts & Studies 69, pp. 363–69. Binghamton: Center for Medieval and Early Renaissance Studies, 1990.

Schlauch, Margaret. "The Marital Dilemma in the Wife of Bath's Tale." *PMLA* 61 (1946), pp. 416–30.

Schmidt, Otto E. "Die Visconti und ihre Bibliothek zu Pavia." *Zeitschrift für Geschichte und Politik* 5 (1888), pp. 444–74.

Schofield, John. *Medieval London Houses*. New Haven: Yale University Press, 1994.

Seabourne, Gwen. *Royal Regulation of Loans and Sales in Medieval England: Monkish Superstition and Civil Tyranny*. Woodbridge: Boydell Press, 2003.

Shatzmiller, Joseph. *Shylock Reconsidered: Jews, Moneylending, and Medieval Society*. Berkeley: University of California Press, 1990.

Silverman, A. H. "Sex and Money in Chaucer's *Shipman's Tale*." *Philological Quarterly* 32 (1953), pp. 329–36.

Silverstein, Theodore. *Visio Sancti Pauli: The History of the Apocalypse in Latin together with Nine Texts*. Studies and Documents 4. London: Christophers, 1935.

Simoni, Anna E. C. "Terra Incognita: the Beudeker Collection in the Map Library of the British Library." *The British Library Journal* 11 (1985), pp. 143–75.

Singer, Kuratorium, ed. *Thesaurus proverbiorum medii aevi. Lexikon der Sprichwörter des romanisch-germanischen Mittelalters*. 13 vols. and supplement. Founded by Samuel Singer. Berlin: De Gruyter, 1995–2002.

Smarr, Janet Levarie. *Boccaccio and Fiammetta: The Narrator as Lover*. Urbana: University of Illinois Press, 1986.

Soly, H. "The Growth of the Metropolis." In van Isacker and van Uytven, *Antwerp*, pp. 84–92.

Spargo, John Webster. *Chaucer's Shipman's Tale: the Lover's Gift Regained*. FFC 91. Helsinki: Suomalainen Tiedeakatemia, Academia Scientiarum Fennica, 1930.

——. "The Shipman's Tale." In Bryan and Dempster, eds., *Sources and Analogues*, pp. 439–46.

Spufford, Peter. *Handbook of Medieval Exchange*. London: Royal Historical Society, 1986.

——. *Money and Its Use in Medieval Europe*. Cambridge: Cambridge University Press, 1988.

Steele, Robert. "Practical Chemistry in the Twelfth Century, Rasis *De aluminibus et salibus*. Translated by Gerard of Cremona." *Isis* 12 (1929), pp. 10–48.

Sternbach, Ludwik. *The Kāvya-Portions in the Kathā-Literature*, 3 vols. New Delhi: Meharchand Lachhmandas, 1971–76.

Stillinger, Thomas C. "The Language of Gardens: Boccaccio's 'Valle delle Donne.'" 1983. Reprinted in Stillinger and Psaki, eds., *Boccaccio and Feminist Criticism*, pp. 105–27.

Stillinger, Thomas C. and F. Regina Psaki, eds. *Boccaccio and Feminist Criticism*. Chapel Hill: Annali d'italianistica, Studi e Testi 8, 2006.

Stollreither, Eugen. *Quellen-Nachweise zu John Gowers* Confessio Amantis. *T. 1.* Munich: Kastner & Lossen, 1901.

Szittya, Penn. "The Green Yeoman as Loathly Lady: The Friar's Parody of the Wife of Bath's Tale." *PMLA* 90 (1975), pp 386–394.

Thompson, N. S. *Chaucer, Boccaccio, and the Debate of Love: A Comparative Study of* The Decameron *and* The Canterbury Tales. Oxford: Clarendon Press, 1996.

———. "Local Histories: Characteristic Worlds in the *Decameron* and the *Canterbury Tales*." In Koff and Schildgen, eds., *Decameron*, pp. 85–101.

Thompson, Stith. *The Folktale*. New York: Holt, Rinehart and Winston, 1946.

———. "The Miller's Tale." In Bryan and Dempster, eds., *Sources and Analogues*, pp. 106–23.

———. *Motif-Index of Folk-Literature: A Classification of Narrative Elements in Folktales, Ballads, Myths, Fables, Medieval Romances, Exempla, Fabliaux, Jest-Books, and Local Legends*, 6 vols. Copenhagen: Rosenkilde and Bagger, 1955–58.

Thorndike, Lynn. *A History of Magic and Experimental Science*. 8 vols. New York: Macmillan, 1923–58.

Thrupp, Sylvia L. *The Merchant Class in Medieval London 1300–1500*. Chicago: University of Chicago Press, 1948.

Thundy, Zacharias P. "Matheolus, Chaucer, and with Wife of Bath." In Edward Vasta and Thundy, eds., *Chaucerian Problems and Perspectives: Essays Presented to Paul E. Beichner, C.S.C.*, pp. 24–58. Notre Dame: University of Notre Dame Press, 1979.

Thurneysen, Rudolf. *A Grammar of Old Irish*. Translated by D. A. Binchy and Osborn Bergin. Dublin: Dublin Institute for Advanced Studies, 1946.

Tillyard, E. M. W. *Poetry Direct and Oblique*. Revised edn. London: Chatto & Windus, 1945.

Tupper, Frederick. "The Pardoner's Tale." In Bryan and Dempster, eds., *Sources and Analogues*, pp. 415–38.

Twomey, Michael. "Medieval Encyclopedias." In Kaske, *Medieval Christian*, pp. 182–215.

Tyrwhitt, Thomas. *The Canterbury Tales of Chaucer, to which are added an essay upon his language and versification and an introductory discourse, together with notes and a glossary.* 5 vols. London: T. Payne, 1775–78.

Uther, Hans-Jörg. *The Types of International Folktales: A Classification and Bibliography based on the System of Antti Aarne and Stith Thompson*. FFC 284–86. Helsinki: Suomalainen Tiedeakatemia, Academia Scientiarum Fennica, 2004.

Van der Poel, D. E. *De Vlaamse Rose en* Die Rose *van Heinric. Onderzoekingen over twee Middelnederlandse bewerkingen van de* Roman de la Rose, Middeleeuwse Studies en Bronnen 13 (Hilversum: Verloren, 1989).

Van Isacker, Karel and Raymond van Uytven, eds. *Antwerp: Twelve Centuries of History and Culture*. Antwerp: Fonds Mercator, 1986.

Van Mierlo, J. "Jacob van Maerlant." In Frank Baur *et al.*, eds., *De letterkunde van de Middeleeuwen tot omstreeks 1300*. Deel 1. *Geschiedenis van de letterkunde der Nederlanden*, pp. 286–303. Brussels: Standaard, 1939.

Van Uytven, R. "The Port on the Rhine and Regional Market with International Fairs." In van Isacker and van Uytven, eds., *Antwerp*, pp. 50–55.

Vande Weghe, R. *Geschiedenis van de Antwerpse straatnamen*. Antwerp: Mercurius, 1977.

Vaughan, Míceál F. "Chaucer's Imaginative One-Day Flood." *Philological Quarterly* 60 (1981), pp. 117–23

Verlinden, O. "Markets and Fairs." In M. M. Postan, E. E. Rich, and Edward Miller, eds., *The Cambridge Economic History of Europe. Volume III. Economic Organisation and Policies in the Middle Ages*, pp. 119–54. Cambridge: Cambridge University Press, 1963.

Voet, L., G. Asaert, H. Soly, A. Verhulst, F. de Nave, and J. van Roey. *De Stad Antwerpen van de Romeinse Tijd tot de 17de EEUW: Topografische studie rond het plan van Virgilius Bononiensis, 1565*. [Brussels: Gemeentekrediet van België], 1978.

Wakelin. Daniel. Review of *S&A*, volume 1. *Review of English Studies* 54 (2003), pp. 516–17.

Wallace, David. *Chaucerian Polity: Absolutist Lineages and Associational Forms in England and Italy*. Stanford: Stanford University Press, 1997.

——. "Chaucer's Italian Inheritance." In Boitani and Mann, eds., *Cambridge Companion to Chaucer*, pp. 36–57.

——. *Giovanni Boccaccio:* Decameron. Cambridge: Cambridge University Press, 1991.

——. "Italy." In Peter Brown, ed., *A Companion to Chaucer*, 2nd edn, pp. 218–34. Oxford: Blackwell, 2008.

Walther, Hans. "Beiträge zur Kenntnis der mittellateinischen Literatur (aus Handschriften süddeutscher und österreichischer Bibliotheken)." *Zentralblatt für Bibliothekswesen* 49 (1932), pp. 269–83 and 325–41.

——. *Proverbia sententiaeque Latinitatis Medii Aevi. Lateinische Sprichwörter und Sentenzen des Mittelalters*. 5 vols. Göttingen: Vandenhoeck & Ruprecht, 1963–67.

Ward, H. L. D. *Catalogue of Romances in the Department of Manuscripts in the British Museum*. 3 vols. London: Printed by order of the Trustees, 1883–1910.

Watanabe-O'Kelly, Helen. "The Early Modern Period (1450–1720)." In Watanabe-O'Kelly, ed., *The Cambridge History of German Literature*, pp. 92–146. Cambridge: Cambridge University Press, 1997.

Watts, J. A. "Approaches to the History of Fourteenth-Century Ireland." In Cosgrove, ed., *New History*, pp. 303–13.

——. "Gaelic Polity and Cultural Identity." In Cosgrove, ed., *New History*, pp. 314–51.

——. "The Anglo–Irish Colony under Strain, 1327–99." In Cosgrove, ed., *New History*, pp. 352–96.

Wenzel, Siegfried. "The Parson's Prologue and Tale." In Benson, ed., *Riverside Chaucer*, pp 955–65.

Wheatley, Edward. "The Nun's Priest's Tale." In Correale and Hamel, eds., *S&A*, 1.449–89.

Whiting, Bartlett J. "The Wife of Bath's Tale." In Bryan and Dempster, eds., *Sources and Analogues*, pp. 223–68.

Wilcockson, Colin. "The Book of the Duchess." In Benson, ed. *Riverside Chaucer*, pp. 966–76.

Wissowa, Georg, ed. *Paulys Real-Encyclopädie der classischen Altertumswissen-*

schaft. 2ⁿᵈ edn, vol. 5. Stuttgart: J. B. Metzler, 1905.

Withrington, John and P. J. C. Field. "The Wife of Bath's Tale." In Correale and Hamel, eds. *S&A*, 2.405–48.

Wood, Margaret. *The English Medieval House*. London: Phoenix House, 1965.

Woody, Kennerly M. "John Gualberti, St." In *DMA*, 7.123.

Wright, Christopher James. "Ibn 'Abd al-Hakam's *Futuh Misr*: An Analysis of the Text and New Insights into the Islamic Conquest of Egypt." PhD diss., University of California, Santa Barbara, 2006.

Yeager, R. F. "John Gower's French." In Echard, ed., *Companion to Gower*, pp. 143–44.

——. *John Gower's Poetic: The Search for a New Arion*. Cambridge: D. S. Brewer, 1990.

Zingerle, Ingaz V., ed. *Bericht über die Sterzinger Miscellaneen-Handschrift*. Vienna: Gerold, 1867.

Internet Sources

http://aalt.law.uh.edu/ : Anglo-American Legal Tradition. Documents from Medieval and Early Modern England from The National Archives in London, digitized and displayed through the O'Quinn Law Library of the University of Houston Law Center.

http://archivesetmanuscrits.bnf.fr/ : portal for documents and manuscripts at the Bibliothèque nationale de France.

http://gallica.bnf.fr/ : portal for the Bibliothèque nationale de France.

http://hdl.huntington.org/cdm / : Huntington Digital Library.

http://image.ox.ac.uk/ : Early Manuscripts at Oxford University, digital facsimilies of complete manuscripts scanned directly from the original.

http://lodel.ehess.fr/gahom/thema/ : *Thesuarus Exemplorum Medii Aevi* (ThEMA), hosted by *Le Groupe d'Anthropologie Historique de l'Occident Médiéval*.

http://manuscripta.at/ : Mittelalterliche Handschriften in Österreich.

http://quod.lib.umich.edu/m/med/ : Middle English Dictionary.

http://sites.trin.cam.ac.uk/james/ : manuscripts at Trinity College, Cambridge.

https://sourcebooks.fordham.edu/ : Internet History Sourcesbooks Project, ed. Paul Halsall, Fordham University.

http://tlion.sns.it/ : Tradizione della letteratura italiana online.

http://tlio.ovi.cnr.it/TLIO/ : Tesoro della lingua italiana delle origini.

https://www.antwerpen.be/nl/overzicht/felixarchief : FelixArchief; Antwerp's online archive.

http://www.bl.uk/catalogues/illuminatedmanuscripts/ : illuminated manuscripts at the British Library.

http://www.dil.ie/ : Dictionary of the Irish Language.

http://www.handschriftencensus.de/ : Handschriftencensus: Eine Bestandsaufnahme der handschriftlichen Überlieferung deutschsprachiger Texte der Mittelalters.

https://www.isos.dias.ie/ : Irish Script on Screen. School of Celtic Studies, Dublin

Institute for Advanced Studies.

http://www.mss.vatlib.it/ : manuscripts at the Biblioteca Apostolica Vaticana.

http://www.musmed.fr/ : Musicalia Mediaevalia (MusMed): Ressources électroniques pour l'étude des sources manuscrites de la musique et de la théorie de la musique médiévales.

http://www.musmed.fr/CMN/CMN.htm/ : Catalogue des manuscrits notés du Moyen Âge des bibliothèques publiques de France (CMN), ed. Christian Meyer (Brepols).

http://www.sd-editions.com/AnaAdditional/HengwrtEx/images/hgopen.html/ : The Henwyrt Chaucer Digital Facsimile.

http://www.sd-editions.com.ezproxy.york.ac.uk/AnaServer?PROME+0+start. anv+id=GENINTRO : *The Parliament Rolls of Medieval England, 1275–1504*, ed. Chris Given-Wilson, et al.

http://www.ub.uni-heidelberg.de/helios/digi/digilit.html/ : Manuscripts at the University of Heidelberg.

https://www.ucc.ie/celt / : CELT: The Corpus of Electronic Texts, hosted by University College, Cork.

http://www.vanhamel.nl/codecs/ : CODECS: Online database and e-resources for Celtic Studies.

Index of passages from the works of Boccaccio, Chaucer, and Gower, and from *Heile van Beersele*

Index

CHAUCER STUDIES